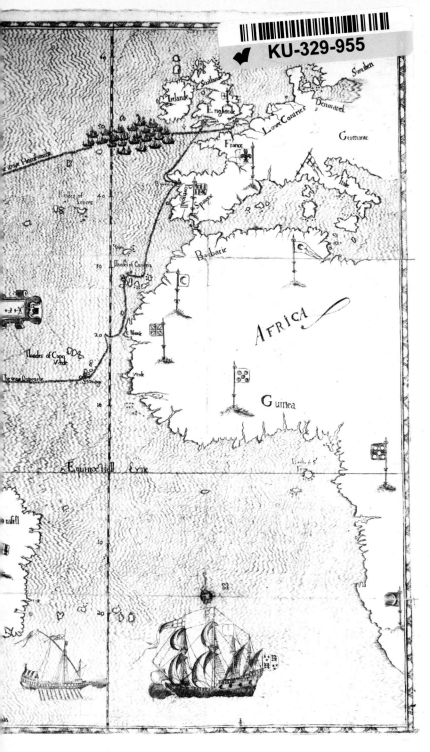

yadge', by Baptista Boazio
e J.C.B Library)

SIR FRANCIS DRAKE'S
WEST INDIAN VOYAGE
1585-86

EDITED BY

MARY FREAR KEELER

THE HAKLUYT SOCIETY
LONDON
1981

ISBN 0 904180 01 8

Printed in Great Britain
by Robert MacLehose and Company Limited
Printers to the University of Glasgow

Published by the Hakluyt Society
c/o The Map Library
The British Library: Reference Division
London WC1B 3DG

CONTENTS

v

CONTENTS

PREFACE

Plans for editing several unpublished documents relating to Drake's West Indies voyage have evolved with the advice and assistance of many persons and institutions. Louis B. Wright, Director Emeritus of the Folger Shakespeare Library, gave me early and continued encouragement, and to the present staff of the Folger Library I am indebted for countless courtesies. David B. Quinn supplied from his own notes references to other unpublished materials and has generously guided my plans for bringing them together in a volume devoted to the voyage. Without his assistance the project could not have been completed. To K. V. Thomas for his early advice, and to K. R. Andrews for numerous suggestions regarding both form and content I am grateful. My thanks for assistance with some problems of transcription are due to Laetitia Yaendle, Curator of Manuscripts at the Folger, and to her and to J. P. Hudson, Assistant Keeper, Department of Manuscripts, of the British Museum (now the British Library), I am indebted for establishing that the handwriting is indeed the same in two important documents, one in the Cotton MSS which is printed as Document 6, and one in the Harley Collection which has been collated with Document 11, *A Summarie and True Discourse*. Edith F. Ridington of Hood College translated the Latin edition of the *Summarie* and collated it with the English text. Invaluable assistance with the Spanish edition of the Castellanos poem regarding Drake's voyage, the *Discurso*, was given me by Juana Amelia Hernández and her students.

To the officials and staffs of the British institutions in which I have spent many pleasant hours I owe particular thanks. Photographic copies of each of the early editions of the *Summarie and True Discourse* owned by the British Library's Department of Printed Books enabled me to make the close textual study which the editing of that narrative required.

P. H. Hulton, Assistant Keeper, Department of Prints and Maps, was helpful with answers about drawings. Reproductions of pages from Cotton MS Otho E. VIII, Harley MS 2202, Harley MS 6221, and Egerton MS 2579, which have been included among the illustrations, have been printed by courtesy of the British Library Board. The staff of the Public Record Office, London, also have provided much assistance. The inclusion among the illustrations of the Map MPF 13 has been made possible under the ruling that 'Reproductions of Crown-copyright records in the Public Record, London, appear by permission of the Controller of H.M. Stationery Office'. To P. A. Penfold, of the Research Department, I am particularly indebted for his checking the probable connection of that map with Christopher Carleill's despatch which is among the State Papers.

An unpublished 'Trial Bibliography' on the *Summarie and True Discourse* and the related Boazio maps, along with correspondence pertaining to them, is now at the John Carter Brown Library, Brown University. For permission to consult this important material I wish to thank Thomas R. Adams, the Librarian. Especially helpful, both while I was there and afterwards, was Jeannette D. Black, Curator of Maps, who has given many suggestions for my study of the Boazio maps. The J.C.B. Library has generously granted permission for use as illustrations their fine copy of Boazio's so-called 'general' map, the four maps from their copy of the *Summarie* (Field edition, 1589), and also the four town maps from their copy of the German text, *Relation* (1589). In connection with the map study I express my appreciation also to Carey S. Bliss, Curator of Rare Books, the Henry E. Huntington Library, who provided photographic copies of the smaller sized maps with legends in both Latin and French; and as well to the staffs of the map rooms of the New York Public Library and the Library of Congress, and to Mr H. P. Kraus of New York, who permitted me to examine parts of his fine Drake collection. Permission to reproduce as illustrations portions of two rare undivided broadside texts of the Santo Domingo map, part of the Elkins Collection, has been granted by the Rare Book Department of the Free Library of Philadelphia.

For their helpfulness in many ways I am continually in debt to Marion U. Rueth and the staff of the Joseph Henry Apple Library of Hood College, as I am also for the kindly interest and suggestions of other associates, both at Hood College and at the Folger Library. I am happy to acknowledge a grant from the American Philosophical Society by which some costs of travel to libraries and preparation of a typescript have been financed. Special thanks are due to Mrs Doris A. Titus for her careful typing of material which was often difficult. Finally, to the Council and the Honorary Editors of the Hakluyt Society I am grateful. Their encouragement for my work with documents pertaining to a voyage in which Richard Hakluyt himself was deeply interested will, I trust, be justified by the publication which has received the Society's endorsement.

MARY FREAR KEELER

Frederick, Maryland
June 1974

ILLUSTRATIONS

ILLUSTRATIONS

MAPS

ABBREVIATIONS

Acts P.C.	*Acts of the Privy Council of England.*
Andrews, *Eliz. Priv.*	Andrews, K. R., *Elizabethan Privateering . . .* [1585–1603].
Andrews, *Last Voyage*	Andrews, K. R., *The Last Voyage of Drake & Hawkins.*
A.O.	Audit Office.
B.L.	British Library, formerly referred to as British Museum.
B.M.	*see* B.L.
Castellanos, *Discurso*	Castellanos, Juan de, *Discurso de el Capitán Francisco Draque . . . 1586–1587.*
Church	Cole, G. W., *A Catalogue of Books . . . in the Library of E. D. Church.*
Corbett, *Sp. War*	Corbett, J. S., ed., *Papers Relating to the Navy during the Spanish War 1585–1587.*
C.S.P.D.	*Calendar of State Papers, Domestic.*
C.S.P. For.	*Calendar of State Papers, Foreign.*
C.S.P. Ireland	*Calendar of State Papers, Ireland.*
C.S.P. Span.	*Calendar of State Papers, Spanish.*
C.S.P. Ven.	*Calendar of State Papers, Venetian.*
DNB	*Dictionary of National Biography.*
Harl.	Harley Manuscripts, British Library.
E.H.R.	*English Historical Review.*
H.M.C.	Historical Manuscripts Commission.
Hakluyt, *Prin. Nav.*	Hakluyt, Richard, *Principal Navigations, Voiages, Traffiques, and Discoveries.*
J.C.B. Library	John Carter Brown Library.
Lacour	Lacour, L., ed., *L'Expédition de Fr. Drake.*

Laughton, *Armada*	Laughton, J. K., ed., *State Papers Relating to the Defeat of the Armada Anno 1588*.
Morison, *European Disc. of Amer.*	Morison, S. E., *The European Discovery of America: The Northern Voyages*.
MS, MSS	Manuscript, manuscripts.
OED	*The Oxford English Dictionary*.
Oppenheim, *Naval Tracts . . . Monson*	Oppenheim, M., ed., *The Naval Tracts of Sir William Monson*.
P.C.	Privy Council Register.
pr.	printed.
P.R.O.	Public Record Office, London.
Quinn, *Gilbert*	Quinn, D. B., ed., *The Voyages and Colonising Enterprises of Sir Humphrey Gilbert*.
Quinn, *Roanoke Voyages*	Quinn, D. B., ed., *The Roanoke Voyages*.
Read, *Walsingham*	Read, C., *Mr. Secretary Walsingham and the Policy of Queen Elizabeth*.
S.P.	State Papers.
S.T.C.	Pollard, G. W. and Redgrave, G. R., *A Short-Title Catalogue of Books . . . 1475–1640*.
Summarie	Bigges, W., *A Summarie and True Discourse of Sir Francis Drake's West Indian Voyage*.
Taylor, *Writings . . . Hakluyts*	Taylor, E. G. R., ed., *The Original Writings and Correspondence of the Two Richard Hakluyts*.
Wright, *Further Eng. Voyages*	Wright, Irene A., ed., *Further English Voyages to Spanish America*.

INTRODUCTION

Four years after Sir Francis Drake returned from his voyage of circumnavigation, and more than three years before the Armada left Spain, Drake was preparing for a new expedition, ultimately the West Indies venture of 1585–86. This enterprise, which included a stop on the Spanish coast, raids on towns in the Caribbean region and Florida, and a call at Roanoke, is viewed not merely as a voyage of exploration but also as a chapter in the developing antagonism between England and Spain in the New World and in the Old. While Drake was away tales of his exploits filtered back to England, mostly by way of Spain,[1] and in less than a year after his return late in July 1586 Thomas Greepe's newsballad, *The True and Perfecte Newes . . . 1587*, published along with news of the latest venture at Cadiz,[2] was extolling Drake's achievements in the West Indies. Presently there followed a longer prose narrative, *A Summarie and True Discourse*, issued in the Armada year at Leyden in both French and Latin, and in 1589 in English, with Captain Walter Bigges designated as the principal author.[3] This is the account which Richard Hakluyt included in his second edition of the *Principal Navigations*, in 1600.[4] It became the basis

[1] 'Advertisements' from Spain, often exaggerated, were circulating as early as January 1585/6. See Julian S. Corbett, ed., *Papers Relating to the Navy during the Spanish War* (Navy Records Society XI, London, 1898), pp. 56–69. This will be referred to hereafter as Corbett, *Sp. War*. Other examples are in *The Fugger News-Letters . . . 1568–1605*, ed. by Victor von Klarwill, First series, London [1924, 1928]; second series, London [1926].

[2] Thomas Greepe, *The True and Perfect Newes . . . Syr Frauncis Drake . . . 1587*, London [1587] (*S.T.C.* 12343); facsimile ed. by David Watkin Waters, Hartford, 1955. On the date of publication see below, p. 7.

[3] See below, p. 7 and Document II. An account of the several editions of this narrative is in Appendix III, Bibliographical Note on *A Summarie and True Discourse*. The narrative will be referred to hereafter as the *Summarie*.

[4] Richard Hakluyt, ed., *The Principal Navigations, Voiages, Traffiques & Discoveries of the English Nation . . .* (3 vols., London, 1598–1600), vol. III. The Drake venture of 1585–86 was noted briefly, in the 1589 edition, as if in an editorial note at the conclusion of 'The Voyage of John Oxnam of Plymouth to the West Indies' (Facsimile ed., London, 1965, II, 596). References to Hakluyt hereafter are to the modern printing by

for all descriptions of the expedition, from the time of the early historians such as William Camden[1] and Van Meteren[2] until the present. The text has been untouched since Hakluyt's work.

More recently, additional information about the voyage has been accumulated. Particularly important was J. S. Corbett's volume, *Papers Relating to the Navy During the Spanish War, 1585–1587*, in which he presented a second narrative which is familiarly known as the '*Primrose log*', and numerous related documents from the State Papers and collections at the British Library.[3] Other English records have been edited by naval historians.[4] Spanish sources also have become available, including the long-lost portion of the contemporary poem by Juan De Castellanos,[5] several other works related to it,[6] and valuable

---

J. MacLehose & Sons (12 vols., Glasgow, 1903–5), in which the *Summarie* is in vol. x. The citations will be to Hakluyt, *Prin. Nav.*

[1] Camden's account of the voyage (in his *Annales . . . Elizabetha*, London, 1615) follows closely the outline of the *Summarie* as printed in England. William Camden, *The History of the Most Renowned . . . Princess Elizabeth* (4th ed., trans., London, 1688), pp. 322–4.

[2] Emanuel van Meteren, *Historia Belgica* [1598, 1600?], included in his *Historie der Nederlandscher* (Delft, 1599; rev. eds. 1609, 1611). Van Meteren was a consul in London for a time (C. Read, *Bibliography of British History, Tudor Period* (Oxford, 1959), p. 77), and was a friend of Richard Hakluyt (E. G. R. Taylor, ed., *The Original Writings and Correspondence of the Two Hakluyts* (2 vols., Hakluyt Society, 1935), p. 52, hereafter cited as Taylor, *Writings . . . Hakluyts*). (R[obert] Robinson's notes on this voyage, from Van Meteren's *Historia Belgica*, are in B.L., Royal MS 18A. lxvi, fols. 25v–6.)

[3] See p. 1, n. 1 above. Since Corbett used modern spelling for his edition of the *Primrose* journal, it is included with its original spelling as Document 10 of this volume. It will be alluded to hereafter as the *Primrose* journal.

[4] Most notable of these is Michael Oppenheim, ed., *The Naval Tracts of Sir William Monson*, vol. 1 (Navy Records Society, 1902); hereafter cited as Oppenheim, *Naval Tracts . . . Monson*.

[5] Juan de Castellanos, *Discurso de el Capitán Francisco Draque . . . 1586–7* [Extracted from Pt. 3 of his *Elegias*; edited with historical introduction by Angel Gonzalez Palencia], Madrid, 1921. This work will be referred to hereafter as Castellanos, *Discurso*. For further description see below, p. 8.

[6] The Castellanos poem or the documents with which it is related was evidently the source for most of what Fray Pedro Simón wrote about this expedition in his *Noticias Historiales de la Conquistas de Tierre Firme* (1623). The poem, *La Dragoneta*, by Lope de Vega (1598) deals with Drake's last voyage rather than with this one. See G. Jenner, 'A Spanish Account of Drake's Voyages', *E.H.R.*, XVI (1901), 46–66; A. K. Jameson, 'Some New Spanish Documents', *E.H.R.*, XLIX (1934), 14–31; Kenneth R. Andrews, ed., *The Last Voyage of Drake & Hawkins* (Hakluyt Society, 1972), p. 3; hereafter cited as Andrews, *Last Voyage*.

documents from the official archives of Spain. Particularly important are those edited by Irene A. Wright for the Hakluyt Society.[1] Additional English materials, still in manuscript, which throw new light on various aspects of the voyage have now been located, partly by David B. Quinn[2] and partly by the present editor. It seems appropriate therefore that a selection of documents relating to the West Indies voyage be set forth in a single volume in order that the nature and significance of the enterprise may be more fully understood. In addition to materials not previously published, this volume includes new editions of the *Primrose* journal and the *Summarie* in their early spelling. There follows a brief description of the kinds of sources, in this volume and elsewhere, that are now available concerning the voyage.[3]

THE SOURCES

Furnishing Lists, Accounts, and Plans

The 'Furnishing List' (Folger MS L.b. 344) in Document 1 provides the most satisfactory list of the ships, and new information about several captains and about Sir Philip Sidney's involvement. A less well preserved list (Harl. MS 366, fols. 146–7) adds information which has been compiled in the Table of Ships in Appendix I.

Documents 2–4, which relate to fiscal matters, include

[1] Especially valuable are the documents appended to the 1921 edition of Castellanos, *Discurso* (see p. 2, n. 6), and the depositions, reports, and other documents that were translated and edited by Irene A. Wright, *Further English Voyages to Spanish America* (Hakluyt Society, 1951); hereafter referred to as Wright, *Further Eng. Voyages*.

[2] David B. Quinn's research on explorations and colonization attempts of the period is well known. Especially useful with regard to the 1585–86 voyage is *The Roanoke Voyages* (2 vols., Hakluyt Society, 1955). Professor Quinn referred me to several of the documents that have been edited for the present volume.

[3] Because they are readily available most of the supplementary documents provided in Corbett, *Sp. War*, have not been included. The Spanish documents printed with the Castellanos poem and in Wright's volume, though they have been used for this introduction and in many footnotes, have likewise not been reprinted. With the exception of Documents 5 and 11, all of the materials edited here are from manuscripts.

Exchequer records from the Public Record Office, particularly from the Pipe Office and the Audit Office, which pertain to the queen's share in the venture and which recite various orders by which the voyage was authorized. Portions of the reports of the auditing commissioners, now at the British Library, are given also. Because Corbett published these reports in full, in a slightly rearranged form,[1] only selections are included here.

Also published by Corbett, but not reprinted now, is a document (Lansdowne MS 100, fols. 98–9), which, while it bears the date of 25 April 1586, represents an outline of the proposed voyage with estimates of amounts of booty to be expected at each stop.[2]

Ship Logs and Journals

Journals from three ships of this expedition give much information about the course of the voyage, and add accounts of military actions and observations about the regions visited. Documents 6 and 9, the fragmented journals from the *Tiger* and the *Leicester*, contain several portions which are virtually ship logs, with regular notations on sailing conditions, sometimes watch by watch. Each, however, is extended into a journal with more elaborate accounts of events than the usual ship log provides. The more complete journal from the *Primrose* (Document 10), although sometimes referred to as a log, is even more concerned with a record of events than it is with navigational matters.[3] Each of these journals came from a ship commanded by an officer of the expedition, the lieutenant general, the rear admiral, and the vice admiral, respectively.

Document 6 (B.L., Cotton MS Otho E. VIII, fols. 229–34),

[1] Lansdowne MS 52, fols. 92–100, pr. in Corbett, *Sp. War*, pp. 86–96.

[2] Pr. in Corbett, *Sp. War*, pp. 69–74.

[3] Ship logs, or navigational notebooks, are described in Andrews, *Last Voyage*, p. 263. See also the Appendix in that volume on 'The Art of Navigation', by D. W. Waters. Because each of the three documents listed above contains material beyond that relating to navigation, the term *journal*, rather than *log*, will be used for identifying them in this volume. Sample pages from the *Leicester* journal and the *Tiger* journal are in Plates IV and IX below.

is the journal of the *Tiger*, Christopher Carleill's ship, and was kept under his direction by Edward Powell.[1] Although the manuscript is badly damaged, its day-by-day record is especially valuable for dating events in the early part of the voyage, and Carleill's comments provide insight into Drake's administrative procedures at the start of the expedition. Related to it, but less complete, is Document 7.

Document 9 (B.L., Harley MS 2202, fols. 55–70v), the *Leicester* journal, is by an anonymous officer, possibly the master, on the earl of Leicester's galleon, which was listed as the 'Rear Admiral' of the fleet and was captained by Francis Knollys. Although it has survived only in fragments, with the record of the early weeks and various later parts missing, this document provides the most complete account of several events and is the only one that describes a bitter quarrel between Knollys and Drake. Supplemented by an accompanying letter from Knollys to Drake (Document 8), the journal offers much new material.

Document 10 is the journal of the *Primrose* (B.L., Royal MS 7 C. xvi, fols. 166–73).[2] Kept by an author whose name possibly was Henley, it is the record of the ship captained by Martin Frobisher, vice admiral of the expedition. Although not a daily record, its account extends over almost the entire voyage and supplies much information about the places visited. Its dates are not always reliable, and it gives relatively few details about individuals.

Fragments from two other ships' records have been edited in relation to these documents. One consists of two pages of an anonymous journal from an unidentified ship (Cotton MS Titus B. VIII, fols. 251–251v).[3] The other is a letter from Philip Sparrowe to Captain Wilson (Lansdowne MS 100, fols. 81–2), which is essentially an abbreviated log of the ill-fated *Speedwell*

---

[1] The references for this MS and for Document 7 were supplied by D. B. Quinn.

[2] Edited with modern spelling by Corbett, *Sp. War*, pp. 1–27.

[3] See p. 73, n. 3. D. B. Quinn supplied this reference. It is erroneously listed in the Catalogue of Cotton MSS (B. L. Department of Manuscripts) as fol. 241.

from the start of the voyage until her return to Weymouth for repairs on 11 October 1585.[1]

Despatches and Newsletters

Many letters relating to the voyage have remained among the State Papers and other collections. Among those printed by Corbett in his volume on the Spanish War of special significance is Carleill's despatch to Walsingham from Vigo in October 1585, which has a close relationship to the *Tiger* journal.[2]

In Document 7 is a hitherto unpublished newsletter (Cotton MS Otho E. VIII, fols. 235-6). Internal evidence suggests that it may have been written by an associate of Carleill and have been intended for Walsingham.[3] Also in the nature of a letter, and in the same hand as the *Tiger* journal, are several explanatory paragraphs in Harley MS 6221, a variant of the *Summarie*, which have been edited with Document 11.[4]

Among the documents in the Spanish national archives are various letters of which many have been presented in Wright's volume. These include reports from the president and the royal factor at Santo Domingo, and from the governor and other officials at Cartagena, Havana, and St Augustine. Especially useful is the report of Diego Hidalgo Montemayor, the official investigator of affairs at Cartagena.[5]

Contemporary Narratives

Document 5, sometimes referred to as the 'Map Log', but in this volume as the 'Map Text', is not a ship log but rather a calendar of the major events of the voyage which was provided

[1] This reference was supplied by D. B. Quinn. See also pp. 71, n. 3; 81, n. 6; 281.

[2] S.P. 12/183: 10, ff. 21-4v (pr. in Corbett, *Sp. War*, pp. 29-49). See also Wynter's letter to Walsingham, S.P. 12/183: 49-49v (pr. in Corbett, *Sp. War*, pp. 49-51); and Drake's despatch to Burghley of 26 July 1586, Lansdowne MS 51, fols. 27-8 (pr. in Corbett, *Sp. War*, pp. 83-5).

[3] See p. 106, n. 5. The reference was supplied by D. B. Quinn.

[4] See pp. 217, n. 2 and 277, n.4.

[5] The report is printed in Wright, *Further Eng. Voyages* (pp. 129-36), under date of 23 May 1586. A slightly different version bearing the date of 6 May is printed as Appendix IV in the 1921 edition of Castellanos, *Discurso*. The documents in these collections have been drawn upon freely for the editing of the English narratives.

as a text to accompany the general map of the voyage.[1] It is associated with the English edition of the *Summarie*.

For the most famous narrative, *A Summarie and True Discourse*, the English version printed by Field in 1589 has been used for Document 11. A manuscript variant of the *Summarie* has been located in Harley MS 6221, which appears to the editor to be closer to an original account that is no longer extant, with the consequence that the printed versions, whether the two foreign-language editions of 1588 or the English ones of 1589, represent the results of considerable editing.[2]

The newsballad published by Thomas Greepe in 1587, *The True and Perfecte Newes . . . 1587* (see above, p. 1), despite the difference in form and tone, follows so generally the pattern of the *Summarie*, particularly of the MS variant, that one may conjecture that it is the earliest printed derivative from the original.[3] Portions of the ballad have been used in notes.

Another narrative, possibly derived also from some version of the *Summarie*, found its way into France, where in the form of two manuscripts it remained until it was published in 1855 by L. Lacour.[4] This account is so similar to the *Summarie* that it

[1] See p. 63, n. 1 and also the Note on Maps, Appendix IV.

[2] See above, p. 1. On the several editions of the *Summarie* and on the MS variant see p. 210 n. 7, and the bibliographical note, Appendix III.

[3] See p. 213, n. 1. Since the publisher was able to refer in his title to Drake's exploits at Cadiz as well as in the West Indies, and also to print, after his ballad, a copy of Drake's letter of 27 April 1587 to John Fox from Cadiz (pr. in Corbett, *Sp. War*, pp. 111–12), the date of issue was probably not long after that letter arrived in England. It can be surmised that several MS copies of the narrative attributed to Bigges were in circulation by this time. Other accounts may have been circulating also. Bernardino de Mendoza, writing from Paris on 26 September 1586 (N.S.), said that the French ambassador had sent a special account of Drake's voyage in Latin, along with Drake's portrait, to Secretary Villeroy. Mendoza secured a copy of that account which he sent on to Madrid. *C.S.P.Span. 1580–1586*, p. 626. D. B. Quinn was unable to locate this document when he was preparing his volume on the Roanoke colony. Quinn, *Roanoke Voyages*, p. 756, n.

[4] Louis Lacour, ed., *Mémoire du Voiage en Russie . . . par Jehan Sauvage suivi de L'Expédition de Fr. Drake en Amérique . . .* [from MSS in the Bibliothèque Nationale], Paris, 1855. D. B. Quinn, who compared the MS at the Bibliothèque Nationale (MS français, anciens fonds, 704) and a similar one in Archives de la ministère des affaires étrangères (MS 24270) with the printed *Summarie*, has described them in *Roanoke Voyages*, p. 309, n. Despite occasional differences and insertions, the resemblance between this account and the *Summarie* is strong. Even if the writer was a

has not been included separately in this volume, but it has been used for numerous notes, especially in relation to Document 11.

Contemporary also, but representing the Spanish point of view, is the narrative poem, *Discurso de el Capitán Francisco Draque*, by Juan de Castellanos.[1] The author, who was a resident of New Granada at the time of Drake's raid, had the opportunity to talk with Spanish officials and eye witnesses and, at least for his account of Cartagena events, seems to have had access to the report of the judge who investigated the situation there. As in the case of the Greepe ballad, this poem includes embellishments and gives a nationalistic interpretation, but its general reliability is confirmed by the official documents.[2]

Maps

Supplementing the narratives are a number of valuable maps which depict places at which the fleet stopped and, in four cases, show the military action of the raids. Especially important are those associated with the printed *Summarie* and attributed to

---

Frenchman who participated in the expedition, as his comparisons with French places in his geographical notes suggests, he appears to have followed the outline of the *Summarie* in writing his own account. His mention of the use of cattle as a hindrance to the attackers at Santo Domingo, unless he witnessed it himself, suggests that he had at hand a printed copy of that narrative containing the Boazio map (see p. 100, n. 4, and Plate V(B). See also p. 213, n. 1.

[1] See p. 2, n. 5 above. Although the portion of the *Elegias*, in which Castellanos included his *Discurso*, was printed as early as 1589, the *Discurso* itself was omitted from publication by direction of the official censor, apparently because the account revealed too realistically the weakness of Spanish administrators in America. Missing thereafter, and considered lost when the Madrid (1850) edition of the *Elegias* was prepared, the censored pages of *Discurso* were found in the Phillipps collection in England later, and were subsequently purchased and returned in 1919 to Spain. Their publication in 1921, with supplementing documents, added important evidence on Drake's activities in 1586. Summaries of different portions of the poem are given by the editor in his introduction, and in at least two English articles: Geoffrey Callender, 'Fresh Light on Drake', *Mariner's Mirror*, IX (1923), 16–28; and A. K. Jameson, 'Some New Spanish Documents Dealing with Drake', *E.H.R.*, XLIX (1934), 14–31.

[2] On the slightly later Spanish narrative, Fray Pedro Simón's *Noticias Historiales* . . . (1623), a summary of which was provided by G. Jenner in *E.H.R.*, XVI (1901), 46–66, see p. 2, n. 6 above.

Baptista Boazio. These include, besides two versions of the town plans for Santiago, Santo Domingo, Cartagena, and St Augustine, a general map which depicts the whole course of the voyage. The maps are reproduced in Plates I, III, V, VI, VII, and are more fully described in Appendix IV, Note on Maps.

PLANS FOR THE VOYAGE

Soon after his voyage around the world Drake had proposed new ventures, possibly into the Azores under the flag of Don Antonio, the Portuguese pretender,[1] and also toward the east. But there were delays. Elizabeth and Lord Burghley were not yet ready for so open a challenge to Spain.[2] By 1584, however, the arguments of the 'war party' advisers[3] and advocates of colonizing ventures north of Spain's settlements in America began to succeed.[4] Elizabeth agreed on 29 July 1584 to permit

---

[1] James A. Williamson, *Sir John Hawkins* (Oxford, 1927), p. 398. Correspondence in Cotton MS Otho E. VIII (fols. 97–103) shows that Frobisher and the earls of Leicester and Shrewsbury also were interested. Drake's letter of 14 October 1581 is printed in Taylor, *Writings . . . Hakluyts*, pp. 169–70.

[2] On Elizabeth's cautious policy, dictated by concern about both France and Spain, and about costs, see Richard B. Wernham, 'Elizabethan War Aims and Strategy', in *Elizabethan Government and Society: Essays Presented to Sir John Neale*, ed. by Stanley T. Bindoff et al., London, 1961, pp. 340–68.

[3] Among these were Leicester, Sir Francis Knollys, Treasurer of the Household, and especially Sir Francis Walsingham, 'Mr. Secretary'. Another was John Hawkins, now Treasurer of the Navy. In July 1584 he sent to Burghley a renewal of his 1579 memorial, arguing that war with Spain was inevitable, and urging that attacks be planned on Spain's interests in the northern fisheries, in her Atlantic islands and the East Indies, and possibly on her own coasts. (James A. Williamson, *Hawkins of Plymouth* (London, 1949), pp. 225–6.) Drake's voyage became a part of this plan, and Sir Philip Sidney, according to his friend and biographer, Greville, promoted it, secretly intending to go on it himself. Ronald A. Rebholz, *The Life of Fulke Greville . . .* (Oxford, 1971), p. 70.

[4] Active proponents of colonization included such West Country men as Sir Humphrey Gilbert, whose ventures of 1578 and 1582–83 failed, and Sir Walter Raleigh, his half-brother, who continued his efforts. Walsingham's stepson, Christopher Carleill, wrote in 1583 *A Briefe and Summary Discourse . . .*, arguing the commercial gains to be derived from such ventures (see p. 291); and in 1584 Richard Hakluyt's *Discourse Concerning Western Planting* was presented to the queen. See also Quinn, *Roanoke Voyages*, pp. 225–6.

a new voyage by Drake toward the Moluccas to strike at Portuguese interests there, and to venture £17,000 herself toward the proposed total cost of £40,000.[1]

While arrangements for this voyage were going forward late in the year, parliament in December gave its formal approval for Raleigh's proposed colony in North America. Plans began to stir also for a strike against Spanish shipping in the Newfoundland fisheries and for armed assistance to the Dutch.[2] In April 1585, however, while Raleigh's colonists, led by Sir Richard Grenville, set out from Plymouth, Drake was held at London because the queen had changed her mind.[3] Richard Hakluyt wrote to Walsingham from Paris on 7 April, urging that, even though Drake's voyage had been stayed, 'yet the rumour of his setting forth' should be continued because of the vexation such news was causing Spain.[4] That country's annoyance stemmed partly from uncertainty about what was planned beyond the obvious threat to the Indies treasure fleets.

[1] See p. 52, n. 3; also, Oppenheim, *Naval Tracts ... Monson*, I, 125; Williamson, *Sir John Hawkins*, p. 411. Drake's commission to organize the fleet was signed on Christmas Eve. Corbett, *Drake and the Tudor Navy* (2 vols., London, 1898), II, 9.

[2] Having secured the renewal of Gilbert's patent in March 1584, Raleigh sent out his first reconnoitering expedition in the spring (Samuel Eliot Morison, *The European Discovery of America* (N.Y., 1971), pp. 619–26; hereafter, Morison, *European Disc. Amer.*); and parliament formally approved Raleigh's plan and patent on 18 December (Simonds D'Ewes, ed., *The Journals of ... the Parliaments ... of Queen Elizabeth* (London, 1682), pp. 338, 340. See also Conyers Read, *Mr. Secretary Walsingham* (3 vols., Oxford, 1925), III, 102–3, 116 (hereafter, Read, *Walsingham*).

[3] Although orders in England had called for secrecy about Drake, the English ambassador wrote from Paris on 16 October 1584 that 'here it is in everyone's mouth' (*C.S.P.For. 1584–1585*, p. 108). With remarkable accuracy Mendoza reported to King Philip from France, 22 February 1585, of the queen's plan to supply Drake with £20,000 for an expedition of 24 large vessels and 20 pinnaces which were to go for the West Indies, intercepting the treasure fleets, and possibly landing at Nombre de Dios (*C.S.P.Span. 1580–1586*, pp. 531–2). Other informers reported extensive preparation in March and then, in early May, that Drake was not to go. *C.S.P.For. 1584–1585*, pp. 353, 455, 467. See also Roger B. Merriman, *The Rise of the Spanish Empire* (4 vols., N.Y., 1962), IV, 517–18; and Wright, *Further Eng. Voyages*, p. 8.

[4] *C.S.P.Span. 1580–1586*, p. 532, n. 5. By 4 May (N.S.) Mendoza learned that the plans were still proceeding, and that the queen was assisting the fitting out of Leicester's galleon, a ship called *Primrose*, and several others besides a royal ship. Ibid., p. 537. Document 2 below shows that payments were being made from Exchequer, but also that Elizabeth knew the delays were troubling the adventurers.

In various places it was thought that open war between Spain and England was about to begin.[1]

Events of May and June finally caused Queen Elizabeth to take bolder measures. King Philip's act of embargoing English grain ships that had come to his coast – the *Primrose* of London only managing a spectacular escape – was the immediate occasion.[2] The Privy Council now authorized the issue of general letters for reprisals against Spanish shipping,[3] and on 1 July Drake's commission for his voyage was renewed.[4] The ostensible purpose, as his stop at Bayona shows, was to secure the release of the embargoed ships,[5] but he wanted also to meet the treasure fleets,[6] and then to ransack various Spanish posts in the Caribbean area, and possibly to establish a base by which English interests in the Western Hemisphere might be furthered.[7] Anti-Spanish feeling was running high in England by this time, and Drake's preparations, resumed in haste, attracted great interest.[8]

[1] Attacks at various points, some possibly in the name of Don Antonio, were imagined. *C.S.P.Span. 1580–1586*, p. 535; *C.S.P.Ven. 1581–1591*, p. 116; *C.S.P.For. 1584–1585*, pp. 610, 642.

[2] *C.S.P.Span. 1580–1586*, p. 543; Corbett, *Drake and the Tudor Navy*, II, 10–11. A Fugger newsletter (11 July 1585) reported that Philip was massing a fleet to move toward the Netherlands, and that war was to be expected. *The Fugger News-Letters*, 2nd series (1926), p. 92.

[3] The Council order of 9 July 1585 (S.P. 12/180:15) is pr. in Corbett, *Sp. War*, pp. 36–8.

[4] See p. 53, and Corbett, *Drake and the Tudor Navy*, II, 11. It was heard at Cologne by 9 August (N.S.) that Drake was already at sea, awaiting the Peru fleet and seizing ships from Newfoundland. *The Fugger News-Letters*, 2nd series (1926), p. 93.

[5] See the negotiations at Vigo, pp. 78–87 below.

[6] The lateness of his start and the storms of late September prevented this. See Drake's letter of July 1586 to Burghley (Lansdowne MS 51, fols. 27–8, pr. in Corbett, *Sp. War*, pp. 83–5); and below, p. 127, n. 2.

[7] The plan dated 25 April 1586 (see above, p. 4) indicated the amount of plunder to be expected at each place. A few minor errors occurred in Corbett's transcription of this document (*Sp. War*, pp. 69–74). Naval historians have thought that Drake wished to take Cartagena as a base from which traffic about the Isthmus of Panama might be controlled and English settlements to the north encouraged. Kenneth R. Andrews, *Elizabethan Privateering* (Cambridge, 1964), p. 192; Corbett, *Sp. War*, p. xiv; Oppenheim, *Naval Tracts...Monson*, I, 123.

[8] The English view that Spaniards were a cruel and treacherous people, as well as supporters of Papists, appeared even in Hakluyt's writings. See William S. Maltby, *The Black Legend in England ... 1558–1660* (Duke Univ. Press, 1971), especially

ADVENTURERS, SHIPS, AND PERSONNEL

The expedition, though royally sponsored and including among its ships two from the royal navy and others fitted out at the navy's expense,[1] was organized as were most of the voyages of this period as a joint-stock enterprise. The adventurers, representing a capital investment of some £40,000 in addition to the queen's £20,000,[2] included royal officials, noblemen, merchants of London, Plymouth and Bristol, and seamen such as Drake and members of the Hawkins family, who were risking themselves as well as their fortunes.[3] They must have included the backers of the 'Moluccas voyage' as it had been proposed in 1584: Sir Christopher Hatton, the earl of Leicester, and Raleigh, along with Drake himself and the Hawkins brothers, John and William.[4] Further, ships and possibly capital were ventured now by Charles Lord Howard, the Lord High Admiral, Sir William Wynter, Surveyor of Ships, the earl of Shrewsbury, and a Cornish gentleman and M.P., Sir William Mohun. The earls of Bedford[5] and Rutland,[6] too, may have had shares. Sir Philip Sidney was interested

---

pp. 63–5. Examples of such feeling occur in several documents in the present volume, particularly in the *Primrose* journal and the *Summarie*.

[1] Cf. n. 4, p. 10 above; and Corbett, *Sp. War*, pp. 242, 247–8.

[2] See Drake's accounts in Document 4. The voyage plan dated in April 1586, see p. 4, shows an optimistic expectation that booty amounting to 2,610,000 ducats, or roughly £717,750, might be taken.

[3] On backers of voyages of this period see Ronald Pollett, 'John Hawkins's Troublesome Voyages', *Journal of British Studies*, XII (1973), 26–40; and G. V. Scammel, 'Shipowning in the Economy and Politics of Early Modern England', *Historical Journal*, XV (1972), 385–407.

[4] Cf. n. 3, p. 52.

[5] See Document 1 and Table of Ships. On Leicester's investments in this and other voyages, and on Shrewsbury's ventures, see also Lawrence Stone, *The Crisis of the Aristocracy* (Oxford, 1955), p. 376, and E. G. R. Taylor, ed., *The Troublesome Voyage of . . . Fenton* (Hakluyt Society), 1959.

[6] Rutland's interest is indicated by letters sent to him regarding Drake's preparations and on his return. H.M.C., *Rutland MSS*, I, 176–8, 200. Mentioned for shares of £200 to £500 for a voyage Leicester was promoting, probably Fenton's of 1582, were the earls of Oxford, Lincoln, Pembroke, and Warwick, Lord Hunsdon, and Walsingham. Cotton MS Otho E. VIII, fols. 105–7. Some of these were probably adventurers also in 1585.

personally, as was his father-in-law, Sir Francis Walsingham, although evidence of capital investment by either has not been found;[1] the same may be said of Sir Francis Knollys, senior,[2] and even of Lord Burghley.[3]

Of lesser men we have few names, but the voyage attracted numerous gentlemen as active participants, and shares were probably bought by well-to-do members of the gentry, who were learning the value of investments at this time. Besides Sir William Mohun of Cornwall, who seems to have supplied a ship, another may have been Sir William More of Loseley, friend of the Lord High Admiral.[4] London merchants sent the *Primrose* and possibly the *Tiger*, as well as a number of pinnaces.[5]

[1] Sidney's interest in Atlantic voyages and colonization plans is well known, and his active role in Drake's new venture is shown not only by Greville's *Life* (Fulke Greville, *The Life of . . . Sir Philip Sidney* (London, 1652; Oxford, 1907), pp. 70–8), but by Documents 1 and 6 below. Strong evidence of Walsingham's interest in every aspect of the voyage, from its planning stage until after its return, is found in Documents 2, 6, 7 and 11. See also Corbett, *Drake and the Tudor Navy*, II, 14; Read, *Walsingham*, III, 162, n., 370–410.

[2] Two of the elder Knollys's sons had planned to go on one of Gilbert's voyages. D. B. Quinn, *The Voyages . . . of Sir Humphrey Gilbert* (2 vols., Hakluyt Society, 1940), pp. 40, 42, 208–9, 218; hereafter, Quinn, *Gilbert*. The elder Knollys had been an adventurer in Frobisher's 1578 voyage (G. B. Parks, 'Frobisher's Last Voyage', *Huntington Library Bulletin*, no. 7 (1935), p. 183), and with his son and namesake commanding the ship belonging to their relative, Leicester, it is probable that he made some investment in 1585 also.

[3] Burghley noted in his journal in August that Drake was at Plymouth, preparing to go to the Indies (Corbett, *Drake and the Tudor Navy*, II, 14), and it was to him that Drake addressed his letter of the next year explaining why he had missed the Spanish treasure fleet (see above, p. 6, n. 2).

[4] See p. 45, n. 1.

[5] The London merchants, angered by Spain's embargo, were rumoured to have offered to provide a whole fleet of ships, with their own admiral (H.M.C., *Rutland MSS*, I, 176). Frobisher and the *Primrose* may have represented their interest. Cf. Document 1 and Appendix I, Table of Ships. Indicated as possible shareholders for the Fenton voyage (Cotton MS Otho E. VIII, fols. 106–7) were Luke Ward, 'Mr. Cust[omer] Smythe', Thomas Heneage, Alderman Martin, and various other aldermen, and they may have subscribed also for 1585. Members of the Muscovy Company, with which Christopher Carleill and his ship *Tiger* had been associated in 1582 (see p. 291), probably bought shares.

Named by the Privy Council in 1586 to go to Drake's ships as soon as they should arrive at Woolwich and Blackwell and to begin the appraisal of them and their cargoes were: Sir William Wynter, Alderman [Richard] Martin, Alderman [John] Harte (a director of the Muscovy Company), Thomas Smythe (Farmer of the Customs), Mr I. Hussey, Richard Drake, Martin Frobisher, and Christopher Carleill. P.R.O., P.C. 14:170. (For those who actually functioned see Document 4, p. 60, n. 1.) If these

The Plymouth merchants were represented by the *Minion* and several pinnaces. Both Drake and John Hawkins contributed ships,[1] and Drake must have invested money also, since the auditors' accounts mention his charges during the preparations for the voyage.[2]

The fleet as it left Plymouth on 14 September numbered about twenty-five sail, with eight or more pinnaces besides.[3] It was larger than the one planned in 1584,[4] and rumours of the time had its size running from twenty-four to thirty-five ships.[5] Besides the two royal ships, *Elizabeth Bonaventure* (600 tons) and *Aid* (200–250 tons), the larger ships were the galleon *Leicester* (400 tons), *Primrose* (300–400 tons), and *Tiger* (150–200 tons).[6] Ten more were in the range of 100 to 200 tons, most of them 100 to 150 tons,[7] and the rest ran in size from the *Francis*

---

were the same commissioners named to hear complaints by the men about their pay, they were adventurers (see the Council's letter of 18 September appointing a different group of men, not adventurers, to hear further and act upon those complaints. P.R.O., P.C. 2/14: 189).

[1] Cf. Document 1 and Table of Ships.

[2] See p. 60.

[3] Cf. Document 1 and Table of Ships. The *Summarie* mentions the figure of twenty-five ships, but gives an inaccurate list. The figure was twenty-five, according to the Greepe news-ballad, but twenty-three, according to the Map Text (see pp. 214, n. 1, 64). The anonymous journal (Cotton MS Titus B. VIII, fol. 251) states the number as '22 Sayll of shippes grett and small and one small gallye & 8 pinesses'. Philip Sparrowe noted '20 to xxv [ships] . . . besides the galley with the Mathue [and] pinisses' (Lansdowne MS 100, fol. 81). The *Primrose* journal combined all in the figure of twenty-nine ships and pinnaces (see p. 180).

A pinnace was generally an oared craft, somewhat larger than a ship's boat, but constructed for the use of sail as well as oars, and ranging from 20 to 60 tons. It was valuable for reconnoitering and for landing operations. Corbett, *Sp. War*, pp. 1, n., 340.

[4] Projected then were eleven ships, four barks, and fifteen pinnaces. P.R.O., E. 351/2222.

[5] *C.S.P.Span. 1580–1586*, pp. 531, 543, 548; *C.S.P.Ven. 1581–1591*, p. 116; *The Fugger News-Letters*, 2nd series (1926), p. 92. Mendoza received his information through a Frenchman who posed as planning to go with Drake and then deserted. *C.S.P.Span. 1580–1586*, p. 551.

[6] Of these the *Bonaventure* was designated as 'Admiral', the *Primrose* as 'Vice Admiral', and the *Leicester* as 'Rear Admiral'. The titles referred to the ships, not necessarily to their captains.

[7] See nos. 6–15, Table of Ships. Several of the barks were in this group, though others were smaller. The term *bark* was used loosely, according to Corbett (*Sp. War*, pp. 98, n., 340), and included 'all sailing vessels of lower degree'.

or the 'little *Elizabeth*' (60–70 tons) to the galliot *Duck* (20 tons).[1]

Changes in the fleet occurred as the voyage progressed. Additions were a French prize ship that was renamed the *Drake*,[2] a Spanish prize that was held briefly and then destroyed,[3] and ships that were taken or exchanged at Santo Domingo and Cartagena.[4] Among these was the *New Year's Gift*, which had to be abandoned afterwards at Cartagena. The little *Speedwell*, forced from the fleet by the storm at Bayona, limped back to England;[5] and several others, of which one was the *Francis*, were driven to sea by the Hatteras storm in June and went straight for home.[6]

Distinguished owners of private ships in the fleet were the earl of *Leicester*, who may have owned the *Speedwell* as well as the galleon bearing his name; the earl of Shrewsbury; Lord Howard, the Lord Admiral; and Sir William Wynter. John Hawkins seems to have owned four, and to have had a shared interest in five more. Drake owned three (*Francis*, *Mathew* and *Thomas*) and possibly the *Elizabeth*, and may have shared with Hawkins in others. Merchant groups in London and the West Country owned the rest.[7]

The list of ship captains is impressive. Vice admiral of the fleet and captain of the *Primrose*, sent on the voyage by the queen's command, was Martin Frobisher, the distinguished

[1] 'A large pinnace or small galleon fitted with oars' (Corbett, *Sp. War*, p. 5, n.). She is referred to occasionally in the narratives as a galley.

[2] See Table of Ships.

[3] See p. 76 and n. 3.

[4] See p. 157. Three older English ships, *Hope*, *Benjamin*, and *Scout*, were replaced by prize ships at Santo Domingo. The *Primrose* journal (pp. 197, 202) states that two ships were exchanged there, and two others at Cartagena.

[5] See p. 221. Sparrowe's letter (see p. 5) described her return voyage, which ended on 11 October.

[6] The separation of the *Francis* from the fleet hastened Governor Lane's decision to leave Roanoke (see p. 273). Four ships were forced out to sea, according to the *Primrose* journal (see p. 209). Among expenses reported by Drake after his return to England were victuals and a new cable for the *Francis*, a cable for the *Talbot*, and both anchors and cables for *Sea Dragon* and *White Lion*. Lansdowne MS 52, fol. 100, pr. in Corbett, *Sp. War*, pp. 95–6.

[7] For further evidence regarding owners see Table of Ships.

explorer and naval officer. Serving as captain of the *Tiger*, as well as lieutenant general for all land operations, was the experienced Christopher Carleill, Walsingham's stepson, just back from Ireland for this service.[1] A veteran seaman, Thomas Fenner, was captain of the *Bonaventure* under Drake. Captain of the *Leicester*, and listed as rear admiral during parts of the journey, was Francis Knollys, younger son of the Treasurer of the Household and brother-in-law of the earl of Leicester, who had sailed with his brother Henry in privateering and other ventures. Known for his court connections, but of less experience, was Sir William Wynter's son Edward, captain of the queen's ship *Aid*. Fulke Greville, who had had some limited sea duty but was known chiefly as a courtier, was listed for a time as captain of the *Hope*, but he was replaced by the more experienced Edward Careless when, with Sidney, he withdrew.[2] Robert Crosse, mentioned as 'a man of Mr. Vice Chamberlain's' (i.e. Hatton's), had also known earlier action at sea and soon gained Drake's confidence.[3] Another gentleman-captain was the Cornishman, James Erisey, commanding the Lord Admiral's ship *White Lion*. Henry Whyte, recommended by Sidney to replace the elder William Hawkins as captain of *Sea Dragon*, was probably trained in the royal navy. John Vaughan, to whom the prize ship *Drake* was later assigned, was an experienced captain, as was 'old Cely' of the *Minion*, a Bristol man who had suffered as a prisoner in Spanish galleys. Others were men whom Drake knew well: his brother Thomas, the younger William Hawkins, who had been around the world with him, and young Richard Hawkins, son of John, in charge of the tiny *Duck*; and at least three more companions of the global voyage: George Fortescue, John Martin and Thomas Moone.[4]

As to the military officers,[5] Carleill's continental experience

[1] See p. 9, n. 4 above, and Appendix II, Personnel.
[2] See Document I and Appendix II, Personnel.
[3] See pp. 49, 87, and Appendix II, Personnel.
[4] For further identifications, see Appendix II, Personnel.
[5] On the errors in the list in the printed *Summarie* see p. 47, n. 4, and p. 215, n. 1.

eminently qualified him to be lieutenant general, and his principal aids, Anthony Powell, the sergeant major, and Matthew Morgan and John Sampson, the two corporals-of-the-field, were professional soldiers. Sampson, whom Carleill regarded highly, had been with him in Ireland and perhaps before. Of the eight captains of companies, at least five or six had served in the Low Countries or in Ireland.[1] Among their subordinates some may have been gentleman adventurers,[2] but it is clear that those who planned the voyage envisaged military actions that would require seasoned commanders.[3]

Among the personnel also were men with special abilities of different kinds, many of whom remain anonymous. Accompanying Drake was his chaplain, Philip Nicholls,[4] and among his 'gentlemen' was one Jonas, who had enough knowledge of Spanish to act at times as interpreter.[5] With Carleill was Baptista Boazio, whose skills in language and in drawing were useful during the expedition and afterwards.[6]

Besides these there were in the company numerous gentlemen who possibly lacked particular skills but had joined in pursuit of adventure.[7] As early as his globe-encircling voyage Drake had stated the need to have gentlemen in addition to common seamen with him, 'for government's sake'.[8] Now,

[1] Barton, Bigges, Goring, Pew, Platt, and probably Marchant were professional soldiers. So, too, may have been Cecil and Hannam, both of whom died during the voyage and about whom fuller evidence is lacking.

[2] e.g. Nicholas Wynter, younger brother of Edward; Captain John Grenville, younger son of the famous Sir Richard; or Richard Stanton, who went out as Knollys's lieutenant and became a captain during the voyage. On these and others, chiefly lieutenants, see Appendix II, Personnel.

[3] The list of military equipment supplied for the voyage is further evidence of this kind of planning. See Corbett, *Sp. War*, pp. 27–33; also, J. H. Parry, *The Spanish Seaborne Empire* (1966), p. 255.

[4] See p. 139 and Appendix II, Personnel.

[5] See p. 178 and Appendix II.

[6] See Plate VIII(A), (B), Appendix II, and Appendix IV, Note on Maps. Cf. also p. 31, n. 1.

[7] Of this type probably were Messrs Chamberlain, Longe, and Thorowgood, who had been recruited by the earl of Leicester for his ship, and who stood by their captain, Francis Knollys, in his dispute with Drake. See Document 9.

[8] 'As gentlemen are very necessary for government's sake in the voyage, so have I shipped them for that, and to some farther intent', he had declared at the time of the

for a venture that held political and anti-Spanish appeal, as well as hope of lucrative gain, many gentlemen were eager to go.[1]

Two gentlemen who did not sail were Sir Philip Sidney and his friend, Fulke Greville. Sidney had been interested early,[2] and as an officer in the ordnance department he assisted with the preparations. Drake even deferred to Sidney's preferences on some appointments,[3] and he entertained both young men when they hastened down to Plymouth as departure time neared. That he ever intended to divide his command with Sidney, as Greville related it, however, is doubtful,[4] and any such possibility ended when, apparently as a result of Drake's intervention, Queen Elizabeth recalled Sidney from Plymouth. He and Greville were aboard ship with Drake on the very eve of sailing,[5] but the continued presence of Sidney would have made difficult, if not impossible, Drake's full exercise of command.

ADMINISTRATION AND AUTHORITY

Even without Sidney, Drake encountered problems in organizing his fleet and managing so diversified a complement of men and officers. After the many delays, his departure from Plymouth on 14 September was in haste, in order both to catch a favourable wind and to avoid the risk that the queen might again change her mind. He sailed without full supplies of water

---

Doughty crisis, which had involved controversy between sailors and gentlemen, according to John Cooke's account (Harl. MS 540), pr. in W. S. W. Vaux, *The World Encompassed by Sir Francis Drake* (Hakluyt Society, 1854), p. 213.

[1] It was reported to Spain in April 1585 that many 'special gentlemen' were preparing to go. Quinn, *Roanoke Voyages*, p. 732.

[2] See above, p. 12.

[3] See Document 1.

[4] On the question of Sidney's involvement see Greville, *Life of . . . Sir Philip Sidney*, pp. 70–8; Roger Howell, *Sir Philip Sidney* (London, 1968), pp. 232–6; and Rebholz, *The Life of Fulke Greville*, p. 20.

[5] See p. 70.

and victuals, and without having drawn up orders for his captains. Parts of the latter were not completed until the stop at Bayona, and orders about the conduct of the men were issued even later.[1]

As the voyage proceeded Drake frequently called a council of captains, with shipmasters sometimes included, to decide on a change of course or to set plans for an attack. The council functioned in an advisory capacity; how well Drake accepted advice, if in his own mind he had settled on a course, may be open to question.[2] The council acted also in handling matters of discipline, taking on the function of a court in such cases.[3] In these ways Drake was developing practices that were later accepted as naval procedure.[4] At other times he relied on a kind of inner council of his highest officers, using especially

[1] Cf. pp. 71, 82, and Carleill's despatch to Walsingham, pr. in Corbett, *Sp. War*, pp. 39–49. The *Leicester* journal reproduces several of the sets of orders (e.g. pp. 130, 140).

Orders prepared for the Fenton voyage mentioned a council to be appointed by the 'general', and added: 'Above all thinges, order is to be taken for amitie, and good obedience, amongst the General, Captaines, gentlemen and the rest'. Cotton MS Otho E. VIII fol. 105. Possibly similar instructions were included in Drake's orders of 1585.

[2] William Borough, whom Drake removed from his post as vice admiral on the Cadiz expedition, declared that the council was expected to accept decisions Drake had already made, and that he relied for advice chiefly on two men who were closest to him, his chaplain (i.e. Philip Nicholls) and Captain Fenner. Corbett, *Sp. War*, pp. 124, 143. See also p. 170 below. Examples of council decisions on policy in 1585–86 are those before the Palma incident, the attacks on Santo Domingo and Cartagena, and the offers made at Roanoke.

[3] See the case of sailors disciplined for neglect of duty (p. 96); and the protracted problem of Francis Knollys (see below, pp. 20, 144, 147, etc.). On at least one occasion the form of verdict by a jury was used (see p. 148); and some regular court procedures were evidently followed during the long stays at Santo Domingo and Cartagena (see pp. 151, 169).

[4] Borough declared that in his case Drake 'panelled a jury, and upon their verdict (by his law and himself the judge) pronounced sentence of death against me'. Supporters of Drake in that case, however, denied that his conduct was so highhanded. Corbett points out that the trial of Doughty in 1578 was the first known precedent for a maritime tribunal, and that it became a model for the orders for Fenton's voyage, but without provision for capital jurisdiction over superior officers. After the Borough affair of 1587, it became customary for special judicial powers to be inserted in the commissions of commanding officers. Corbett, *Sp. War*, pp. xlviii–xlix, 152, 163. As to Drake's authority in the Knollys case of 1585–86, cf. the wording in Knollys's letter, p. 118 below.

Carleill and Frobisher,[1] but not the next in rank, Francis Knollys.[2]

It must be borne in mind that none of his ranking officers had sailed previously with Drake, and that both Carleill and Knollys had high family and court connections. The former, Walsingham's stepson, was a man of greater experience and reputation than Knollys and, though he had had differences with his superiors in Ireland, he soon gained Drake's confidence. With Knollys, however, the matter was different. The son of Elizabeth's puritanical Treasurer of the Household,[3] he was related by blood to the queen herself, and by marriage to Leicester. His designation as rear admiral, attributable possibly to these connections but also to the size of his ship, seems to have counted for little in Drake's view at the start, and for several months of the voyage Drake suspended him from the rank for insubordination, and threatened to send him home. Knollys was not inexperienced at sea, as he protested in a letter to Drake in January 1586.[4] He had been with his brother Henry in ventures of 1578 and 1582, planning at the earlier date to go out with Sir Humphrey Gilbert,[5] and his name was next to Frobisher's in the January 1586 list of captains fit to command ships for the queen.[6] Drake must, however, have heard about how the Knollys brothers deserted from the Gilbert expedition of 1578, and have had some concern about how loyal Knollys

[1] Carleill noted in the *Tiger* journal several conferences during the first few days of the voyage (see pp. 71, 72). Carleill and Frobisher were the officers who vouched for the accuracy of Drake's accounts after their return. Corbett, *Sp. War*, p. 92. Cf. p. 19, n. 2.

[2] On the matter of Knollys's rank, see p. 16 and also pp. 152, 170.

[3] The elder Knollys's outspoken Puritanism was well known. Although he was considered one of Walsingham's allies, his influence was less great than the secretary's. Read, *Walsingham*, I, 13; II, 264; III, 81, n.

[4] See Document 8, p. 116. Only the *Leicester* journal provides details about this case.

[5] See Appendix II, Personnel; also, *C.S.P.For. 1579–1580.* p. 464; *1581–1582*, pp. 418, 433–4; Corbett, *Drake and the Tudor Navy*, I, 378; Quinn, *Gilbert*, pp. 40–2, 208–9, 218.

[6] S.P. 12/186: 19. His name was written there as 'Fraunces Knowles gentle*man*', without the title of *Sir*; Corbett (*Sp. War*, p. 292) misinterpreted a mark on the MS in reading the title. Knollys was not knighted until December 1587. W. A. Shaw, *Knights of England* (2 vols., London, 1906), II, 86.

would be on this new voyage. Further, Drake may have regarded him as representing interests at court, especially those of his brother-in-law, Leicester, whose ship he commanded. As such, though less conspicuously than in Sidney's case, his presence may have been viewed by Drake as a potential for problems in the chain of command. It is understandable that Drake, as Carleill's account indicates, chose not to include Knollys among his confidants. It is likewise understandable that Knollys resented that exclusion, and that he became jealous of Drake's increasing reliance upon Carleill.[1] The test of Drake's authority came early, during the occupation of the Cape Verde town of Santiago in November.

Carleill had assisted Drake in drawing up various sets of orders during the stop at Vigo, and rules about pillage were announced in early November.[2] Later, at Santiago, there were put forth additional rules on the relationship of military officers to the high command, and of their soldiers to them with oaths of obedience to be sworn.[3] Most of these Knollys regarded as inapplicable to him, a ship captain. A heated argument quickly developed, first between Knollys, supported by some of his followers, and Drake's chaplain, and then with Drake himself. Although their protest was based partly on the ground of religious scruples about the oaths, it seemed to rest also on the requirement that men of their station must take oaths designed for common soldiers. Drake, angered at their criticism, charged Knollys with defending his men against their general, adding, 'They were a pack brought a purpose'. Although an attempt at conciliation was led by Frobisher and

[1] Evidence of this distrust on the part of Knollys and others aboard the *Leicester* appears frequently in Document 9. Frobisher, who seems not to have been directly involved in the quarrel, undertook at one time to intercede on Knollys's behalf (see p. 145).

[2] See pp. 82, 130. On Carleill's previous experience in military administration see Rachel Lloyd, *Elizabethan Adventurer . . . Carleill* (London, 1974), pp. 49–50.

[3] See pp. 140–1. The decision to require such oaths probably resulted from Drake's experience with Doughty in 1578, and his orders for the voyage may have mentioned such procedure (see above, p. 19, n. 1). Possibly he consulted Carleill about them, but they were actually drawn up by Drake's chaplain, Philip Nicholls. On the latter, see Appendix II, Personnel, and p. 19, n. 2 above.

several other sea captains, the issue was not resolved. Plans were proposed for shipping Knollys and his staunchest supporters home, but were postponed when the fleet needed to move on. Several of his men were transferred to other ships, however, and Knollys, relieved of his rank, was apparently held under the supervision of a marshal until January, awaiting a firm decision by Drake. A compromise of some sort was arranged at Santo Domingo, partly through the intercession of Edward Wynter, and at Cartagena Knollys performed certain non-military duties once more as rear admiral.[1]

No reference to this quarrel appears in English accounts except that for Knollys's ship, the *Leicester*, but a Spanish official at Cartagena noted in May 1586 that there had been disagreements between Drake and some of his officers, some of whom were removed from their posts.[2] Spain's ambassador, Mendoza, heard later that the quarrel between Drake and Knollys recurred after their return to England, with the result that the queen ordered Knollys to be kept under arrest for some days.[3]

Another feature of administration for the fleet was the keeping of records. A 'book' of the voyage was mentioned by both Carleill and Drake. The survival of copies of various sets of orders in the *Leicester* journal suggests that each officer, or

[1] See pp. 142–5, 155, 170. Throughout this controversy Drake called his council for consultations, but his own views were evidently the determinants. Various gaps in the MS of the *Leicester* journal prevent the telling of the full story. See also n. 3 below.

[2] Wright, *Further Eng. Voyages*, p. 135. A newsletter from Madrid, dated in July 1586, noted a report that some of Drake's captains had 'sailed away home from him, ships and all, because he had broken his word over the partition of the booty'. The same letter, however, had faulty news about Havana. *The Fugger News-Letters*, 2nd series (1926), p. 114.

[3] Mendoza, writing to King Philip from Paris, 8 November 1586 (N.S.), stated that delays in Drake's plans for Cadiz were caused by the disappointments about profits from the previous voyage, and by Drake's bad treatment of seamen and others who had gone with him, and also because of Francis Knollys, relative of the queen and of Leicester, 'who has always taken out ships of plunder and went with Drake on his last voyage. In consequence of the small profit they made and the loss of so many men, they had high words on the voyage, and the quarrel had been renewed since they came to London. The queen ordered Knollys to be kept under arrest for some days, and Drake in consequence has become much disliked. . . .' *C.S.P.Span. 1580–1586*, p. 650.

INTRODUCTION

possibly each ship's captain, kept not only the daily log of the journey but copies of orders as they were issued.[1] In Drake's case there must have been also fiscal accounts, not only for expenses in fitting out the voyage and buying supplies, as during the stop at Vigo, but for records of ransoms collected. The death of his secretary prevented the orderly completing of his book, and his accounts for the auditors were assembled with difficulty after his return.[2] As he approached England, Drake wrote to Burghley requesting cash for payment to his men. The Privy Council on 5 September 1586 ordered that the men's wages should be paid,[3] and on 18 September set up a special committee to hear some further complaints and arrange for payments,[4] but other participants waited even longer for reimbursement.[5] The poor return for the voyage, with the adventurers, including the queen, receiving only 15s. on a pound of their investment, should probably be attributed, however, not to mismanagement of the accounts, but to the delays and hardships the expedition encountered and to the reality that the Spanish colonies did not possess wealth in the amounts that had been anticipated.[6]

[1] See *Tiger* journal, p. 71, and Drake's comment, p. 61; and Corbett, *Sp. War*, pp. 88, 93.

[2] See Document 4. The more detailed accounts of the ransom negotiations in the *Leicester* journal (Document 9) are in general confirmed by the Spanish records printed in Wright, *Further Eng. Voyages*.

[3] This order was issued as a special instruction to the auditing commissioners. Cf. p. 55.

[4] On 18 September the Privy Council appointed a special committee of Londoners who were not adventurers, as were the auditing commissioners, to hear the complaints of soldiers and mariners against Drake for default of payment, and to arrange for some proportionate payments to be made. The letter added that, if any of the mariners and soldiers showed themselves obstinate they should be committed to prison. P.R.O., P.C. 2/14:189.

[5] At least Frobisher and Carleill had to wait. *Acts P.C. 1587–1588*, pp. 75–6; *1588*, p. 63.

[6] See the estimates in the plan dated in April 1586, above, p. 11, n. 7.

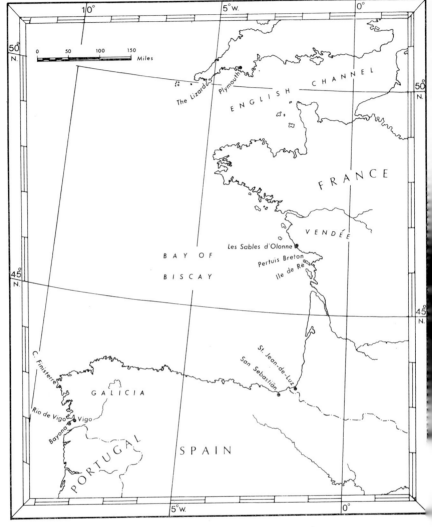

Fig. 1. Area of Drake's Voyage, 14–27 September 1585

INTRODUCTION

THE VOYAGE TO SPAIN,
14 SEPTEMBER–11 OCTOBER 1585

Since the publication of the narrative known as the *Summarie* in four languages, 1588–89, the main events of the West Indies voyage have been familiar, and the text for the general map prepared at the same time (Document 5), shows the sequence of events.[1] More details about the crossing to Spain are supplied by the journals from the *Tiger* and the *Primrose* (Documents 6 and 10), and permit corrections of parts of the account as given in the *Summarie*.

After leaving Plymouth on 14 September, and staying close to the English coast, the fleet reached the Lizard by the afternoon of the 16th, and then turned southward. On the 18th they met French ships bringing fish back from Newfoundland, and they passed an unidentified vessel on the night of the 19th. On the 22nd, not far from Cape Finisterre, they overtook another ship laden with fish, homeward bound to a Biscay port. Although her master declared she was from St Jean-de-Luz in France, Drake determined by other evidence that she was instead a Spanish vessel from the region of San Sebastián, and therefore a lawful prize.[2] Soon after passing Cape Finisterre, they met some English armed merchantmen that were hovering about the coast in the hope of recovering others embargoed by the Spaniards. These now joined forces with Drake for a time.[3] On 25 September they intercepted a group of French ships carrying salt from Spain. The newest of these Drake appropriated, although, since she belonged to a French merchant of Sables d'Olonne, she was not a legitimate prize. This is the ship subsequently named the *Drake*.[4]

[1] Modern summaries, based mainly on the evidence of the *Summarie*, supplemented by the *Primrose* journal and other materials edited by Corbett, are included in: K. R. Andrews, *Drake's Voyages* (London, 1967); Corbett, *Drake and the Tudor Navy*, II, 1–59; and Oppenheim, *Naval Tracts . . . Monson*, I, 127–33.

[2] See pp. 75–6. The sequence of events in the *Summarie* is incorrect.

[3] See p. 77, n. 1.

[4] The French king shortly afterwards demanded reparation, and it is stated in the *Summarie* that she was paid for after Drake's return. Whether Drake did this is not known. See pp. 77, 217, 289.

Arriving at the entrance to Vigo Bay on 27 September, the fleet anchored in the Cies Islands at Bayona. Here Drake began a series of conferences with Spanish officials regarding King Philip's embargo upon English shipping, using Captain Sampson as his spokesman. An English merchant, Short, served as the local governor's emissary. The proceedings were interrupted, however, by a heavy storm, so severe as to drive several ships from their anchorage and to threaten disaster for the whole venture. After three days, however, Drake sent Carleill with some smaller ships up the Vigo River, seeking supplies and possibly plunder, and also a more protected anchorage. The whole fleet followed presently to Tysus, above Vigo. Here, with the Spanish officials who had now assembled troops on the shore, Drake agreed to an exchange of hostages, and carried on further conferences.[1] Learning that the king had lifted the embargo and freed the goods of the English merchants, Drake contented himself with an agreement for watering his ships and buying food peacefully. He was thus able to make up partially for the inadequate supplies with which he had left England. Returning to Bayona on 7 October, the fleet awaited a favourable wind for making its departure. On 11 October Drake sailed once more, this time heading for the real purposes of the voyage, a possible encounter with the treasure fleets and raids upon Spanish towns beyond the seas.

THE CANARIES AND THE
CAPE VERDE ISLANDS

When Drake left Bayona the Spaniards were uncertain as to his intentions. Some thought he would go to Brazil by way of

---

[1] Accounts from Spanish sources indicate the fear that Drake had come to open a war between England and Spain. Some plundering was done by the English, mostly men by from the merchant vessels that had attached themselves to the fleet, before Drake moved up to this position. These acts tended to increase the alarm. Drake seems to have ordered restitution of the valuables that had been taken, and to have conducted himself so as to impress the Spaniards with the size and excellence of his fleet. See pp. 84-7 and Plate II.

the Canaries and the Cape Verdes, sacking as he pleased. Others expected him to strike, possibly with only part of his force, into the West Indies, with attacks at Santo Domingo, Puerto Rico, Cartagena, and on to Nombre de Dios and Havana, with threats to the treasure fleets of the next year. Warnings needed to be sent, therefore, to the endangered towns, and a fleet must be organized for their relief.[1] Preparations for such action were hampered, however, by uncertainty concerning the plans of Don Antonio and the dangers with which Spain's European interests were being threatened.[2]

The encounter with the 1585 treasure fleets for which Drake had hoped did not occur. The last one had reached Spain safely a few days before the English left Bayona.[3] Unaware of this until later, Drake steered for the Canaries. There he had planned to water before going on to the Cape Verde Islands. After reaching the first of the Canary group on 24 October, he called a council, at which it was decided to attempt a landing at Palma. When the ships were met there with cannon fire from the shore on 3 November, however, and were unable to find a suitable landing place, Drake abandoned the effort. The fleet touched next at Ferro (Hierro), where they tried but failed to secure provisions, and then moved on to the Barbary Coast. Here they were becalmed for several days, and spent the time in fishing to replenish their supplies. They finally reached Santiago in the Cape Verde Islands on 17 November, and prepared for their first raid.[4]

After a night landing beyond the range of the town's forts,

---

[1] These were the views of the Marqués de Santa Cruz, the Spanish high admiral, expressed in his letter of 16/26 October 1585. Hakluyt, *Prin. Nav.*, x, 92–7; *C.S.P.Ven. 1581–1591*, pp. 128–32.

[2] *The Fugger News-Letters*, 2nd series (1926), p. 102; *C.S.P.Ven. 1581–1591*, pp. 144, 145–6; *C.S.P.For. 1585–1586*, p. 233.

[3] See pp. 89, n. 2; 127, n. 2.

[4] For these events and dates, particularly that of the arrival at Santiago, see Documents 5, 9, and 10, which are more exact than the narrative in the *Summarie* (Document 11). The arrival was almost two weeks behind the projected time (4 November) in the schedule as shown in April 1586. Corbett, *Sp. War*, p. 70.

and a difficult inland march under Carleill's leadership,[1] the troops made their entry into the town of Santiago on the morning of 18 November, only to find it almost completely deserted. They took up quarters there and busied themselves for the next ten days with collecting what they could find to carry to their ships. Oil and meal and fresh fruits they found, but little else of value except the town's brass ordnance and powder, and bells from the churches. Rules governing pillage had by this time been distributed, and on 19 November the military captains were assigned to their specific companies. At a council on that day also oaths of obedience to commanders were announced, with the ceremony of oath-swearing scheduled for Sunday, the 20th. This was the occasion for the protest by Captain Knollys and his followers, who refused to be sworn, the beginning of the quarrel that continued without settlement for the rest of the stay.[2]

The English had almost no contact with the inhabitants of the island or their officials, although a few men who came close to the town were taken prisoner. Near the end of the occupation, Drake and Carleill led a march inland to the town of Santo Domingo, where they hoped to find treasure, especially at the house of the Portuguese bishop, but they were disappointed, and fired the town upon leaving. The loss of two stragglers during the return march represented almost the only English casualties of the stay, but the tale of the barbarous mutilation of their bodies by islanders became a dramatic feature in the edited *Summarie*.[3] Finally, having set fire to the town of Santiago, and also to the smaller town of Praya, which they had searched for military equipment, the English put to sea once more on 29 November.[4]

[1] The military action is well portrayed in the maps of Plates III(A), (B), (C). Two of these are attributed to Baptista Boazio, but the name of the other artist is unknown. See Note on Maps, Appendix IV.

The *Summarie*'s account appears to have been tampered with for propaganda purposes. See p. 225, n.1.

[2] See above, pp. 20-22, and Document 9, pp. 139-50.

[3] See below, pp. 148, 189, 235.

[4] See p. 99. No ransom efforts were attempted here. The chief commodities taken away, besides food, were brass ordnance and other metals.

TO THE WEST INDIES, DECEMBER–JANUARY

Little is known of the eighteen days or so required for the voyage to the first landfall in the West Indies except the disastrous epidemic of fever, the *calenture*, which struck the fleet a few days out from Santiago. The heavy drain upon its manpower by death and debilitation – estimated in one account as close to five hundred lives – affected much of the later action of the expedition.[1] The fleet arrived about 18–21 December at Guadeloupe and Dominica, and made a landing at St Christopher's. Here they spent Christmas, resting the ill men and airing the ships. Moving on once more, skirting the other eastern islands, they headed for Hispaniola and its famous city of Santo Domingo. Since they had fallen behind schedule,[2] if Drake wished to have the advantage of surprise before letters from Spain could warn of his coming, he could afford no more delay.

The city was ill prepared for his coming. The officials had not taken seriously news that had come from the Cape Verdes, and the royal warning had not been received. When the fleet which they saw approaching on 31 December was identified as English, some hurried defences for the harbour on the Ozama River were attempted. Several ships were sunk in order to block the channel, and the single royal galley, not yet fully repaired from a previous misfortune, was placed across the entrance so that its guns might fire toward the sea. Most of the citizens withdrew to plantations or other places of safety in the country, leaving behind only a small number of defenders. No one expected the English to try an attack from an inlet nine miles west of the city. To this place Drake was guided by a Greek(?) pilot from a ship he had intercepted, and his soldiers made a night landing, losing a pinnace in the operation. Carleill

[1] See pp. 99, 235.

[2] By this time the prepared plan had had to be altered, for they were over a month behind. The decision to omit Margarita and other points on the 'Main' and to go directly for Hispaniola was probably dictated by this fact. Cf. Corbett, *Sp. War*, pp. 70–1.

then led the march of some thousand men toward the town while Drake returned to his ships, preparing to open fire from their guns in support of the land attack.[1]

About mid-morning on New Year's Day, 1586 (English calendar), the city officials, surprised and confused by this approach from the west, made some frantic efforts to resist, and planted a few guns at one gate of the inadequate west wall.[2] The elderly President Ovalle rode out with a small troop of possibly one hundred and fifty men, only to retreat ignominiously; two younger officers attempted in vain to hold their men against the attack, but had to fall back. The English and Spanish accounts agree that attackers and defenders entered the city gates together. The few shots fired from the artillery there had little effect. The English poured in, Carleill and Sergeant Major Powell leading them through two entrances, and meeting at the central open space near the cathedral. Gunfire from the English fleet outside had meanwhile been battering the town, the ships being out of range of Spanish guns in the galley and the fort at the harbour entrance. By late afternoon the English had taken all the chief points in the town except the fort, and had started to entrench their positions. Soon afterwards the few Spanish officials, including those at the fort, escaped by boat up the river and scattered into the country. With the exception of occasional forays on English troops venturing into the outskirts thereafter, all armed resistance was over.[3]

The search for provisions and for booty began promptly, and

[1] See below, p. 101; and also, Wright, *Further Eng. Voyages*, pp. xxxiv, xxxviii, n., 16–17, 20, 22, 24, 26.

[2] Walls had not been built to protect the whole west side, as the Boazio map indicates (see Plates V(A), (B)), although a hedge may have marked the boundary. Wright, *Further Eng. Voyages*, pp. 18, 34, 222.

[3] Wright, *Further Eng. Voyages*, pp. xxxviii, 19, 22–3, 178–80; and President Ovalle's letter, printed as Appendix III in the 1921 edition of Castellanos, *Discurso*. There is no evidence in either English or Spanish documents of efforts by Drake to turn the native population or the maroons (*cimarrones*) against the Spanish, although he may have hoped for such aid and the Spaniards were said to fear such an uprising. Wright, *Further Eng. Voyages*, p. xxv; Corbett, *Sp. War*, p. 79; Corbett, *Drake and the Tudor Navy*, II, 35; and below, p. 198.

valuables were taken from the various religious houses, including the cathedral, and from the government house and private residences. Drake made the cathedral his headquarters, and in time sent a messenger into the country to seek the president or other official who could negotiate about a ransom.[1] First to come was a group headed by the city sheriff, and with him Don Francisco Maldonado, a visitor from Rio de la Hacha on the mainland, but they withdrew after a few days of ineffectual bargaining. The English now began a systematic process of destruction, firing portions of the town each day and carrying to their ships quantities of hides, copper money, brass ordnance, and church bells. Finally García Fernández de Torrequemada, factor for the Crown, became spokesman for the citizens, and arranged for a ransom of 25,000 ducats to be paid for the portion of the town still standing – less than half or possibly a third of the old city.[2] Drake declined to return a silk escutcheon he had taken from the government house; he was said to have felt its value as a token of the damage he had done to Spain's pride was greater than any ransom he might be offered for it. Certainly the description of it became a strong bit of anti-Spanish propaganda as it was printed in the versions of the *Summarie* that were published in 1588 and 1589.[3]

The ransom payments were completed on 30 January. As the English prepared to leave they exchanged three of their older ships for better ones which they found in the harbour. They confiscated a large one belonging to Antonio Corço of Seville, which they renamed the *New Year's Gift* and loaded with

[1] One messenger for this purpose was Carleill's 'page', Baptista Boazio. See Plate VIII(A), (B). The Spanish official who later negotiated with Drake regarding the ransom stated that, because Drake knew only English, interpreters were used, in Latin or French or Italian. There was one Englishman who knew a little Spanish and sometimes acted as interpreter (i.e. Jonas; cf. Appendix II, Personnel). Wright, *Further Eng. Voyages*, p. 225.

[2] Wright, *Further Eng. Voyages*, pp. xlvi, 30, 223–4; Castellanos, *Discurso*, Appendix III; and below, pp. 153–5, 195, 243–4.

[3] The incident is described in the Castellanos poem (*Discurso*, p. 96); see also the account in the *Summarie*, p. 245 below. See also Maltby, *The Black Legend*, p. 70.

heavier items of booty, and then burned most of the rest. They burned also the royal galley, having first freed the slaves, whom they offered to take away with them.[1]

During the month's stay at Santo Domingo, besides sacking the city and negotiating for ransom, Drake dealt with various other matters. The disagreement with Francis Knollys and his followers was considered again, though it was not resolved; and some form of court was used for handling matters of discipline among the troops. Quarrels among officers occurred, as well, but not all may have come to trial.[2] Two Spanish clerics were hanged by the English, as various records show, and at least one narrative besides the *Summarie* mentions the killing of Drake's negro servant by a Spaniard,[3] but the connection between the two incidents as asserted in the printed versions of the *Summarie* may be open to question.[4]

Tales of the damage to the city and of enormous riches taken there got back to Europe by the spring.[5] Whether the value of the booty collected, over and above the official ransom and the quantities of brass ordnance, was as high as rumour had it or not,[6] Drake's success in taking so easily this city, which prided itself as the centre for the royal government of the region, was of major importance. Word of its fate hastened plans for defence in other endangered places in the Caribbean –

[1] See p. 195 and Plate V(B). One slave so taken was an Indian from Cuba whom Drake may have used later as a scout (Wright, *Further Eng. Voyages*, p. 170). Some of the French and German slaves made their way back to Europe (*C.S.P.For. 1581–1586*, p. 711). Many negro and Turkish (Moorish) galley-slaves appear to have gone along with Drake, possibly intended as reinforcements for his now depleted manpower, or perhaps to be used to aid the colonial enterprise in Florida or Roanoke. Wright, *Further Eng. Voyages*, p. 172; Quinn, *Roanoke Voyages*, p. 722.

[2] See below, pp. 151, 243.

[3] See p. 196.

[4] On these incidents see pp. 112, 196, 242–3 and notes. Wright (*Further Eng. Voyages*, p. xxxvii, n.) comments on the lack of reference to these incidents in the Spanish records. See also Castellanos, *Discurso*, p. xxxviii. Once more one may suspect some editorial licence in the interest of propaganda in the *Summarie*.

[5] A newsletter from Madrid, 5 April 1586, telling of events at Santo Domingo, stated, 'They say he has carried off and done damage to the tune of over two millions. He killed or ill-treated all priests and monks he could get hold of, and is fortifying himself in San Domingo'. *The Fugger News-Letters*, 2nd series (1926), p. 103.

[6] On the ransom see p. 156 and n. 5; also Wright, *Further Eng. Voyages*, pp. 55, 223–5.

Cartagena, Havana, and elsewhere.[1] And in Spain the news seemed disastrous. It spurred preparations for retaliation, either in the West Indies or in European waters.[2] Probably even more than the subsequent capture of Cartagena, the fall of Santo Domingo was a stinging blow to the King of Spain.

CARTAGENA

Leaving Hispaniola at the end of January, Drake sailed directly toward the mainland and Cartagena, omitting stops along the coast. He may have considered an attempt at Rio de la Hacha, but conditions of the sea prevented it.[3] Having reason to believe that Cartagena had been warned of his approach and that a surprise attack would be difficult,[4] he sailed boldly along the sea approach to the city on Wednesday, 9/19 February, in full view of the defenders, and entered the fine outer harbour with ease.[5]

Cartagena had indeed received warnings from Spain in early January, and by the end of the month from Hispaniola.[6] On 6/16 February Don Francisco Maldonado, who had been at Santo Domingo, arrived with exaggerated reports on Drake's strength. The city officials sent away the women and children and all but the heaviest valuables. Then they built barricades at street openings, planned ways to block entrance from the sea, and brought in Indians to help with the defence. A chain was prepared at the blockhouse guarding the inner harbour to

[1] Wright, *Further Eng. Voyages*, pp. 47, 161, 164, 180.

[2] *C.S.P.Ven. 1581–1591*, pp. 162, 165; *The Fugger News-Letters*, 2nd series (1926), pp. 106, 108–9. A letter from Seville, 18/28 March 1585/6, spoke of the English capture of 'that strong thing, Santo Domingo, which is the key to all of the Indies'. *C.S.P.For. 1585–1586*, p. 462. See also ibid., pp. 575, 595, 609, 610, 623.

[3] See below, pp. 157–9.

[4] He must have known of the departure of Francisco Maldonado from Santo Domingo, and of the probability of warning despatches from Spain. See pp. 198, 260.

[5] On the disagreements among officials about defence plans, the ineffective role of the governor, Don Pedro Fernández de Busto, and the failure to fortify the harbour entrance at Hicacos Point, see Wright, *Further Eng. Voyages*, pp. xlv–xlviii, 71–3, 195–7, etc.; see also p. 198 below. On the place of entry, see p. 160, n. 4.

[6] Oppenheim, *Naval Tracts . . . Monson*, I, 128–9; Wright, *Further Eng. Voyages*, pp. xlv, 47.

prevent entry there by ship. On the Caleta, the long stretch of land extending westward to the main harbour entrance (see map, Plate VI(A), (B)), at the narrowest point near the town a barricade with a trench was constructed to check an approach by land. But there were weaknesses in the defences: the citizens were not trained soldiers; no guns were stationed at the far end of the land strip to guard the main harbour entrance (Boca Grande); and the barricade nearer the town was not finished all the way to the sea. Furthermore, over the objections of some, the governor and citizens had persuaded the commander of the two royal galleys to station them within the inner harbour so that their guns might fire upon any force approaching by the Caleta. Also, for fear of a rear attack, some of the defence forces were dispersed to more distant points. Morale was weak, with officials disagreeing among themselves and few trusting the elderly governor, Don Pedro Fernández de Busto; and alarming reports had been spread about Drake the pirate.[1]

With his fleet anchored in the outer lagoon by late afternoon, Drake called a council. Then, during the night, he sent a heavy contingent of men ashore to undertake a march under Carleill's command along the Caleta.[2] The Spaniards, who seem not to have expected a massive attack before daybreak, became confused as their plans for an early attack from ambush failed.[3] The English also had their difficulties. Lacking an adequate guide and endangered by poisoned stakes which had been emplanted

[1] Most of the Spanish documents, including the depositions taken by the investigating judge, reveal the confusion and ineptness of the defence plans. See Wright, *Further Eng. Voyages*, especially Document 27, and *passim*.

A valuable narrative of the judge, Diego Hidalgo Montemayor, dated 23 May 1586 is in Wright, op. cit., pp. 129–36 (from A. de I., 72–5–18, Santa Fé 89). A somewhat different version of it, certified as a copy of Hidalgo's report and dated 6 May 1586, is printed in App. IV of Castellanos, *Discurso*, pp. 299–309 (from A. de I.: Est. 2, caj. 5, leg. 2/21). The narrative in Cantos 4 and 5 of the poem by Castellanos suggests that he had seen this report.

[2] A description of Cartagena and its defences, prepared in 1587 by Baptista Antonio, royal surveyor (i.e. Bautista Antoneli, the military engineer), is printed in Hakluyt, *Prin. Nav.*, x, 137. According to the *Tiger* journal, 1,700 men were in the march. Other estimates put the figure at nearer 1,000 (see p. 103, n. 4). The *Leicester* journal (p. 161) tells of the council and plans to start landing about 2 a.m.

[3] Wright, *Further Eng. Voyages*, pp. xlix, 49, 75; and below, p. 162.

along the way, they found an orderly march impossible.[1] However, keeping close to or in the water, which was at low tide, and aided by heavy darkness, the vanguard reached the narrow point near the lagoon well before dawn. Firing from the guns on the galleys and the barricade began, but did small damage. Scarcely able to see either enemy or friend, both attackers and defenders fought in confusion. Carleill, however, rallied his followers and broke through at the sea end of the unfinished wall, where only wine butts hastily filled with sand had been placed. Neither the governor nor Don Pedro Vique, the galley commander who was with him at the Caleta barricade, could hold their forces together and, after only a brief resistance, most of them retreated into the city, and through it to the other side. In hand-to-hand combat the English killed the ensign-bearer of the remaining commanding officer, Captain Alonso Bravo de Montemayor, and then wounded the latter and took him prisoner. Pursuing the retreating Spaniards into the city, the English overcame what feeble resistance was attempted, and by daybreak were in possession. Only the little blockhouse held out for a day and then, with reinforcement impossible, it was evacuated.[2]

During the night march along the shore, Drake had sent a diversionary attack by water against the blockhouse and the chained entrance to the inner harbour. A group of pinnaces and small boats under Frobisher made the attempt, but were beaten back by shattering fire. The Spanish commander thought that Drake himself tried a second time, but no English documents report such action. The fort was fired on through the following day both from ships of the fleet and from the city's own guns which the English turned upon it after entering the town.[3]

The two royal galleys also were lost. Having been used

---

[1] See pp. 103-4.

[2] Wright, *Further Eng. Voyages*, pp. li–liii, and the depositions in Document 27, especially pp. 69, 81–3, 108–10, 118–19. See below, pp. 161–5, 250–3.

[3] The best description from the English side is from Frobisher's ship, the *Primrose* (see p. 198). On the Spanish, see Wright, *Further Eng. Voyages*, pp. l, li, and Captain Mexia Mirabal's deposition, pp. 82–3.

ineffectively at the Caleta approach, they attempted to move toward the fort and out into the main harbour, but were prevented by the shallowness of the water at that time, and by mutiny among the crews. One galley was accidentally set on fire by a powder explosion, whereupon its slaves were un-chained and many escaped to the English. Both ships then ran aground, and both were burned shortly afterwards by order of their commander to prevent the enemy from taking them and their guns.[1]

The English now established and fortified themselves in the city. Drake chose Alonso Bravo's house for his headquarters, and the fleet moved in closer to the town. During the search for valuables Drake was angered at finding in the governor's house King Philip's warning letter that referred to him as a pirate, *corsario*.[2] As ransom negotiations began, Drake summoned from the country both the governor and the bishop, but the talks progressed slowly, since Drake's demands were far beyond what they were willing to pay. Again Drake pressed his victims by burning outer and poorer sections of the town,[3] and he busied his men with loading aboard the *New Year's Gift* ordnance taken from the town and from the sunken galleys.

The delays in the ransom talks, however, became costly. Two of his captains, Varney and Moone, lost their lives in trying to intercept a vessel carrying food for the city, and a

---

[1] See the map (Plate VI(B)), and Wright, *Further Eng. Voyages*, pp. liii, 58, 76–8, 110–11. With regard to their guns the move was not a success.

[2] Wright, *Further Eng. Voyages*, pp. liv, 114, 134, 140, 157; and below, pp. 176, 258, n. 1.

[3] According to Spanish accounts, a merchant, Tristan de Orive, broached the subject first, within a day after the city fell, and then Drake demanded that the officials come in. Wright, *Further Eng. Voyages*, p. liv, and n. For the names of those who came in on 15 February see the *Leicester* journal (p. 165–6) and also Wright, op. cit., pp. 113, 134, 142–3.

The *Leicester* journal notes that Drake demanded 400,000 ducats and the city proposed only 5,000. Although Tristan de Orive, the chief negotiator, mentions the figure of 500,000 gold pesos, the sum of 400,000 ducats shows in most of the other documents; and the city's offer is quoted as being 25,000 ducats. Wright, *Further Eng. Voyages*, pp. lv, 43; and below, p. 166, n. 5

The damage by burning was probably less than had occurred at Santo Domingo, and the injury to the cathedral, which the Spanish thought was intentional, seems to have occurred by accident. See below, pp. 167, 201; and Castellanos, *Discurso*, p. 211.

return of the epidemic of fever claimed many more.[1] Restlessness and jealousies broke out also, and courts had to be held to deal with these matters.[2] The English were aware, too, that a fleet from Spain was expected, and were concerned about their own weakness and disappointed about the low yield in treasure and in ransom that could be gained. Although the sea captains seemed willing to await the challenge of a Spanish attack by sea,[3] the land captains drew up a set of resolutions in which they urged Drake to compromise on the ransom figure, and to begin the journey homeward, omitting the further action that had been planned for the Isthmus of Panama.[4]

The Cartagena officials continued to argue among themselves about the propriety of yielding on a ransom and how the sum Drake required could be raised, but individual citizens were permitted to start bargaining on their own. Drake eventually agreed to accept a figure of 110,000 ducats for the city, with payments to start on 10/20 March, and two gentlemen became hostages for the settlement.[5] Since Drake would take only a small part in jewels, demanding the bulk in bullion, the officials

[1] See p. 168. Captain Fortescue was among its victims (see pp. 174, 254). The resolutions of the land captains indicate that there were among the English by this time not over 700 able-bodied men, and that 150 were sick or wounded. See p. 254, n. 9; and Wright, *Further Eng. Voyages*, p. lvii, n. 4.

[2] The courts dealt with matters of food, with decrees about who might keep a negro or other slave, and about the 'strangers' from the royal galleys (see p. 169). The Spanish became aware of quarrels among Drake's followers, and that some kind of agreement about them was being drawn up. Wright, *Further Eng. Voyages*, pp. lvii and n., 52, 135.

[3] Proposals for a relief armada were discussed in Spain after the Vigo incident (Corbett, *Sp. War*, pp. 65, 67, 77–8); and the Cartagena officials hoped for its early arrival. Wright, *Further Eng. Voyages*, pp. xlvii and n., 47. One Spanish document mentions that the English ship officers, during the second stay at Cartagena, expressed their readiness to hold the city against a sea attack. Wright, *Further Eng. Voyages*, p. 145. A fleet started out from Spain late in the spring with instructions to meet Drake, but it turned back because of an epidemic of illness. *C.S.P.For. 1585–1586*, p. 700; *1586–1587*, p. 11. Not until 18/28 July did a fleet from Spain arrive at Cartagena. Wright, *Further Eng. Voyages*, pp. 192–3.

[4] See pp. 171–3. The plans for attacking at Nombre de Dios and, with the help of the *cimarrones* there, possibly crossing to the Pacific, were now abandoned. See Corbett, *Sp. War*, pp. 72–3; Wright, *Further Eng. Voyages*, pp. lviii, 55; and below, p. 255.

[5] See p. 175. Although the names of the hostages do not appear in the printed Spanish documents, a narrative by one of them is in Wright, *Further Eng. Voyages*, pp. 46–52. For comparative money values of the period see p. 259 and n. 2.

decided to 'borrow' from a store of silver ingots belonging to the Crown.[1] Additional sums were paid by Alonso Bravo for his own release, and by the Franciscan friary outside of the city. One Spaniard declared afterwards that probably 200,000 ducats more were turned over by wealthy citizens to recover their properties,[2] and it may be assumed that considerably more than the official ransom and pieces of ordnance were taken away from Cartagena.

Drake moved his fleet out on Thursday, 31 March/10 April, sailing toward Cuba. But he returned a few days later because the ship laden with the captured ordnance was leaking dangerously. The English stayed at Cartagena for another ten days, transferring the heavy cargo, and baking bread supplies for the homeward voyage. On 14 April they sailed once more.[3]

CUBA AND FLORIDA

After touching briefly at the Caymans, the English stopped at Cape San Antonio on the western end of Cuba for water and firewood. Finding insufficient water, they moved along the northern coast, where they spent about two weeks, with unfavourable winds, and then returned to the cape. Now they went about collecting rain water for their needs. Again setting sail toward the east, they passed Havana without attacking, and then turned north along the Florida coast.[4] Their goals were

[1] See below, pp. 173–8; also Wright, *Further Eng. Voyages*, pp. lvi, 143, etc.; and Castellanos, *Discurso*, pp. 317–18.

[2] Letter of Francisco de Avila to the Crown, pr. in Wright, *Further Eng. Voyages*, pp. 195–7. Avila argued that official reports had been falsified, at the expense of the poorer inhabitants. Others referred to booty taken in addition to the official ransom, one estimating that it was as much as 200,000 ducats more. Wright, op. cit., p. 212. The officials' estimate of damage amounting to 400,000 ducats included the losses by fire. Wright, op. cit., pp. 146, 192. See also Castellanos, *Discurso*, pp. xlviii, 213–14.

[3] Wright, *Further Eng. Voyages*, pp. lvii, 51–2, etc.; Castellanos, *Discurso*, pp. 223–5, 307, 320; and below, pp. 106, 202–3.

[4] For events of the stay about Cuba, approximately 27 April to 20 May, see pp. 68, 204, n. 4, below, and Wright, *Further Eng. Voyages*, pp. lviii–ix, 168–74. Drake may have had some hope of intercepting the 1586 treasure fleet, but there was no possibility of this, for its departure had been delayed. Corbett, *Drake and the Tudor Navy*, II, 55; Wright, op. cit., p. lix.

now the Spanish posts in that region and a stop at Raleigh's colony farther north.

The fleet reached the position of the Spanish settlement of St Augustine on 27 May, and men were landed the next day, preparing to attack first the small fort of St John, recently built on the river bank for the defence of the town. The governor, Pedro Menéndez Marquéz, having been warned from Santo Domingo, had evacuated the town and was waiting in the little fort with some seventy or eighty men. The Spanish held out against the English during the day, while Drake brought up reinforcements and planted ordnance across the river from the fort for battering it. Then, concerned about hostile Indians near the town, and about the weakness of his garrison, the governor withdrew his men by night. For the next several days Drake stayed at St Augustine, utterly destroying the fort and ransacking and burning the settlement and its fields. He offered no ransom negotiations, but carried away cannon, a royal treasure chest containing 6000 ducats, tools, food, and other items of utilitarian value. He lost several officers in the attack, including Sergeant Major Powell, and some of his negro captives escaped; but he took away with him at least one Frenchman who had been held prisoner by the Spaniards, Nicholas Burgoignon.[1] Before leaving, a council of the captains decided to attack the Spanish post at Santa Elena farther north and then to seek out the English colony.[2]

During the first week of June the fleet moved along the coast, keeping close to shore. They stopped at least twice, making some contacts with the Indians, but were unable to go in at Santa Elena because they lacked a pilot to take them through the dangerous shoals.[3]

[1] Wright, *Further Eng. Voyages*, pp. lx–lxiii. 164–5, 180–90, 198–203; Quinn, *Roanoke Voyages*, pp. 295–8; and below, pp. 206–7, 264–9. See also the maps (Plates VII(A), (B)).

[2] See p. 269. Earlier plans about this stop seem to have been made. The negroes transported from Cartagena and the household supplies from St Augustine were possibly intended for the colonists' use.

[3] See pp. 209, 270; Wright, *Further Eng. Voyages*, pp. 190–1, 203; Quinn, *Roanoke Voyages*, pp. 299–300, 306, n.

ROANOKE AND THE RETURN

On 9 June, responding to a signal fire at Croatoan, Drake encountered a small band from the English colony, and with their guidance pioceeded to the settlement at Roanoke Island. Because most of the ships were too large to move into the channel there, the fleet anchored at sea, outside the sand banks.[1] Here Drake conferred with Governor Ralph Lane about the serious conditions at the colony, and the discouragement because supplies promised from England had not arrived. Lane gladly accepted Drake's offer of supplies for a month or more, until the relief ship should come, and of a ship,[2] with able masters, by which his company might return to England on their own if necessary. But three days of Hatteras storms, so violent as to force many of Drake's ships out to sea, changed the plan. Some of the ships, including the one that had been assigned to Lane, never rejoined the fleet but returned home separately. The disheartened colonists now accepted an alternative offer of Drake and his captains, transportation for all of them back to England. Accordingly, with the hundred and five men distributed among the remaining ships, they sailed from Roanoke on 18 June.[3] They reached Portsmouth on 27 July.[4]

The news of Drake's return spread quickly after Richard Hawkins arrived at Exeter on 22 July and Drake appeared with the rest of the fleet at Portsmouth five days later. While some word had come to England late in 1585 about his reaching the Canaries,[5] later news had filtered in only by way of Spain or

[1] See pp. 209, 271 below; and Lane's narrative in Hakluyt, *Prin. Nav.*, VIII, 342.

[2] The *Francis* and some smaller craft. See below, p. 272, and Lane's narrative, Hakluyt, *Prin. Nav.*, VIII, 343.

[3] See p. 274. For more details on the Roanoke stay, see also Quinn, *Roanoke Voyages*, pp. 288-303.

[4] The edition of the *Summarie* printed in England gives the date as 28 July, but it was the 27th, according to Lane, the Harl. 6221 variant, and the two Leyden editions of 1588. See note 7 on p. 274. Of the other ships, the one carrying Richard Hawkins reached the Cornwall–Devon coast on 21 July (see p. 273 and n. 1.)

[5] William Camden, in a letter to Abrahamus Ortelius from London, 31 January 1585/6, commented that Drake had not been heard from since he left Lanzarote in the Fortunate Islands in December. *Abrahamus Ortelius . . . Epistulae*, ed. by J. H. Hessels (Cambridge, 1887), pp. 334-5.

France, mostly with exaggerated reports of the rich treasure he was collecting.[1] Not until the ships had been brought to the Thames for unloading and the work of the auditing commissioners had started was it finally realized that the 'great wealth'[2] he brought back was insufficient to cover the costs of the expedition, and that even the soldiers and sailors would have to wait for their pay.[3]

Nevertheless, the news of Drake's raids on such places as Santo Domingo and Cartagena caused rejoicing wherever Spain's power was feared. Whereas there had been alternating rumours in the spring of 1586, some that Queen Elizabeth was hoping for peace and that Drake would return quietly, others that she was equipping a new supply fleet to go to his aid,[4] in July the Scottish queen complained to Mendoza on how news of the exploits of Leicester and Drake 'lifts the hearts of his Majesty's enemies all over Christendom'.[5] In time reports began to circulate about the expedition's poor financial returns and the heavy loss of men.[6] But Palavicino, agent for Walsingham in Germany, wrote to the latter on 11 September,

[1] Many of these news items, now in the State Papers, are pr. in Corbett, *Sp. War*, pp. 66–7, 75–82. Similar rumours reached Germany (*C.S.P.For. 1586–1588*, pt I, p. 42) and France (H.M.C., *Salisbury MSS*, III, 142, 144). See also *C.S.P.Span. 1580–1586*, p. 584.

[2] News from London to Antwerp in late August still reported the high expectation. *The Fugger News-Letters*, 2nd series (1926), p. 117. Stafford wrote to Walsingham from Paris about the same time, however, saying that one of the negroes who had come back with Drake was circulating reports about meagre accomplishments. *C.S.P.For. 1586–1588*, pt I, p. 73.

[3] See Document 4 below, and Corbett, *Sp. War*, pp. 85–96.

[4] *C.S.P.For. 1586–1587*, pt II, p. 144; H.M.C., *Salisbury MSS*, III, 147–8. A newsletter dated at Antwerp, 15 July 1586 (N.S.), reported that Queen Elizabeth 'asserts that she never gave Drake orders to make those attacks upon places belonging to the King of Spain. . . . This occurred at the instance of Don Antonio'. *The Fugger News-Letters*, 2nd series (1926), p. 111.

[5] *C.S.P.Span. 1580–1586*, p. 596.

[6] Mendoza sent such a report to King Philip, 26 September 1586 (N.S.), saying that Drake had lost 1,000 men, that his booty amounted to less than 200,000 crowns, and that the English ambassador was spreading word that too much of the booty had been taken by the soldiers as they sacked the towns. He gave as his source of information an account of the voyage written in Latin which the French ambassador in London had sent to Secretary Villeroy. See above, p. 7, n. 3. See also *C.S.P.Ven. 1581–1591*, pp. 201–2.

declaring his view that the amount of booty was of less importance than the disturbance Drake had caused to Spain's plans, and that it was now 'certain that one year of war in the Indies will cost the Spaniards more than two or three in the Low Countries'.[1] Plans for Drake to return to the West Indies, possibly with the help of the Dutch, were being made that autumn. These were abandoned, however, when the execution of Mary of Scotland heightened the threat of a Spanish invasion, and the departure of a fleet for so extended a voyage became unthinkable. Drake's range then was shortened to Cadiz.[2]

In the view of his English contemporaries, Drake's strike into the West Indies had been a success, and the impression must have been strengthened by such literary tributes as Greepe's newsballad of 1587 and the versions of the *Summarie* that appeared in 1588 and 1589.[3] At least one early naval critic, however, Sir William Monson, argued a few years later that England's interests would have been better served if Drake had held Cartagena instead of leaving it, providing by his stay the means to divert Spain's attention from England. Further, because Spain became more energetic about protecting her outposts after the raid, he declared that Drake had awakened rather than weakened Spain; and he argued that the voyage, though momentarily successful, probably should not have been undertaken except with better preparation and greater manpower.[4] Later historians have tended to believe that Drake's decision to leave Cartagena was wise, in view of his weakened forces. As to the effects of the voyage upon Spain, it not only brought a rude shock to her pride and prestige at the time but the money that now had to be spent on strengthening the fortifi-

[1] *C.S.P.For. 1586–1588*, pt I, pp. 76–7, 88. Roger Manners wrote on 30 July from London: 'Surely he [Drake] hath don great hurt to the King of Spayne and won great credit to himself'. H.M.C., *Rutland MSS*, I, 201.

[2] Corbett, *Sp. War*, pp. xvi–xvii.

[3] Most of Camden's account in his *Annales* . . . , 1615 (see above, p. 2, n. 1) follows the *Summarie* narrative closely.

[4] Oppenheim, *Naval Tracts . . . Monson*, I, 123. Even while writing in this vein Monson noted that the voyage had 'proved both fortunate and victorious'. His lament was that more had not been accomplished.

cation of the colonies was drained away from use at home, and King Philip's difficulties in securing loans for his troops in the Netherlands and for setting out the Armada were increased.[1]

The significance of the West Indies voyage can indeed not be judged if it is looked upon as a single venture. As an example of a joint-stock enterprise for financial gain, it was disappointing, for the adventurers suffered a loss. As one of a series of voyages, with larger forces than Drake had previously commanded, it tested severely his talents as a leader and a naval commander, but during the course of the expedition procedures for better administration were used and developed. As a voyage of exploration, the reports concerning geographical features of the places visited, their products and their peoples, especially as published in the narrative known as the *Summarie*, expanded the knowledge of places with which Englishmen might later hope to trade. Also, although some of the colonists whom Drake brought home from Roanoke spread tales that might have dampened enthusiasm for colonial enterprise,[2] the longer effect of the voyage was to encourage such activity, particularly if it might be attempted near the regions where Spain had succeeded. Finally, as an action of undeclared war, in that hazy ⟨7 yrs war⟩ zone which Elizabethan policy permitted, the West Indies raid was an important part of the series of events that brought Spain and England into open confrontation. The needling of Spain's authority with regard to English shipping in her home ports and the exposure of the weakness of her defences in her colonies overseas served not only as a spur to Spain's naval preparations, but as a support for the arguments of the war party in England. In this connection the early publication of the *Summarie*, with its strong anti-Spanish slant, may well be viewed as a propaganda device.[3] The voyage was, as Corbett interpreted it when

---

[1] Williamson, *Hawkins of Plymouth*, p. 292. See also Corbett, *Drake and the Tudor Navy*, II, 52–3. According to Irene Wright (*Further Eng. Voyages*, p. lxvi), 'Drake's raid was of immediate benefit to the Spanish colonials [i.e. in securing better defences], and also played its part in ruining Spain. This was the end of a period.'

[2] Cf. Taylor, *Writings . . . Hakluyts*, p. 40; and Quinn, *Roanoke Voyages*, pp. 312–13.

[3] See Document 11 and Appendix III.

he edited his volume of documents for 1585-87, the opening action in the naval war between England and Spain.

EDITORIAL POLICY

The documents that follow have been edited so as to preserve as much of their original form as possible. Abbreviations have been extended, capital letters have been inserted for place names as well as for the names of persons, and some punctuation has been added when it has seemed necessary for clarification, but peculiarities of spelling and form have been retained. Square brackets have been used to indicate words introduced by the editor. In some cases these represent the editor's interpretation of the sense of a passage, especially in cases of manuscripts that are torn or otherwise damaged. In others, words have been supplied from parallel readings of contemporary documents. The special practice used for Document 11, dictated by the several versions of the *Summarie* that have been compared, is explained in the notes at the beginning of that narrative.

Italics which appear in a text in most cases indicate that a word, usually a place name, was written in italics in the manuscript. In a few instances in Document 9 they have been used to indicate direct quotations. Marginal notes, particularly those of Document 9 relating to dates, have been retained in the margins.

On matters of dates, the English calendar (O.S.) has been followed generally, since this is the form appearing in the English documents. In the case of Spanish records, where the dates appear according to the new Gregorian calendar that was used on the continent (N.S.), it has been necessary to cite both the English and the Spanish reckoning (e.g. above, p. 33).[1]

[1] No attempt has been made to adjust dates for the nautical day, which customarily ran from noon to noon, and was, therefore, for the twelve hours following midday, a day in advance of the civil date. The only cases in which the difference might have been important are those of 17 November and 27 July (see pp. 97, 225, 274, and notes); but other evidence as well has been used by the editor in the decisions regarding those dates.

For checking the accuracy of dates in the documents, the *Handbook of Dates for Students of English History*, ed. by C. R. Cheney (London, 1945), has been used.

Document 1
Furnishing List for the Fleet

'Sir *Francis* Drake. Names of Ships & number of men in each, with Sir *Francis* Drake. Captains for land service' (Folger MS L. b. 344).[1]

[fol. 1]

The number of men appoynted for every Shype bounde in
        the vyage with Sir Frances Drake . . . [   ][2]

1	The Elizabeth Bonaventure	250
2	The Prymrose	180
3	The Gallyon Leycester	180
4	The Ayde	120
5	The Tygere	100
6	The Sea Dragon	090
7	The Thomas als the Barke Hastynge	100
8	The Mynyon of Plymmothe	100
9	The Barke Talbot	085

[1] This MS, which was called to my attention by D. B. Quinn, was previously Loseley MS 477, before its acquisition by the Folger Shakespeare Library. In addition to the original outside sheet bearing the endorsement, now numbered as fol. 2v, it contains three folio sides. On the first is the list of ships, with complements of men; on the second, the provisioning estimates, and a list of land captains; and on the third, notes regarding sixteen of the ship captains. The nature of the latter notes indicates that they were made by someone fairly close to Drake, possibly a 'West Country' man, and that they were compiled near the end of August 1585. The handwriting is identified in the Folger MS Catalogue as that of Sir William More of Loseley, but why this document should be among his papers is not clear. More was himself a vice admiral for Surrey and Sussex and may have had an official, possibly a financial, interest in the venture. He was also a fairly close friend of Charles Lord Howard, the Lord Admiral, owner of the *White Lion* and officially concerned with the expedition. Possibly the furnishing list came through his hands to the attention of More.

There is extant also a second list which, except for the final page, closely resembles this one. It is B. L., Harl. MS 366, fols. 146–7, 'The furniture of Sir Frances Drakes Jorney September 1585.' It supplies the names of captains and also figures for tonnage and for the number of men for each ship, but the document has been badly damaged by damp and is partially unreadable. Relevant parts have been used for editing the more complete Folger MS, and for the Table of Ships in the Appendix. See also p. 3.

[2] Undeciphered.

45

10 The Whyte Lyon ———————————— 075
11 The Barke Bond ———————————— 075
12 The Hope ———————————————— 075
13 The Barke Bonner ——————————— 070
14 The Barke Hawkyns —————————— 070
15 Sir Wylliam Mohons[1] Shype ————— 075
16 The Beniaeman [Benjamin] —————— 045
17 The Vantage ———————————— 040
18 The Frances ———————————— 035
19 The Spedwell ———————————— 030
20 The George ————————————— 030
21 The Scout —————————————— 020
22 The Mathewe ——————— 055 [25][2]
23 The Galley to sayle herewithall [Duck][3] ——— 10
24 Fower smale roweyng pynneses which come from
   London to be sayled with —————— 020
25 Fower pynnases [of P][4]lymothe ————— 025
                     [1]925 men[5]

[fol. lv]

The proporecon of vyctuall for a 100 men[6]
Beef and Porke in hogsheds ——————— 12

---

[1] Probably Sir William Mohun, a Cornish gentleman of ancient family, who was actively concerned with the defences of the county, 1584–86 (*C.S.P.D. 1581–1590*, pp. 211, 304, 305). As MP he was named on 14 December 1584 to the committee on the bill to confirm Raleigh's patent 'for the discovery of Foreign Countries'; serving with him were Walsingham, Sir Philip Sidney, Drake, and Sir Richard Grenville, among others (S. D'Ewes, *The Journals of . . . the Parliaments . . . Elizabeth* (1682), p. 339). Mohun died in April 1587 (J. L. Vivian and H. H. Drake, *The Visitation of Cornwall* (Harl. Soc., 1872), p. 145). On his ship see Table of Ships.

[2] The figure is written as 55 in the MS, but its location suggests that 25 was probably intended. The latter figure permits a total of 1,925, corresponding with that at the bottom of the page. See also Table of Ships.

[3] The name of the galley is in *Summarie*, p. 217.

[4] The MS is torn.

[5] Although the MS is torn, the figure *1925* corresponds with the total of the figures on the righthand column. In the Harl. MS 366, which omits the pinnaces, the total is 1,922. There is an added line in that MS which reads: 'The . . . for usres [or *furnished*?] [. . .] in pieces £3280/'.

[6] In Harl. MS 366 (fol. 146) the items, insofar as they are legible, agree almost exactly with those in the Folger MS.

46

New land Fyshe	30 C[1]
Pylchers in hogsheds	30
Lyngs Cod in Burthens	10 burd*t*hens[2]
Bysket in hundreths	10,000 wayght
Meale in Barrells	$22\frac{1}{2}$
Otmeale in barrells	2
Pese [ ] in hogsheds	15
Canari wyne in pypes	6
French wyne	1 tone
Bere	30 tonnes[3]

Besydes bacon, butter, chese, honeye, oyle, vynegar, Rye, whereof there is provyded a good quantyty, but the partycular proporcens for each Shyp ys not yet set down at the tyme of the wrytynge here of

And yt ys to be understoode that besydes the proporchion of vyctuall all*redye* consumed, theys parcels aforsayd are now furnyshed in these full proporcens, beyng redy by God's good favor to depart from Plymmothe within vii dayes. wrytten at Plymmothe the last of August 1585

Suche Capteyns as are appointed for the Land Service
Christopher Carleill Lieutenant Generall by Lande
George Acres[4]   John Hannam

[1] In Harl. MS 366 the figure is written out as *3000*.
[2] This line in Harl. MS 366 reads: *Lynge & codd in Burdennes*. The last word means loads or bundles (*OED*). *Lynge* was Aberdeen ling (Andrews, *Last Voyage*, p. 54).
[3] The imported wines were probably for the officers, while the beer was for the men. Cf. Morison, *European Disc. Amer.*, p. 131. This list is more complete than the victual allowance, figured for 4 men for 28 days, printed from the State Papers (1581) in Corbett, *Sp. War*, p. 263.
[4] This name appears in no other list of land captains, and is not mentioned in any of the narratives. Powell was Sergeant Major under Carleill, and Morgan and Sampson were Corporals of the Field (see p. 214). Three names from the *Summarie* list do not appear here, Pew, Wynter, and Stanton. The first of them, Pew, who was an experienced army man (see p. 297), may have taken the place of Acres.
In Harl. MS 366 twelve land officers' names were originally written, but some are unreadable. Those which have been identified are: Carleill, Powell, M[organ], Sampson, W. [Cecil], Ed [Wynter?], [March]aunt, Bigges, Robert Pryse [or Pew?], Barton, and Goring.
The omission of Stanton from either list is probably correct. He started out as 'lieutenant' to Francis Knollys on the galleon *Leicester* and became an officer in the

Anthony Powell
Mathewe Morgeyn
Anthony Plotte [Platte]
William Cycell
John Merchaunt

John Sampson
Walter Bygs
George Barton
John Gorynge

The Capteyns of suche Shyps as presently I can remember
In the Elyzabeth [Bon]¹aventure beyng Admyrall ys Sir Frances
Drake, Generall by [Sea] and Land of the voyage. In which
Shype ys apoynted for h[is lieut]enant Master Thomas
Fenner.²

[fol. 2]

1 In the Prymrose beynge Vyceadmyrall ys Capten Marten
Furbussher³
2 In the Galleon Leycester now caulled the Lettyce Leycester
beynge Rere Admyrall ys Capteyn Frances Knolles⁴
3 In the Ayde ys Capteyn Edwarde Wynter⁵
4 In the Tyger ys Capteyn Chrystofer Carleill
5 In the Sea Dragon which ys Sir William Wynters paynted
Shyp was apoynted William Hawkyns thelder for
Capteyn, but at the request of Sir Phyllip Sydneye and

---

land forces while the voyage was in progress (see p. 298). Edward Wynter, captain
of the *Aid*, was permitted to change to a land command at Cartagena (see pp. 165, 253).
The list of land officers in *Summarie* was evidently compiled retroactively and the
number of captains below the rank of corporals of the field was probably eight,
rather than ten.

¹ Tear in the MS; the letters have been supplied from other sources.
² i.e. second in command of the flagship, and usually referred to as Captain Fenner.
In the *Summarie* variant (Harl. MS 6221, fol. 94), Fenner is described as 'Vice admirall
by office, and captain in the Bonaventure under the Admiral', but that MS assigns no
ranks for Frobisher or Knollys.
³ Cf. *Summarie* (p. 215): 'Captain Martin Frobisher, Viceadmiral, . . . being nowe
shipped in the Primrose.' In Thomas Greepe's newsballad, *The True and Perfecte Newes*,
Frobisher was referred to as 'Vice General', with Carleill being 'Lieutenant Generall
on the mayne'.
⁴ Cf. *Summarie* (p. 216): 'Captaine Francis Knolles, Rieradmirall in the Gallion
Leicester.' The Spaniards at Cartagena noted one of the larger ships as being rear
admiral. Wright, *Further Eng. Voyages*, p. 51.
⁵ The son of Sir William Wynter. See p. 47, n. 1 above and p. 299.

Master Grenevyle Capteyn Henrye Whyte[1] ys nowe placed ther and Master Hawkyns apoynted by the Generall to be another Lieutenant for hym in hys own shyp and shalbe the first of the Lieutenants ther.

6 In the ship which sometymes was cauled the Barke Hastinges[2] ys Capteyn Thomas Drake, the Generall's brother

7 In the Mynyon of Plymmothe was first placed old Seely[3] of the garde, a man that hathe byn long prysoner in Spayne, and thus he hathe taken to hym for companyon Jo Newsome of the Wygth.

8 In the Barke Talbot ys one Bayly a man of my Lord of Shroseberyes[4] who hath servde in the same Shyp when she was ymployed at the Ilandes in the service of Don Anthony.[5]

9 In the Whyte Lyon my Lord Admyralls Shyp[6] ys one James Erizo of this Contrey[7] an honest proper man aged and lyke to do well but not of anye experience.

10 In the Barke Bonde is Capteyn Robert Crosse a man of Master [. . .] vice-chamberlains[8] who long sense hathe medled at Sea but not of late, very lyke to do well.

11 In the Bark Bonner ys one Fortescue[9] a gente of thys Contrey and with the Generall in hys last voyage

[1] Whyte appears as captain of *Sea Dragon* in the *Summarie* list, but the elder Hawkins is not mentioned. This change is evidence of Sidney's intervention in the decisions of August 1585. On Grenevyle (i.e. Greville) see p. 50, n. 1 below.

[2] i.e. the *Thomas, alias* the *Hastings*. See Table of Ships.

[3] i.e. Thomas Cely. See p. 292.

[4] On the *Talbot* and the earl of Shrewsbury's interest see pp. 15, 285.

[5] i.e. the pretender to the throne of Portugal.

[6] Not a royal ship, but one of several belonging to the current Lord High Admiral, Charles Howard, Baron Howard of Effingham, who had entered his office in 1585 (*DNB*). See pp. 15, 286.

[7] On Erisey, of Cornwall, see p. 293.

[8] Sir Christopher Hatton, a prominent courtier and Privy Councillor, afterwards (1587) Lord Chancellor. Though somewhat out of favour between 1584 and 1586 (*DNB*), his interest in voyages and his distrust of Spain were well known. It was in his honour that Drake renamed the *Golden Hind* during his voyage of circumnavigation. On Crosse, see p. 292.

[9] George Fortescue, who died at Cartagena (see p. 174).

12 In the Hope ys Capteyne Grenevyle of Oxfordshyre[1] sometymes my Lord of Bedfords Servant.

13 In the Barke Hawkyns ys William Hawkyns the younger[2]

14 In the Beniaeman ys one John Marten of Plymmothe who was with Sir Frances in the last voyage

15 In the Frances ys Capteyn Thomas Moone[3] of Plymmothe who was in the last voyage

16 In the Speedwell ys one Wylson whom I thinke ys of Plymmothe and belongs to my Lord of Leycester[4]

Document 2

Drake's Account to the Queen for her Share in the Venture (P.R.O., A.O. 1/1685/20 A).[5]

The Declaration of the Accompte of Sir Frances Drake knighte, for so much of her Maiesties Treasure as was to him

[1] Fulke Greville, first Lord Brooke (1554-1628), the courtier and Sidney's friend. Through his connections with Walsingham and Sir Henry Sidney he had been granted in 1577 the reversion of two offices associated with the Council of Wales, from which he began to receive income in 1581; this doubtless explains the reference to his employment under the earl of Bedford (H.M.C., *De L'Isle and Dudley MSS*, II, 96, 97; Rebholz, *The Life of Fulke Greville*, pp. 20-1; *C.S.P.D. 1581-1590*, p. 399; *DNB*). Bedford, as one of the strongly puritan Privy Councillors and Lieutenant of Cornwall until his death in July 1585 (*C.S.P.D. 1581-1590*, pp. 139, 249, 309), may have been a promoter of the voyage. In his *Life of Sidney*, however, Greville stated that his interest in the expedition resulted chiefly from his friendship with Sidney.

As to sea experience, Greville had spent a few months in 1580 as captain of a ship in Sir William Wynter's unsuccessful mission to prevent the arrival of Spanish reinforcements for western Ireland (Rebholz, op. cit., pp. 42-5). His name appeared in a list of captains qualified to examine the state of the navy in 1583 (Williamson, *Hawkins of Plymouth*, p. 266), and he was named also in the January 1585/6 list of captains (Corbett, *Sp. War*, p. 292).

[2] The name of this bark, though missing from the printed *Summarie* list, is in the MS variant (Harl. 6221), and it is mentioned in the narratives. See p. 286.

[3] Moone died at Cartagena. See pp. 168, 297.

[4] The *Speedwell* is not in the *Summarie* list, but she was with the fleet until the storm at Bayona (see pp. 81, 287). The account of her voyage, ending with her arrival at Portsmouth on 9 October, is in a letter from Philip Sparrowe to Wilson, a badly damaged document, B.L., Lansdowne MS 100, fols. 81-2.

[5] Few documents relating to fiscal accounts are available, and it must be borne in mind that the existing records relate only to what was officially declared. Spanish

prested out of the Receipt of her highnes Exchequier, in parte
of Adventure with diverse her Maiesties subiectes to the
furtheraunce of A VOYAGE by him made anno Domini 1585,
in the xxvii[th] yeare of her highnes Reigne, with the assistaunce
of a competente Fleete of her Subiectes Shippes and pinnaces,
so authorised and warranted successivelie[1] from time to time by
sundrie her Maiesties orders and directions, as hereafter vpon
everie occurrence Verbatim is rehersed. Firste for her highnes
pleasure concerninge a preste of her Treasure to be made in
Forme as followeth ELIZABETH &c. To the Treasurer and
Chamberlaines of our Exchequier greetinge. Wee lett you witt
our pleasure and Commaundemente is, that yee deliver and pay
or cause to be delivered and paide of such of our treasure as
remayneth in your charge and custodie vnto such person or
persons as shalbe appointed and directed vnto you by lettres
vnder the handes of you our sayd Treasurer y[e] Baron Efingham
Lord Chamberlaine of our house, and Sir Frances Walsingham
Knight our Principall secretarie, the summe of TENNE
THOUSANDE POUNDES – to be issued from time to time
in our causes and affaires[2], as by them, he, or they shalbe further
ordered and assigned, and these our lettres shalbe your sufficiente

---

reports, although they were probably exaggerated, indicate that much more than the
official ransoms and captured ordnance was carried away by Drake and his men (see
pp. 156, n.; 177, n.). See also Oppenheim, *Naval Tracts . . . Monson*, I, 133.

As to official records, the reports of the Royal Commission for auditing Drake's
'book', preserved now among the Lansdowne MSS, were printed by Corbett
(*Sp. War*, pp. 86–92, 94–6); excerpts from these appear below (pp. 60–2). Among the
Exchequer papers at the Public Record Office are two additional documents, one from
the Audit Office (Declared Accounts Navy) and the other from the Pipe Office. The
latter (P.R.O., E 351/2222), which is a separate roll for this voyage, is a duplicate
of the other, with a few slight variations in wording, but has been somewhat damaged
because of folds in the parchment. For this reason, the Audit Office record (P.R.O.,
A.O.1/1685/20 A), which consists of four large sheets of paper with writing on both
sides, has been chosen for the basic text for the record of Drake's account with the
queen. Because the plan by which items are listed is inconvenient for printing, some
condensing of various sections has been done by the editor, and Arabic numerals have
been substituted for the more cumbersome Roman forms.

[1] Written as *sufficientlie* in the Pipe Office roll.

[2] The word order in the Pipe Office roll is: '. . . in our causes and affaires from time
to time. . . .'

warrante, and discharge in this behalfe. Given vnder our privie
Seale at Nonesuche the xxix daye of Iulie 1584[1] in the xxvj[th]
yeare of our Reigne./ Concerninge her Maiesties further orders,
and directions thus. FIRSTE we are pleased with the preparation of this fleete of Eleven Shippes fower Barques and twentie
pinnaces to go vnder ye conduction of Sir Frances Drake
knighte. wee are further pleased that whatsoever commoditie,
or gaine shalbe gotten by the Adventure of this charge in ye
said voyage to be conducted by the said Sir Frances Drake, the
Adventurers shall enioye their portions thereof accordinge to
the quantities of their Adventure, portion and portion alike,
without anie question to be made to them for the same. And
further wee are pleased, that if vpon anie consideration wee
shall staie this enterprise, to promise hereby, that the Adventurers shall beare no losse, So as the hoole provisions and
thinges prepared be at our disposition, to vse and converte the
same at our pleasure. At our manor of Sainte James the xxiii[th]
daye of December 1584 in ye xxvij[th] yeare of our Raigne./[2]
And further warrante also thus. WHEREAS our Trustie and
welbeloved servante SIR FRANCES DRAKE KNIGHTE
hath made Offer vnto vs of some speciall service to be by him
executed, tendinge gratelye to the Benefite of vs and our
Realme, Towardes the charges which in the same and to the
performaunce thereof, are by the said Sir Frances Drake to be
susteyned, diverse of our lovinge subiectes are of them selves
willinge to be Contributaries,[3] and yett vpon some doubte

---

[1] In the Pipe Office roll the date is written as 'the xxx[th] daie of Iulie 1584'. The
earlier date is probably correct, since it is repeated in the documents cited regarding
payments of cash out of the Exchequer (see below).

[2] Oppenheim noted Elizabeth's Letter of Privy Seal, 23 December 1584 as being in
Chancery Misc. Rolls 928/35 (*Naval Tracts . . . Monson*, I, 125, n.). Although the voyage
was still being projected for the Moluccas, as notes dated 20 November show
(Williamson, *Sir John Hawkins*, p. 411), other developments were occurring to shift
the focus westward. It was on 18 December that the House of Commons passed the
bill confirming Raleigh's letters patent 'for the discovery of Foreign Countries'.
S. D'Ewes, *Journals of all the Parliamnents . . . Elizabeth*, p. 340.

[3] Ventures listed in November for the Moluccas voyage, with the estimated cost
being 40,000 *l.*, included the queen's venture of 17,000 *l.*, of which 7,000 *l.* was
represented by two ships; Drake, 7,000 *l.*; the earl of Leicester, 3,000 *l.*; John Hawkins,

conceyved by them that the same service should not go forwarde, They are lothe (as we are enformed) to yelde their Contributions, leaste (the service not proceadinge) it turne to their greate losse, and hinderaunce:/ Wee have therefore bene pleased by theise presentes to declare our good likinge of the Offer of the said service, and to assure also our lovinge subiectes, that our meaning is: not onlie, that the said Sir Frances Drake shall proceade to the execution of the saide service, but also that such of our subiectes as shalbe Adventurers, and Contributaries therein, shall receyve suche benefite as shalbe agreed vpon by the said Sir Frances Drake and them./ Given vnder our Signe manuell the firste daie of Iulie in the xxvij[th] yeare of our Raigne.[1] OF ALL which summe of x[m] li. aforesaide, prested out of her Maiestie treasure in the Receipte of her Exchequier accordinge to the order before prescribed cominge of his owne acknoweldgemente hoolie, and entierlie to his handes, the said Sir Frances Drake knighte yeldeth this his Accompte and ioyntlie withall of a further Charge of twoo her highnes Shippes, the ELIZABETH BONAVENTURE, and the AIDE, committed to him in that voyage, with all their Brasse Ordinaunce, cables, anchors, tackle, and other furniture valued also at y[e] summe of x[m] li. and by him likewise acknowledged in his Bill of Adventure.

2,500 l.; William Hawkins, 1,000 l.; Sir Christopher Hatton, 1,000 l.; and Sir Walter Raleigh, 400 l. Williamson, *Hawkins of Plymouth*, pp. 225–6.

[1] With the queen's formal consent at this late date, 1 July 1585, Drake could now hasten his preparations for departure. Not until 9 July, however, did the Privy Council issue the general letter of reprisal against Spanish shipping (S.P. 12/180: 15, pr. in Corbett, *Sp. War*, pp. 36–8), as Elizabeth's response to the seizure of English ships in Spain in May.

The saide Accomptaunte is Charged with

Readie Money (money *prested* out of the Receipt of the Exchequer, accord- to letters to the Receipt, dated 4 August 1584, by warrant under Privy Seal for 10,000 *l.*, dated 29 July anno 26 Eliz.)[2]

Easter term (26 Eliz.)
To Sir Francis Drake kt.,
1200 *l.*
To John Hawkins,
1600 *l.*
To Carey Rawley, esq.[1]
400 *l.*
To William Hawkins, esq.
300 *l.*
Total   3500 *l.*

Mich. term (26 Eliz. and 27)
To Sir Francis Drake, kt.,
5400 *l.*
To John Hawkins, 800 *l.*
To Carey Rawley, 150 *l.*
To William Hawkins,
150 *l.*

Total   6500 *l.*

In all prested out of the Receipte of the Exchequier for those causes . . . , in regarde of her highnes Adventure in that voyage ──────────── ────── 10,000 *l.*

The value of two of her Maiesty's ships

The *Elizabeth Bonaventure* and the *Aide*, with their brass ordnance and other furnishings, valued at   10,000 *l.*[3]

In Total of the Charge aforesaide// ──────────── 20,000 *l.*

---

[1] Carew Raleigh, elder brother of Sir Walter, and active in naval matters (Corbett, *Sp. War*, pp. 292, 296). He was probably acting as his brother's representative in the voyage preparations.

[2] Supplies of ordnance for the two royal ships, on the basis of a warrant dated 12 June, were delivered from the Master of Ordnance on 17 July; other supplies that month included powder and munitions for the fleet. See Corbett, *Sp. War*, pp. 27-33.

[3] The valuation of the ships at 10,000 *l.*, higher than the figure planned in 1584 by 3,000 *l.*, was termed by Oppenheim (*Naval Tracts . . . Monson*, I, 126) 'ridiculously extravagant'. The *Aid*, which had had a declared value in 1577 of about 839 *l.* (Morison *European Disc. of Amer.*, I, 518), had recently been reconstructed (Williamson, *Hawkins of Plymouth*, p. 262), but hardly up to this 1585 value.

Against the which [are allowances for the return of the two
    ships, for brass ordnance, for pearls, and an abatement for
    charges sustained in the voyage, which are described as
    follows]:

Abatement & defalcation . . . [for] charges susteyned and
    defrayed in the adventure of the said voyage, passage, and
    return to and fro, so authorised as well by letters directed
    from her Maiesties honorable Privie Counsaile to certaine
    Commissioners, by them appointed to take vieu of the
    ladinge of that hoole fleete then returned,[1] as also agreed
    vpon and so testified by the same Commissioners by
    returne of their Certificate, concerninge the true value and
    praisement of the said ladinge, as it was founde after the
    arrival at Woolwich, and Blackewall within the River
    Thames, and as may evidentlie appeere by the tenor and
    purporte of the saide Lettres, and Certificate hereafter
    followinge./ viz. of the lettres directed from her Highnes
    honorable Privie Counsaile verbatim thus./ AFTER our
    hartie commendacions./ Whereas yow have bene speciallie
    appointed, and receyved direction to make a praisemente
    of the gooddes broughte by Sir Frances Drake in this late
    voyage, in which direction it was omitted to authorise
    yow that yow should likewise make payemente of the
    Wages due to the Captaines, Souldiers, and Mariners that
    were imployed in the same voyage; These are nowe to
    requier yow, that yow shall by vertue of these our lettres
    disburse all such summes as by Sir Frances Drake shalbe
    sett downe and requiered at your handes for the said
    payementes./ And so wee bidd yow hartelie farewell./ At
    London the vth of September 1586.[2] Of the Certificate

---

[1] i.e. the royal commissioners for auditing Drake's account, whose names appear
below. For portions of their report, see Document 4 below.

[2] There has been some question as to whether Drake's men were paid. This letter
shows that the Privy Council authorized the payment. The amount, as determined by
the Commission in calculating the net proceeds of the voyage, was 17,000 *l.* or
17,500 *l.* (see below, pp. 59, 62). Oppenheim assumed that the payment was made
(*Naval Tracts . . . Monson*, I, 133).

On 18 September the Council appointed a separate committee of Londoners to hear returned by the Commissioners verbatim thus./ THE Commissioners whose names hereafter followe, viz. Sir William Winter, Sir Francis Drake, and Sir Richard Martin, knightes, Thomas Smith, Customer of London, John Harte Alderman, and John Hawkins, esquiers, appointed . . . [by Privy Council] for the determininge of the hoole charge of the late voyage of Sir Frances Drake into the West Indies in anno *1585* outewarde, and also for the receyvinge of an Accompte of all Bullion, pearle, Golde, plate, Brasse Ordinaunce, and other Merchandizes returned from the said voyage in anno 1586./ And havinge with manie meetinges and greate deliberation and advice broughte ye hoole charge outewarde to a certaine summe, and the value of all that was returned to the like, they founde, and have sett it downe vnder their handes, that there mighte be paide to everie Adventurer in the saide voyage ye summe of xv *s.* for everie pounde by him so adventured./ The Originall copies of which bothe the *Lett*res of directio*n* and of the Certificate before rehersed remaine of Recorde in the Eschequier./ Wherevpon by consequence it ap*p*eereth that in her Maiesties foresaide Adventure of xx^M *li.* there is to be ABATED & allowed (correspondente to the rate and proportion so allowed by the reste of the Adventurers) in regarde of his charges afore remembred, a fourthe parte,[1] rising to ————— 5,000 *l.*

The value of her Maiesties twoo Shippes . . . were founde worth by the Officers of the Navye, at the time of their returne & redeliverie at Chatham, . . . with the consente and allowance of vs Sir John Hawkins knighte, and William Borough esquier, by the Commissioners for that voyage appointed, valued in the summe of EIGHTE THOUSAND poundes . . . ————— 8,000 *l.*

---

some further complaints and to arrange a final settlement with the men. P.R.O., P.C. 2/14: 189 (see n. 4, p. 23 above).

[1] Compare the June 1587 report from the Commissioners (p. 60).

Brasse Ordinaunce [over and besides those belonging to the two royal ships] viz. of such strange pieces as were gotten in the voyage, and deliuered at Woolwich vpon her Maiesties Wharfe there to her Highnes owne vse . . . , valued also by them appointed Commissioners, vpon conference with men of skill and iudgemente in matters of Metalles, accordinge to such direction as by her Highness commaundemente was given. . . . Viz. in names, number, weightes, and price, as followeth./[1]

Serviceable

Basilisco	1	[81 pieces, weighing
Canons	4	174,079 lbs., at 60 s.
Canon pierrers	13	per cwt., worth
Demi Canons	16	5222 l. 7 s.]
Culveringes	3	
Demi Culveringes	8	
Sakers	15	
Minions	21	

Unserviceable

Sakers	3	[104 pieces, plus 55
Falcons	21	chambers, weighing
Falconettes	8	59,060 lbs., at 50 s. [Total weight,
Portebases	72	per cwt., worth 233,139 lbs.]
Chambers	55	1476 l. 9s. 4d.]

[Total value] —— 6698 l. 16s.4d.[2]

[Weights and values certified by Roger Monox, 'late servante to Sir William Winter knighte'.][3]

Pearles . . . of sundrie values . . . since delivered into her Maiesties possession, after deligente vieu thereof hadd by

---

[1] A description of various types of naval ordnance is in Appendix A, 'Guns and Gunnery in the Tudor Navy', Corbett, *Sp. War*, pp. 315–36. Two ordnance reports for 1585 are included in the same volume (pp. 300–11).

[2] The figures for weights and values of these two items correspond with those in the reports of the Audit Commission (see p. 62), although the totals differ by 2 l. The figure is written as 6696 l. 16 s. 4 d. in Lansdowne MS 52, fol. 96 (pr. in Corbett, *Sp. War*, p. 94).

[3] i.e. an employee of Wynter as Surveyor of Ships.

the foresaide Commissioners, vsinge also the assistaunce of skilfull lapidaries, for the better distinguishinge of them in their severall kindes, and competent prices . . . The particularities whereof are herevnder sett out as followethe./

At 20 *l.* the piece	7 pearles	140 *l.*	
At 10 *l.* the piece	2 pearles	20 *l.*	
	pend*a*nt		
At 40 *s.* the piece	82 pearles	164 *l.*	
At 30 *s.* the piece	192 pearles	288 *l.*	315 pearles
At 20 *s.* the piece	32 pearles	32 *l.*	
		[Total] —— 644 *l.*[1]	

Sum*me* Totall of the Discharge aforesaide

Abatement and defalcation. ————	5000 *l.*
The value of her Maiesties twoo shippes . . . ————	8000 *l.*
Brasse Ordinaunce . . . . ————	6698 *l.* 16 *s.* 4 *d.*
Pearles . . . . . . ————	644 *l.*
[Total] ——	20,342 *l.* 16 *s.* 4*d.*

And so the said Accomptaunte, vpon the determination of this his Accompte, is in Surplusage the summe of ———————————————————— 342 *l.* 16*s.* 4*d.*[2]

[At the end are the signatures of two auditors (Bartholomew Dodington, deputy for William Dodington, and John S[otherton?], and also of Lord Burghley and Sir John Fortescue. There is a memorandum, dated 13 November 1596, at the end of Pipe Office roll (E 351/2222), as follows]: Memorandu*m* that the abovesaid Surplusage of [342 *l.* 16 *s.* 4 *d.*] was released

---

[1] The corresponding figure in the auditing report of 1587 is 654 *l.* (Lansdowne MS 52, fol. 96, pr. in Corbett, *Sp. War*, p. 94). Evidently the largest pearls, out of a total valued at over 3,200 *l.* (see p. 61), were delivered to the queen.

[2] In the report from the Commission, where the valuation of the ordnance is 2*l.* less and the valuation of the pearls is 10 *l.* higher than in the figures from the Audit Office (see notes above), the amount of the surplus was stated to be 350 *l.* 16*s.* 4*d.* (Corbett, *Sp. War*, pp. 87, 95). The Audit Office figure, which is based on more detailed accounts, and is confirmed by the notation on the Pipe Office roll in 1596 (see below), is doubtless correct.

& remitted in the Courte of Eschequier before the Barons there, by Thomas Drake esquier Executor to Sir Fraunces Drake knighte Accomptaunte abovesaide deceased. before the delyverie in of this Accompte.

Document 3

Estimate of the Proceeds of the Voyage
(S.P. 12/191:38).

A valuation of the goods brought home by Sir Francis Drake[1]

The plate and Bollyon	42000
The perle	03500
The Ordenaunce	05500
The shipps	12500
The hydes	01800
The Iron and lead, etc.	00600
	62100[2]

[A second column, not itemized, is written below, with the figure for hides being 800 instead of 1800. It shows a corrected total of 64,900. From this is deducted the amount of 17,000 (probably the one-third estimated as due to the men), and net valuation of 47,900.][3]

[1] This document was printed in modern form by Corbett (*Sp. War*, p. 85). The endorsement has been identified in a note by a later hand as Walsingham's writing.

[2] The total given here, in which a 6 was substituted for a 7, or *vice versa*, is incorrect. Corbett omitted it, and he printed the figure for hides as 800, corresponding to the figure in a corrected second listing that was written below, on the same document.

The rough total, though slightly larger than that found by the auditors, is much smaller than the estimate of the value of the cargo as given in the French narrative of the voyage (Lacour, p. 26), in which the amount was said to be five or six hundred thousand *escuz*, or roughly 166,000 *l*. to 200,000 *l*.

[3] The document bears no date, but the records of the Audit Commission show that it relates to this voyage. See Corbett, *Sp. War*, p. 85, n., and Document 4 (below). This estimate shows 17,000 *l*. for the men's pay, whereas in the Commission's report the figure appears as 17,500 *l*. (see p. 62).

Document 4

Excerpts from the Reports of the Royal Commission, June 1587 (B.L., Lansdowne MS 52, fols. 92-100).[1]

[In their letter of June 1587, transmitting to the Privy Council their itemized report, the Auditing Commissioners noted their difficulty in arriving at a figure for Drake's charges outward.] ... but in the ende wee agreed to allow the Chardge outwarde to be 57000 *li.* Althoughe his Demaunde was by the booke, 60400 *li.* . . . [They have set valuations upon the various commodities brought back.] In which accompte the money taken out for the thirde payde vnto the company and the Chardges otherwise since theire retorne into England being Deducted theare remayned to be devided 45908– 18–6 ... [Hence they concluded that the adventurers should be paid 15*s.* on each pound invested, with the possibility at most of 12 *d.* per pound more. The queen's dividend would be 15 *s.* for each pound ventured, with an additional amount of 350– 16 –4.][2]

[The itemized accounts follow, with an opening statement showing Drake's charges which the Commissioners accepted as 'an honest and true accompte'. It continues]:

[1] This document, which includes a copy of the letter of transmittal, as well as an itemized report, with portions in duplicate, was printed by Corbett (*Sp. War*, pp. 86–92, 94–6), with some rearrangement of the material. Hence only excerpts from the original are given here, selected because of their relationship to matters in the texts of other documents.

The Commissioners were Sir William Wynter (Surveyor of Ships), Richard Martin (London alderman and Master of the Mint), John Harte (London alderman and director of the Muscovy Company), Thomas Smythe (Farmer of the Customs and Master of Mining Works), and John Hawkins (Treasurer of the Navy and certainly one of the adventurers). (Corbett, *Sp. War*, p. 95.) Assisting them, in addition to Drake himself, were Carleill and Frobisher. A separate note regarding the accounts (dated in December 1586), in which the latter two joined with the five Commissioners, is in S.P. 12/195: 79 (pr. in Corbett, *Sp. War*, pp. 92–4).

Besides these, the Privy Council order of 6 August 1586 naming the commission to begin appraising the ships and their contents (P.R.O., P.C. 14/170) included two other names, I. Hussey and Richard Drake; but these seem not to have served. John Hawkins, though not named in this 6 August list, may have acted officially as Treasurer of the Navy as well as an important adventurer.

[2] Lansdowne MS 52, fol. 92. A separate tabulation concerning the queen's venture of 20,000 *l.* (fol. 96) shows a different figure for her 'surplus' (see above, p. 58, n. 2).

Firste the Chardge of the booke was ————— 60400 *l.* 0 *s.* 0 *d.*

Item sundry sommes stood in the booke in blancke and weare not sommed vp, which did seeme to be of good valew.

Item he hath demaunded nothing for his Chardges during the whole tyme of the preparaccion of the Ieorney in the sayde accompte, which Could not be but a great matter the thing hanging soe long.

Item his man Cottell dyed in the Ieorney whoe had the Chiefe Chardge of his accomptes, wheareby he Could not but forgette much, and soe recewe great losse theareby.

Neverthelesse he hath vpon the reasons, and debatinges had betweene vs and him as aforesayde Concluded that the Chardge outwarde ended the xiiij^th^ of September 1585 shalbe set downe to the Certainty of 57000 *li.* Soe that we are persuaded for any thing that we Can percewe, that he dealeth very liberally, and truly with the adventurers, and beareth him selfe a very great loss thearein. . . .[1]

[The list of 'assets', given in duplicate on fols. 94 and 99 includes several categories, some of which, such as brass ordnance that was turned over to the queen, show up in the Exchequer accounts. The main items are as follows]:

	L.	*s.*	*d.*
For the gold beinge of severall finesse, coined by Alderman Martin which doth amount vnto, the charges Deducted in weight	5146–	5–	10
For blockes of silver fyne and course, Ryalles of plate *coriente* of the Indies and Florida, gilte & white plate, beinge fyned and coined by Alderman Martin, amounting vnto, the charges Deducted	34133–	9–	10
For Pearle of all sortes, great and small, as they were solde, with 6 ounces of Emeraldes	3205–	3–	8

[1] Lansdowne MS 52, fol. 93 (pr. in Corbett, *Sp. War*, pp. 88–9). The cost outward may be compared with the figures for the Hawkins–Drake voyage of 1595, with the outfitting costs for an expedition of 2,500 men then coming to 31,000 *l.* and wages to some 12,000 *l.* Andrews, *Last Voyage*, pp. 48–9.

The brasse ordenaunce . . . [at 3 l. per
    cwt., 174,000 lbs, 3 qrs. 4 lb.]   5222–   7–   0[1]
For all Basses and those out of order . . .
    [59000, 2 qrs., 10 lbs. at 50 s. per cwt.]   1476–   9–   4
[Additional items in the list are 36 pieces
    of iron ordnance, 317 gold buttons,
    copper, $93\frac{1}{2}$ cwt. of copper money,
    sheet lead and sow lead, pewter; and
    'shippes Deliuered backe to their
    owners' (14520 l. 1 s.);[2] and a list of
    items not yet sold, as well as certain
    amounts of money due to the
    enterprise, which brought the grand
    total to]:   67017– 11– 1.[3]
[In conclusion]:
    Charges after the ships arrivall[4]   3608– 12– 7
            Rest nete   63408– 18– 6

    Abate for the thirde   17500–   0– 0[5]

Rest nete all Deductions Defaulked 45908– 18– 6

[1] Cf. the figures for ordnance and large pearls turned over to the navy and the queen, pp. 57–8.

[2] This may refer to some of the prizes, or to ships chartered in England, possibly to both (Corbett, *Sp. War*, p. 91, n.). The French prize, *Drake*, was apparently not restored to its owner. See Table of Ships.

[3] For the list in full see Corbett, *Sp. War*, pp. 90–1.

[4] Among these charges were food allowance for the *Francis*, which came back alone from Roanoke, and Richard Hawkins's expenses in travelling from Cornwall to London with news of the voyage (see p. 273, n.); charges including clothing, for 'the Turkes' (the word in the MS is in the plural, not in the singular as Corbett thought (see *Sp. War*, p. 95, n.), and must refer to the former galley slaves); customs duties; and the cost of replacements for various ships' cables, anchors, etc., and of repair work. See Corbett, *Sp. War*, pp. 95–6.

[5] The one-third for the men appears here higher than the earlier estimate of 17,000 l., but there is no explanation as to why it is below one-third of the total (i.e. 21,136 l.). Possibly the remaining 4,136 l. was held for officers, as Corbett suggests (*Sp. War*, p. 85, n.).

Some wages had been distributed at Portsmouth. In his letter of 26 July 1586 to Burghley, Drake had requested an advance of 6,000 l. in bullion from the Tower, if necessary (Lansdowne MS 51, fols. 27–8, pr. in Corbett, *Sp. War*, pp. 83–5). Some bullion remaining from Drake's 1577–80 voyage was still in the Tower in December

Document 5

Voyage Text from the General Map[1]

Sir Francis Drake knight Generall of the *whole Fleete of the West Indian voiage in 1585.*

1585 (H.M.C., *Salisbury MSS*, III, 116; and William Murdin, *Collection of State Papers . . . Lord Burghley* (2 vols., London, 1740–59), pp. 539–40). It was heard in London in August 1586 that, 'He [Drake] had received from the merchants of London, against bills of exchange, the sum of 60,000 sun-crowns to pay his soldiers, and has given to each gentleman who accompanied him 100 *l.* sterling.' (*C.S.P.Span. 1580–1586*, p. 620). Listed among the expenses after the fleet's return is an item: 'For the charges of 6000 *l.* taken up and carried to Portsmouth for payment of the Company—100 *l.*' (Lansdowne MS 52, fol. 100). Furthermore, the Privy Council's letter of 5 September 1586 directed the Commissioners for Drake's accounts to pay the wages due to the 'Captains, Souldiers, and Mariners' of the voyage (see above, p. 55).

Some delays occurred, however, perhaps only with the captains or officers. The Privy Council records show that one shilling for each pound of the proceeds (here mentioned as being 56,000 *l.*) had been reserved 'for satysfaccion of certaine particular captaynes and other gentlemen that bare chardge' in the voyage, in consideration of expenses incurred in setting out, and that this reserve had been left in the hands of Sir William Wynter. The Council wrote to Wynter on 8 May 1587, directing that 280 *l.* out of the 400 *l.* Carleill claimed as his expenses should be paid, although he deserved more. Carleill was then preparing to leave for Ireland. (*Acts P.C. 1587–1588*, pp. 75–6.) Another letter on 12 May 1588 ordered Wynter to pay to Martin Frobisher 150 *l.* in partial satisfaction of his 'expences outwardes', since he had received no repayment up to this time, and had gone on the voyage at the express command of the queen. The letter indicates further that the accounts had not yet been perfected with regard to what was 'due to every man'. *Acts P.C. 1588*, p. 63.

1 Although there has been some question as to whether the Boazio general map, known as 'The Famous West Indian Voyadge . . .', was planned for publication with *The Summarie and True Discourse* (see Note on Maps, Appendix IV), the accompanying Map Text suggests that this was so. There are several strong points of agreement in dates or in wording (e.g. 3 November, 1 January, 9 February, 27 April, 28 May); and in the case of Cartagena there is a reference in the Map Log to 'the book of discourse of that voyage'. But the Map Text provides as well a valuable supplement in the form of specific dates, some for incidents not reported in the *Summarie*. A comparison of these dates with those in other accounts, English as well as Spanish, shows that they are quite reliable, at least until the departure from Cartagena in late March, and for some of the later events. In its own right the Map Text has value for the chronology of the voyage.

The rather close resemblance, especially in the earlier parts, to matters noted in the *Tiger* journal (Document 6) and the related newsletter (Document 7) suggests that the compiler of the Map Text may have compared his notes with those of someone aboard Carleill's ship. If Baptista Boazio, the cartographer, was indeed associated with Carleill (see Note on Maps), such collaboration in planning for his large map would seem not unreasonable.

SEPTEMBER.

The 14. of September departed out of the Roade of Plimmouth with 23.[1] Ships and Barkes in all.

The 27 of September we entred in the Roade of Bayon.

The 30. of September our Lieftenant Generall Captayne Carleill went vp from the Roade of Bayon to the Riuer of Vigo with some Ships and Pinaces.

OCTOBER

The 1. of October, all the rest of our Fleete came and ankred vp in the Riuer of Vigo from the Roade of Bayon.

The 7. of October we set sayl and departed out of the Riuer of Vigo and came to anker agayne at the Ilands or Roade of Bayon.

The 11. of October the winde came at North North West,[2] and so we departed from the Roade of Bayon alongst some part of the Spanish Coast.

The 24. of October in the morning, we fell with one of the Ilands of Cannaria called Lançarotte.

NOVEMBER.

The 3. of Nouember we came within Cannon shot of Palma, being also one of the Ilands of Canaria, where by reason of the great surge of the Sea[3] we could by no meanes land our men, but were fayn within an howre after to depart from thence.

The 5. of Nouember we landed 700. men in Ferro,[4] also one of the Ilands of Canaria, but seeing the commodity thereof

---

Since the text is in English, and since the date of 28 July for Drake's return agrees only with that given in the London editions (differing from the MS variant of the *Summarie* and the 1588 Leyden editions), the indication is strong that both map and text were planned in relation to the English editions rather than for those published abroad. The failure to adjust another date (17–18 November) to agree with the English publication was perhaps an oversight. On these matters see Note on Maps. The text used here is from the B.L., Field copy. A text marred by several printer's errors is on the separate copy of the map at the John Carter Brown Library which appears as Plate I.

[1] In the *Summarie*, the figure is twenty-five.   [2] Cf. p. 89.

[3] The *Summarie* text (p. 223) mentions the dangerous 'sea-surge'.

[4] Cf. pp. 95, 131.

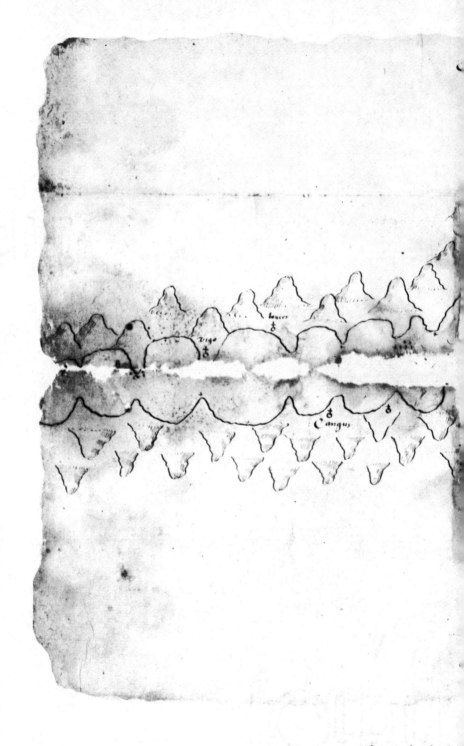

Plate II. Sketch of th
(P.R.

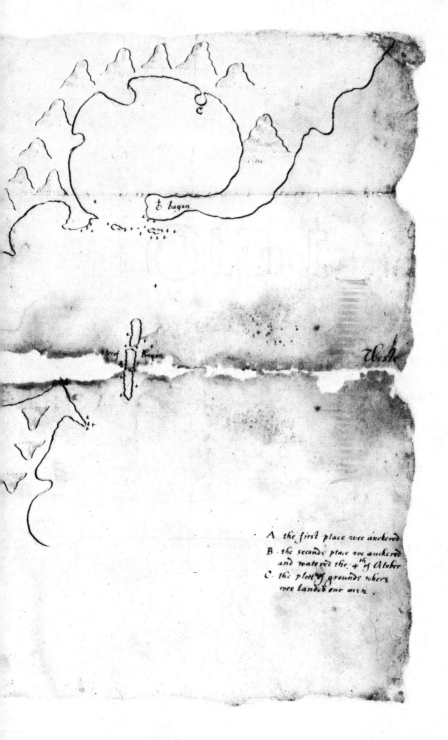

E bayon

Hog of Bayon

Wesse

A the first place wee anckred
B the seconds place wee anckred
and watered the 4th of October
C the plott of grounds where
wee landed our men

woulde little auayle vs, we put to Sea in the same afternoone, the wynd at South South East,[1] towards the coast of Barbary.

The 8. we descryde the coast of Barbary, and made our course towards Cape Blanke.

The 11. we bore somewhat neere with the coast of Barbary, and so continued alongst the shore till our comming to Cape Blanke.

The 13. we fell with Cape Blanke, where putting into the Bay, we found certayne French men of Newhauen, we departed thence that day shaping our course towards the Ilands of Capo Verde.[2]

The 16. of Nouember we descryed one of the Ilandes of Capo Verde called Bona Victa.[3]

The 17. of Nouember we saw and fel with the Iland of Maye.

The 17. of Nouember we also recouered the Iland of Saint Iago,[4] where we landed 1000. men, betweene the Town of Saint Iago and the Towne of Playe, vnder the chiefe charge of Captayne Carleill our Lieutenant Generall.

The 18. we entred and tooke the Towne of Santiago.

From the 18. of Nouember to the 29. of the same moneth, wee remayned in the Towne of Saint Iago.

The 29. of Nouember we departed from Saint Iago,[5] putting ouer the great Ocean and making our course continually west ward for the west Indies.

DECEMBER

The 18. of December we arriued to Guadalupe, one of the Ilands of the west Indies, hauing made our passage ouer the Ocean in 19. dayes.

[1] Cf. p. 95. In the *Summarie* text the statement is, 'We put off to sea south Southeast' (see p. 224).

[2] Cf. pp. 110, 224. This encounter occurred on 11 or 14 November, according to other accounts (see pp. 133, 186).

[3] i.e. Buena Vista. Cf. pp. 133, 186.

[4] On the significance of the dates of 17–18 November, and the apparent changes made for the London edition of the *Summarie*, see notes on pp. 97, 134, 225, 228.

[5] This date agrees with that in the Carleill records (see pp. 98, 111), and corrects the error in the *Summarie* (p. 231). See also p. 191.

The 18. of December we came to the Dominica,[1] an other Iland where we watred and refreshed vs with such things as the Saluadges of the Iland brought vnto vs.

The 19. of December we set sayle and departed thence towards another Iland lying to the Northward of Guadalupe.

The 20. we descride two Ilands more, called Mançarotte and Rotunda.[2]

The 21. we came to another Iland, called Saint Christophers, where we landed and refreshed our sicke men for three or foure dayes.[3]

The 25 of December we departed thence, and set sayle West and by South.

The 27. of December being Munday, we descryde an Ilande called Sancta Crux.

The 28. we came to the sight of Saint Iohns Iland.[4]

The 29. we descride two small Ilands to the Westward of Saint Johns Iland called Mona [and] Monica,[5] which Ilands lye iust betweene the Iland of Hispaniola, and Saint Iohns Iland.

The 30. being Thursday we recouered the Iland Hispaniola.

IANVARIE.

The 1. of Ianuary we came to the bay of Saint Domingo, wher we landed 1000. men on shore on the Westermost part of the Bay, 9. or 10. miles distant from the Towne of Saint Domingo,[6] the same day our men (by Gods helpe) tooke and spoyled the Towne, vnder the conduction of Captayne Carleill our Lieutenant Generall. In this Towne we remayned the space of one moneth.

[1] Cf. pp. 100, 236.

[2] i.e. Montserrat and Redonda.

[3] Cf. p. 111. The *Primrose* journal (p. 193) places the arrival at St Christopher's on 24 December.

[4] The places passed, 27–9 December, are noted also on pp. 84, 111. St John's Island is the present Puerto Rico.

[5] i.e. Monito I.

[6] Hispaniola had been sighted on 29 December (see p. 111). The landing at the mouth of the Hayna River was begun on the night of 31 December (see pp. 101, 238).

FEBRVARIE.

The 1. of February we departed out of the Bay of Saint Domingo,[1] keeping our course South and South and by West.

The 5. of February we came to Cape la Vela, on the firme land[2] of the West Indies, we thence sailed West and West South West.

The 6. of the same moneth we came before Rio de la Hacha, where we ankred all that night.[3]

The 7. of February being Monday, in the morning we set sayle and went West North West to the sea, the Viceadmirall with hys Skiffe and other Pinaces, being gone to the shore side, to see if he coulde get any guyd of Cartagena, but could finde none.[4]

The 9. of February we came to the sight of Cartagena,[5] where we recouered and ankred in the harbour, and landed our men 4. or 5. miles to the Westward of the Towne, vnder the conduction of Captayne Carleill our Lieutenant Generall, our men marched close by the wash of the Sea, vntil our comming to the Towne, where we found the Enemy strongly fortified and wel prouided of Artillerye and small shot, that continually for the space of halfe an howre played vpon vs, (but by Gods prouidence) we von theyr fortresse and so presently entred and won their Town, as the book of discourse of that voyage doth more playnly declare,[6] we remayned in thys Towne of Cartagena the space of 6. weekes.

MARCH.

The 26. of March we departed out of the harbour of Cartagena towards Cape Saint Antonie in the Iland of Cuba.[7]

[1] This date was probably 31 January. See notes on pp. 103, 157.

[2] i.e. Tierra Firme, the continental coast. Cf. p. 158.

[3] Drake's original plans may have included a plundering raid here. Lansdowne MS 100, fol. 98, pr. in Corbett, *Sp. War*, p. 71.

[4] Cf. p. 159.

[5] Cf. pp. 103, n. 2, 160.

[6] This may be a reference to *The Summarie and True Discourse*, as edited by Cates.

[7] The sailing date was Thursday, 31 March (see pp. 105, 202). This is the first case of serious discrepancy in the dates provided by the Map Text.

APRILL.

The 20. of Aprill ve fell with two Ilands called Caimanes,[1] vhere we refreshed our selues with many Allagartas and greate Turtoises, being very vgly and fearefull beasts to behold, but were made good meate to eate, and so the next day we departed thence towards Cape Saint Antony.

The 27. of Aprill we came to Cape Saint Antony,[2] being the Vestermost part of Cuba, where ankering but a while because fresh water could not be speedily found, and so departing thence within two howrs after our arriual, we put to Sea alongst the coast of Cuba, and plying vp and downe with contrary winde, hoping still to recouer the Matances,[3] a good harbour to the Eastward of the Hauana, with intent there to water our shipps at ease, we were in the ende after 14 dayes beating vp and down, put downe to Cape Saint Antony againe, where the scarsety of fresh water being growen somewhat greater with vs, we were fayn to take such water as we found in the Moorish[4] ground, by making of pits, and out of them to take vppe the water that would gather together in them.

MAY.

The 13. of May we departed the second time from the Cape Saint Antony,[5] and proceeding about the Cape of Florida, wee neuer touched any where, but kept the coast alongst.

The 28. of May earely in the morning we descrie the Riuer of Saynt Augustine in Florida, in 36 degrees of Latitude,[6] wher some small Spanish Garrison was planted, of some 150. men,

---

[1] Grand and Little Cayman. The date agrees with that of the newsletter (p. 113), but the less reliable *Primrose* journal (p. 203) dates this on 22 April. The stop is not mentioned in the *Summarie*.

[2] Cf. pp. 113, 263.

[3] i.e. Matanzas.

[4] In the *Summarie* (p. 263), where the wording is very similar, the word is printed *as marrish*, meaning marshy. *OED*.

[5] This is the date in the *Summarie* (p. 264), but the *Primrose* journal (p. 205) gives it as 19 May.

[6] The 36° is probably a printer's error for 30° (see p. 265). In two days the fort was taken and then the town was occupied. The total stay was six or seven days. Cf. pp. 206–7.

or thereabouts: Here we spent two dayes in taking the fort and spoiling the Town, and so departed agayn keeping as nigh the shore as might be, to haue a sight if it myght be of our English men planted in Virginia.

IVNE.

The 9. of Iune in comming alongst the coast, we discouered some part of Virginia, and found some of our English men, and the next day spake wyth more of them, & so afterwards with them al.[1]

The 18. of Iune we departed from the coast of Virginia,[2] and so betweene Virginia and the first sight of England, we were in sayling one whole moneth, or thereabouts.

IVLY.

The 22. of Iuly we fell in sight of the Sorlinges, or the Ilandes of Sylly, being the westermost part of all England.

The 28. of Iuly 1586[3] God be thanked we arriued all in good safety at Portesmouth.

Document 6

The Record kept aboard the Ship *Tiger* by Christopher Carleill and Edward Powell, 13 September 1585 to 14 April 1586. British Library Cotton MS Otho E. VIII, fols. 229–34.[4]

[1] Cf. pp. 209, 270.

[2] On this date see p. 274 and n. 5.

[3] Although this is the date given in the English editions of the *Summarie*, it was probably 27 July. See p. 274 and n. 7. By error the date is printed as 22 July on the map used for Plate I.

[4] This MS, consisting of six consecutive folios, twelve sides, has been badly damaged by fire, so that both upper right- and left-hand corners and a portion of one edge of each page are missing. Lost as well are at least one page, possibly more, which must have noted preparations for the expedition, and also the 'orders for the voyage' which were to have been placed 'towards the end of my book' (see entry for 15 September). The record was kept less steadily as time passed, and the final entry was on 14 April 1586.

The handwriting is consistent throughout, a somewhat difficult Elizabethan hand,

[September 13]

[fol. 229]

...¹ afternone ... plyenge up & down[e] ... [w]e came in the eveninge to a [   ]² ... N.N.E: and thereaboute.³

[Tu]esday the. 14.

... [   ]le with the whole flete about eyght of the clocke ... [a]n howres saylinge or twoo Ser Philipe Sydney with ... (torn) [S]ydney, Master Foulke Grevile, Master Rychard Drake and oth[er] ... vs aborde the admyrall, they went to the shore⁴

---

probably that of Edward Powell, who noted on 2 October (see p. 86) that he was taking over from 'my captain' the keeping of the record. The captain, who apparently dictated the earlier pages to his clerk, was Christopher Carleill, Drake's lieutenant general and captain also of the ship *Tiger*. This identification is established by the use of the personal pronoun *I* in relation to conferences with Drake and to actions of both Carleill and his ship. It is corroborated by the close similarity between the account of events off the Spanish coast and that provided in Carleill's despatch to Walsingham of 4–11 October 1585 (PR.O., S.P. 12/183: 10, printed with modern spelling in Corbett, *Sp. War*, pp. 39–49). In the present account (see p. 81) Carleill mentioned his desire to send a description of Bayona to 'Master Secretary'. Because the wording of certain paragraphs of the two accounts is identical, the despatch has been used to fill in some of the words missing from the damaged MS.

Important relationships between this record and several other accounts of the voyage should be noted. The distinctive hand of this Cotton MS is that also of a MS copy of *The Summarie and True Discourse*, Harley MS 6221, fols. 94–8v (see pp. 213, n. 1; 307 and Plates Nos. IX, XI). The recorder of the *Tiger* journal was evidently engaged in assembling materials about the voyage, possibly for Carleill's distinguished stepfather, Walsingham.

There appears to be a connection also between the *Tiger* account and the newsletter (possibly prepared also for Walsingham), which is contained in Cotton MS Otho E. VIII, fols. 235–6, bound immediately after the *Tiger* fragment (see p. 106 and note 5, Document 7). There may be a relationship also with the record which was printed as the Map Text for the general map of the voyage (see p. 63 and n. 1).

¹ Words missing because of damage to MS.

² Undeciphered word.

³ This entry obviously refers to embarkation procedures on 12 and 13 September. It was reported in Spain that bad weather had postponed the departure planned for 12 September. *C.S.P.Ven. 1581–1591*, p. 122. The departure was at 8 a.m., 14 September. Letter of Phillip Sparrowe (Lansdowne MS 100, fol. 81).

⁴ Confirmation that Sidney and Greville were aboard Drake's ship as it left Plymouth, and that they then returned in obedience to the queen's command. As late as 13 September Sidney's father-in-law, Walsingham, wrote to Davison that Sidney had gone to join Drake, despairing of the appointment as governor of Flushing. 'There is some order taken for his stay, but I fear it will not take place; and yet I pray you make me no author of this unpleasant news.' *C.S.P.For. 1585–1586*, pp. 23–4.

& we plyed l[   ] ... *o*ur smale sayles attendinge the retourne
of some boates that ... the shore/ The wynde in the morninge
at no:east: and ther aboute ... [n]one tyme the wynde come
to the so: west: This after noone the ... aborde the Admyrall
agayne where we spente sometyme in settinge ... some articles
of order for the governement aswell of the fleet as of the ... in
perticular[1] and after supper I returned to my owne shipe agayne.

Wedensday, the. 15.

All this mornynge the wynd in slender gale with some fogg
was at n[   ] ... and towards none we were shette before
Falmowthe,[2] at which tyme I w[ent] aborde of the admyrall/
who aftar mornynge service / havynge called all *the* Captaynes
and mastars aborde of hym delyvered vnto eche man the ordars
and direction of the flete/ which I have placed towards the end
of my bok*e*.[3] In the evenynge we had the wynde at W. & by
north/ a good freshe gayle/ at which tyme the Lyzard bare us
w. and by sowthe, but in the nyght the wynde standynge
angayne to the sowth west cawsed us to put Rome/[4]

Thursday the. 16.

In this last nyght the wynde beinge so badd and the shipe in
travers,[5] it hapend the Minion [   ][6] to fawle aborde of us by

---

[1] The body of rules being prepared by Drake and his chief officers which were
subsequently announced to the fleet. Work on the rules continued at Bayona.
Although general sailing orders were announced on 15 September, other rules
pertaining to land actions were not announced until later (see pp. 130–1, 140). See also
Carleill's despatch to Walsingham (Corbett, *Sp. War*, p. 42).

[2] Mendoza, writing from Paris, 7/17 October, placed the departure at nightfall on
17/27 September. He stated that all the next day and night they were in sight of land,
becalmed, that they reached Falmouth the following day and then had good weather,
though with many calms, until the end of the month. Afterward there were furious
westerly gales. *C.S.P.Span. 1580–1585*, p. 551.

[3] This portion of Carleill's record has not survived.

[4] The meaning of *rome* corresponds with such usage as *sea room*, or open sea, with
room to move about. Hawkins, in 1564, *went roomer* until morning. *OED*. See also
the verb *romer* used on p. 91 below.

[5] i.e. in *traverse*, relating to the zig-zag course, or tacking, because of a contrary
wind. *OED*. In Sparrowe's account (Lansdowne MS 100, fol. 81) is reported: 'O*ur*
travis vpon the Englishe co*a*st was tell Thorsday ... none, 16th of the sam*e* and the
Lysard Barr. N.W.'

[6] Undeciphered word: *C* (or *E*) *Eleame*; possibly *Elean*[*o*]*re*.

theyr fowll negligence, for ye want of theyr lookynge to the mattar so sone as we ded/ They came still bearing [upon] vs, and albeit we put owr shippe on stayes, yet they not doinge the lyke also were cawse of this fowld dyscorde/ where in theyr bolt spritt hapened to enter owr foresayle and to rent the same all to peces/ Somewhate they broke owr beakehead and a pece of owr lower wale, but [there] was no greate hurt. beinge clere agayne we were fayne to strike all owr sayles and to take owr forsayle from the yard to mend, where of we gave warninge to the Admirall and the rest of the flete by sho[o]tynge of a pece of ordinaunce and hanginge out a lyght which cawsed them all to staye vntyle we had fitted vp owr tope sayles and so afterwards owr forsayle within two or three howres was put to yarde agayne/ We bare in towards Falmowthe all this night vntyll in the mornynge the wynde comynge fayre to the easteward and growinge afterward to East sowth easte/ About.3. of the cloke after none the Lizard bare of vs northe and beinge seaven leags from it we set of sowthe/

Friday the .17. of Septembar/

The wethar fayre and clere I went aborde the Admirall and aftar dynnar [Drake] takynge Captayne Furbushar and my selfe asyde,[1] declared vnto vs his disposition to put [in] eyther with Fraunce or Ireland, vpon any forced occasyon rathar then with England, thereby to be the better assured from any staye which hir maiestie by any alteration of opinion might happen to lay vpon hym/[2] he proceded with longe discorce of many things conserninge the voyadge and with earnest protestation amonge the rest of the trust which he ded and dayly had to repose in vs two: above all men elce, and with all requiringe in

[1] Drake's consultation with these two, his vice admiral and his chief military officer, seems to have become customary. No special consideration appears to have been given at this time to Francis Knollys, an omission which doubtless contributed to the distrust of Drake and Carleill which the *Leicester* journal reveals.

[2] Carleill referred again to this uncertainty about the queen's firmness when, in his despatch from Vigo, he stated that they had left Plymouth hastily, not only to catch a favourable wind, but because they were 'not the most assured of her Maiesties perserverance to let vs go forwarde'. S.P. 12/183: 10, f. 22.

frindly sorte to be advartysed by vs of any thinge which we
coulde wyshe to have altered or amended/ In so muche that for
my owne parte I can not say that evar I had to deale with a
man of greatar reason or more carefull circomspection/
The ships way was .16. leagwes in .29. howres sowthe west,
and sowth west and by sowthe/[1]
Towards the eveninge we descryed three sayles to leaward, and
comyning nere the [Admirall][2] [fol. 229v] . . . all roome to the
ho[   ] . . . he browght vp by a towa[   ] . . . [undeciphered]

Satterday yᵉ .18. of Septembar/
This night we had some rayne and the wynd continu[ing] . . .
tyme we met a pore Frenche ship of Normandy w[hich]
. . . and bownd with his fishe homeward, whom the gener*all* . . .
[   ]chinge any thinge/ aftar he had enqwired of hym the
news . . . from whence he came , which was no more then in
the Grand . . . xiiij. sayle of Spaniards/[3]
The bowrds were cleared .[4] Three watches[5] sowth sowthwest/
the sh[   ] 13: leages/ more two wattches sowthwest and by
sowthe/ and one . . . west and by west hir way good sowth
west. 9 leagus/ The latitud[e] . . . day at a resonable g[u]ess
was .52. minutes. The elevation beinge .39– 10 minutes.[6]

[1] According to Sparrowe's notes, 'tell Friday non[e] 12 leiges S.W. Then from
non[e] the Fridaiy tell Satterday non[e] 18th . . . 40 Leigges.' Lansdowne MS 100,
fol. 81.
[2] The word *Admirall* is supplied from the catchword written at the bottom of
fol. 229. Because of fire damage it is missing from the top of the next side.
[3] Cf. p. 180. In another fragment of a journal (Cotton MS Titus B. VIII, fol. 251):
'a 40/ or 50/ Leges of the Costee of England whee DissCried & met with a small shipe
a Normand homeward Bound frome the Neve Flound Land Laden with whall oyell
whome the . . . generall Relessed within 2 owers.'
[4] This refers to the 'traverse board', the device having marked at the top the
32 points of the compass and, below, the rows of holes in which pins or pegs were set
for keeping records, usually a pin for each half-hour, of the time during which a ship
travelled on a particular course. Cf. Morison, *European Disc. of Amer.*, pp. 155–6.
[5] Three watches of four hours each. Typical of a naval log are notes for each watch
of wind direction and force, the ship's progress, and any special event. See the appendix
on 'The Art of Navigation' by D. W. Waters in Andrews, *Last Voyage*. Cf. records by
watches in the *Leicester* journal (e.g. p. 120 and Plate IV).
[6] This relates to a calculation, probably by use of an astrolabe, to determine the
degrees of latitude. See William Bourne, *A Regiment for the Sea* (ed. by E. G. R. Taylor,
Camb., 1963), pp. 84–5; and Morison, *European Disc. of Amer.*, pp. 151–3.

Sonday the .19. of Septembar/

At none tyme the boord was clered as folowithe/ .16. pinns sowthwest and . . . hir way[1] sowth west. 6. leages, 32 pyns sowth, sowthe west, hir way good sowth west and by sowthe .6. leagues.[2] Toward the eveninge we discrie[d] . . . kepinge hym selfe to wyndward of vs and ronnynge owr cowrse alongst [where]vpon I repayred to the admirall to knowe his pleasure, who imagininge that it was some Frenche man of warre that watched [for] the faw[llinge be]hynd of some of owr flete and so to prize hymselfe of some one of them [at] break of day/ wherevpon the generall willed me to gett vp agayne . . . wethar of the flete and so nere as I could to kepe an eye vpon this . . . but not to gooe out of syght of his owne lyght, vntill it were within . . . or twayne of daye breake and then to strike vp into the wynd of this stra[nger] so to deale furthar with hym as I shuld find good/ but when it was two . . . aftar shuttynge in of night/ the moone yet shininge/ this fellow came s[o] neare the flete as thoughe he would have put hym selfe amongst them, [where]vpon I approched as neare hym as I might conveniently [so] that I might be[tter] know hym from the rest/ when he shuld get amongst them, but he findy*ng* that I followed hym so directly packed on all the sayle he could make, and [in the] thike myste which presently ensued we lost syght of hym and so could hea[r no] more of hym/[3]

Monday the .20.

The borde cleared, viz .28. pin*n*s, hir way good . 17. leags sowthe, 4 pinn[s] . . . 4. pyns sowth sowth west, hir way good sowth and by west 3 leags more . . . pyn*n*s sowth sowth west, hir way good. 2. leagues/ The latitude the same d[ay] at a reasonable gweste[4] .46. degrees 46. minutes.[5] The elevation taken at 40:30 minutes/

[1] In MS, *was*.
[2] According to Sparrowe's record, they had travelled twenty leagues from noon on 18 September until 6 a.m. on Sunday. Lansdowne MS 100, fol. 81.
[3] Cf. p. 180.   [4] i.e. *guess*.
[5] Sparrowe's account (Lansdowne MS 100, fol. 81), noted the latitude Monday noon

Twesday the .21.

The wethar fayre I went aborde the admirall and supped with hym & aftar suppar returned aborde myne owne shippe agayne. The borde clered, viz 48 pinns sowth and by west, very lytle wynd, hir way good. 6. leages:

Wedensday the .22. of Septembar

In the morninge we descried towe sayles, the one a heade, the other a greate way to lee ward/ About .ij. or .iiij. of the cloke aftar none the shippe¹ that was a heade was made to strike by vs of the Tygar,² we beinge the first shipe that recovered her/ albeit the sayde chase was lykewyse vndartaken by the Admyrall, and bycawse he was not fare a starne [of] vs we ded forbeare to put any man aborde vntill the Admiralls comynge vp, who presently cawsed his longe skyffe to fetche the mastar of the price aborde of hym selfe, whithar my selfe with the mastar of my shippe went also with my pinnace/ to see how the generall would [fol. 230] . . . [   ]ongs . . . Seint Iohn de Luce³ . . . and there to remayne vn[til] . . . [   ]yne . . . *caw*sed me to remayne aborde of hym that . . . [fu]rther examination which he ment to take vpon . . . *part*icularly. The boorde of my shipe was clered th[   ] . . . west/ her way good. 28. leagus.

Thursday the .23. of Septembar/

[Partic]ular examination taken of the men of this prize afore-sayde . . . confessyon of all suche as had ben of any continewance in hir that . . . [bei]nge now laden with dried New Land fishe, of the bowrden of .vij. or viij . . . bownde to Passadge, and Saint Sebastians,⁴ both which places are in Sp*ain*

---

at 46¾ degrees; at 45½ degrees by Wednesday noon; and at 44 degrees by Thursday noon.

¹ In MS, *of* was written after *shippe*, but crossed out.

² This is the first identification in the MS of the ship in which the writer travelled. It confirms that this is the record of Christopher Carleill, captain of the *Tiger*.

³ i.e. St Jean-de-Luz, in France.

⁴ i.e. Pasaje (Spain), near St Jean-de-Luz; and San Sebastián, on the northern coast of Spain, near the French border.

. . . confessynge with all that as she was but nowe .4. yeres olde
so th[   ] . . . fowrthe voyage that she had made, havynge
never bene employed other . . . then between Passadge, and the
Newfound Land, and that when she made hir retourne it had
bene every yere before to Passadge, and that there the shipe
remayned alwayes vntill the next season of goinge to fishe
agayne withowt evar comynge to Seint Iohn de Lucye/[1] Albeit
that this moche was confessed by dyvars of the shipe/ and was
also particularly confirmed by the mastar of hir in his owne
confessyon, yet becawse he pretended to be ownar of hir/ he
named hym selfe and the shippe boathe to be of Seint Iohnn de
Lucie, and in dede ded beare the flagge of Seint Iohn de Luce/
but dyvars bulls from the pope beinge found in hir graunted to
sondry of the companye/ the same beinge all in the Spanishe
tonge,[2] and the shape of hir playnly declaring [her] to be
Byscayne, with sondry other tokens ovarlonge to be written,
ded conclude the whole to be Spanishe goods and intended to
be imployed for theyr service/ And therefore as lawfull prize
to be reserved for the service of owr selves/[3]
The bords clered viz .16. pynns sowth and by west/ hir way
good .6. leagus/ more sowth easte and by sowthe/ 32 [pynns]
hir way good. 18. leagus my selfe continuynge still aborde the
Admirall/

---

[1] St Jean-de-Luz is a French port on the Bay of Biscay. The encounter was reported
in a journal fragment (Cotton MS Titus V. VIII, fol. 251) thus: 'aboute/ 70/ or 80 Leges
of the Coste of Ingland whee mete with a tall shipee a Biskayne homewarde bound
frome the New Found Land fishee whome named them Selves of Bayon in Fraunce
nere unto Byskeye. shee had 40 men & boyes. Whee carryed here alonge to Bayon in
Galyziae.'

[2] In his despatch to Walsingham Carleill added that the papal 'bulls' were made out
with blank spaces in which names could be inserted. He stated also that the cargo of
fish was a welcome prize for Drake, he being 'somewhat more charged with men then
he thought on'. S.P. 12/183: 10, f. 21. See Corbett, Sp. War, p. 40.

[3] The capture was dated on Wednesday, the 22nd, in Sparrowe's letter (Lansdowne
MS 100, fol. 81). The Primrose journal (p. 180) reported for 22–3 September the capture
of this 'good new shipp' of 150 tons. Her cargo of fish was especially valued (see p. 108)
and was ultimately distributed among the fleet, while the ship was broken up for
firewood (see p. 88 below). Drake may not have wished to account for two possible
French claims after he seized a French salt ship on 25 September (see below).

Friday the .24.

In the morninge early was had syght of Cape Finister and it bare of vs sowth sowth easte. 7. leagus of/[1]

Satarday the .25.

Vndar the shore of the Mores[2] we discovered .vij. small Frenche shipps which we cawsed to be taken by owr pinnice, and the same beinge examoned were all found laden with salte for the whiche they had browght wheate into Spayne/ but the admirall released them all presently, one excepted which was newe and thowght fitt for many services, intendinge to paye for hir at his returne yf so it be adiudged. we ded this rathar becawse we were informed by the othar barques of the companye that she belonged to a very riche man that was a papiste and greate enemye of those of the relygion/[3] my selfe kept by the admyrall still aborde of hym.

---

[1] Edward Wynter, in his despatch to Walsingham (S.P. 12/183: 49, pr. in Corbett, *Sp. War*, p. 50), placed the arrival at Cape Finisterre on 23 September. According to Sparrowe, the fleet remained about the cape all day (the 23rd) and doubled the cape that night. He mentioned meeting there with four English 'men of warre', i.e. armed merchantmen (Lansdowne MS 100, fol. 81).

The anonymous journal fragment (Cotton MS Titus B. VIII, fol. 251) noted for 27 September: 'In the morninge whee haud sighte of capee Fenester where whee met with the Gorge Boneventer of London & another small Baurke hir Consserte as also the Mary Goolld of Hampton.' Cf. p 180.

[2] i.e. Muros, below Finisterre.

[3] In reporting the appropriation of this ship to Walsingham (S.P. 12/183: 10, pr. in Corbett, *Sp. War*, p. 40) Carleill omitted reference to the last mentioned reason. The *Summarie* (p. 217) states that Drake planned to pay for her, 'as accordingly he performed at our returne: which barke was called the Drake' (see p. 289). The anonymous journal (Cotton MS Titus B. VIII, fol. 251), which refers to the salt ships as 'five Birtons', noted that on the same day three or four of the English ships chased briefly a French 'man of war', but it escaped. Sparrowe referred to the salt barks as being *Ollennois* (Lansdowne MS 100, fol. 81).

The King of France complained to Queen Elizabeth in a letter of 11/21 October about Drake's seizure of a French ship, *La Magdelaine*, near Cape Finisterre, and stated that she belonged to Jacques Piocheau, marine merchant of Sables d'Olonne, was just returning from her first voyage to Portugal, and was valued with equipment and cargo at 2,800 crowns (*C.S.P.For. 1585–1586*, p. 79). Les Sables d'Olonne is on the French coast in the Vendée, to the north of the Pertius Breton.

Sonday the .26.

We had syght of the Iles of Bayon, which bare of vs sowthe easte and by sowthe. 4. leages of.[1]

Monday the .27.

We yet within the Ilands of Baion[2] & there cominge to anker about one of the cloke, the wethar as then very calme.[3] It was thowght mete forthwith to make some show of owr force and good meanes to put the same on the land vpon any sodayne [need], and therefore [we] manned our pinaces and longe boates & rowed directly towards Bayon towne which was two leagues of,[4] meaninge to take some viewe of the towne for[5] [fol. 230v] ... *t*he Governor of ... was one Short, an English [merchant][6] ... and of .x. or .xij. yeres resydence in these [partes[7]

[1] Sparrowe's letter stated that they 'fell' with Bayona on Sunday, the 26th, in fair and calm weather. It adds that Drake took here another 'Barke Ollennoise' and also one from London which was bound for the town. Lansdowne MS 100, fol. 81.

[2] The Cies Islets at the mouth of the Vigo River. Corbett, *Sp. War*, p. 40 n.

[3] The Sparrowe letter stated that the fleet put into Vigo Sound on the 27th and came to anchor about 2 p.m. in the islands. 'A litell befor*e* in a fysher Boat o*ur* Generall a[nd] *Maste*r F[robisher (?) went] ashore.' Later, 1,000 men were landed. (Lansdowne MS 100, fol. 81v.) On the date the Map Text (p. 64) and the *Primrose* journal (p. 181) agree. See also note 7 below. The newsletter (p. 108), however, gives the 28th; and the anonymous journal (Cotton MS Titus B. VIII, fol. 251), in which the dating is not reliable, gives it as the 29th.

[4] Carleill's despatch (S.P. 12/183: 10) states that the fleet anchored at the islands two leagues out from the town. Cf. pp. 181, n. 2, 219, and Plate II.

[5] The last two words appear at the bottom of this folio as catchwords, and are missing from the top of the next side.

[6] Because large portions of this journal were used, at times *verbatim*, in Carleill's despatch to Walsingham (S.P. 12/183: 10, pr. in Corbett, *Sp. War*, pp. 39–40), it has been possible to supply in square brackets many words lost from the damaged Cotton MS of the *Tiger* journal. The words supplied at this point are from fol. 22.

This first encounter, according to the despatch, occurred when Drake's boats were met by a boat sent out by the Governor from the town. Cf. p. 219.

[7] This merchant wrote on 4/14 October to a regular correspondent in England, sending his letter by Titus Johnson, the captain who carried Carleill's despatch for Walsingham (S.P. 12/183: 10). Excerpts from a Spanish version of the letter are printed in *C.S.P.For. 1585–1586*, pp. 63–4. Telling of Drake's arrival on 27 September/ 6 October, he continued, 'I was called before Senor Pedro Bermodis who requested me to go aboard and know what ships they were. When I came aboard I was half amazed, but like a stout man I did come before Sir Francis, who I promise you did give me a friendly courtesy, and did ask me what I did come for.' Then followed the inquiry as to possible warlike intentions, and assurance that if the English came in peace they would be allowed to obtain necessities. After commenting on the English actions

78

and with hym some ij or iij] Spanyardes¹ whereof one
was a soldyer of some Iudgm[ent. Their Instructions weare]
thus: the Governor² seeinge so many shipps come to A[ncker
togeather sent] them as his ordynary messengers in the lyke
occ[asions to see what shi]pps we were, and whether there
were any corne in [them or] not whereof the Contrye hathe
some nede already [and is like to have] great deale more before
it be longe, In so mvtch as th[ey greatlie feele] [   ]ntly a sore
dearthe to come amongst them/ This . . . vs that our merchantes
and there goodes were newly sett . . . but because wee had
begon to make showe of our forces and Inten[ded] . . . some
nere view of the towne as convenyently as we myght . . . [the
Generall] retorned all these men back agayne as messengers and
with [them Captain] Sampson, whome we chose the rather
because of his good abyly[ty and] Iudgment and to take
particular notyce of the place and people . . .³ Capt. Sampson

---

on one island (see p. 181), the writer stated that he was sent four times that day between
the two officials, 'and with much trouble made a peace that they should join together
on the day of their meeting at Tyse above Vigo' on the 11th, at which time the
governor was to deliver all merchants and their goods. He mentioned the two days of
stormy weather, the movement of part of the fleet to Tyse and seizure of church goods
there (see p. 182), and the general alarm about further plundering. He stated that he
had gone back and forth between the officials for the past eight days, and that Drake
had promised to restore all that had not been spoiled if, 'tomorrow,' the governor gives
'his firme that we do live at liberty'.

¹ On this folio, beginning with the fifth line and continuing to the middle of the
twenty-fifth ('. . . Spanyardes . . . question . . .') the handwriting changes (see Plate IX).
The new hand resembles that of the newsletter (Document 7). (See Plate X.) On this
matter see p. 106 and n. 5.

² Pedro Bermudez, Governor of the Islands of Bayona, wrote on 28 September/
7 October to the Marqués de Santa Cruz about this first conference. Having word that
Drake had landed 1,500 men in launches, 'I sent a recognisance to see who they were,
and Drake sent back one of his officers in company with my messenger. This officer
was ordered to tell me that in my hands lay peace or war, that he came in the name of
the Queen of England to gather together all the English and to abolish all the
impositions which had been laid on them, and his action would depend on my
answer.' His reply was that he had no power or order to make war, but that if Drake
intended to levy war, 'he would find his hands full.' A copy of this letter was included
in the Venetian ambassador's despatches to the Doge. *C.S.P.Ven. 1581–1591*, p. 124.

³ In Carleill's despatch to Walsingham he explained further regarding Sampson,
'whome I brought with me out of Ireland and was with me there all the time of my
beeinge there, but could not have meanes to present hym to your honour duringe my
Last beeing in England by reason of his long absence from London emongest his
frendes in the Countrey.' S.P. 12/183: 10, f. 22v.

was geven this Instruction that synce the Governor [had sent]
to know what we were, he was to certyfye hym that we were
[English] shipps sent from her Majestye to demavnde the cause
of empryson[ing her] subiectes & takynge ther goodes from
them as yf it were open war [and in] case it were the Intention
of the Kynge of Spayn to hold them t[hus by force] and therby
to geve cause of warr, then we were lykewyse redy [to
proceede] accordynglye with his people and contrye as farr as
wee myght/[1] Ca[ptain Sampson] began his messadge with
question[2] to know of the governor whithar he w[ould make]
warre or peace/ for sayth he owr generall is come hethar to
your owne h[oame to lett] yow have peace/ yf yow satisfye his
reasonable demaunds, and with . . . [the contrarie] to gyve you
warre to the vttermoaste/ whiche vehemencye, he presum[ed
to use the] rathar when he saw theyr weakenes in every
respect/ And so procede[d to the] mattar of owr marchaunts
staye, where vnto the Govornor answered/ [that to] make
warre or peace betwine the two princes was more then his
mea[ne condi]tion might do/ Agayne, his Comissyon stretched
not so farre/ The mer[chantes weare] not (as he sayde) vnder
any arrest, but that they myght dispose them selves and th[eir
goodes] at theyr owne pleasures. If the wateringe or any freshe
victuals of the[ir Contrey] might stand our Generall in any
stede, he was readye to pleasure hym there[with] as one
Captaine in honest Curtesie might and owght to do one to an
othar, theyr [prin]ces beinge in league togethar/[3] In this meane
while the bettar to countinan[ce] the intencion of the message
we advanced still, with oure pinaces, and my selfe [with] some

[1] The words in square brackets are supplied from the Carleill despatch, S.P. 12/183:
10. (An abbreviated version of Sampson's message is in the *Summarie* (see p. 219) and
in Document 7 (see p. 108). The anonymous journal (Cotton MS Titus B. VIII, fol.
251v) states merely: 'messengers [were sent] to intrete favore from spoilinge or Raun-
sakinge the towne vppon condicion all ouer Inglishe marchants & goods should be
Relessed.'

[2] With the word *question* the second hand used on this folio ends and the familiar
hand of Powell resumes the narrative in mid-sentence with *to know*. This suggests that
the report on these talks may have been written in some earlier form and then copied
by two different persons into the *Tiger*'s record.

[3] Cf. Short's letter, above, p. 78 and n. 7.

THE *Tiger* JOURNAL

othars beinge sent a good waye before them all in five¹ rowinge
small skyf[fs] to take the beste viewe I might of the place/
which I send discribed to mastar S[ec]retarye/² The Generall
vpon this answere put hym selfe and his people on shore in a
place of good assurawnce,³ and sent the marchaunt Sharpe⁴ to
the towne agayne for some of the Englyshe marchaunts/ and
with all to tell the Govarnor that yf his answere would be
approved trwe, then of his parte he would lykewyse vse all
peasyable means/ And therefore he cowld wishe that the
Governor shuld come hym selfe vnto vs for the bettar
conclusyon of all things/ where vnto was returned by the sayde
Shorte and othar marchaunts, who came with hym that the
next day the Governour would come hym selfe to owr
Generall and make that firme conclusion which weare requisite/
by this tyme it was mydnight and the weathar threateninge to
alter we presently altered owr determination/⁵ and shippinge
owr selves and people agayne retorned with all spede to owr
shipps/ when as the storme began and put some of owr pinacis
to their shiftes, and the next day grew to be so greate that
albeit we ryd vndar the lee and favor of the yllands, yet many
of owr shipps made very fowle weathar/ In so moche that the
barke Talbot, the barke Hawkens, and an othar small barke,
with a Carvell, the sayd barke beinge called the [fol. 231]
[Speedwell]⁶ ... distaunt from the Ilands of [Bayon] ... and

¹ Written in MS as *fine* or *five*, obviously referring to a number.
² In his despatch to Walsingham Carleill changed the wording slightly, to read:
'... the best viewe I might of the place, Which I sende herewith described aswell as
may be permitted for the present.' S.P. 12/183: 10. The wording suggests that a sketch
of some sort accompanied the letter. It probably refers to the rough sketch of Vigo Bay
which is now in the map collection at the Public Record Office (MPF 13). It shows the
first anchorage in the islands outside of Bayona, another place where men were landed
within the harbour, and also the point, up river from Vigo, where the ships watered
on 4 October. See Note on Maps and Plate II.
³ On the Island of 'Our Lady of the Borge'. Cf. p. 181, n. 4.
⁴ In Carleill's despatch his first reference to the merchant messenger was 'one Shorte
or Sharpe'. S.P. 12/183: 10, f. 23.
⁵ Sparrowe's letter stated: 'the weather Beganne to brew up'. Lansdowne MS 100,
fol. 81v.
⁶ Sparrowe, whose ship *Speedwell* was forced out to sea, noted that the *Talbot* lost
her anchor first, then the *Hawkins*, and also a 'small man of warr of London and a
carvaill, which was pin[nace to] the Barke Ramaldes of London and her' (Lansdowne

puttynge in with the Iland ... occasyons, first we dowbted
some stor[   ]¹ ... prove a very sore tempest, and of [any(?)]
... we thowght good while it was yet fayre and ... [   ]¹ghe
dowbtynge the contraye wynde whiche als[   ]   ...
[   ]vinge to be any whit greatar would at the leaste dryve
... [   ]pe, yf it ded not disparse vs/² The refurnishinge owr
selves ... [gev]inge to many of owr shipps theyre nedefull
wantes out of the [store, which store is] dispersed into severall
shipps and was moare hastely sent ... it myght be so ordarly
ymployed to every shipe becawse the wynde [beeing fa]yre
vpon owr cominge from Plimouth/ we were lothe to lose the
same ... [for an]y small mattars, comynge so rarelye as it dothe
there/ and with all we not [the] moste assured of hir maiesties
perseveraunce to let vs goo forward/ The se[tting d]owne some
furthar direction to owr people, I meane articles of ordar for
th[eir] good behavioure both by sea and land³ [and lastly]
which was not the leaste to m[ake] owr procedings knowne to
the Kynge of Spayne/ that he may find and see m[ore]
apparauntly that we nothinge feare any intelligence he hathe

MS 100, fol. 81v). Carleill's despatch, which follows the narrative from the *Tiger*
through the portion on fol. 230v, added notes that the *Hawkins* had returned but not
the *Speedwell*, and that the *Talbot* was understood to have found safety in the harbour
of Pointa Fedra, two or three leagues distant from Bayona. S.P. 12/183: 10, f. 23.

The *Summarie* (p. 221) noted that the *Speedwell* got back to England. Sparrowe's
better gave her arrival, after much difficulty, at Portsmouth on 9 October. Corbett,
on the basis of expense accounts (*Sp. War*, pp. 45, n., and 91), concludes that she was
refitted but did not rejoin the fleet. See also p. 287.

¹ Word undeciphered.

² At this point the meaning is garbled, partly because of the poor condition of
the MS. When Carleill organized his despatch for Walsingham he stated, before
reporting on the negotiations with the Spanish, the following reasons for the stop at
Bayona: first, concern that the approaching storm might disperse the fleet; second,
the need to refurnish the ships with water and complete the distribution of stores,
which the hasty departure from Plymouth had prevented; third, writing the Articles
of Order for the expedition; and fourth, informing the King of Spain of their purpose.
With regard to the latter point, and through the remainder of the paragraph, the two
accounts are identical. Missing words have been supplied from the despatch
(S.P. 12/183: 10, f. 22).

³ Another evidence of Drake's hurried departure. There had been time to formulate
directions for the ship captains (see above, p. 71), but now rules of conduct for the
men were being prepared. Only in Carleill's narrative is there a record of these early
administrative decisions.

gotten by the spialls he hathe eythar in England or els where/
And trewly, were owr sowldours so trained men as to knowe
but some parte of theyr ordar, I would thinke (yf it might be
so purposed) to make owr selves mastars of his towne of Bayon
once within fyve dayes at the moaste with that nomber whiche
we have here, and the provisyon of munition [which] owr
shipps are well able to spare and furnyshe./

Tweseday the .28.

The storme continued very greate still, inso moche as all this
day no boates durst passe betwene shippe and shippe, vnless it
were the Generals longe skyffe or rowinge pinase/ which was
ymployed vpon some extreme necessytie and verye vrgent
occasyon which were the fetchinge of some men from the
Galley beinge in some daungar/ and the carienge aborde a
Cable and anker to the barke Hawkens which was now in the
eveninge of this day come from sea into the roade agayne. This
want was signified by hir shootinge of two pieces of ordinaunce/
and accordingly supplied with expedition. For which service
the Generall gave an angell to every marinar that rowed in
the skyffe/

Wedensday the .29.

The storme continued still with very muche wynde at sowth
sowthe west/ In so moche that this day lykewyse there was no
sturringe with any boates/

Thursday the .30. day of Septembar/

The fury of the storme beinge alytle abated, owr boates began
to make resorte vnto the admyrall, whithar my selfe beinge
also come It was advertysed by the capitayne of the barke
Hawkens that there shuld be gone[1] vp the ryvar above Vigo,
three or fowre Carvels, which [it] was to be supposed myght be
laded with some good mattar/[2] Where vpon the Generall

---

[1] In Carleill's despatch *gotten* is written, instead of *gone*. S.P. 12/183: 10, f. 23.
[2] Corbett (*Drake and the Tudor Navy*, II, 22) suggests that these boats were trying to escape into the interior, fearing the English at Vigo.

directed my selfe to goe aftar them to seeke them out and to see what theyr myght be in them avayleable for owr servyce. And leaste their shuld be any Attampte geven from the land to interrupte the performaunce of this purpose, the generall appoynted me these foarces, that is, my owne shippe, the Tyger,[1] with hir pinnace, the barke Thomas with her pinnace, the barke Fraunces, and the Galley/ whereinto Captayn Fenner[2] was appoynted Cappitayne for that tyme.[3] I went vp with these ships above Vigo to a place called Tysus where fyndinge convenient roade and safe harbor for my shipps, I lefte them all at anckar and with the Galley, pinaces, and shipps boates well armed and manned for the purpose I undertooke to beat vp the [ ]⁴ [fol. 231v] . . . that they were very sy[ ]⁵ . . . they . . . of salte. thothar of hoopes . . . onions and garlike, many othar small . . . theyr mariners vpon the syght of owr comynge . . . howsholde stuffe and suche othar lyke vsuall pillage of . . . flienge with the same towards Rendondela and othar . . . ways/ Amonge othar things I happened with my [ ]⁵ . . . a boate where in was a Chest⁶ filled with Coapes . . . and suche othar Churche trashe belonginge to the hyghe churche . . . withought any othar mattar of Importaunce.⁷

---

¹ A further confirmation that this record is by Carleill. His role as commander of the party is reported also in the *Summarie* (p. 221), in Document 7 (p. 108), and in Carleill's despatch (S.P. 12/183: 10).

² Thomas Fenner, captain of Drake's flagship.

³ The Map Text (p. 64) gives 30 September as the date. While the other ships remained at Vigo, they examined another foreign ship that came in during the storm. She purported to be from St Malo, carrying sugar from the Madeiras. The English suspected her of having captured Spanish or Portuguese goods, however, and that there had been mutiny aboard. When Carleill wrote of this to Walsingham, he said he did not know what the outcome would be, 'although I must confesse I would have more willinglie wisshed them to taste none other then playne rencounters of meere Inglishe and meere Spanishe.' S.P. 12/183: 10, f. 21v.

⁴ Undeciphered word. Carleill's despatch reads: 'Wee beate vpp as farr as was convenient, but fownde none other then some badd Carvells, the one laden with hoopes and Wood, an other with Salte, and the thirde with Onyons and Garlicke.' S.P. 12/183: 10, f. 23v.

⁵ Undeciphered.

⁶ In the MS, before *Chest*, the word *Cross* was written and then crossed out. This refers to the 'great crosse of silver', for which see *Summarie*, p. 221.

⁷ Carleill estimated the value of the crosses and plate in the chest as not under

I returned to owr ship*s* in the harbour in Tysys/ whithar I fownde also arrived two or thr*ee* . . . *of* the flete/¹

Friday the first of Octobar/

The admyrall with the rest of the Flete forsoke the roade of the Il[land to come] to vs in the harbor of Tysus/² Early in the mornynge some of those ship[s that] had bene in the harbor all night put men a shore vndar the collar of [getting] balla*st* to ketche what they could from the contrye people/ Where vp*on* . . . leaste they myght receyve some foyle or disgrace (a thinge verye inc[   ] . . . so busi*l*ye set forward) I thowght good to send Captein Sampson with a f[orce of] . . . some .iiij.ˣˣ men to see them safeley retired and browght back to ther sh*ips*, who vpon the advauncinge hym selfe some what forward to the heigh hill was there set vpon and charged by a troppe of .C C. men/³ But makynge his retrayte in good ordar beinge dryven sometyme to ch[   ] . . . his whole troope he recovered the lowere ground by the watar syde, with*out* hurte savinge that one man was shote throwghe the arme of his owne [and] . . . of the enemyes ovarthrowe/ There was also

---

500 marks (S.P. 12/183: 10). In the *Primrose* journal (p. 182), the cross was valued at 3,000 ducats, and other items at another 3,000 ducats.

The English merchant, Short, wrote: 'On their way they did find the great cross of Vigo, with other two crosses, and all their chalices and their rich copes and all there plate. . . .' He reported the spoiling of the church in Tyse, the church of the Cobras, the friars of Redondela, with other churches. *C.S.P.For. 1585–1586*, p. 63. Another report (*The Fugger News-Letters*, 2nd series (1926), pp. 96–7) noted that Drake's men had looted and done much damage to convents and churches. See also p. 109.

¹ As the storm began to abate on 1 October the ships moved up to Vigo. See pp. 64, 182.

² Cf. pp. 64, 109. Carleill's despatch confirms the date. S.P. 12/183: 10, f. 23v.

³ In his despatch Carleill stated, 'I sente Captain Sampson to retire theis men from the shoare with some lxxx men of my owne shipp and an other whoe was rencowntred with 200 of the Spaniardes. . . .' S.P. 12/183: 10, f. 23v. Cf. p. 109.

Edward Wynter, who also wrote to Walsingham (S.P. 12/183: 49, pr. in Corbett, *Sp. War*, pp. 49–51), said that there 'came downe 8 or 9 ensygnes of ye enemye with purpose to have letted oure landinge for water (w*hi*ch was our pryncypall cause why wee putte in heere) where after some lyghte skirmishe havinge loste iiij or v of theyre men and wee one, belyke mistrustinge theyre forces, the Governor sent to parleye w*i*th oure Generall. . . .'

one yonge fellowe belonging [to the] George Bonaventure[1]
who whiles the Trowpe was marchinge forthe st[rayed from]
the rest into a howse, busyed hym selfe and seekynge aftar
tryflynge pill[age with]out eyther Companion or Armes for
his owne defence was at vnwares [seized by] the enemye and so
his head cut of, vnknowne to Captayne Sampson or any [of
the] troupe vntill it was a good while aftar/

Aftar my Captayne lefte of and gave the charge of kepinge
this b[ook] . . . tyme to come, vnto me Edward Powell/[2]

Satarday the .2. of Octobar/

About tene of the cloke the Governor of Bayon sent downe to
the watar sy[de a flag] of truce,[3] wherevpon owr Generall sent
a skyfe a shore to knowe the mean[ing of] the sayde flagge. The
messengar[4] brought worde that the Governor was at . . . syde
and would speake with owre generall. So Captayne Sampson
was sent a[shore] . . . to fet[ch] hym aborde, and comynge to
hym, he told Captayne Sampson that the gentlemen about
hym would not suffer hym to go aborde of owr shippes, but yf
[it] wolde please the Generall to send two of owr Captaynes to
the shore, then hym selfe would enter the same skyffe and
mete owr generall a Calivar shot from the shore, which
message he returned to owr Generall/ our generall was content

[1] 'The George Bonadventure a shipp of warr of London whome wee mett withall
vpon the Coaste.' Carleill to Walsingham. S.P. 12/183: 10. Four men were left
beheaded, according to the *Primrose* journal (p. 182). See also p. 109.

[2] These lines are inserted, with an indentation, apparently to indicate a change in
authorship of the record. Since the handwriting does not change, it can be assumed
that the same scribe had written all of the earlier part, with the exception of a few
lines on fol. 230v (see above, p. 79, n. 1), probably acting as Carleill's secretary. It is
the same hand as that of the *Summarie* variant, Harl. MS 6221 (see Appendix III).

[3] The new meeting occurred on 1/11 October, according to the letter of the
English merchant (*C.S.P.For. 1585–1586*, p. 63). The anonymous journal (Cotton MS
Titus B. VIII, fol. 251v) states that two days before this parley (for which the date of
4 October is given), three 'caveleros of Spain' had visited the 'admerall', and that the
next day there came aboard the chief townsmen of Vigo and Bayona, '& the treasurer
of Galyziae & Andoleza, as it was bruited that the generall entertayned them.'

[4] Carleill's despatch does not identify the messenger. According to the *Primrose*
journal (p. 182), Frobisher was sent to shore on this occasion, but it seems likely that
Sampson was used for making the arrangements.

to send Captayne Erezo and Captayne Crosse[1] vpon theyr
owne intreatye, willynge with all Captayne Sampson that
when the Governor was entered the boate he shuld hold out a
handkerchyfe/ which sygne beinge done the Generall put of,[2]
and so they mett and had two howres talke and conference/[3]
At whiche tyme they concluded a peace, and that we mowght
come a shore to watar and trafaiqwe for any victuall/[4] For the
bettar performaunce where of owr two Captayns were sent a
shore vnto them, and they sent aborde owr Generall two
gentlemen for pledges, dwellynge about Vigo/ These things
beinge thus browght to passe they shewed .viij. ensignes with
men in the syght of owr ships.[5] The wethar some what rayny/.

Sunday the .3. of Octobar/

This day many of the Spaniards came abord owr shipps and
owr people in lyke sort to the shore, and furnished them selves
of watar/ The wethar for the moaste parte contynuynge verye
wett, in so moche as we could make no dispatche of any othar
thynge almoste more then wateringe. at the leaste wyse what
was done was yᵉ worse for the rayne that fell, and the wynd
still as contrary as mowght be/[6] [fol. 232] . . . places/ Those
which . . . selves havynge fayre . . .

[1] James Erisey and Robert Crosse. See p. 109 and Appendix II.
[2] The French narrative (Lacour, pp. 19–20) states that this parley was between the Marqués de Santa Cruz, and Drake, and that it lasted for an hour and a half, each man being in a small boat, with Drake a cannon-shot from his vessels, and the marquis the same distance from the shore. Edward Wynter commented that this meeting was conducted 'with farre lesse mystruste then ys commonlye seene'. S.P. 12/183: 49.
[3] According to Carleill's despatch (S.P. 12/183: 10, in order to complete the agreement discussed earlier, the governor was brought in an English boat to meet Drake, and the conference was held in Drake's boat, only Frobisher staying in it with them. Cf. pp. 182, 222, and 86, n. 4, above.
[4] The terms were 'that peace should be wholly entertayned of all partes and that restitution should be made of all thinges which might possibly be fownde'. S.P. 12/183: 10. Cf. *Primrose* journal, p. 182.
[5] Cf. p. 182. The anonymous journal (Cotton MS Titus B. VIII, fol. 251v) notes that they made 'a bravado' with seven or eight ensigns.
[6] The words of this paragraph are practically identical with the concluding lines of Carleill's despatch (S.P. 12/183: 10; see Corbett, *Sp. War*, p. 46). The *Primrose* journal (p. 183) states that the Spaniards 'came thicke abowte our shippes'. Short's letter, referring to Drake's entertainment of visitors, notes: 'His royalty, it is a world to see;

Tweasday the .5. of Octobar

[The gener]all about .x. of the cloke comaunded the whole fl[eet] . . . vp to the Ilands of Vigo/ where finding the wynd . . . ankre before the towne of Vigo/[1]

Wedensday the .6.

. . . [cont]inued all this day in Vigo roade, beinge comaunded by our Gen[eral to go] aborde of the first prize/[2] and to fetche thence certayne fishe . . . [pro]visyon/ As also eche one of the flete ded the lyke.

Thursday the .7.

. . . the morninge by owr generals appoyntement all the flete wayed [anchor] from Vigo[3] and came vpp to the Ilands of Bayon. At which tyme the barke [Talbot][4] who throwghe fowle wethar before was put to sea was now come in and [joined] vs about three of the cloke in the aftarnone/ The prize[5] wherein the fishe was beinge then hauled to the shore, and havoke made of hir hull for fiar wood [and] what vse else they would dispose of hir/

Friday the .8.

Remaynynge in the Ilands of Bayon we fitted owr selves from

---

with all that do come, great and small, he doth keep as open house.' *C.S.P.For. 1585–1586*, p. 63.

[1] According to the anonymous journal (Cotton MS Titus B. VIII, fol. 251v), on 5 October, 'whee came with ouer shipes beffore Vigo & there where detayned 20/ or more of poure Spanyerds abourd the admerall for it was bruyted they had imprissoned ower Inglishe marchants at Bayon. But they where immedatlye Relessed. See also p. 183 and n. 3.

[2] In MS, *prise*. This was the Biscayan vessel taken 22–3 September.

[3] Cf. Map Text and also p. 183. Writing from Bayona on 10 October, Carleill stated, 'Two daies synce wee turned from Vigo to this place.' S.P. 12/183: 10, f. 24.

[4] The MS is torn. The *Talbot* had been forced out to sea on 27 September (see p. 81). Her return is dated on 9 October in the *Primrose* journal (p. 183).

[5] In MS, *prise*. Both the Biscayan prize and the caravel taken at Vigo were destroyed (see p. 183). The action is dated on 8 October in the anonymous journal (Cotton MS Titus B. VIII, 251v): 'Whee towkee in the New Foundland fishe out of the Biskane deviding into everye shipe a pourcion & broke & burnt the shipe & sunkee the Portingall shipe.'

one shipe to *an*othar of suche things as were necesarye/ And this day in the aftarnone the George Bonaventure of London departed for England/

Satarday the .9.

This mornynge Capitayne Furbussher and my Capitayne were sent towards Bayon with thr*ee* pinacis and with them the Spanishe pledges that they mowght demaund and bringe aborde owr owne pledges, and delyvar the Spanyards/ The govornor hym selfe was content to come and bringe owr Englyshe pledges with hym/ and vpon owr comynge from owr pinacis in a small roweinge boate of owr owne to mete vs in a lyke small rowinge boate of his/ which done the pledges on bothe sydes were delyvered.[1] The Lyon and the little Elyzabeth were also willed to turne vp and follow the direction of their Viceadmyrall/[2]

Sonday the .10.

We continued in the Roade of the Ilands of Bayon attendinge a fortunate wynd, beinge readye to set sayle/

Monday the .11.

The wynd beinge now come northerlye about .viij. of the cloke in the morninge the *w*hole flete ded set sayle from the

[1] The date agrees with that in Carleill's despatch and also in Document 7 (see p. 109). The *Primrose* journal (p. 183) places this exchange of hostages on 8 October. The anonymous journal (Cotton MS Titus B. VIII, fol. 251v), which agrees here with the Carleill documents, adds for this date: '[There] came in to the Road a Frenche mane Lauden with New Found Land fishee taken by a shippe of London whom our generall relessed.'

[2] This suggests a division of the fleet, with Frobisher in the *Primrose* to lead one group. *Lyon* was the *White Lyon*, captained by Erisey. On the 'little Elyzabeth', see p. 289. A sea captain who reached Spain later with news of events at the Canaries (see p. 92, n. 4), stated that Drake's fleet approached there in two squadrons of seventeen and thirteen ships (report enclosed with the Venetian ambassador's despatch, 1/11 January 1586. *C.S.P.Ven. 1581–1591*, p. 133). The separation may have been for the purpose of searching more widely for the expected treasure fleet from the Indies, of whose safe arrival by this time Drake was not yet aware. (On the dates for the treasure fleets see below, p. 127, n. 2.) The subsequent pages of the *Tiger* journal, however, do not indicate that the two squadrons were ever widely separated (see pp. 90–1).

sayde Ilands/[1] saylynge alonge the coaste all day, bearing a good sayle the wynd large, and at nyght we shortened owr sayles to get the flete togethar/ At owr departure [from] the rode/ we sanke owr two prizes.[2] Master Martyn[3] departed from vs for England in Tytus Johnⁿson his barke, beinge accompanyed with a small Englishe fly boote/[4] My Capitayne at that instant went aborde the Generall where he lay all night.

Twesday the .12.

We ded lye of to sea havynge the wynde sotharly for the moaste parte of the day, but at nyght it came northerlye with fowle weathar and stormy and towards day it began to be fayre/ My Capitayne lay aborde the admyrall the same nyght/

Wedensday the .13.

We kept owr cowrce sotherly not seeinge any more sayles then owr owne, and at nyght the Primerose was a weathar of owr shippe/ and in owr first watche we might easely discrye a standinge lyght the space of an howre in a shipe that was to weathar of vs which we thowght to have bene the Primerose.[5]

Thursday the .14.

Kepinge owr cowrse we fell sotherly without syght of any othar sayle savynge of owr owne company/ In the morninge lookynge for the assembly of owr flete/ we missed[6] the

---

[1] Carleill reported that the fleet expected to sail on the 10th, but the wind 'skanted'. At the end of his despatch he wrote: 'The xjth readye to set sayle.' (S.P. 12/183: 10.) Cf. Map Text. The anonymous journal (Cotton MS Titus B. VIII, fol. 251v) agrees, but the newsletter (Document 7), which is closely associated with Carleill's account, gives 12 October as the sailing date (see p. 109). The *Primrose* journal, less accurate for dates, places the departure on 9 October (p. 183).

[2] In MS, *prises*.

[3] Martin's identity is uncertain, but the reference to him here suggests that he was a man of some importance. Whether he was John Mart in, captain of the *Benjamin* (see pp. 287, 296), has not been determined.

[4] Titus Johnson, master of the *Jonas*, of London, carried Carleill's despatch for Walsingham. One of his missions at Bayona had been to secure the release of 'a smale flye boate' which had been detained there (S.P. 12/183: 10). See also p. 78, n. 7.

[5] i.e. Frobisher's ship, *Primrose*, which was missing the next day.

[6] In MS, *miste*.

Primerose¹ and the Burton barke² whiche we ded not see all
the day aftar/

[fol. 232v]   Friday [the 15] of Octobar³
... we had kepinge owr cow*rse* ... g*re*ate gustes with rayne
by w[   ] ... [   ]me/⁴ and so in lyke maner owr gen*eral* ...

[Sunday] the .xvij. of Octobar.

... the assemblye of owr Flete, we myst the Sea Dragon a[nd
the White] Lyon ... West cowrse all day and night/

[Monday] The xviij.

... the mornynge the wynde became sowthe, so that we were
for[   ] ... sowthe w*ith* the steme, whiche made a lee ward
waye ... of the cloke we discried a sayle, and the generall
willed the Gall[eon to put out] the flage in the mayne toppe,⁵
and to leade a waye the flet*e*, [while he him] selfe ded go with
the sayd discried sayle comaundinge the George, [and] the
Scoute to followe hym/ and fettynge⁶ vpp the sayle they found
it [was the Sea] Dragon, a shipe of owr flete/ and all the fleet
ded beare romer⁷ with ... the wynd not betteringe mutche
all night/

[Tuesday] the .xviiij. of Octobar

The Primerose and the Burton barke ded fall amonge the Flete,
who had [been lost from] the xiiij. of Octobar vntill thys day/⁸

¹ The *Primrose*, according to her own journal (p. 184), 'lost' the fleet on 11 October.
Her record continues to disagree with the *Tiger* journal on dates.
² i.e. the French prize, afterwards renamed *Drake* (see pp. 77, 289). The *Leicester*
journal reports the loss of the *Francis* and the *Primrose* on one day, of Captain
Vaughan's ship (the *Drake*) on the next, and the return of the latter and the *Primrose*
together on 19 October (see pp. 120, 123).
³ *Friday* appears as a catch-word at the bottom of fol. 232, but has been lost from
the next side.
⁴ Undeciphered word.
⁵ Cf. p. 122. With Frobisher in the *Primrose* missing, the *Leicester* thus became
temporary flagship for those not in the chase.
⁶ Possibly intended for *setting*, or *fetching*.
⁷ i.e. gained sea room.
⁸ See above. The *Primrose* journal (p. 184) dates the return on 17 October.

about .xi. of the cloke the generall com[manded the] Tygar to runne west of to the sea the Fraunces/¹

[Wednesday] the .xx.

At night we haïled the Vice admirall to welcome hym to the flete agay[ne, who] then told vs that durynge his absence he had dyscryed land/² And all nyght owr cowrce sowth sowth west/³

[Thursday] the .xxi.

We kept owr cowrce toward the Grand Canaries without syght of any sayle then owr owne.

[Friday] the xxij.

Our generall discryed two sayles to the east warde/ and gave chase to them [the space] of .vi. howrs, but could not fetche them,⁴ and so ded beare his cowrse west[ward] the whole flete with hym all the next morning/

[Saturday] the xxiij.
[Sunday] the xxiiij.

We fell with the easternmost Iland called Lancerota, havynge at that tyme [passed] of anothar Iland more greatar then the first, called Fortaventura,⁵ where vp[on our] generall put owt his

¹ Although not entirely clear, this probably refers to the search for the *Francis*, which was missing at this time (see p. 91, n. 2).

² Frobisher had sighted the Madeiras. See p. 184.

³ The notations in the various ship records do not always agree. The *Leicester's* notes on the course for this date, however, are south or south-west (see p. 123).

⁴ This incident is mentioned also in the journals of the *Leicester* and the *Primrose* (pp. 124, 184). Possibly it was the one reported later by a Spanish ship captain, although the date of 15/25 November which he gave for his encounter with English ships in the Canaries must have been incorrect. He said that he met with a group of English corsairs off Teneriffe, and that he fled to the port of Lanzarote, where some of the English ships found him the next day and stripped him of all provisions and sails. He reported that the English came together again off Teneriffe, sailed on to Palma, and later to Ferro. This report was sent with the Venetian ambassador's despatches to the Doge. *C.S.P.Ven. 1581–1591*, pp. 133–4.

⁵ One of the Canaries was sighted on the 23rd, according to Document 7 (p. 109), and the arrival at Lanzarote was on the 24th (see pp. 64, 125, 184).

flage of Counsell/ where it was agreyd vpon by them [all] to
land of force vpon the Ile of Palma/[1] and all the nyght the flete
w[as ordered] to beare a small sayle, the which was done, and
the first parte of the nyght [we] ded lye by the lee/

[Monday] the xxv of Octobar
[Wednesday] the .xxvij.

fallynge with the grand Canarie[2] we saw a sayle to the
easteward, the which we made chase to/ and comynge up to
hir we found it was the Fraunces the which had loste owr flete
from the .xvij. tyll the .xxvij. she browght with hir the generals
longe boate and skyffe.

[Thursday] the xxviij

We were betwixt the Tenerift[3] and the Palme/[4] We ded see a
shipe into the westward, to the whiche we sent owr pynnases/
and they found hym to to be a French man of warr of New
Haven/[5] and they browght hym alonge to the generall/[6] The
day was very fayre, whereby we myght see the pike[7] of the
Iland of Tenereft which is a marvaylous height, where lyeth
snow continually/

[Tuesday] The second of Novembar/

We bare to the yland of Palma vndar owr small sayles, and
this night the Hope lost the flete/[8]

[fol. 233] . . . [   ]em [   ]ndinge the . . . *n*orthern parte of
the Iland . . . the admyrall bare in/ and [they des]crying . . . and

---

[1] Palma was not on the original plan as described in the schedule dated in April 1586.
Lansdowne MS 100, fol. 98.

[2] The *Leicester* journal (p. 126) states that the 'Grand Canaria' was sighted on
Tuesday (i.e. 26 October).

[3] i.e. Teneriffe. The newsletter (p. 109) notes that Teneriffe was seen on the 28th. The
description of Teneriffe's peak is inserted in the *Leicester* notes for the 26th. (See p. 126.)

[4] i.e. Palma.

[5] i.e. Le Havre.

[6] This was the occasion which brought Drake definitive news that he had missed
this year's treasure fleet. Cf. pp. 127, n. 2, 184.

[7] i.e. peak.

[8] Cf. p. 128. The *Hope* returned on 5 November (see below).

93

... there of ded make two shute at hym[1] ... by the towne
and comynge with in dangar of ... first shot was ovar vs in
the Tygar/ and the next ... h[it] ... [the gallery where] owr
generall then stode/ havynge in companye with hym ... and
yet none sore hurt/ The third shot ded hit the generalls [ship]
goinge thrwght but stucke fast/ The Galyon Lestar also
recey[ved a shot, without h]urtyng of any person/[2] where vpon
owr generall fyndinge that [he could not] conveniently come
to an ancre nor saffely land his men/ comaunded [the fleet] to
make retrayte/ The towne in all shote .xxiij. pieces.

[Thursday] the iiij of Novembar/
... mornynge we came hard by the Iland of Gomera,[3] plyeing
vp and downe by the sa[   ] ... it was two of the cloke in the
aftarnone/ The Generall ded then put out his flagg o[f counsel.]
At which tyme it was agreed to leave the Gomera and beare to
the Iland of Fero ... [beari]nge what sayle we might all night
recovar the sayde Iland of Fero/ willing at [the s]ame tyme the
barke Hawkyns and the Fraunces to put back agayne with the
Palma ... [to seek] the Hope which had lost the flete the second
of [November],[4] and the Scowte, which lost [the fleet on]
28 October.[5]

[1] This was on 3 November (see pp. 64, 110, 184). Words inserted within square
brackets to fill gaps caused by damage to the MS are based upon the *Leicester* journal
(pp. 128–9).

[2] The somewhat unreliable report brought back by a Spanish ship captain (see
above, p. 92, n. 4) noted that warning of Drake's approach had been sent from
Lanzarote to both Teneriffe and Palma. He stated that Drake lowered boats to attempt
a landing at Palma, but that the defenders 'prevented a landing and sank one of the
boats with all the troops in it, while they rattled up the captain's ship and another in
such a way as they became unmanageable and had to be lightened ... and taken in
tow by the others'. *C.S.P.Ven. 1581–1591*, p. 133.

The hitting of two large ships, although the English accounts minimize the effect,
probably gave rise to other Spanish reports that Drake lost two ships here. For reports
circulated at Cartagena see Castellanos, *Discurso*, pp. xxxvi, 59, 300. The Castellanos
report was the basis for that written later by Fray Pedro Simón. See the summary by
G. Jenner, *E.H.R.*, XVI (1901), 53 and A. K. Jameson's criticism of Simón in 'Some
New Spanish Documents', *E.H.R.*, XLIX (1934), 14–15.

[3] On the decision not to land at Gomera see p. 131.

[4] In the MS *November* was written, but crossed out, and *October* superimposed. The
Hope was lost on 2 November.

[5] Cf. p. 127. All four missing ships returned on 5 November (see below).

[Friday] the .v. of Novembar[1]

[   ]vynge in the morninge recovered the Iland of Fero owr generalls pinnace with oth[er b]oates went to the shore with about seven hundred men/ Where vpon the inhabytaunts seeinge suche a force sent some of theyr people with an Englyshe boye which they had dwellynge amongst them vnto owr Generall, who made theyr peticion, that they myght not be cruely delt with all in deprivynge them of theyr lyves or otharwyse with inforcynge them by stroke, and they would resigne all that they had with in the Iland which in effecte they sayde was very smalle, so meane as they thowght it would not serve the expences of the flete for two dayes/[2] where vpon owr Generall lookynge thrwghly into so[me] sclendar estates willed all men to repayre aborde/ the which was done accordingly, and hym selfe went to another landynge place where he expected the comynge of some of the Inhabytaunts of the Iland, but there came none/[3] Then he repayred aborde thinkynge the next day to have sent some a shore to have spoyled the Iland/ and there to have stayed about the Iland tyll the rest of the Fleete had come vp/ so the eveninge approching, we discried the barke Hawkens, the Hope, the Fraunces, and the Scowte cominge towards vs/ which havyng fetched vs/ the Generall comaunded to set sayle from Iland/ so we put of sowth sowth easte/[4]

[Saturday] the .vi. of Novembar

The barke Hawkens with certayne othar of owr Consortes beinge now lefte a sterne of the Generall/ he lay a hull tyll they came to hym/ and so all the Flete beinge come togethar owr Generall put out his flagge of Counseyll/ where havynge assembled all his Captaynes that day before dynnar there were

---

[1] Cf. pp. 64, 110, 131 for the date. The *Primrose* journal (p. 185) gives it as 4 November.

[2] The same estimate is given in Document 7 (see p. 110).

[3] Similar accounts are in other journals. See pp. 110, 132, 185, 224.

[4] The Map Text (p. 65) states that the wind was at South Southeast.

two marinars dowked[1] at the yarde armes becawse havynge charge to kepe the pinnace, they forsoke the same straglynge vp to the Iland to have gotten some pillage/ And so in the eveninge the rest of the flete were come vp and then we set sayle togethar toward Cape de Blanck.

[Monday] the .viij. of Novembar

Kepinge owr sotherly cowrse and the wynde scantynge vpon vs, we laye a hull, beinge vpon the Coaste of Barbarye[2] where soundynge the depth we found owr selves in fifty fadome/ so that dyvars of owr shipps fell to fisshinge with theyr lynes where many were cawght that night and the next day by reason it was so calme/

[Tuesday] the .ix. of Novembar/

We were becalmed/ whereby we went to fisshynge in fiftye fadome where we got good store of fishe to sarve all owr shipps company some two meales/

[Wednesday] The .x.

All day we fysshed, and towards night we had a fayre gayle of wynd at northeast/[3]

[fol. 233v] . . . [   ]ve fall with [the] Coast . . . leagues of the shore . . . Generall, the Drake with other . . . saw to the westward/[4] the wynd beinge then . . . [   ]e haled to the shore agayne to assemble the flete.

[Friday] .The xij.

. . . [   ]d alonge the coaste hard by the shore and so we contynued . . . the afternone/ at which tyme we lay by the lee

---

[1] *Dowke*, obsolete form of the verb *duck*, referring to the punishment of 'ducking' from the yard arm. *OED*. The incident is not mentioned in other accounts.

[2] Cf. p. 65. The *Leicester* journal (p. 132), places the sighting of the Barbary coast on the 9th. The *Primrose* journal (p. 185) does not note it until the 10th.

[3] Cf. p. 132.

[4] This section of the MS is damaged. It probably refers to the events of 11 November that are noted in the *Leicester* journal (p. 133).

to catche fis*he* . . . *w*hich wee stode to the shore and moaste parte of that night we lay. . . .

the xvij. of Novembar, Wedensday/
About fowre of the cloke at night[1] we cam*e* to an anker some two leagu*es* . . . [Seint] Iacobi where landinge owr men, wee marched moaste parte of that nyg*ht* . . .[2] the wayes moaste rockye and stonye/ with great hills and dales very pay[nful] . . . which by computacion was not above fowre myles, but dyvers who had be[en there of] owrs confessed that they nevar marched the lyke/[3] so aboute break of d[ay] . . . to the towne of Seint Iacobi/[4] and at the comynge there we found that th[e inhabitants had] fled/[5] Thursday, Fryday, Satarday, Sonday, Monday, Twesday, Wednesday, [Thursday], Fryday consequently folowinge we continued in Seint Iacobi/[6] where owr men . . . of such things as was lefte behynd/

Satarday the .xxvij. of Novembar/
Early in the morninge we cam*e* to Seint Domingo[7] a towne

[1] i.e. in the late afternoon.
[2] The arrival at Santiago in the Cape Verdes on 17 November and the entry into the town the next day is confirmed by the Map Text, the *Leicester* journal, the *Primrose* journal, the MS variant of the *Summarie* (see pp. 65, 134, 186), and also by a despatch forwarded to the Venetian Doge (*C.S.P.Ven. 1581–1591*, p. 140). Regarding the date which appears in the English editions of the *Summarie*, see p. 227, n. 1.
[3] On the nature of the terrain see the Boazio town plan (Plates III(B), (C)), and also 135. Because the town was unapproachable for an attack at its harbour, its defences had to be attacked from the rear. T. Bentley Duncan, *Atlantic Islands* (Chicago, 1972), pp. 174–6.
[4] The town now known as Ribeira Grande (Duncan, op. cit., p. 174). The island itself was designated as *S. Jacamo* on the African map in Ortelius, *Theatrum orbis terrarum* (reproduced in Eldred D. Jones, *The Elizabethan Image of Africa* (The Folger Shakespeare Library, 1971), p. 38). See also the *Primrose* journal (p. 186).
[5] None of the English narratives supports a statement by Castellanos (*Discurso*, p. 59), that the population fought bravely.
[6] The brevity of the notes concerning the first ten days here may be explained by Carleill's preoccupation with his duties as chief commander of the land forces ashore, with Powell, his scribe, staying aboard ship except for the inland march to Saint Domingo. References to the oaths (seep. 110) may have been left for the 'book', as were other rules about the voyage, and the scribe seems not to have been aware of the difficulties which the *Leicester* journal reports (pp. 141–8). His earlier concerns about nautical matters, and his silence on these points suggest that he was more of a sailor than a soldier.
[7] Both Document 7 (p. 111) and the *Summarie* (p. 230) give 24 November as the date

supposed to be three l[eagues from] Seint Iacoby: where
fyndinge the people to be fled without any thynge f[ound
worth] the writynge/ havynge the wayes moaste hilly and
paynfull we taried [for] fowre howrs/ and vpon owr comynge
awaye we set the town on fier/ And as we [returned] being
some .v. Englyshe myle from Seint Iacobi/¹ certayne Spaniards²
lurkyng ... of a hill made out vpon owr rerewarde, which
beinge encountered by owr men [were there]wythe made to
retire/ where vpon they offered a flagge of truce vnto vs, but
w[   ] ... to parley with vs/³ where vpon owr Capitayne
wayenge that the nyght approached ... grew weary/ and that
they showlde be charged vpon in the night, the wayes beinge
... and paynefull to passe as it was, commaunded the whole
troupe to marche forth [towarde Seint] Iacobi and so we came
in good ordar safe to the towne without losse of any man
[except] of one, who, whiles we rested owr selves in Domingo,
stragglynge alone in a howse, was taken vpon some advauntage
by the enemye and his hedd cut of ... hym besydes in dyvers
partes of his body/⁴

[Sunday] the xxviij. of Novembar/

We set fiar on Seint Iacobi and toward night moaste parte of
owr men shipped [them]selves havynge already watered and
dyspatched suche busynes as they had to do/

[Monday] the .xxix. of Novembar/

Toward three of the cloke in the aftarnone, we came to Praye,⁵

of the march, and the *Primrose* journal is less definite (see p. 189). The *Leicester* journal,
however, seems to support the later date. Since some of the *Summarie*'s dates for this
period are erroneous (see pp. 148, 230, 231 and notes), and since the *Tiger* journal
gives both day of the week and of the month, its date of 27 November appears to
be correct.
    ¹ The distance was six or seven miles, according to the *Leicester* journal (p. 148);
twelve miles, according to the *Primrose* journal.
    ² Cf. p. 189.   ³ Cf. p. 231 and n. 6.
    ⁴ Cf. pp. 148, 189. This is a detail on which the several versions of the *Summarie*
do not entirely agree (see p. 235, n. 3).
    ⁵ i.e. the town of Porto Praya. Lying seven or eight miles east of Santiago, it had a
population of 500 in 1572. Duncan, *Atlantic Islands*, pp. 173- 175. Cf. pp. 190, 232.

where the Generall an*d* othar boates goinge a shore, findinge the people fledd, set fyar on the towne & forwi*th* returned to owr shipps agayne, and put to sea, and kept owr cowrse westerlye/[1]

[Saturday] The fowrth of Decembar

Many of owr men thrwghe out the whole flete about this tyme began to fall sicke[2] whereby *ea*che shippe as they passed by the admirall made reporte there of unto hy*m* who then cownsayled the capitaynes and mastars there of to have speciall care of them for the so*o*ner recoverye of theyr he*a*lthes, and therefore thowght it good to lett them blood/[3] this daye the wynd was west halfe a poynt northerly, and the shipps way was .40. leag*ue*s/

[Tuesday] the .vii.

The wynd continuynge at west and by north/ we kept on owr cowrse with very fayre we*a*thar.

[Thursday] the .9.

havynge the wynd still to continue on owr dwe cowrse it was no small comforte vnto v*s* the rathar becawse we hoaped thereby so moche the so*o*ner to fall with the land which great*l*y was desyred by tho*se* which already were sicke/ who were perswaded yf they myght come once agayne to the shore they showlde become *w*hole men/

---

[1] The departure date is confirmed by the Map Text (p. 65), Document 7 (p.111) and the *Primrose* journal (p. 191). The *Summarie* date of Monday, the 26th (p. 231) is evidently erroneous.

[2] Cf. pp. 191, 235.

[3] Reports circulating at Cartagena, including one by an Italian captive taken by Drake at Santiago, estimate the losses by death from this illness as close to five hundred. Wright, *Further Eng. Voyages*, pp. 46, 52, 55, 121. The heavy losses are mentioned in the other English narratives, and became a decisive factor in the later changes of Drake's plans.

The contemporary explanation for the 'calenture' is given in the *Summarie* (p. 254). J. A. Williamson (*Hawkins of Plymouth*, p. 292) suggests that the epidemic of 'island fever' came rather from overcrowding in the ships (see p. 282 on the ratio of men per ton).

99

[Saturday] the .xviij. of Decembar

We fell with the land, but on what Iland I know not the name,[1] but certeyne of owr men went ashore . . . them . . . [ ]ere very courteously entertayned of them r[ ]² . . ./ /bies [fol. 234] . . . [ ] in the . . . [ ]ment that all the [ ] . . . [ ]ingly havynge the wynd then . . . nyght, still kepynge owr selves within . . .³

[Monday] the .27. of Decembar

. . . we ded see an Iland called Seint Cruse, and bare of . . . [ ]s of/ It rysed in many partes beinge not very highe . . . [part]e of it very lowe with trees vpon it, and [ ]⁴

[Tuesday] the .28.

. . . Seint Iohnns Iland,⁵ and it risethe in partes and reasonable highe . . . west a longe the land/

[Wednesday] the .29.

We sawe an Iland called Mona which risethe flate land/ and by it lyeth . . . and hard by the same a litle hyer then that but very smalle, and then we . . . coast/

[Thursday] The .30.

We contynued in syght of the land which the othar day we discovered,⁶ and toward . . . of the cloke by yll fortune the Thomas['s] pynnace bearinge too moche sayle (as it was

---

¹ The fleet sighted both Guadalupe and Dominica, and made their stop at the latter (pp. 65, 111, n. 7). The arrival date is given as 21 December in the *Primrose* journal (p.191).

² The MS is badly damaged here. For accounts of the courteous dealings with the inhabitants see pp. 111, 191–2.

³ Missing, probably because of damage to the MS, is mention of the stop at St Christopher's at Christmas. See pp. 111, 193, 237. On the other islands passed, 27–9 December, see p. 66.

⁴ The sentence is incomplete in the MS.

⁵ i.e. Puerto Rico.

⁶ i.e. Hispaniola, which had been sighted on 29 December and 'recovered' on the 30th. See p. 66.

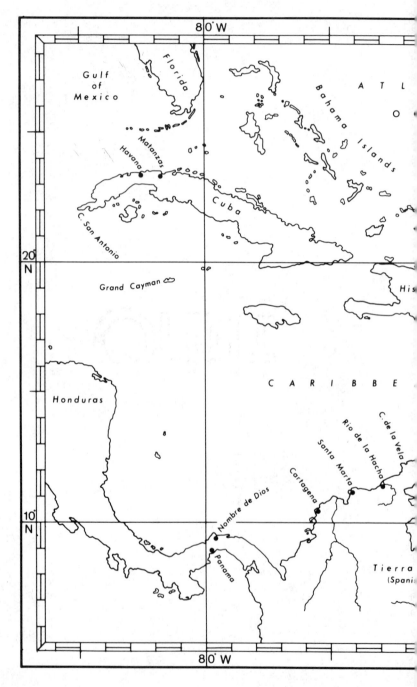

Fig. 2. The Carib

THE CARIBBEAN

AND

THE SPANISH MAIN

0   100   250
Miles

20˚
N

Mona

San Juan Bautista
(Puerto Rico)

T I C

N

A T L A N T I C

Santa Cruz

St. Christopher's

Montserrat

Guadeloupe

Dominica

S E A

Margarita

O C E A N

10˚
N

ie Spanish Main

supposed) was ovarwhelmed, havynge in hir about syx persons/[1]

[Friday] the .31. of Decembar/[2]

About three of the cloke in the aftar none we ymbarqwed owr selves into owr pinn*aces* . . . and so kept the sea all that nyght/ and in the mornynge we landed beinge about eyght myles from Seint Domingo/[3]

Satarday the first of Ianuary/

The mornynge aftar we were landed/ we marched towards Seint Domingo and approaching nere the towne certayne horsemen advaunsed them selves vpon owr forward who aftar some small encountar were dryven to retyre/[4] and at the vppar

[1] This was Thomas Drake's command. A Spanish account mentions the loss of a ship and the narrow escape of Drake's brother during the landing at Hayna River. Wright, *Further Eng. Voyages*, p. xxxviii, n. 5.

[2] The city officials had regarded as false a tale brought in December about Drake's deeds at the Cape Verdes (Castellanos, *Discurso*, pp. 60–6); and the king's advice boat sent after the Vigo incident may have been intercepted by Drake (Castellanos, *Discurso*, pp. xxxvii, 67, 300; Wright, *Further Eng. Voyages*, pp. xxix, n., 16–17, 130; Oppenheim, *Naval Tracts . . . Monson*, I, 128 and n.). Word of the fleet's arrival east of the city on 30 December reached the officials about 10 a.m. on the 31st, but not until late that afternoon did Don Diego Osorio's reconnoitering trip confirm that it was English (Wright, op. cit., pp. xxix, 32, 38).

Drake declared later that the officials had been forewarned (*C.S.P.Span. 1580–1586*, pp. 612–13), but all indications are that few serious preparations were made. The chief act was to block the harbour and to locate the single disabled galley across the entrance so that its guns might be used against any attackers (Wright, *Further Eng. Voyages*, pp. 20, 26; cf. p. 195 below). On the city's poor defences see also R. Boulind, 'Shipwreck and Mutiny in Spain's Galleys on the Santo Domingo Station, 1583', *Mariner's Mirror*, LVIII (1972), 297–335.

[3] The Spaniards had been so sure that no landing was possible except near the harbour and castle that no guard had been placed elsewhere. 'To have landed there [Hayna] is to the natives of this land a thing more incredible than I can express,' went one report (Wright, *Further Eng. Voyages*, pp. xxxiv, 22). Although they observed the movement of the small ships at night, they did not understand it (Wright, op. cit., p. 39). The English narratives tell of no attempt to enter the harbour by night, as President Ovalle afterwards reported (Wright, op. cit., p. xxxvii, n. 5; Castellanos, *Discurso*, p. 293). The distance from Hayna to the city was about nine or ten miles. Cf. pp. 66, 111, 193, 238.

[4] About noon on Saturday news of the forces approaching from Boca de Hayna reached the city, from which already many of the citizens had fled. Such armed men as were available (only 110, according to the governor, but 210, including 50

gate[1] where my capitayne enteryd there was a great shott made from thence, amongst vs, which kylled two of owr men/[2] where vpon we rann maynely vpon the Enemye and entered the Towne/ and beinge in the towne, a certayne Spanyard crossed the way from an othar strete/ where vpon one of owr men made a shott at hym, but myssed hym and he there vpon bent his pike agaynst us/ which when my capitayne perceyved, hym selfe havynge then nothinge but his leadynge staffe encountered with hym hand to hand vntill such tyme as a sowldiour seeinge the great odds that the Spaniard had stepped to hym and with his piece ovarthrew the Spaniard/[3] so enteringe the towne without any furthar resystaunce we continued there in .xxxj. dayes/[4]

The ordinaunce in the towne were .lxvj. [pieces] all brasse very fayre/[5]

---

horsemen, according to another official) went out to meet them, but found they could do nothing, 'owing to the enemy's speed and impetuosity,' and promptly retired (Wright, *Further Eng. Voyages*, pp. 18, 20-1, 33; Castellanos, *Discurso*, p. 294). Nor were they diverted by a herd of cattle driven toward them to throw them into disorder. (This tactic is mentioned in the French narrative (Lacour, p. 23), and is pictured on the Boazio map (Plates V(A), (B)), but is not referred to in the Spanish documents (Wright, *Further Eng. Voyages*, p. xxxvi, n.) or in the English narratives.) One official attributed the speed of the advance to the presence among the English forces of twenty 'traitors' who had fled from Spanish punishment (Wright, *Further Eng. Voyages*, p. 26). A brief description of the city's fall, based upon a report dated 24 February and received on 14 May is in the *C.S.P.Ven. 1581–1591*, pp. 167–8.

[1] The city gates on the west side were flanked by weak walls for not more than fifty feet, the rest of the boundary being marked only by shrubbery, and usually had no artillery (Wright, *Further Eng. Voyages*, pp. 18, 34, 222). The type of wall shown on the Boazio map is therefore incorrect.

[2] Three artillery pieces were hastily planted at the Lenba gate, and one of them was fired, killing two or three of the English, 'among them an ensign' (Wright, *Further Eng. Voyages*, pp. 18, 21, 34), but otherwise provided little resistance. Cf. pp. 193,240.

[3] The Spanish documents do not report this encounter. Their report of fighting as late as 5 p.m. is inaccurate (Wright, *Further Eng. Voyages*, p. 24).

[4] More details regarding the stay appear in other accounts. The dating in the *Leicester* journal seems to be more reliable, and the February dates in the *Tiger* journal appear to be off by two days. See p. 157 and n. 2.

[5] Cf. pp. 197, 277. A Spanish report noted 'over 70 pieces of artillery, including five culverins and eleven cannon larger than Little Saint Lorenzo, and three extra large perriers'. Wright, *Further Eng. Voyages*, p. 27; also pp. 134, 142.

[Wednesday] The second of February[1]

The towne durynge owr resydence therein, beinge sacked to the full, *with* such consyderation drawne from them as it was thowght good by owr generall, we all embarqwde owr sel*ve*s this day by eyght of ye cloke in the mornynge, havyng a fayre wynd, which caryed us *on* owr dwe cowrse sowth and by west/

The .xi. of February[2]

havynge kepte owr cowrse at west norwest all that day we came to an anker about .v. of the cloke at nyght.[3] At which tyme we put all owr sowldiours in pinaces and boates to the nombar of seventeen hundred,[4] and landed about myd nyght havynge then some iiij. Englyshe myles to the Citie of Cartagena,[5] which done we marched all that nyght towards the sayde Citie. but fortune not favoringe eche leadar or Captayne in suche sorte as myght have bene wisshed/ dyvars of them who were in the rerewarde thrwgh theyr often stonds which they made, and the neglygence of theyr officers who weare verye remisse in lookynge to theyr charge, were not only lefte behynd, but also were dryven into suche an amaze thrwghe the losse of the forwarde, beinge them sel*ve*s altogethar then without any guyde, as none of them all knewe which way to folow to ioyne with the rest of the armye/ beinge thus distressed and hearinge nowe and then a warnynge p*ie*ce discharged by the enemye, it ded not a litle greve vs to have suche evell fortune so to be bothe lost and lefte behynd/[6]

---

[1] See p. 102 n. 4 above.

[2] This date also is inaccurate. It was Ash Wednesday, 9/19 February, according to the Spanish documents (Wright, *Further Eng. Voyages*, pp. xlvii, 73, 118, etc.). See also pp. 67, 160.

[3] At three or four o'clock (*Summarie*, p. 248; and Wright, *Further Eng. Voyages*, pp. xlviii, 58, 106).

[4] The number in the English landing force, as given in Spanish reports, varied between 550 and 1,200 (Wright, *Further Eng. Voyages*, pp. 49, 61, 119, 141, 153). Considering the losses from fever and the need for men to stay on the ships or to join in Frobisher's attack on the fort, 1,700 seems high.

[5] Cf. p. 248, n. 1.

[6] Cf. pp. 160–3, 248. The Spanish accounts confirm the darkness of the night, and confusion within their ranks as well. Wright, *Further Eng. Voyages*, pp. 49–50, 53, 75, etc.

fearinge leaste that owr lyeftenente generall who then was in the forward, beinge so slenderly backed, myght there by be put in great daungar, but God who moaste graciously defended vs browght vs within one howre [fol. 234v] ... *ap*proche w[   ] . . . *b*est advauntage/ for had . . . the bulwarke and the Galleys . . . *l*osse of owr men then (God be thanked) . . . to [   ]en the towne was not only a place m[   ] . . . [   ]y directly vpon vs beinge a way of narrow passage and . . . placed .vi. greate brasse peeces, but also two greate Gal*leys* . . . hand as we cam*e* in wherein were no lesse then ix. greate br[asse pieces] . . . shote besyd*es* who played vpon vs to owr great anoyaunce[1] and . . . be they had had the day[2] to have had but some reasonable ayme at vs . . . Lieut*en*aunt Generall/ with good co*u*rage not fearinge the roaring of the ca[non] from the Galleys, nor the Rente of sworde/ havynge God on his syde, ded [brave]ly enter with thes*e* wordes, *God and Seynt George*/[3] who then had not above xx [men] . . . waytynge on hym/ and so havynge entered the sconse,[4] and beaten the ene*mye* . . . bulwarke, vpon his enteringe the skonse, moaste co*u*ragiously slewe the [chief ensign bea]rar who then advaunsed hym selfe agaynst vs with his owne hands/[5] by this [time it was] day lyght and moaste triumphantlye we entered the Citie of Cartagena[6] . . . wh[ere we con]tynued from the xij. of Februarye[7] tyll the .xxj. of Marche[8] Towch[ing the]

[1] Cf. pp. 162, 250 below, and Wright, *Further Eng. Voyages*, pp. xlvi, 58, 73, 92, 102, 107, 109, etc. Besides the two royal galleys, *Capitana* and *Ocasion*, there was also in the inner harbour a galleon or frigate, the *Napolitana*. Wright, op. cit., pp. 76, 106, 110, 117; Castellanos, *Discurso*, pp. xlii, 151. See also the Boazio Map (Plates VI(A), (B)).

[2] That is, *if they had had daylight*.

[3] The words are underlined in the MS.

[4] i.e. the area behind the wall and trench. The English had rushed around the unfinished end of the wall. See Bravo's deposition in Wright, *Further Eng. Voyages*, p. 119.

[5] Cf. pp. 163, 251. The ensign bearer was Juan Cosme de las Sal(a). Wright, *Further Eng. Voyages*, pp. li and n., 56, 69, 119; Castellanos, *Discurso*, pp. xlvi, 193.

[6] Although most of the resistance in the city ended quickly, the fort held out until evening. See p. 199, n. 2.

[7] Again the date is off by two days. It should be Thursday, 10 February.

[8] About 21 or 22 March Drake moved his men outside of the town to await the ransom payment. The stay in town was approximately five and a half weeks. See pp. 200, 202.

state we found the Citie in when we entered, It is well knowne
th[at in the] .xx. dayes warninge which they had of owr
comynge/[1] theyr ryches and [treasures were] conveyed awaye/
the towne left vnvictualed and nothinge at all in effe[ct left]
savynge some wyne whiche stode vs in some steade/ Not
withstandinge . . . to satysfye vs with all, we cawsed them to
raunsome them selves at .xxx. thous[and pounds][2] before we
would departe theyr citie/ havynge contynued in theyr ci[tie
five] wekes and three dayes/[3] It was thowght good by owr
generall and lieveteau[nt general] to leave the same/ and to
fortifye owr selves in a certayne priorye very near the Citie,
where there were apoynted certayne captaynes with .ij C. men[4]
. . . the same place who contynued there three dayes/[5] The
forte by the watarsy[de was] kept by owr sowldiours tyll the
Spaniards had performed suche furthar co[mpounding] as by
owr generall was layde vpon them/ The ordinaunce which was
from the towne, forte, and Galleys were in all three score and
two brasse pieces.[6] . . . Maunday Thursday[7] early in the
mornynge owr generall and the whole flete wayed [anchor] and
put owr selves to sea havynge the wynd at sowthe easte/
where we continued then . . . beatynge vp and downe the seas
with contrary wynds and fowle weathar besyde . . . yll happe
wherewith we were all combred[8] in asmoche as the Newe Yers
Gyfte lost owr companye/[9] and besydes had so greate a leake

[1] The Spanish documents show that by early January a series of general warnings
had come from Spain, and that by 10/20 or 14/24 January news from Hispaniola had
arrived. Wright, *Further Eng. Voyages*, pp. xlv and n., 47. See also p. 198, n. 4, below.

[2] The newsletter also states the ransom figure in this form (see p. 113), which is
less than the equivalent of 110,000 ducats at 7s. or 8s. 6d. per ducat (see pp. 175, 259 n. 2).

[3] See below, and also Document 7 (p. 113). The departure date was 31 March,
according to the *Primrose* journal (p. 202), the French narrative (Lacour, p. 25), and
the Spanish records (Wright, *Further Eng. Voyages*, pp. lvii, 135, 159).

[4] i.e. 200 men.

[5] Cf. the *Primrose* journal (pp. 201, 202), which places the additional stay at
ten days.

[6] These pieces, with those from Santo Domingo, were among the most valuable
products of the expedition. See pp. 57, 62, 277.

[7] Maunday Thursday in 1586 was 31 March. Cf. above, n. 3.

[8] i.e. *encumbered*.

[9] This was Corço's ship from Santo Domingo, used to transport the captured
ordnance. Cf. p. 262, and Wright, *Further Eng. Voyages*, pp. lvii, 51–2, 160, 167.

as meetynge with vs by good fortune agayne we were forced to returne to the mowthe of Cartagena,[1] where we lay by . . . the sayde New Yers Gyfte was discharged of all suche things as were worth the carryinge awaye/ which was finished on Wednesday the .xiij. of Aprell[2] & immediatly set on fyar by vs/

[Thursday] The .xiiij. of Aprill/[3]

Earlye in the morninge about fowr of the cloke we all wayed ankors and came vndar sayle, havynge the wynd sowthe east with a small gale for a while, but aftarwards [a] stiffe gayle/[4]

Document 7

A Newsletter (British Library Cotton MS Otho E. VIII, fols. 235–236v).[5]

[fol. 235] . . . The l(?)etter . . . [   ]ynges[6] are I am sure, as I . . . at my handes/ I besech y[ou] who althoughe vnadvysedly and vn[   ] you/ yet such a one as in good will & sy[   ] . . . geveth place no not to your derest or nev[   ] . . . whatsoever/ And because our generall Sir Fran[cis Drake] promysed a whole and perfect booke of all such th[ings that] have happened throughout our whole voyadge[7] . . . this present [will] comvnycate no more then the effective tymes and manner of our procedynges, referryng the rest [to the] promysed booke, or to our next famylyar talke if ever w[   ] & lybertye it may be my fortune to talke with y[ou].

Thus then it was/.

For the Servyce of our Prynce, the welth & honor of our cou[ntry] & the commodytye of our selves & the adventurers

---

[1] The return was on 4/14 April. Wright, *Further Eng. Voyages*, p. 135. One document (ibid., p. 159) dated it a day earlier.

[2] The 13th of April (English calendar) fell on Wednesday in 1586.

[3] This date agrees with that given in the Spanish records (Wright, *Further Eng. Voyages*, pp. lvii, 136, 145, 160; Castellanos, *Discurso*, p. 307). The *Primrose* journal, however (p. 203), erroneously places it on 18 April.

Footnotes to page 106 continued.

⁴ The record in this MS ends here, with about three and one-half inches of the page unused.

⁵ This document, consisting of two folios, four sides, is bound in the Cotton MSS immediately after the account from Carleill's ship *Tiger*, Document 6 (Cotton MS Otho E. VIII, fols. 229–34), and has suffered the same type of damage from fire. It proclaims itself in the opening paragraph as a newsletter or abbreviated narrative of the voyage, and it serves to fill in occasionally for missing parts of the other document, and to supplement it after the date in April 1586 at which the *Tiger* narrative stops. It has been printed in full here especially because of its apparently close connection with that account and its writers.

Several features of the newsletter point to tha trelationship. One is a strong similarity between the hand in which this document is written and that which appears for several lines on fol. 230v (see notes on pp. 69, 79 above). Although a positive identification is less easily established than was the case of the more distinctive hand in which the other parts of Document 6 were written, there are signs of identity in the spelling of a number of words (e.g. *demavnd, retorned, shipps*, rather than *shippes*), and in the form of various capital letters (e.g. *D, G, I, S*). See Plates IX, X).

Other points of similarity are in the order and form of reporting of events or incidents of the voyage, in matters of dates, and in figures on ransom payments (e.g. incidents in the Canaries, especially at Palma and Ferro; observations in the West Indies; dates and incidents at Santo Domingo; and the Cartagena ransom). There are occasional differences, most of which are pointed out in the notes below, but these are less striking than the similarities.

Furthermore, there are indications that this narrative came from, and was addressed to, someone who had official connections with the expedition. Its author refers in the first paragraph to Drake's promised 'book' of the voyage, for which the present account was to represent a kind of advance report. The insertion at two points in the text of 'Mr S' or 'Mr Sr' suggests that the person for whom the report was prepared may have been the 'Mr Secretary' (Walsingham), to whom Carleill's despatch from Vigo was addressed (see above, p. 69, n. 4. Compare with the printed copy in Corbett, *Sp. War*, pp. 39–49). The tone of the opening paragraph of the newsletter suggests that the writer was personally acquainted with the addressee. If the latter was indeed the Secretary, then it may be concluded that either Carleill or someone close to him, whom Walsingham knew, wrote this report. The penmanship itself does not appear to be Carleill's (the hand differs in several respects from that in documents presumably written by him, such as his letter to Walsingham from Ireland in 1584 (S.P. 63/112: 173), and the spelling of his name as Carleyl (see p. 108 below) differs from the spelling of his customary signature, *Carleill*), but, as in the case of the *Tiger* journal, Carleill may have used another member of his entourage to write this abbreviated report (cf. note 4, p. 69).

For these reasons the editor believes that the newsletter, as well as the *Tiger* journal and the MS variant of the *Summarie* (see p. 213, n. 1 and also Appendix III) must be associated with Christopher Carleill, and through him with Walsingham. Whether the report ever reached Mr Secretary cannot be established. It is not among the State Papers, where the dispatch from Vigo is found. Possibly it was never sent, or the Cotton MS may be the copy of the newsletter which its author retained among his papers.

⁶ Because the top corners of the MS are badly damaged, many words are missing or incomplete.

⁷ See reference to the book also in the *Tiger* journal, p. 71.

the 14 [of] September 1585 with 22 shipps, barkes, & pynasses,[1] we put to sea from Plymouthe & contynewed our coorse til the 28 daye on which we anckered in the Iles of Bayon/.[2]

I may not omyt (Master Secretary)[3] a peece of servyce performed in our waye, namely a ship of Saint John de Luce[4] taken and spoyled. it was Laden with New Land fysh which in scorne our men called (poore John).[5] this victuall supplyed our necessytyes many wayes and our people repented they had not Chrystened it by a moore gloryous and rych name/.

Rydinge at the Iles of Bayon our generall manned his Gally, longe boate and pynasses, with 700 men towardes the towne or Cytye of Bayon,[6] where mett hym a messenger demavndyng what he was and what he sought/ answer was made we were men of warr & sought nothyng butt what we could winn by force/ with this man Captayn Sampson returned and demavnded whether K. Phyllyp had warrs with her Maiestie or nott, & why our shipps & marchantes were Imbargued[7] & stayed/ to the fyrst answer was made by the governor that he nether could tell any such matter nor would meddle in it/ as for the shipps and merchantes [they] were at lyberty to go & come at there pleasure, which answere brought to the generall he landed his men hard by the towne, where by Captain Carleyl/ Levetenant generall, they were ordered, with watch & gardes placed for theyr sure defence/[8] presently after [fol. 235v] ... Talbott & the Speedwell from the fleet. Two ships retu[rned] to us but the other one [   ][9] ... the L[ieutenant] generall

---

[1] On the number of ships see p. 180 and the Table of Ships.

[2] The fleet actually reached the islands on 27 September. Cf. pp. 64, 78.

[3] In the MS, only the first bracket shows plainly. The *M*[r] is clear. The second letter could be read either as *S* alone, or as *S*[r], with the superscribed *r* unclear because the ink splattered into dots on the page.

[4] i.e. St Jean-de-luz. See pp. 75–6 above.

[5] On 'poore John' see p. 156, n. 4.

[6] Cf. the *Tiger* journal, p. 78. The account which follows resembles that in Document 6 and other records, but gives fewer details.

[7] i.e. *embargoed*.

[8] Cf. the *Tiger* journal, p. 81.

[9] Because the MS is damaged, its description of the storm has been lost. The *Talbot*, *Hawkins*, and *Speedwell* were blown out to sea, and the last named never returned to the fleet. See p. 81.

with other Captayns were [sent with cer]tayne shypps to go down the ryver of F[igo[1] where they] fovnde certayne small Frygattes or boates [laden with] church stuffe & others with howsehold [stuffe] which were . . . bvrnte. we landed also in an Islett called Saint [   ] . . . [where] was a relygyous howse which we spoyled[2] & so w[   ] . . . which by this were come into the harbovr of Tysys or Vygo/ The fyrst of October Captain Sampson with a C men [went] to view the Covntrye betwixt Fygo & ovr shypps/[3] and w[   ] . . . where after a few shott & each party returned only [one] maryner straglynge from his company for pillag[e was] slayn & hys head cut of./[4]

The enemy the next daye presented a Flagge of t[ruce and] demavnded parley/ which being gravntted ovr gen[eral and the] governor mett in ij boates a Calever shott from the shore/ [they] agreed I wott not on what Condytions but for pledges[5] . . . [We] sent to the towne Captain Eryzy & Captayn Crosse, & [two] of them were left aboorde with vs/ where they were till the 9 daye that the Lieutenant generall & Captain Furbusher . . . were sent for with them [and] so ovr men returned.

The 12 of October we sett sayle and contynewed till the 23, on which day we espyed land, namely one of the Isles of the Canaryes/.[6]

The 28 we saw the Teneryffe, an excedying hye movntayn on the top wherof lyeth snow contynuallye. We saw also the Grand Canarye.[7]

---

[1] Probably intended for Vigo. The writer uses either *F* or *V* in his references to the place (see below). It was Carleill in his ship *Tiger* who led the way to Vigo. The wording here suggests that the writer participated in that action. Cf. pp. 84–5.

[2] Cf. p. 84 and n. 6.

[3] Cf. pp. 64, 85.

[4] Cf. p. 86.

[5] For details on the negotiations of 2 October see the *Tiger* journal (pp. 86–7) and the *Primrose* journal (p. 182). Frobisher, rather than Carleill, stayed with Drake during the talk with the governor. Details may have been omitted from the newsletter in view of the fuller account which Carleill had sent back to Walsingham in his October despatch.

[6] The departure was dated 11 October in the Map Text and the *Tiger* journal (see pp. 64, 89). Lanzarote was first sighted on 23 October, according to the *Leicester* journal (p. 125), and the fleet arrived there on the 24th (see p. 92).

[7] The fleet was between Teneriffe and Palma on the 28th (see p. 93).

The 3 of November we beare alongst the shore and came before Palma where the bulwarke made shott at vs & h[it] the gallery of our admyrall, the generall hym selfe standynge in it/ and other shott also hytt her broade syde but the bullet [stuck][1] fast in it. the Galeon Leycester receyved a shott a[lso]. they spent at least 23 shott at vs & did no hurte/[2] the generall fyndinge no ankerynge for his shypps/ left the Iland and sayled till we came to Fero.

The 5 day our men Landed, and the Inhabytantes sent an Englysh boy to vs[3] desyrynge that they myght not be delt with cruelly concernyng there lyves, as for the Cattell & goodes[4] they resygned being not suffycyent to serve the fleet/ 2 dayes[5] in respect[6] wherof everyman was commavnded aboard. So we left the Canaryes & sayled alongst the Coast of Barbary.

The 13 day we fell with Cape Blanke, where we sawe certayn French men of warr.[7] [fol. 236] ... [   ]ynge w[   ] ... orderyng our men ... approched the towne/ which we ... quartered and gvardes placed in places [under the] dyrection of the Lieutenant generall.[8]

The next day search was made for victuall ... wyne, oyle & meale fovnde besydes in there [forts] good store of brasse ordynance.

The 20 daye a covnsell was called & each man was ...[9] full aucthoryty of his offyce as the Viceadmyrall, the [Lieutenant] generall & other captayns & offycers[10]/. and everyman [was] sworne to the vttermost ...[11] ther of.

---

[1] In MS, *stack*.   [2] Cf. pp. 94, 128–9.   [3] Cf. pp. 95, 131.

[4] The word is crossed through in the MS, but no other word was inserted.

[5] Cf. the *Tiger* journal, p. 95.   [6] In MS, *respett*.

[7] The date agrees with that in the Map Text (p. 65) and the *Summarie* (p. 224), and also with Cheney's *Handbook of Dates*. The fleet had been off the African coast since the 8th or 9th (pp. 96, 132). The *Leicester* journal places the encounter with a French man-of-war (possibly an armed merchantman) on 11 November.

[8] These notes refer to the land actions at Santiago in the Cape Verdes.

[9] References to the oaths of loyalty announced on this date (see pp. 139, 233). The missing words are probably, *was sworn to the*. This incident is not in the *Tiger* journal.

[10] There is not enough space on this page for a reference to the rear admiral, but in mentioning the vice admiral this version of the oaths differs from that in the *Leicester* journal (see pp. 140–1), which emphasizes officers for land operations.

[11] Words are illegible because of a tear and the folding of the MS.

Whyle we aboade in this towne one Thomas Ogle . . . of the barke Talbott was hanged for commyttyng Sodomy. . . .[1]

The 24 we marched toward a village called Saint Domingo which we also fovnd abandoned.[2] the village was burned . . . the byshops howse and as we retorned the people made s[how] of some force but not any such as was able to encovnter . . . vs/ the towne of Pray was also burned & 2 pieces of ordyn[ance taken].

The 29 of November we sett sayle[3] and sayled till the 18 [of] December with out syght of Land/

In this space, Master S:[4] befell a Lamentable and grevous sycknes amongst our men so that great nombers dyed and many were syck to the great astonyshyng of the rest.[5]

The 28 daye we fell with an Iland called Saint Domynica[6] inhabyted with savadge people, with whome our people that went ashore exchanged beades, & other trashe & receyved agayne, tobaco, rootes. Then sayled we in syght of other Ilandes, as Moncerate, and Guadelupe.[7]

The 21[8] we landed our syck men being 260 in an Isle called Saint Chrystovall & taryed there till the 25 in which space most of them recovered/ then passed we by Saint Cruse, Saint Johns, Mona & the 29 we set syght [of] Hyspanyola & bare in with the shore.[9]

On New Yeres Daye by 8 of the Clock in the mornynge we Landed our men 3 leauges[10] from the Cyty of Saint Domyngo

[1] Cf. p. 148.

[2] The date of the march agrees with that in the *Summarie* (p. 230), but other accounts place it on the 27th. See pp. 97, 148 and notes.

[3] This date agrees with that in the *Tiger* journal (see p. 99).

[4] Possibly *Master Secretary*. See above, p. 106 and n. 5.   [5] Cf. p. 99 and n. 3.

[6] In the MS, the date appears to have been written first as *28*, and then corrected to *18*; the date immediately following is the 21st. The Dominica events are placed on 18 December in the Map Text (p. 66) and the *Tiger* journal (p. 100).

[7] Guadeloupe on 18 December, Montserrat on the 20th, according to the Map Text (pp. 65–6). On the trade with the islanders see p. 192.

[8] The date, written first as *31*, was changed to *21* in the MS. The Map Text (p. 66) also dates this stay as 21–5 December.

[9] Santa Cruz on 27th December, St John's on the 28th, and Mona and Monito on the 29th (see pp. 66, 100).

[10] i.e. about nine miles.

and comynge within a myle of it a troupe of horsemen shewed
them selves, but perceyvyng our strength retyred/ our battayl
ordered & our men placed/ we approched the Cytye. our men
wer devyded into 2 partes which, entryng in at the 2 gates
[were] appoynted to mete in the markett place/ the enemye
perceyvynge our comyng discharged the greate ordynance that
was planted at the gate[1] and killed a soldyer or 2 & with all
fledd, so we entred the Cytye/ About 12 a clock at mydnyght
we entred the Castell and fovnd in it great store of brasse
ordynance/[2] 7 dayes we sacked the Cytye and fovnd therein
plenty of wyne, oyle, sugar, gynger, hydes, etc.
[fol. 236v] . . . we stayed . . . hapned 2 Clerkes that came . . .
were hanged.[3]

[An] Irishman also hanged for kyllyng his offycer . . .[4] and
brought to the gallows for mvteny & per[   ] . . . The last
daye we burned a gally that was in th[e harbor and took] a way
with vs 2 shypps the New Yeres Gyft & the [new Hope,
which we] had rygged & trymed for our purpose.[5]

Then sayled we from the [cytye][6] 2 of February[7] till the . . .
daye our men were landed about 4 myle from th[e city of]
Cartagena/ who havyng had warnyng of our comyng . . . vs
in such sort as had not God blessed vs . . . fully in gr[   ] bene
fayled (?)/[8] and because you shall [see] how and with what
davnger this Cyty was won I have . . . sent you a modell or
platt wherin is descrybed the manner of entrye/[9] The end was
we tooke it and fovnd in it . . . brasse ordynance, and for

---

[1] In the MS, written first as *gates*, but the *s* is crossed out. The main resistance was
at the gate by which Carleill entered. Cf. p. 102.

[2] Cf. pp. 197, 277.

[3] On this incident see pp. 196, 242. The wording here suggests possibly a different
explanation for the execution of the two Dominicans.

[4] Cf. *Summarie*, p. 243.

[5] Cf. pp. 157, 197.

[6] The word *Cytye* is crossed through in the MS, but no word replaces it.

[7] The date agrees with that in the *Tiger* journal (p. 103), for correction of which see
p. 157, n. 2.

[8] A number of words are unreadable here because of a fold and a tear in the MS.

[9] Since no map has been preserved with this MS, there is no way of knowing
whether or not this refers to the Boazio drawing. If it does, then the arguments for
associating this newsletter with Carleill are strengthened. See Note on Maps.

30,000 *li* ransomed it after we [burned] at least a quarter of it/
5 wekes & 3 dayes we t[arried in] it & the . . . we set sayle
homewardes.[1]

The 21 of March[2] the New Yere Gyft receyved a leak, so t[hat
with] much hazard of her losse we came agayne to the harbor. . . .

The 20 of Apryll we Landed our men at Cuny Grand[3] [and]
tooke plenty of turtles, Alygathaes,[4] Coneys,[5] etc.

The 23 we set sayle agayne.

The 27 we saw Cape Saint Anthonye/[6] The generall land[ed
but] fovnd no water so set sayle agayne, plying vp and dow[n
with a] contrary wynd till the 10 of May we came agayne *to*
Saint Anthonye where in 2 or 3 dayes we watered, & *set* sayle
agayne laboryng yet in vayne to reach the Ma[tanzas].

The 23 of May we saw Cape Floryda and runnyng along by
the shore the 28 daye we anchored before Saint Augustyne[7]
and landed our men before the watch towre/[8] The fort of
Saint [John] de Pynes being betwyxt us & the towne,[9]
we encamped our[selves] ag[ainst] it and the same nyght
planted a peece of ordynance/[10] The levetenant generall going
in aboute in the nyght to discover was descryed and the alarm

[1] Several words are unreadable here, some having been written and then crossed through. The departure date was 31 March. The ransom figure agrees with that in the *Tiger* journal (see p. 105).

[2] This date is incorrect. See p. 105.

[3] i.e. the Grand Cayman. The *Primrose* journal (p. 203) places the arrival here on 22 April.

[4] i.e. *alligators*.

[5] *Coneys*, a kind of shell fish of the West Indies. See *OED*.

[6] i.e. Cape San Antonio. On the two stops at the cape see pp. 68, 204–5, 263, and Wright, *Further Eng. Voyages*, pp. 167, 169. The fleet was outside of Havana for several days from 19/29 May (Wright, op. cit., pp. 168, 171). For incidents in the Cuban area see p. 204 and n. 4.

[7] The English were off St Augustine by 27 May, and attacked on the 28th.

[8] Cf. Map Text, p. 68. See also the Boazio map (Plates VII(A), (B)), and p. 68.

[9] The fort, newly built of timber, had been erected only after warnings of Drake's approach had come. In it the governor, Pedro Menéndez Marqués, had eighty men, having sent the women and children inland for safety. Wright, *Further Eng. Voyages*, pp. lx–lxi, 164.

[10] The English made two approaches to the fort that Saturday, retreating for reinforcements after being fired on the first time. They returned in greater numbers and brought up guns, preparing to batter the fort and then to make a major assault. See p. 265, and Wright, *Further Eng. Voyages*, pp. 181–3, 198–9.

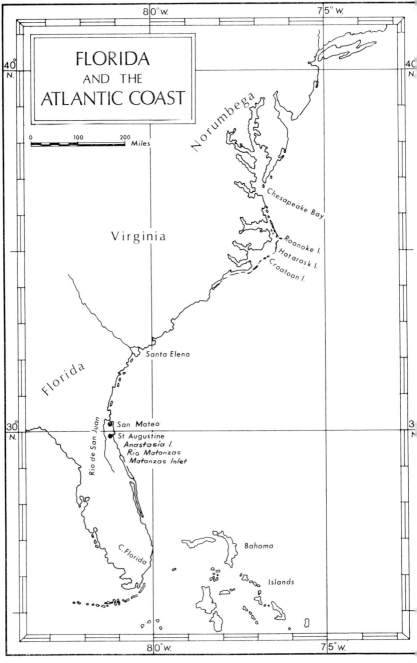

Fig. 3. Florida and the Atlantic Coast

gevne.[1] Within 2 hours after the enemye abandoned the forte wherof the generall was advertysed by a Frenchman & a Dutchman that escaped from them.[2] The generall with other captaynes going to it, the enemy discharged 2 peeces of great ordynance at hym and so fled. in this fort was fovnd 8 or 9 peces of brasse ordynance very well movnted/ also a chest with at leaste 1000 *li* of sylver/[3] store of meale.

The 28 we landed at the towne & with no resystance recovered it.[4] Captain Powell our Sergeant maior, getting a horse and followynge the execution was stryken with a bullett & slayne.[5] His body was recovered/ at whose funerall performed with a volley of shott as the manner is one Grene was by mishap slayn.[6] Master Waterhowse, Levetenant to Captain Goryng,[7] was also slayne by the enemye & there [buryed].[8] The towne & fort were bothe burned.

The [2]th of June we set sayle etc.[9]

[1] On Carleill's night reconnoitering see p. 266.

[2] The *Summarie* (p. 266) mentions a Frenchman; the *Primrose* journal (p. 206) mentions a Frenchman and a Dutchman. The Spanish reports speak of three deserters, French, Flemish and Spanish. Wright, *Further Eng. Voyages*, pp. 182, 183, 186. On the identity of the Frenchman see p. 206, n. 2.

[3] The chest had been taken from the town to the fort for better protection. It contained some 5,000 or 6,000 ducats, according to Spanish reports. Wright, *Further Eng. Voyages*, pp. lxii, 165, 181. See also pp. 207, 268.

[4] Having taken the fort early on Sunday, 29 May, the English entered the undefended town. The governor and the men with him from the fort had withdrawn to the place where the women and children were, fearing possible damage from the Indians as well as from the English. Wright, *Further Eng. Voyages*, pp. lxii, 181, 183.

[5] On Powell's death see also pp. 206, 269.

[6] Green has not been identified.

[7] Waterhouse was Goring's lieutenant, possibly assigned to Frobisher's ship. See pp. 206, n. 5, 299.

[8] In MS, *byryed.*

[9] The page is torn here. The departure was on 2 June (see p. 207). With the *etc,* the newsletter ends.

Document 8

Letter from Francis Knollys to Sir Francis Drake, January 1586
(British Library Harley MS 2202, fols. 54–54v).[1]

[fol. 54]

The copy [of the] letter ... sente by *Master* Knowlles to the generall[2]

[Jan.][3]
6

The 6 daye in the morninge my *master* sent a *lettere* to the *generall which* was as followeth

Sir, I fynd my self soe infynetlye iniured by the hard courses you vse daylie both vnto my self and as many as any waie affect me I say Infynetly because yt is without end, as in truth I knowe

---

[1] Two documents from the ship *Leicester*, bound consecutively in B.L. Harl. MS 2202 as fols. 54–70v, include Document 8, a letter addressed by her captain, Francis Knollys, to Drake in January 1586, while the fleet was at Santo Domingo (fols. 54–54v); and Document 9, sixteen folios of narrative (fols. 55–70v) which were kept by someone in Knollys's employ aboard the *Leicester*, whose name has not been discovered. This journal, portions of which constitute a genuine ship's log, extends from October 1585 through March 1586, with breaks at intervals where pages are missing. Folios 55–62v bear earlier page numbers 9–16, and include events from mid-October through 27 November 1585; fols. 63–4v (earlier numbers 23–4) deal with events of 9–18 January 1586; fols. 65–8v (earlier numbers 27–30) concern 26 or 27 January into early February; and fols. 69–70v (earlier numbers 33–4) relate to late February and early March, the last noted date being 15 March. There is a break at mid-sentence as the page ends.

The handwriting of the letter, which is presumably a copy kept for Knollys himself, differs from that of the narrative. The notation across the top of the letter, however, appears to be in the same hand as that of the later narrative pages. The nature of the notes, both while at sea and on land (e.g. pp. 132, 137, 158) suggests that the keeper of the *Leicester* journal was a man of education as well as experience at sea. His copies of sets of rules at various times (see pp. 130, 140) indicate that he held some administrative responsibility, and his reports of conferences between Knollys and Drake suggest that he had access to the inner circle of commanders. He may have been master, or second in command under Knollys, aboard the *Leicester* (see pp. 147, 151, n. 1); certainly he shared his captain's distrust of Drake and Carleill. His is the only record of the case of near mutiny that developed on this voyage, and his notes regarding ransom negotiations, especially at Cartagena, are the fullest that are known, outside of Spanish accounts.

[2] A line written across the top of the page, probably by the keeper of the narrative pages. Although the name is spelled Knowlles here, the alternate spelling, *Knollys*, has been used throughout by the editor, since this is the form generally used for the family.

[3] This record contains dates in the margin, shown here simply as 6. The name of the month has been inserted by the editor.

not what waye I maye take either to your satisfaccon or my
owne quyett for I protest vnto youe, ther is nothinge I desyre
more beinge never accounted seditious or mvtinous in any place
or companye in all my lyffe hethervnto as is well knowen. Yet
have I passed my tyme not obscurely havinge tassted as many
waters as most have donne in this and that I thanke God
without any blote or dyscredite.[1]

But touchinge [my] present estate, the oftener I looke into yt
the more amased I stand for when I see honest love and
vnfayned affeccon rewarded with dysgraces in dispyte
wroughte by the fynes of flatterye, and founded vppon the
vncertayne grounds of poysoned Ieloses,[2] when neither places
of chardge dischardged without cause of blame nor pryvate
estate ledd in quietness without offence [are considered], when
all the whole worlde canne not touch me with any dysorder or
mysbehavior towardes the action of our General or any man
else, when what soever, I doe well is either not regarded or is
ill taken, when accordinge to equitie & Iustice I can nether be
accused openly as an offender nether yt excused accordynge to
the innocencye of my accions, when I may nether remayne
here in any estate or condicion in quyettness nor yet be sent
home agayne as vnworthye of this socyetie what wytt can
advice me, or what tonge will counsell me in this my perplexed
dystresse? yet of this I doe assure you that no course that can be
taken whatsover shall make me playe the dysymblynge hipocrit
nether carrye ij faces vnder one hoode, thoughte yt would fall
oute greatlye to my advantage for if I have favoure shewed me
I can acknowledge yt as farre forth as any man, howsover[3] I
have deserved yt, yf [on][4] the contrarye, with the which I ame
the more famyliarlye aquaintede, I cane vse pacyence &
obedyence because I knowe yt is my dewtye here, but love is

---

[1] A reference to Knollys's previous experience at sea, but ignoring his involvement
with his brother Henry and their withdrawal from Gilbert's expedition of 1578. See
pp. 16, 296.

[2] i.e. *jealousies.*

[3] In MS, *whatsoever* crossed out, and *howsoever* substituted.

[4] In MS, *of.*

not to be forced nor boughte but by love and this much more
I assure youe, were you possest of all the Indyans[1] (as thanckes
be to God you have opened a fayre gate towardes yt), yet if
my self might have a good portion in the same in doinge
somethinge agaynst my conscience, I protest vnto you I woulde
not [do so] for more then I canne expresse esteemynge yt vyle
tromperye & trashe in respecte of the imcomperable treasure of
an vnpoluted mynd,[2] but lett me not be mystaken in this as in
all thinges allmost I ame as if I shoulde chalendge[3] to my selfe
a pryvilee[4] of puertye above all others for I knowe I am as
others are as full of imperfeccions as maye be, but this I said
that one measure cannot meate all mens consciences, for that
maye be lawfull to me which is a scruple to another, the
lybertye whereof God forbed but should be lawfull to everye
honeste & true subiecte of her Maiestie. but fearinge to be
troublesome vnto youe this is the chiefest cause of my
wrytinge, the which I will knytt vp in as few Wordes as I canne/
[fol. 54v]
At my last beinge ashore with you dyninge at Captayne
Plattes,[5] you did openlie pronounce these wordes in generall,
havinge before this sed particular speeches to Master
Chameberlain & Master Longe touchinge ye same matter, the
some & conclusion of all which was that no man whatsoever
should proceed any farther in this action that did refuse to be
sworne, in manner and forme as is sett downe for him &
thought at that tyme I saide nothinge yet did I see yt
pryncipallye directed vnto me, and as I did then refrayne to
annswere only because I would not interrupte youe from any
of yoer busyness soe doe I beseche you havinge the lawe in
your owne handes, to take some such order as both myself and
such as you hold troublers of your quyett may have our

---

[1] Thus in MS, probably meaning *Indies*.

[2] The wording here suggests that religious scruples may have been a real factor in Knollys's decisions regarding the oaths of 20 November (see p. 141).

[3] Meaning *claim*?

[4] *Privilege* (?); or possibly, *privity*, meaning *priority*.

[5] Anthony Platt, the land captain to whom charge of Knollys's company had been committed, and who thereafter had sailed in Knollys's ship. See pp. 139, 149.

doome,[1] and y^t in such quiettness[2] as your procedyngs be not hyndered by any of vs for I assure you for my owne parte that I desyre nothinge more then the happye successe of this honorable action and if at any tyme I had bynne of other mynde I could have shewed yt longe before in other sort then I have done/ But I wilbe honest when others that you hold in better estymacion shall shewe them selves in ther ryght coullers. Thus, not expectinge any annswere but that at your convenyent leasure you will resolve vppon somme such course as I may knowe what to trust to/ I end, prayinge hearteley for your good successe. From abourde the Lettuce Lecester the 6 of Ianuarye.

Your most unhappy folower

Fraunces Knowlles/

Document 9

The Record kept aboard the Ship *Leicester*, October 1585 to March 1586 (British Library Harley MS 2202, fols. 55–70v).[3]

[The fragments of the journal from Knollys's ship, the *Leicester*, begin on fol. 55, the ninth page by the original numbering. Missing is the account of events between the departure from Plymouth on 14 September until the voyage from the Spanish coast to the Canaries. The first entry, according to the calculation by days, is that for the pre-dawn watch (4 a.m. to 8 a.m.) on 14 October.[4] The marginal entries on the later pages

---

[1] i.e. judgment pronounced.

[2] Meaning *quickness*, perhaps; or without further debate.

[3] For a description of this document and its relationship to the Knollys letter in Document 8, see p. 116, n. 1.

[4] The dates follow those established by the detailed record from Document 6, and in a few instances, by other accounts. Exact references in this document to events for certain days, such as 14, 19, and 26 October, and 3 November, have been useful. The four-hour watches have made it fairly simple to follow the records for a day, and the observations on latitude, made at midday, are recorded for the 12 noon to 4 p.m. watch. In a few cases, where the several accounts do not agree, the *Tiger* journal, with its more frequent statement on dates, has been preferred.

of the manuscript confirm dates thereafter and indicate locations.]

[fol. 55 (MS 9)][1]

October [14, a.m.]

From 4 to 8 we Caped[2] south w & by south & south amongst 8 glasse 6 leages, the windes at north a stife galle. In that watch we lost our viceadmerall & Capten Moone./[3]

From 8 to 12 we Caped south south w & south w amongst 8 glasse 6 leagues. in that watch we stroke our maine saile & went round with the Fleett. the winde at north a stout gale.[4]

[noon, 14 Oct.]

From 12 to 4 we caped s.s.w. 8 glasse 6 leagues in that watch we gave chasse [for] 2 glasse and put out both our topsailes but could not fettch him vp so we gave him over. the winde at north. a stife gale

From 4 to 8 we caped s.s.w. 8 glasse 6 leagues the winde at north a fresh gale. in that watch we tooke in our bonnet & hoysted our forcorse a flier./

From 8 to 12 we caped s.s.w. 8 glasse 5 leagues the winde at north a fresh gale.

[15 Oct. a.m.]

From 12 to 4 s.s.w. 8 glasse 5 leagues the winde at north, a freshe gale we put out our sprite saile & missen

From 4 to 8 s.s.w. 8 glasse 6 leagues the wind at north a stife gale we lost Captain Vaughan[5]

From 8 to 12 s.s.w. 8 glasse 5 leagues the winde at north, a freshe gale. all this waye good

[noon, 15 Oct.] Lat. 38 deg. 36 mintes.

From 12 to 4 s.s.w. 8 glasse 2 leagues the winde at north north w., litle winde. her way good.

From 4 to 8 s.s.w. 8 glasse 4 leagues the winde at north w., a freshe gale./

---

[1] The entries give first the Harley MS folio number, with the earlier page number in round brackets. Marginal notes from the MS appear without brackets, but editorial insertions have been bracketed.

[2] Cape is an obsolete verb meaning 'to head, to keep a course, bear up; to drift'. *OED*.

[3] Martin Frobisher, sailing in the *Primrose*, and Thomas Moone, Captain of the *Francis*.

[4] Gale, in Elizabethan English, meant a good sailing breeze.

[5] John Vaughan, captain of the *Drake*. He rejoined the fleet after several days.

From 8 to 12 s. and by w. 8 glasse a league & a halfe the winde at west, a litell breath

From 12 to 4 s.s.w. 8 glasse 4 leagues the winde at no*rth* & by east, a faire gale, her way good [16 Oct. a.m.]

From 4 to 8 we caped s.s.w. 8 glasse 5 leagues, the winde at no*rth* and by e*ast* a stiffe gale

From 8 to 12 s.s.w. 8 glasse 5 le*agues* the winde at no*rth* & by e*ast* a faire gale. we laide our shipp by the lee to make fast our bote

From 12 to 4 we capet s. and by w. 8 glasse 6 leagues, the winde at no*rth* and by E*ast* a stiffe gale. her waite good [noon, 16 Oct.] Lat. 37 deg. 35 mintes.

From 4 to 8 s. and by w. 8 glasse 6 leagues the winde at no*rth* a stiffe gale. in that watch we had a gust & tooke in our tope sailes & stro*o*ke our mainsaile & foresaile and tooke of our maine drabler[1]

From 8 to 12 s.s.w. 8 glasse 9 leagues and a half the winde at no*rth* and by e*ast*, a freshe gale.

From 12 to 4 s.w. & by s. 8 glasse 6 leagues the winde at no*rth* east & by no*rth* a fresh gale [17 Oct. a.m.]

From 4 to 8 s.w. and by s. 8 glasse 6 leagues the winde at no*rth* north E & by no*rth*/ we stoke[2] our for saile to fleett our tyes[3] & put out our topgall*ant* saile

From 8 to 12 s.w. and by s. 8 glasse 5 leagues and a halfe the winde at no*rth* e*ast* and by no*rth* a fresh gale.

From 12 to 4 s.s.w. 8 glasse 6 leagues the winde at northeast a stife gale. [noon, 17 Oct.] Lat. 35 deg. 39 mintes.

From 4 to 8 we caped s.s.w. 8 glasse 5 leagues, and when 4 glasse of that wa*t*ch was out we tooke in our maine saile & went henc*e* with our foresaile striken halfe mast downe the winde N e*ast* much wynde.

[fol. 55v (MS 9v)]

[1] The drabbler is a piece of canvas, laced to the bottom of the bonnet of a sail, to give greater depth. *OED.*

[2] i.e. *struck*?

[3] To 'come up' the tyes (ropes used in hoisting the topsail yards), so as to haul to more advantage, especially to change the situation of a tackle when the blocks are drawn together.

October

From 8 to 12 s.s. west 8 glasse 5 leagues, the winde at north E, much winde.

[18 Oct. a.m.]

From 12 to 4 s s w 8 glasse 5 leagues the wind at north E, much winde. our forsaile half mast downe

From 4 to 8 we caped s s w 8 glasse 4 leagues the winde at north E, a stife gale. the Ammirall[1] lost her great boate & her skife, and the Tigar his pinasse[2]

From 8 to 12 s s w 8 glasse 4 leagues the winde at north E much winde In that watch we had two great gustes and showers of raine in so much y[t] we tooke in our topsaile & sprittsaile & spanned hence before the sea. We lost the Fraunces[3]

[noon, 18 Oct.]

From 12 to 4 s.s. 8 glasse 4 leagues, the winde at north E, a faire gale./

From 4 to 8 s w & by s 8 glasse 4 leagues the winde at N E and by N a faire gale & when that watch was out the winde begayne to faynt

From 8 to 12 s s w 8 glasse 3 leagues the winde at north west a faire gale. in that watch we put out our topesailes./

[19 Oct. a.m.]

From 12 to 4 s s w 8 glasse 3 leagues, the wind at n.w., a faire gale./

From 4 to 8 s s w 8 glasse 2 leagues, the winde at w n w a litle winde./

From 8 to 12 s 8 glasse 2 leagues the winde at w and by s little winde. that day our generall commanded vs to put out our flagge in the mainetoppe & he himselfe with the George & the galley went round to gyve chayse, and the shippe which he chaysed was the Sea Dragon./[4]

[noon, 19 Oct.]

From 12 to 4 we went round with the Ammiral. the winde wexed to the s w & by w. we caped E 3 leagues and when that watch was out we laide hit [   ][5] with our maine saile & caped s her Leeward waye was s.E. and by E. So I saye frome the daye

[1] i.e. the 'Admiral', or Drake's ship, *Elizabeth Bonaventure*.
[2] The *Primrose* journal (p. 184) notes the loss of the *Tiger's* pinnace, and also that of the admiral, with six men aboard.
[3] Moone's ship, once more.
[4] The *Sea Dragon*, captained by Henry White, had been missing since 17 October (see p. 91).
[5] Word omitted in MS.

aforesaide vntill the nine teenth at a south sonne[1] our Leewarde way was East South E 10 leagues. that daye the Viceadmirall and *Captain* Vaughan came into the Fleete agayne./[2]

From 12 to 4 w and by s[3] her Leeward waye was North west our topemast stroke & by w, the winde at S and by w. a stiffe gale

From 8 to 12 we laye a hull and caped w and by n. her Leeward waye was n & by w 2 leagues, the winde at s w & by s a stiffe gale. in that watch we bare up with the Ammirall 3 tymes[4]

From 12 to 4 we did hull and caped north w. and by west 8 glasse her Leewarde waye north and by East 2 leagues, the winde at w S w much winde [20 Oct. a.m.]

From 4 to 8 we caped north west and by west 8 glasse, her Leeward waye north and by East 2 leagues the winde at w s w, much winde. and when that watch was out we set our forecorse and laide it about to the Southwardes. then the winde vered to the W

From 8 to 12 we caped S S W 8 glasse 2 leagues $\frac{1}{2}$ her way s. in that watch we set our mainecorse./

[fol. 56 (MS 10)]

From 12 to 4 we caped S S W 8 glasse 3 leagues the Leeward waye south & by w $\frac{1}{2}$ to the southwards, the winde at W.N.W., great gustes & raines October [noon 20 Oct.]

From 4 to 8 we caped S S W 8 glasse 3 leagues $\frac{1}{2}$ her waye South & by W. & halfe a poynt to the southwards, the winde at w.n.w. much winde with raine and gustes

From 8 to 12 we caped S S W 8 glasse 3 leagues & a halfe, which waye was good the winde at N W a stife gale. in that watch we put out our fore topsaile./

From 12 to 4 we caped S S W 8 glasse 4 leagues, the winde at [21 Oct. a.m.]

---

[1] i.e. *sun*. For the sailing weather at this time cf. p. 91.

[2] The return was on the 19th, according to the *Tiger* journal, but on the 17th according to the less reliable *Primrose* journal (see pp. 91, 184).

[3] The hours noted are apparently in error; they should be *4 to 8*. The day of the month was still 19 October, as figured by reckoning the watches recorded between this point and the time of specific happenings of 22 to 26 October, below.

[4] Events in the darkness, approaching midnight.

N.W. a faire gale. in that watch we put out our spritt saile & missen

From 4 to 8 we caped S S W 8 glasse 4 le*agues* $\frac{1}{2}$, the winde at N W, a stiffe gale./

From 8 to 12 we caped S S W 8 glasse 5 le*agues* the winde at N.N.W., a stife gale./ In that watch we had 3 or 4 great gustes. We [stooke][1] oure fore topsale. our shipp was very light so that we could beare but littell saile

[noon, 21 Oct.] From 12 to 4 we caped S S W 8 glasse 4 leagues, the winde at N E and by E, a faire gale./

From 4 to 8 we caped S.S.W. 8 glasse 4 leagues, the winde at N and by E, a steady gale./

From 8 to 12 we caped S.S.W. 8 glasse 4 leagues, the winde at N & by E, a steady gale./

[22 Oct. a.m.] From 12 to 4 we caped S.S.W. 8 glasse 5 le*agues*, the winde at no*rth* north w., a faire gale

From 4 to 8 we caped S and by W 8 glasse 3 le*agues* the wind n.n.w., a faire gale.

From 8 to 12 we caped S and by W – 8. In that watch our Generall gave chayse[2] and *our* bo*a*te went abourd *our* generall*s* w*i*th our Captayne./ So I say from halfe an ower past 8 to 12 we caped S E & by E 7 glasse 3 le*agues* $\frac{1}{2}$ the winde at N.N.W., a small gale

[noon, 22 Oct.] Latitude 30 degre*es* 34 min-ett*es* From 12 to 4 we caped S. and by W. 8 glasse 5 le*agues* her way halfe a poynte to the westward*es* of the S & by W the winde at N W, a fresh gale./

From 4 to 8 we caped S and by W 8 glasse 5 le*agues* her waye south and a halfe a poynt to the E*a*stwardes the winde w. and by S, a faire gale

From 8 to 12 we caped S and by W 8 glasse 4 leagues $\frac{1}{2}$, her way south & halfe a poynt E*a*sterly the winde W and by S, a faire stedy gale./

[23 Oct. a.m.] From 12 to 4 we caped S and by W 8 glasse 5 le*agues*, her way south & halfe a poynt E*a*sterly the winde at W. a faire gale./

From 4 to 8 we caped S and by W 8 glasse 4 le*agues* $\frac{1}{2}$, her way

[1] i.e. struck. [2] Cf. pp. 92, 184.

south halfe a poynt to the Eastwards, the winde at the west and halfe a poynt to the westwards

From 8 to 12 we caped S and by W 8 glasse 4 leagues, her way s & halfe a poynt to the Eastwards, and when 6 glasse of that watch was out I saw the lande.[1] Hit bare of me s w & halfe a poynt to the S wards about 14 leagues of, I beinge north east & halfe a poynte to the northwards from it. At one of the cloke I did sett it & it was in this forme.[2]

[fol. 56v (MS 10v)]

Canarys[3]

From 12 to 2 we caped S S W 4 glasses 2 leagues. then we laide it about westwardes. so I say from 2 to 4 we caped N W 1 league & a halfe the winde then beinge at S W & by W & halfe a poynt to the westwardes, a faire gale, & when that watch was out we laide hitt about to the southwardes & caped S S E. presently, the winde vered to the N then we laide it about agayne. So I saye [   ].[4]   October [noon, 23 Oct.]

From 4 to 8 we caped w and west & by north 8 glasse 3 leagues the winde at north, a small gale./

From 8 to 12 we caped w 8 glasse 4 leagues the winde at N, a smale glandering[5] gale./

From 12 to 4 we caped W 6 glasse 5 leagues the winde at N W & by N. a fresh gale   [24 Oct. a.m.]

From 4 to 8 we caped W 6 glasse 3 leagues & a halfe & when the 6 glasse of that watch was out I went up to the toppe & sawe the land which I sawe the day before which was Lancerata, the Easternmost Illand of all the Canaryes./

The next day we dyscovered the Illand of Forteventura,[6] but   [25 Oct.]

---

[1] The date agrees with that in Document 7 (p. 109). The arrival at the Canaries was on 24 October, according to the *Tiger* and *Primrose* journals (pp. 92, 184).

[2] For the drawing at the bottom of fol. 56v see Plate IV.

[3] From this point the writer customarily placed at the top of each page the name of the place at which events occurred. For editorial reasons these notations of place hereafter have been moved to the margins.

[4] The sentence is unfinished in the MS.

[5] i.e. increasing or swelling.

[6] The *Tiger* journal (p. 92) reports the arrival on 24 October at Lanzarote and Fuerteventura, and the decision to move on to Palma.

not knowing certaynly whether it was the Grand Canaria or
hitt, the *generall* sent for most of the Ancient masters *to come*
abourd his shipp to heare ther opinions & finding them not to
agree, he bare in with the lande and by the next day in the
morning we were within 5 or 6 leagues to the lande and then
was it certaynely knowne to be the same.[1] then we cast about
to sea agayne and tooke counsell to make towardes an Illand
called Pallma, one of the farthest of all the Canaryes, by the
Incouragement of a Spaniard borne there and in his youth
banished who promysed to bring vs without danger to
commande the whole Illande

26
[Oct.]
Twesdaye[2] we dyscovered the Grande Canarye & passed
both by it and by the Illand of Teneriffe, the pick[3] of which
Illand is an exceding heighte, the highest that ever I saw, the
toppe of which hill is piked like a steple and thereof called the
pick, always covered with snow being in the cold region. For
you shall in the fairest daye see the clowdes benethe the toppe
of the hill. never man could come nere the toppe but many
have assayed and put it in proof, but few have returned agayne.
it is sayde to be 30 miles high taken by Instruments, for
otherwyse it cannot be knowne. there are many that have
dyscovered this Iland 50 leagues in the sea. I suppose this
Illand to be next in welth and accompt vnto Canaria, being
very well peopled both of horsmen and footmen. and thus
much for the Illand, of which we onely passed allongst by
Sea.

28
[Oct.]
We held one our course south & south and by west towardes
Palma. in the morninge we espied a saile a farr of to which we
gave no chayse because we thought to have taken the benefitt
of the winde to put into Palma. but comming with in 3 or 4
leagues of the land, we were so becalmed that we could not

[1] Fuerteventura which lies between Lanzarote and Gran Canaria.
[2] The marginal dates here are according to days of the month. 26 October 1586
was a Tuesday (C. R. Cheney, *Handbook of Dates*, Table 21). The *Tiger* journal (p. 93)
dates the arrival at Gran Canaria on the 27th (Wednesday), and the voyage between
Teneriffe and Palma on the 28th.
[3] i.e. *peak*.

possebly fetch [fol. 57 (MS 11)] the land, but were constrayned Palma[1]

to ply up and downe. wherefore by commandement of our November
generall the pinasses were made toward the saile before spoke
of which was a French man of warr, the Capten whereof was
well knowne to our Generall and to sum others of our company
by reason he had bene with him in his last viadge. His name was
Monsieur Montayne. this Frenchman with 4 or 5 other sayles his shippe
where of he was Admirall lay of and on of these Illandes having 140 tonne
an intent to take the spoyle of sum one of them, but especially
of Palma as they saide which we meant to attempt. of them we
likewyse heard that the Indian Fleete to the number of 17 sailes
were past a 20 or 22 dayes before.[2] The same night after[3] the
Frenchman had bene spoken withall, the Skout, a smale shippe
of our fleete, was by our generall sent to looke for one of our
pinasses, since which tyme we never harde of her, whether
forecebly taken or voluntary consentinge to goe with him[4]
we know not./

the 29, 30 & 31 the winde being contrary we were compelled [29-31
to ly attry lest we shuld have bin dryven so farr back from the Oct.]
Illand of Palma where we meant to have landed as that we
shuld not have ben able to have recovered it agayne.

[1] *Palma* is at the centre of the top line in the MS. The marginal notation, November,
is also at the top of the page, but obviously relates to the events beginning with the
marginal figure *1* (below).

[2] Cf. p. 93. According to the *Primrose* journal, the French captain, whose ship was
probably an armed merchantman, had hoped to meet the Spanish treasure fleet, and
he told of seeing forty sail of Spaniards at Cape St Vincent. See p. 184. That encounter,
if 20 or 22 days before his talk with Drake, occurred about 6 or 8 October. The first
of the two treasure fleets of this year had reached Spain by 22 September, but that
from Peru, having been delayed at the Azores, met the escorting galleys from Spain
on 6/16 October (Wright, *Further Eng. Voyages*, pp. xxxi–xxxii; Oppenheim, *Naval
Tracts . . . Munson*, pp. 127–8). The Venetian ambassador in Spain, having noted earlier
the arrival of the first fleet, commented in his despatch of 15/25 October, that 'they
think Drake has missed the Peruvian fleet by his staying at Galicia'. *C.S.P.Ven.
1581–1591*, pp. 122, 123.

It was his missing the latter fleet by twelve hours, in a storm, which Drake lamented
in his letter of July 1586 to Burghley (Lansdowne MS 51, fols. 27–8, pr. in Corbett,
Sp. War, pp. 83–5). He told the Spaniards at Cartagena also that he had missed the
Indian fleets 'by twelve hours'. Wright, *Further Eng. Voyages*, pp. 122, 130; Castellanos,
Discurso, p. 300. On his hopes for the fleets of 1586, see p. 263, n. 6.

[3] In the MS the words, *the same night after*, are by error repeated.

[4] i.e. the Frenchman. The *Scout* returned on 5 November, as did the *Hope*. See p. 95.

1
[Nov.]

2

The 1 of November being All Saintes Day, the winde being vered about, we made a gayne towardes Palma & the next night after, we being come within 2 leagues or sum what lesse of the Iland, we lost the Hope, no man knowinge which way or how. All that night we lay before the Iland, where by the fiers & lightes that were made vpon the shore we might perceive we were dyscovered whether by former intelligence or otherwise I know not.

3

The next day we packte on all our sailes & bare alongest by the shore towardes the towne of Palma, before which we came about two of the clocke in the after noone with intent to have landed & taken the towne for the relief of our fleete, beyng the nexte day after All Saintes Day.[1] But when our shippes came before the towne thinking to cast anker out of Danger of theyr bulwarks, the Admirall beyng formost sounded & could finde no grounde under 40 within muskett shott to the Shore, & when our shippes were come within Danger of the towne they bestowed powder & shott franckly vpon vs out of theyre fortes. The first shott was made at our Admirall, which went fayre over. The second being likewise shott at her strake

Palma

atwixte our Generalls legges, [fol. 57v (MS 11v)] standing in his gallery with Captain Frobusher and C. Carlell of the one side and Captain George[2] on the other, the splinters of the planke where on they stod hurte George a litell, but ther was no more hurt done by it being a mynione shott. there were divers other shott bestowed on the Ayde[3] but next to the Admirall the Lettice Lester was the fayrest marke, for at her did they spend most shott & did hitt her, but only with one pece harde by one of her guner rome portes of the larbord with eyther a Canon or a Culvering Shott which entered not past 3 Inches, for the strength of her great beames gave such an

---

[1] For other accounts of the events of 3 November see pp. 94, 110, 184. The date in the margin here, rather than the day after All Saints Day, as noted in the text, is correct.

[2] Probably the land captain, George Barton, to whom the writer at a later point (p. 135) refers as 'Captain George'.

[3] The *Aid*, one of the queen's ships, captained by Edward Wynter.

incounter to the shott that it rebounded a pikes length from her. The Admirall was hitt agayne close by the water, a canon shott in the waist cleane thorow one side, the bullet remayning in the shipp without any hurte done to any man. dyvers other narrow escapes were in the fleet but no shipp hitten. The whole number of the great shott which was shott at vs that day was 18.[1] But the *generall* because he coulde finde no conuenient ankeringe for our shippes in safety, nor good landinge for the soldiers, he sett saile agayne & all the flett & put to the sea, the winde beinge at that instant purposely[2] vered southerly, without spendinge any shott on the towne. This towne lies in the northeast side of the Iland & is no doubt very riche. there is a castell which standes in the middest of the towne but somewhat to the W N W end of it, where there is likwise a Bullwarke scituated lower and nerer the sea side in which is the best ordinance. For from thence came all the canon shott. there is an other bulwarke in the eastern end of the towne which did playe with great ordenance vpon vs. in these 3 doth consist all the strength of the towne for it is not walled neyther hath any other fortification. by coniecture there maye be sum 500 men of all sortes. They did march alonge the East end of the towne by the sea shore with about 5 or 6 ensignes. We were so farr of that we could not descerne the men but in that end of the towne is there greatest strength. The Iland is excedinge high lande, the highest of all except Teneriffe. there growes one the toppe of the hills high trees, with which the highest partes of the hills are covered, beinge so steepe, cragy, and diffuse that it semes a strange wildernes. the trees as we thought are firre. The K of Spayne hath yearly a great tribute for the pitch & tarre had yearly out of those trees. & in the lower parte growe great store of sugar canes yealdinge great comodyty. The same day was there orders made by the *generall* to be observed by all those which shulde beare armes in the voyadge./

[1] The number of shots, according to other accounts, was 20 or 23. See pp. 94, 110 184.
[2] i.e. conveniently for the purpose.

1 In primis, that what person soever shall wander or stragle from
his ensigne without commandment shall receue punishment
according to the law of armes, to wit death

2 That no man offer to take any pilladge or make any spoyle
before proclimation made vppon payne of death

3 That no souldier presume to breake or burne any church chest,
locke, or doore, or any other thing locked or fastened, without
order from his captain of whome chardge of any such thinge
shalbe required

4 That no Captain gyve any such order for any breakinge of
Gomera howses [fol. 58 (MS 12)]¹ or chestes without direction from
Nouember the generall or his deputy for the tyme being

5 That in every pinnasse or boate that shall lande any men the
Captain & master do appoynt sum one especiall man of trust
to kepe the same & that the saide person suffer not any man to
[bring] abourd any pilladge whatsoever without order from
the generall or his deputy and that no pinasse goe from the
shore vpon payne of death

6 That no man of what condition soever retayne or kepe to
himselfe any gould, siluer, Iewellry, or any thinge of speciall
price, for that there shalbe order taken where the same shalbe
deliverede. yf any souch thinge be founde with them or
hereafter vnderstood & iustly approved² that then he shall not
only lose the benefitt that might growe vnto him by the
voiadge, but shalbe reputed as a person non worthy of credit.

7 Item, for as much as we are bounde in conscience and required
also in duty to yielde an honest account of our doinges &
procedings in this action & that her Maiesty [ ]³ shalbe
appoynted & persons of cerditt shalbe assigned, unto whom

¹ The words *Gomera* and *Nouember* occur in the MS at the top of the new page.
The numerals in the margin refer to items in the list of orders, rather than to dates
Plans for the distribution of the orders are mentioned briefly in the *Summarie* (p. 223).
They had been drawn up during the stop at Bayona and Vigo (cf. p. 82) and were
announced as the time for land attacks approached.

² i.e. *proved*.

³ In the MS, the words *Her Maiesty* are repeated and then crossed out. Several
words (possibly *may be served, there*) seem to have been omitted by error as the orders
were copied into the record.

such porcions of goods of speciall price as golde, silver, Iewells, or any other thinge of moment or valew shalbe brought and delyvered, the which shall remayne in chestes vnder the chardge of 4 or 5 severall kayes, and they shalbe committed vnto the custody of souch Captens as are of best account in the Fleet.[1]

Youre loving Frende,
F. Drake

We put of from the Ilande the same eveninge and [came] alongest with the Ilande of Gomera at that night, and by the next morninge we were within 5 leagues of it. our generall meant to have landed there but we were so becalmed that before we shuld have dubled the N W poynt of the Iland we shuld have been sagged with the sea vppon the Lee shore. by which meanes and for not loosing any more tyme,[2] we put of from this Illand and bare with Fiero[3] beinge the most sotherne Ile. The Illand of Gomera is not so bigge as Palma, not so fruitfull. we could see no wood in it & as they say there is but one towne in all the Illande, and in that one castell but Indifferently fortefyed, the which we could not see. neyther can it be verye rich because it is but sclenderly inhabited.

We sayled all that day and night, having verye little winde, and the next daye being the 3[4] of November, we Fell with the Iland [5 Nov.] of Fiero, where there landed 500 men.[5] the generall and most parte of the captens did lande. There came vnto our generall a Spayneard who made offer to present him with the best thinges in the Ile, and [said] that within 5 monethes the Ile had bin twyse spoyled with Frenchmen who had lefte with them an

[1] This list of orders was probably distributed to each officer or ship commander. The rules regarding records of pillage became the basis for later critical comments in this journal regarding some actions by Drake and Carleill.
[2] The *Tiger* journal (p. 94) indicates that Drake consulted his captains on this decision.
[3] i.e. *Hierro*. *Fero* is the spelling in the *Tiger* journal.
[4] The figure resembles 3 in the MS, but 5 was probably intended. Cf. pp. 95, 110.
[5] The other accounts give somewhat larger figures for the landing party. See pp. 64, 95, 185, 224.

131

English boy, who likewise tould our *generall* that there was
some catell in the Illand but they were very poore & leane,
neyther was there any freshe water in the Iland but what comes
out of a tree in most strange manner.[1] we founde certayne cakes
of pitch heaped vp by the sea side & that is thought to be the
chiefest commodyty of the Ile. I could see no wood nor cattell
there. it is the [fol. 58v (MS 12v)] lowest of all the Ilandes and
stones of it showes like dross or pindust comming of the smithes
forge, not vnlike Iron, of which I suppose it takes the name of
Fiero.[2] there is good landinge in the Easterne side of the Iland
and a very good place for ballast but no ankeringe vnder an
100 fedom water hard by the shore./

We set saile towardes the coast of Africa,[3] leaving Fiero with
out taking anythinge from them. neyther did the Spaniard
bringe anything to our *generall* according to promise.

We discovered the coast of Africa[4] by the which we sailed
alonge to Cape Blanke, as well to meete with sum shippes yf
any were sturringe as for the great aboundance of fishe we
were in hope to take for the relevinge of our men, of which
we tooke good store with hookes & lines only, beinge vnder
sayle & som tyme lyinge a hull[5] an hower or two. The fish we
founde most store of was sea Breames and pargoses, beinge of
a bigger sorte but in my opynion all one fyshe.[6] we tooke
likewise dogfishe which did sum what relieue us for the present.
beinge 3 or 4 dayes alongst this coaste, which is a very lowe
lande & a very white sandy grounde, the lande dankishe and
[   ]esky,[7] we found 9 or 10 fadom water in running 10
leagues at 5 leagues or 6 leagues of the shore.

Fiero
Nouember

6 day
7 day
lat. 26
degrees
19 min.
9 day

---

[1] This narrative resembles the other accounts. The MS variant of the *Summarie*
(see p. 224, n. 6) mentions collecting some fresh water from a pit.

[2] This observation suggests that the writer was acquainted with Latin, and that he
had a degree of education beyond that of the common soldier or sailor.

[3] In the MS, after the word *Africa*, the words *by the which we sailed* were written and
then crossed out in order that the statement about leaving Fiero might be inserted.

[4] On these dates of early November compare pp. 65, 96, 185.

[5] 'Sails furled and helm fixed alee'. *OED*.

[6] Sea breams are identified in *OED*. Porgy in Spanish is *pargo*.

[7] Undeciphered letters.

In the morning about 8 a clocke we discovered the cape[1] 11 day
where we sawe at the entringe in *with* the cape a shelfe south
and sumwhat to the westwards from the cape/ We went ouer
it in dublinge the Cape eavning 7 fadom water, but in comming
out our Ammirall had but 5 fadom water/ bearinge sumwhat
nearer the point a league from the cape/ A shipp of 1000 toones
may boldly passe over it. a ship of 50 or 60 toones may at any
tyme double hard by the shore & have yenough to passe ouer.[2]
there was in the Bay a man of warr of 200 toones to whome our
ge*nerall* gave chayse, but vnderstandinge he was a Frenchman,
he sent for the Capten aboard and frendly entertayned him,
by whom our ge*nerall* was certefyed that there was no good to
be done there,[3] who then descried a sayle and gave chayse to
her, being right in our course to Ca*pe* de Verd, but she escaped   12
by reason of the night. So, having a prosperous gale, we   Lat 22
continewed our course So*uth* W.   degrees
                                   49 *minutes*
In the night we sawe great store of herringes. as we sayled
my Capten stooke one with a fis*h*gige.[4] they are farre bigger
than ours vppon the English coast. lickwyse we sawe great
store of flieinge fyshes, sum fallinge into our bo*a*te, sum into
our pinasses, & sum into the chaynes of our shippes, and they
are *as* good meate as hearinges, & rather better and allmost as
great as millets,[5] [fol. 59 (MS 13)] or full so bigge. the 16 daye,   *Saint* Eago
the winde continuing at N*orth* and by E*ast*, we dyscovered   Nouember
lande w*h*ich was one of the Iles of Cape Verde called Bona   15/
Vista, 23 leagues short of S*aint* Iacamo.[6] we passed alongest by   Latitude
the E*a*sternside to*o* farr of to make any dyscripsion of it./   15 degrees
                                                                2 *minutes*
                                                                16

---

[1] Instead of the 11th, other accounts place the arrival at the cape on Saturday, the 13th. See pp. 65, 110, 224. 13 November 1585 was a Saturday (Cheney, *Handbook of Dates*).

[2] Drake's ship, the *Bonaventure*, the largest of the fleet, was of 600 tons (see Table of Ships). Here is further evidence of the diarist's knowledge of seamanship.

[3] This incident is mentioned in other accounts, but they suggest several French ships here. Cf. pp. 65, 110, 186, 224.

[4] A fish spear. *OED*.

[5] i.e. mullets. See *OED*.

[6] The island of Santiago. In the MS, the name was written first as *St. Eago* and then changed to *St. Iacamo*. The Map Text (p. 65) agrees with these dates.

The 17 day in the morninge we passed allongst by the Ile of
Mayo,[1] which is but 4 leagues short of Saint Iacamo, but a
smale Ilande, not altogeather barren. Goates are the chiefest
meates that these Iles do yielde. Beinge passed from thence,
we might dyscover the Iland of Saint Iacamo with which we
bare, lieing from vs S W & by W, & about 5 of the cloke we
came to [anchor][2] very nere the shore on the E N E side of
Ilande,[3] where we landed presently 220 men about 7 a cloke at
night, Captain Carleill Lifftenant generall, Captain Powell
Serieant maior, and Captain Morgan & Captain Samson
corporalls of the Fielde, and divers other captens, eache of them
in there places.[4] my Captain himsealfe went ashore with the
generalls lycense, carryinge with him a 140 men.[5] so all
togeather we marched most parte of the night the waye to the
towne of Saint Iacamo, which was very ill by reason of often
mountaynes & rockes.[6] and beinge come within lesse then an
English mile to the towne we reposed till it was day, not
knowinge where we were, beinge guyded only by the noyse
of people and barkinge of dogges & the hearinge of great pieces
shott of by the townsmen. and at breake of day we devided
company into 3 partes, meaninge to enter into the towne
3 severall wayes, and that in this manner. my Captains company
beinge a 140 was adioyned with the Tygar & Whitt Lyons
company, being in the whole 250 men. these were placed in
the right winge led by my captain, Captain Samson and Captain
Platt.[7] Captain Samson tooke out of the Tygers and White
Lyons company 30, whereof there was 4 rankes of shotte &

---

[1] The island of Maia. Cf. p. 186.

[2] In MS, another.

[3] On the date of arrival, 17 November, see below, p. 135 and note 4 and also pp. 97, 186.

[4] On the organization of the troops for attacking and entering the town see also the MS variant of the Summarie (p. 226 and notes).

[5] Since Knollys was a naval officer, he apparently needed special permission to lead soldiers.

[6] Other complaints about the difficult march are on pp. 98, 226.

[7] Captain Sampson was now performing as one of the two corporals of the field. Cf. p. 226, n. 9. Anthony Platt was the land captain who was afterwards assigned to the Leicester (see pp. 138, 149).

two of longe bowes. Richard Stanton, my *Captains* Lifftenant,[1] tooke out of our company 30 more *of* like sorte. these were winges before our troupe. Cap*tain* Powell & Captain George [Barton] led as many more on[2] the left winge, George and Goringe[3] leadinge 2 troupes as C*aptain* Samson and M*aste*r Stanton did before. in the middest, but sumwhat after the rest came C*aptain* Carlell wi*th* the maine battaile, in which were 600 men.[4] All these shuld have entred 3 severall wayes, but the day being broken and we marchinge, we might see all before vs the people of the town runninge vp into the mountaynes for there better securety, havinge so stepe a bottome & so great a hill betwixte them & vs as it was not possible for vs to cum to them. so comming to the dyssendinge of the hill, the towne we sawe vnder us quite abandoned, & where we thought to have entred 3 severall wayes we found but one waye, w*hich* wold have ben greatly to oure disadvantage yf there had ben many solders or men of valewe to have kept the same, for there was vpon the tope of the hill a plate form or sconce w*hich* stode in the E*aster*n*e*nd of the towne, planted vppon the waye w*hich* we had to descend done to very good purpose, had it bene kept, in w*hich* there was [fol. 59v (MS 13v)] but 3 smale pieces of Iron. our descendinge was so narrow as that but 2 could go togeather and lickwise it was very stepe and open vpon the face of the towne. But M*aste*r Stanton wi*th* 30 of my

Saint Eago Nouember

---

[1] Richard Stanton, eventually promoted to a military captaincy at Cartagena (see p. 174), was not among the land captains at the start of the voyage (see pp. 47, n. 4, 298), although he was so designated in the 1589 editions of the *Summarie* (see p. 215, n. 1).

[2] In MS, *one*.

[3] 'Captain Barton' is the leader named in the *Summarie* (p. 227).

[4] The number of men landed was 600, according to the *Primrose* journal (p. 156), but 1,000, according to the *Summarie* (p. 225).

These events were reported afterwards (9/19 February 1586) by the Venetian ambassador in Spain, as follows: Having arrived on the 27th (i.e. 17/27) November, the fleet anchored at St Martin, half a league away from the city, out of shot of the fort, and landed some 3,000 men. 'At day break, in good order, they marched on the town which offered no resistance except to prevent the English ships from casting anchor in the harbor.' The inhabitants fled by night, with their possessions, and the governor left at daybreak. *C.S.P.Ven. 1581–1591*, p. 140. The *Primrose* journal mentioned that a few shots were fired when the fleet arrived, probably before the night march.

masters men was one of the firste that entred the towne in very
peaceable manner but for 2 or 3 shott, shott of [by] the
Spaniards which fledde when we came into the towne. there
was none lefte but certayne ould women whome we founde at
there beades & others sick in the hospitall.[1] the rest were all fled
with the chiefest of there wealth. Yet was there many good
thinges lefte for the prouision of our flete. the first ansient[2]
displayed was my captens one the tope of the bishops house,
beinge the chiefest and stateliest in all the towne & standinge
so as it had the commandinge of all the rest. the towne was
governed by a Bishop, a man of great account amongst them,[3]
& by a Governor of the K. of Spaine. we learned that vpon
the view of our shipps there fell a division amongest them
bredde by feare. For the Bishope declared himsealfe to be for
Don Antonio of Portingall,[4] thinkinge by like we had bin sent
thether by him. the governor & his sorte were for the Kinge of
Spayne, & in this factious and mutinous manner they all rane
awaye, not daringe to trust one another.

The towne is seated vpon the southwest side of the Iland, the
Bishops [house] standinge above all the rest in the east ende of
the towne right before the harbor, having in each side of it a
platt forme well furnished with brasse ordinance, which belike
was provided for vs, for they say it had not bene there[5] but
2 monthes before our comminge, lefte by the Armathos of the
K of Spayne. all this is in the southeast end of the towne. there
is another platt forme in the west ende of the towne, sumthing
without the towne in which there was likewise very good
ordinance, but the worst of the three. all the ordinance was

[1] Cf. p. 187.
[2] i.e. ensign. The MS variant of the *Summarie* states: 'Captayne Sampson takynge
a bulwarke for his place of stand, and Captayne Barton the market place, the
livetenaunte generall sent presently certayne ensigns to be placed, that our fleet might
see the Seint Georges cross florishe in the enemyes fortresse.' (See p. 226, n. 9.)
Knollys's men were with Sampson.
[3] Cf. p. 188.
[4] i.e. the Portuguese pretender. Rumours of such a connection with Drake's
expedition had been widespread before his departure.
[5] In the MS, after *there*, the word *longe* was written and then crossed out.

Brasse, the greatest parte of them of Portingall brasses, which we found lyinge in the streetes and in dyvers howses vnmounted. But I suppose there was no lesse then 30 or 40 brasse pieces,[1] whereof Captain Carlell had a Culveringe of Brasse gyven him by the generall and Captain Powell another whole culveringe of Brasse for a memoriall of the place. The rest were dystributed and put abourd divers of the shippes [fol. 60 (MS 14)] The Lettice Lester reaceuinge but 2 morter peces which wold, as I thinke, not have ben receaued to any other shipp, being in respect of the rest of litle worth./[2]

St. Eago
Nouember

This towne was divided in the middest with a trench, the hilles in each side vere steepe & marvelous heighe, which height of the hills of nature shulde prove it[3] a valley, but the narrowes betwext these hills shuld rather prove it a trench artificially made. but the most probable reason that I can alldege is the ryver running thorow the botome, the violence where of may be so great after much rayne as it maye weare this bottome more & more.[4] It raynes but seldome in this place, some tymes not in a yeare or 2 or 3, but when it doth fall it is with great violence so that thereby my reason is confermed.[5]

The only waye to invade this towne is to lande secretly in the south East side of the Iland and then to march to this trench, for I finde it the best place of defence to march in the valley to the towne, the which wilbe easy to enter, for that waye there is neyther fortification nor any other strenght but of a many naked men which will make no resistance./

This valley or trench is most fruitfull & pleasante, having great store of Quoques trees[6] which are vere heigh & streyght,

[1] Cf. pp. 186, 227, 276.

[2] This is the first of a succession of comments in the *Leicester* journal that reveal a growing jealousy regarding Drake's relations with Carleill.

[3] In the MS, *at*.

[4] The surmise is correct. The modern name of the town, Ribeira Grande, comes from the stream that flows down a narrow valley toward the sea. Duncan, *Atlantic Islands*, pp. 174–5. See also the maps (Plates III(A), (B), (C)).

[5] Cf. p. 191. In the Cape Verdes there is very little precipitation, the rainy season being short and uncertain. Duncan, *Atlantic Islands*, p. 158.

[6] i.e. the coco palm. Cf. pp. 187, 229.

& the fruite thereof most excellent and wholesome, yieldinge both meat and drinke. one of them is sufficient for 2 men to make a meale of. there is lickwise great plenty of Oranges and the fayrest that I did ever see./

Likewise plantens, a most excellent fruite, figges, dates, suger canes in great store, Corne better then rice, Potatos, Coleworthes, oynions,[1] and many other fruites which I cannot write./

Sainte Ago
Nouember [fol. 60v (MS 14v)] This trench may be very well termed the Nursery of all or the most parte of there wealth. The rest of the Illand cannot be very fruitfull by reason it is stony & for the little raine that falleth there. The only thinge I see it yieldes is cotton, the which in great abundance do growe over the whole Ilande.[2] there is lickwise in sum parte of the Ilande Saten[3] growinge, but I saw no great quantety of it./

18 In the morning, we havinge entred the towne,[4] the generall came from his shipp in his skiffe to the towne, and seeinge it English he reioysed not a little. there were in the harborow seven sailes called carvells loden with divers commodyties,[5] the certayne knowledge & dysposition whereof is only knowne to the generall. I [have] knowne not any made privie to it, but whome himsealfe imployed in takinge out of all thinges within the said Carvells.[6] When the lifftenant generall and all the whole company were come into the towne, every capten was appoynted a quarter for him sealfe and his company by the lifftenant generall who plaied the harbinger himsealfe that day. but the distribution he made was so vnequall as that sum had all, sum nothinge, which was a dyscontentment to many,

[1] i.e. coleworts (see *OED*) and onions.

[2] At this period the crops included fruits, Brazilian maize for export to the West African coast, sugar cane and cotton. Duncan, *Atlantic Islands*, pp. 159-60, 167, 168, 171-2.

[3] This product has not been identified.

[4] The date of entry, 18 November, agrees with that in the Map Text (see p. 65). No reference to a noisy celebration occurs in the *Leicester* account. On the question of the date and the description in the *Summarie*, see pp. 225, 227 and notes.

[5] Cf. p. 190.

[6] The comment points out a deviation from the announced orders regarding booty (see above, p. 130).

Ca*ptain* Carlell himselfe and all the other land Ca*ptains* beinge
placed in howses of greatest wealth, except only Ca*ptain*
Winter, who was appoynted one of the best howses in the
towne,[1] every man pleading possession of what he could get,
all *of which* was caried abourde *with* as much diligence and
cunninge as might be devised. there was, for [avoiding] facions
sake, a dystribution of Wine, Oyle, and meale. For some it had
bene as good neuer a whitt as neuer the better. my Ca*ptain*
warded all that day and watcht all that night vpon the
Plateforme one the westerne ende of the towne.

    The day followinge all officers and Captens were established
in there places & over chardge publickly delyuered them by
the g*enerall*, namely, Ca*ptain* Carlell, Lieftenant g*enerall*;
Ca*ptain* Powell, Serieant Maior, Morgan and Samson, corporall
of the fielde, with other officers also appoynted. & in presence
of them all Ca*ptain* Platt was appoynted to have the chardge of
my Ca*ptains* company, Ca*ptain* Goringe of Ca*ptain* Forbyshers,
Ca*ptain* Sissill[2] of Ca*ptain* Winter*s*, with Marchant and
Hannam, who was [fol. 61 (MS 15)] appoynted other
Companyes in chardge.[3] The same daye, the counsell being
togeather,[4] there was brought by one Master Niccolles, a
preacher,[5] a Draught of certayne oathes,[6] none *of which* was
necessary for vs to be sworne vnto.[7] the first was the vsual oathe
to the supremasy, the second [the oath of] the lyfftenant generall
by lande to the generall, the thirde the Captens oathe to the

19

Saint Eago
Nouember

---

[1] Favoured treatment for Wynter may have been the result of his connections at
court, and possibly a closer acquaintance with Walsingham than Knollys enjoyed.
See pp. 215, n. 1, and 299.

[2] i.e. William Cecil, serving at this time as a land captain.

[3] These were assignments to military officers of men from the various ships, for
periods of operations ashore.

[4] The council of officers, according to Drake's custom.

[5] Philip Nicholls, Drake's chaplain. See p. 297.

[6] The oaths are not mentioned in the *Tiger* and *Primrose* journals, but in the
newsletter (Document 7) is a note about the council of 20 November and the swearing
of loyalty. An oath for the vice admiral is mentioned specifically there, but no dissent
is reported (see p. 110). The account in the *Summarie* also is brief, with a possible hint
of some disagreement appearing only in the MS variant (see p. 233 and n. 2).

[7] The view seems to be that seamen, not regularly land forces, were exempt; or
possibly the writer thought that Knollys's men, on a private ship, need not be sworn.

generall, the fourth and last was the private mans oathe to the
Capten vnder whom he was to serve and all other *of* his officers,
the trwe coppy of all w*h*ich [oaths][1] hereafter followeth:/

The Coppy of Divers o*a*thes ministred to the
generall and all his Company for the most parte the 20 of
Nouember Anno 1585 in the ch*i*efe towne of the Illand
of S*ain*t Iacamo
To her Maiesty

Thou shall sweare in thy conscience thou dost acknowld*g*e
the Queens Ma*i*esty Eli*z*abeth our gratious soueraine is and by
Godes worde ought to be supre*m*e governour[2] ouer all *p*ersons
as well ec*c*lesiasticall as Civill with in her realmes and dominions
next and Im*m*ediately vnder God, and that no forraine prince,
prelate, or potentate hath or ought to have any sup*r*emasy or
Iurisdiction w*i*thin the sam*e*.

The Lifften*n*ant generall

Furthermore, thou shall sweare dilligently and faithfully to
the vtter*m*ost of thy knowledge,[3] experience, and power to
*p*erforme the duty of lifften*n*ant generall in all Lande services
during this action, according to the trust reposed in thee, so
God helpe thee and by the contents of his holy gospell

To all The Capteyns

Further*m*ore thou shalte sweare that y*o*u will truly and
dilligently to the vttermost of [thy][4] abylety during the whole
tyme and course of this action to dyscharge the duty of Capten,
as well in followinge obediently the articles and direction of
the generall and his officers therevnto appoynted, as in doing
right indif*f*erently to every *p*erson vnder [thy][4] charge, so God
helpe thee and by the Contents of the holy gospell

[1] In the MS, *others.*
[2] The word *head* was written, but crossed out, and *governour* inserted.
[3] The word *power* was crossed out, and *knowledge* substituted. These changes
probably represent corrections of slips in copying.
[4] In the MS, *there.*

To every private man

Furthermore you shall sweare that you shall dutefully and faithfully *performe* the partes of trew subiects to her saide Ma*i*esty and to be obedient to your Capten and all other officers appoynted to take charge ouer you during the whole ty*m*e of this action, so God helpe you and by the contents of his holy gospell

The*ise* oathes being read to all the Captens by the generall were well licked of the*m* all, so that the generall wolde presently have had them sworne, to the which all the Cap*t*ains saving mine seemed very willing. To the first he agreed with them presently to have bin sworne. and as for the rest he never sawe nor hearde of before,[1] therefore he requested farther tyme to advise vppon the*m* considering how worthy a matter an o*a*the is and ought to be to them all. the generall seemed to be contented yet not very well pleased. my Capten hisselfe having wroght the*m*,[2] presently out went to M*a*ster Niccols, being ther, which was the penner & deviser of these o*a*thes, to whome my Captayne saide, he merueled that a man of his profession wolde devise o*a*thes that weare so daungerously like to hazard many mens soules, for as sa*ff*ely and with better warrant might you sware not to Commit addultery or any other sinn as great.[3] he [Nicholls] presently fell in a passion, saying he greatly merueled *a*ny man shulde be so simple, for *If I eyther read or harde any thinge I coulde not be so Ignorant,*[4] alleaging certayne heathen and prophane examples,[5] bothe as fallse and as

---

[1] Knollys was willing to take the oath to the queen at once. He had not, however, been included in the earlier consultations about articles for the voyage (see Carleill's accounts, pp. 72, 82, n. 3; and Corbett, *Sp. War*, p. 42).

[2] i.e. *wrote*, or made a copy.

[3] Knollys's meaning is not entirely clear. Possibly religious scruple was being raised against the possibility of being required to act in some way that could offend his conscience. Or perhaps he used the religious argument to protest against an unanticipated order that would clearly subordinate him and his followers to Carleill's commands or to some officer of lesser rank.

[4] The italics, inserted by the editor, represent Nicholls's own words.

[5] The word *matters*, crossed out, is replaced by *example* in the MS.

141

vnchristianable as coulde be. Master Thorowgood[1] and other Gentellmen of my Capteynes company being come, and hearinge those speeches of Nicolls, he being more moued than my Captayne with these wordes [fol. 61v (MS 15v)] sayde vnto him, that he greatly forgetteth him selfe, bothe in the manner of his behauiour towards my Capten and allso in the matter he did reason of, for the one did not beseme him and the other he was not able to maintayne, & fell no further in disputation touching the matter but departed.

Saint eago
Nouember

20

    The 20th day of Nouember being Sonnday,[2] in the forenoone he [Nicholls] made a sermon, but rather an Oration to perswade men how safely they might take these four oathes, for after dinner the oathes shulde have bin adminstred. But in his sermone he saide that If there were any man so foolish or so proud or so fleshly harted as to refuse these oathes beforesaide, he thought him an Ill member in the action, and not worthy of the scocyety. The wordes being publikly pronounced and [it being] openly knowne that my Captayne only did not agree to these oathes, he [Knollys] thought him selfe not a littell touched in reputation. wherefore after Dynner he did charge him [Nicholls] openly before the Generall and all the Captains of the great abuse offered him by this his manner of Drawling. But he excused him selfe, protesting that he had no meaning to touch my captayne nor any other private man. the answere, allthough it were most unlickely, yet was my Captayne content to take that for a satisfaction. Master Thorowgood and the rest of the Ientellmen which weare at the first speeches which passed Betwene Nicols and my Capten were called to wittness. Master Thorowgood was by my Captain requested to resyte the wordes spoken betwene Nicols & them the daye before, who beginning to speak was cutt of by the generall being in his

---

[1] Thoroughgood, of Thorowgood, and several other supporters of Knollys have not been identified. They were probably among the less well known 'gentlemen' who had been recruited for the voyage. See below, p. 146.

[2] The date was the 21st, following the events of the 20th (see above). 21 November 1585 fell on a Sunday (Cheney, *Handbook of Dates*).

acustomed Furies[1] [at] seeing his trusty instrument touched in this manner, saying Niccolls was his [Thorowgood's] better in this place and that in this action there was 500 better men then he, saying that they did nothing but sowe sedition, and y[t] by meanes of there factions[2] he stood in feare of his lyffe, and moreouer he thought they were no well wishers to this action nor true subiects to her Maiesty, but then he [began] reclaiming his speeches, imputing the whole occasion to Master Thorowgood and to Master Willis as chieffe, and Master Chamberlain and Master Longe as accessaryes, to which speeches Master Thorowgood answered, he was as true a subiect to her Maiesty as any whatsoever, and that he was as ready and willinge to do her maiestyes service and wolde to his power do her as good service as any man in this action. The *generall* tooke that to be spoken in comparison with him. Wherevppon he grewe in exceding furye, wishing that neyther my Captain nor any of them had entered into this action. to whom my Captain answered he sawe his choller so much to superbounde that he knew not what to saye, and as for the hard speeches[3] he had gyven him touching himsealfe and his gentlemen which were with him, he sawe no licklehood of remedy, especially where will stood for a lawe.[4] Yea, saide the *generall, you are there defender and mayntane them agaynste me.*[5] My Captaine answered, he had reason to take there partes in any good and honest cause, in respect they lefte there Frendes and all that they had and betooke them selves to go with him in this unhappy voyage booth for them and him. but this, vouchsafed my Captain, that *If either youre selfe or any other man can alleage and prove any thinge agaynst them that may touch them in creddit or reputation, before you all I renounce them and leave them to there own deserts. but one the other side, If I be a wittnes of ther continuall behauiour booth to*

---

[1] Drake's temper had flared often before, as records of his voyages show.

[2] Possibly Drake was referring to some incident recorded in the lost early pages of this MS; or possibly he was thinking of earlier events in Knollys's career, or even of problems associated with the Doughty affair.

[3] In the MS, *speechor.*

[4] Cf. the words used by Knollys in his letter of 6 January (above, p. 118).

[5] The italics indicate direct quotations.

*you and to all men else, and thoughe we have harde speeches[1] yet is
there no proofe of any thing to be obiectted agaynst us, I hope that it
maye be thought reasonable that I have spoken, especially having so
great cause.* the generall answered him, they were a pack brought
a pourpose, wishing he had never seene them,[2] to whom my
Captain answered, his [Drake's] meaning was to weary with
discontmentes, which he might easy do, for rather then he
wolde continnewe such a hellish liff to consume him selfe with
greefe in continuall dysgraces and to remaine still so offensive
in his [Drake's] eyes without any thinge proved against him or
his company, he desired his generall to have a ship or a barke
for him and his company, and he wolde be suer to go farr
yenought from troubling him any more this voyadge. He
[Drake] tolde him presently[3] before all the Captains that he
shulde have [a ship] for him selfe and as many as wolde go
with him, and rather then he shulde staye, he shuld have a shipp
as good as the Ayde,[4] for the which my Captain gave him great
thankes and so departed./

22

Monday the 22 of Nouember the generall commanded all my
Captains company[5] to appear before him and the other captens,
where publickly he demaunded of every man particularly
Sainteago whether he wolde procede of the voyadge or retorne [fol. 62
Nouember (MS 16)] into England with my Captain. Euery one answered
as his affection served him. there was founde 40 or 50 of the
properest men willing to go with my Captain, whethersouer y^t
were, not withstanding the great gyftes which the Generall
promised to divers that wolde leave my Captain. vppon this
Division, such as meant to go with my Captain were exempted
from watch and ward and all other services, and the Fraunces
[was] appoynted for my Captain and his company. he had his

---

[1] In the MS, *speecher.*

[2] Here is a suggestion that Drake suspected some political interest related to
Knollys's place in the expedition.

[3] i.e. at once.

[4] The *Aid*, a royal ship, was one of the larger vessels in the fleet, but smaller than the
Leicester. Drake evidently wished to keep the latter ship in the fleet, seeming not to
fear trouble with her owner, the earl.

[5] In the MS, *souldiours* crossed out, and *company* substituted.

choyse of the barke Bond [or] the barke Bon*ne*r, e*i*ther [or][1] booth, of the burden of 120 townes. Yet did he take the Fraunces. He desired to have the Whitt Lyon, but coulde not, & therefore he chowse the Fraunces. though she weare but smalle, yett was she newe and strong and of 50 tonnes.[2]

Twesday the 23 day next followinge, my Capten being com*m*anded abourd by the ge*nerall's* appoyntment,[3] yet neuerthelesse my Ca*ptain* vnderstanding of sum service to be done one the shore in the Illande,[4] he sent his saide company to repaire to the ge*nerall* w*i*th offer of them selves and there services untill the tyme of there departure, for that there comming out of Englan*d* was to do her M*aies*ty service and there c*o*untry [and] to the furtheringe of that action by all meanes possible to the vttermost of there power. the Ge*nerall* w*i*th all the rest of the captens being sett togeather in counsell,[5] and vnderstanding my Captens company to have sumwhat to say vnto them, willed them to stay a tyme vntill there were returned from my ca*ptain* an answer of 3 Articles sente to him fro*m* the Ge*nerall* by Cap*tain* Furbusher, Ca*ptain* Winter, Cap*tain* Heriza, Ca*ptain* Crosse, Ca*ptain* Foscue, and M*aste*r Cottell, the generalls secretary or clerke,[6] w*hi*ch articles followeth: 23 [November]

Articles sent fro*m* the ge*nerall* to my Ca*ptain* by the viceadmirall & divers other captens An*n*o 1585, 23 of Noue*m*ber at the Illande of S*ain*t Iaca*m*o

1 Whether are you content that youre company shalbe at the disposition of the generall or no

2 Whether are you resolved to departe out of this action and service of her maiesty or no

[1] Written as *of* in the MS.

[2] For comparison of these ships see the Table of Ships. *White Lion* was larger than the others. The *Francis*, probably owned by Drake, was hardly more than half the size of the *Bond* and the *Bonner*, with a capacity for 35 or 40 men.

[3] Knollys was thus relieved of land service.

[4] Probably he had heard of plans for the night march inland (see p. 148).

[5] Knollys, having been sent aboard his ship, was not present.

[6] This was a committee made up, with the exception of Drake's secretary, of important sea captains: Frobisher, Wynter, Erisey, Crosse, Fortescue.

3 Whether If you departe will you go into Englande or no
directly

We do demaunde the directe answer in wrighting of the
foresaide articles foorthwith by reason of the present
service of Importance now in hand.

The Answer of my Capten

1 Touchinge the first, I aunswer that booth my selfe and my
company booth are and have beene at the generalls appoyntment and disposition in any service of her Maiesty as farr fourth
as any others./

2 Touchinge the second, there is none more vnwilling to departe
then mysealfe but rather then I shulde be thought a mvtinouse
or factious person, whereby I remaine an offence and an
hinderance in any Part of this so honorable an action, which
I desire God to blesse and prosper, rather I saye then to be
Imputed a hinderer of this, I desire not only to be out of the
socyety but vnder the waves as deep as there is any bottom./

3 Touching the thirde, I meane nothing lesse then to returne into
my cuntry yf by any meanes I may be vitteled.

This awnswer of my Captens being returned by Captain
Furbusher and the rest of the Captens appoynted for that
purpose, Master Thorowgood, Master Chamberlain, Master Longe,
Master Willis & Master Stanton, who had waited all this
whilles, were sent for to the counsell bourd before the generall
and the rest of the captens. at there comming the generall redd
vnto them the Articles sent vnto my Captain and likewise his
awnswer. after he had read my captains awnswer vnto them he
did lickwise read a decree annexed to the articles which was
decreed vppon by the whole counsell after my captens awnswer
was returned vnto them, which was that without he wold go
directly into England he shulde have no shipp.

Lickwise he read another Decree concluded vppon by them
also conserning the displacing of Master Thorowgood, Master
Chamberlain and Master Willis from my Capten vnto other

shippes. and M*aste*r Thoro*w*good and M*aste*r Cha*m*berlain toulde
our generall that they were placed with the consent and good
like booth of my Lor*d* and my Lady of Lester and therefore
they did hope [fol. 62v (MS 16v)] that without prooffe of some
misbehauiour of therse towardes him [Drake] or any of his
Capt*ains*, or ells any disorderly or vnseemly speeche geven out
by them to any man either preiudicially to there reputations or
hurtfull to there honorable action [that they should not be
transferred; but] that yf prooff of these or any souch like thinges
shuld be brought agaynst them that then they wolde not only
be contented to be seperated from my Capten, but allso abide¹
the shame of yt to the vttermost./

The 24*th* my capten was sent for by the ge*n*erall to come a 24
shore to what end he knew not, but assoone as he came, all the
counsell being assembled, there came a sudden bru*i*te of a great
many shippes w*h*ich shuld be in sight,² vppon w*h*ich the
ge*n*erall in all haste commanded every man aborde. and my
Capt*ain* with his co*m*pany being ready to enter his bo*a*te, the
ge*n*erall in her Ma*i*estys name com*m*anded me³ that I shuld not
carry abourd M*aste*r T., M*aste*r C., M*aste*r W.,⁴ for he had
appoynted them other shippes to go in, the w*h*ich com*m*ande-
ment he [Knollys] obeyed most vnwillingly, for they
were lefte one shore not knowing where to lye or eat any
thinge./

The 25*th* M*aste*r Thorowgood was sent abourd the Whyte 25
Lyon vnder Capt*ain* Heriza by the ge*n*eralls order, M*aste*r
Chamberlayne to the Barke Talbot vnder Capt*ain* Baylisse,⁵
and M*aste*r Willis to the Ayde vnder Capt*ain* Winter. but
before they were com*m*anded abourde Nicols did use these
speeches vnto them, that yf any wold come vnto him in
hu*m*ility to knowe his opinion touching the o*a*the he wolde

¹ In the MS, *abode*.
² The other accounts do not mention this alarm.
³ The personal reference suggests that the diarist was a ship officer of the *Leicester*
under Knollys, possibly her master.
⁴ i.e. Thorowgood, Chamberlain, and Willis.
⁵ i.e. Baily. Drake was separating the 'trouble-makers'.

satisfy them but yf they came in carping manner he wolde not
cast pearles before swine./

**A steward
Hanged**   The same day there was one Thomas Ogle, stewarde in the
bark Talbot, hanged in the west ende of Saint Iacamo for
buggery committed in his stewards rome with 2 boyes, being
convicted by 12 men, whereof Dolober was the foreman. the
man confessed the fact and died very penetently./¹

27   The 27th the generall and most of his Captens with 700 men
went into the Illand.² they went in the night from Saint Iacamo
having 2 or 3 Moores for there guides,³ and in the morning
they came to another houwse of the Bishops at 6 or 7 miles of,⁴
but they were discouered before there comming so that ther
was nothing lefte in the howse for they had conueyed all to the
mountaynes, and that that was anything worth was hidden.
the souldiours spoyled this howse & divers other small cottages
about the same, and at parting they set all on fyer and burnt
[the town]. there was one or 2 of our men killed at this tyme
and there hartes taken out of there bodyes [as they were]
dysorderly seeking for pilledge.⁵ the bishope and the chiefest
of [the] Spaniards or Portingalls wear one horsback to the
number of 15 or 16 horse for there safte ouer flying, but neuer
durst approch neare oure men.

This parte of the Illande is the most pleasante & richest of all
the rest, abounding with store of fruites aforesaide having a

¹ See also pp. 111, 243. In the *Primrose* journal (p. 189) he was said to be from the *Aid*.
No other account gives the date or mentions what appears to have been a full jury trial.
² The date agrees with that of the *Tiger* journal (p. 97 and n. 7) for the night march,
although the 24th is the date given in the newsletter (p. 111) and the *Summarie* (p. 230).
According to the MS variant of the latter, however, the march occurred on the next
to the last day before departure, with a day of rest before sailing (see p. 231 and n. 6).
If 29 November was the departure date (see pp. 65, 98, 111), this would place the inland
march on the 27th. According to the *Summarie* also (p. 232), the search at Praya, just
before the fleet left the island, was conducted on the evidence of a prisoner, and the
Leicester journal (p. 149) indicates that this was the prisoner taken during the inland
march. The report of events sent from Spain to Venice (*C.S.P.Ven. 1581–1591*, p. 140)
also noted that the march occurred just before the departure.
³ The guide was a negro, brought out from England, according to the *Primrose*
journal (p. 189).
⁴ In the town of St Domingo (see pp. 97, 189).
⁵ On this incident see *Summarie*, p. 235 and n. 3. See also pp. 98, 189.

faire and pleasant ryuer running by the bishops house. One of my Cap*tain's* company called Newman did take a Spaniard who was M*aste*r Gunner of S*aint* Iacamo,[1] and this was all in effect that was doone at that ty*me*. The generall and his company returning home as we*a*ry as might be, the ge*nerall* and Cap*tain* Carlell eased them selves somtymes ryding vppon an asse w*hich* they tooke in the Feildes.[2] the foresaide Spaniard taken by Newman, being made offer of sum torment, did confesse that he knew of sum Ordnaunce hidden at Prano,[3] a smalle towne of S*aint* Iacamo./

This daye there was brought aborde divers shippes certayne provision of wyne and oyle according as *it* pleased the ge*nerall* to appoynt of that, that was gotten in the towne, namely there came aborde the Lettice Lester by the generall's appoyntment and order 2 butts of wyne for the shippes provision and on butt for Captayne Platt's owne vse.[4] there came allso 36 Iarres of oyle w*hich* was Indi*ff*erently bestowed thorow the shipp, to every messe in the shipp a Iarr. that was all that was appoynted for the Lettice Lester of all the spoyles of S*aint* Iacamo and of the 7 carvels w*hich* wear all loaden w*ith* good thinges.[5]

This day the Carvels being emptyed by souch as the generall in his secresye had appoynted for that purpose [and] having nothing left in them, there were certayne of them sent to sea to look [for] there fortunes. the rest were broken vp for fyer wood and carried abourd the shippes. this day likwise Cap*tain*

[1] The *Primrose* journal (p. 188) mentions the capture earlier of the *master governor* of the town, but the identification in the *Leicester* journal seems more accurate. His knowledge of military supplies was what the English wanted.

[2] This comment on Carleill differs from that in the *Tiger* journal (see p. 98).

[3] i.e. Porto Praya.

[4] Although Anthony Platt was aboard as commander of Knollys's company (see above, p. 139), the removal of Knollys and his supporters to the *Francis* had evidently not been effected.

[5] Cf. p. 190. It was reported in Spain that the seven ships included two from Lisbon, three from Madeira, and two from Santiago itself, of which only one was laden (*C.S.P.Ven. 1581–1591*, p. 141). It was rumoured afterwards in Amsterdam that seven Spanish ships taken by Drake at the Cape Verdes had been richly laden with treasure, stones, and jewels (*C.S.P.D. 1581–1590*, p. 324).

Winter & *Captain* Morgan[1] fell out, and Winter challenged Morgan but the matter was taken vp yet so as Morgan wolde goe no longer in his shipp, but with *Captain* Carleill, Leifftenant generall.[2]

26   The 26*th* day[3] every man brought abourde there shipps souch provision as they had gotten by the pilladg*e* of the towne. that day in fresh water we brought abourd the Lettice Lester 38 tonnes, but our caske was not very good. there . . . .

[At this point occurs a gap in the narrative, pp. 17–22 of the numbered pages of the manuscript being missing. The record of events from the departure from Santiago until after the capture of Santo Domingo in Hispaniola (29 November 1585 to 8 January 1586), therefore, has been lost. The Knollys letter of 6 January called upon Drake for a decision on his case, and Drake's response was the convening of his council, to act in some semblance to a court martial, on 9 January. With the meeting on that date the *Leicester* journal resumes, with plans being made again for sending Knollys and his supporters home.]

Saint
Domingo
Iannuarii
[9]

[fol. 63 (MS 23)] [They shall prepare] them selves to go abourd the Barke Hawkins, haveing 2 dayes limeted to make them selves ready and the 3 day to depart & so they were dyscharged. but they being in the church yarde when the g*e*nerall came downe,[4] he saide vnto them, *Gentlemen, ye maye take your pleasure where ye lest vntill souch tyme as the barke Hawkins*[5] *be ready, which shalbe with all spede possible.*[6] So they gave him

---

[1] Edward Wynter, captain of the *Aid*, and Matthew Morgan, one of the two corporals of the field.

[2] In the *Tiger*.

[3] The date should probably be 28th instead of 26th. It is out of order, and it refers to preparations for the departure, which occurred on the 29th. See p. 148, n. 2.

[4] The cathedral was utilized by the English as their centre of business and for keeping prisoners. Wright, *Further Eng. Voyages*, p. 28.

[5] The *Hawkins* was larger than the *Francis*, which had been assigned earlier. See Table of Ships.

[6] The italics, inserted by the editor, represent a direct quotation.

thankes. my m*aste*r continued all this day and night in the Martials chardge vntill the next day in the morninge.[1]

The 10*th* day in the morninge the g*enerall* sent for my master to the place aforesaide where the court war kept, and there he discharged my m*aste*r from the martiall, and when he had so donc the g*enerall* having no more to saye vnto him, he [Knollys] dep*a*rted, leavinge him and all the rest of the captens descydinge many Quarrells betwext C*a*p*tain* and C*a*p*tain,* namely C*a*p*tain* Powell, Seriant maior, and C*a*p*tain* Platt, who vppon wordes passing betwene them, Powell strok him w*it*h his leading st*aff*e twise or thrise and ran him into one of his armes. Platt bare all as he said because of his o*a*the.[2] there was lickwise a combat required betwene C*a*p*tain* Heriza and M*aste*r Burle, an Ensigne bearer.[3] there was allso a great Quarrell betwene Waterhowse, Liuete*nant* to C*a*p*tain* Goring, and Ha*m*pton, M*aste*r of the Primrose,[4] and divers others w*hi*ch I omitt, but at this towne the Captens leading staves did walke about the shoulders of the poor souldeours & this I dare say, whilst we weare there, there wear 30 or 40 souldiours com*m*itted to the Marshalsy[5] for contempt and disobedyence to there captens, there o*a*the being considered. How lamentable a matter this is I refer it to the Iudgment of others.

This day C*a*p*tain* Fenerd[6] feasted the G*enerall* and all the rest

---

[1] The diarist referred to Knollys during the stay here as *my master*, rather than *my captain* (see pp. 152–5), which indicates that Knollys was still relieved of his command. He was probably in special custody until 10 January, in the charge of a marshal (see below). The notes of the diarist about officers' quarrels suggest that he, as temporarily in command of the *Leicester*, may have been present for the council meetings.

[2] Powell, the sergeant major, was Platt's superior among the military officers.

[3] James Erisey, captain of *White Lion*. This was a quarrel between a ship captain and a soldier.

[4] Hampton, possibly *Hamplon* (see p. 294), Master under Frobisher. Goring had been assigned command of the soldiers aboard the *Primrose* (see p. 139). On Waterhouse, see pp. 206, 299.

[5] i.e. Marshalsea. Evidently the prison cells at the cathedral (see above, p. 150, n. 4) were used for Englishmen as well as Spaniards. For other cases of discipline and punishment see pp. 112, 243. A Spanish official at Cartagena wrote in May 1586, 'They say there was disagreement between Francis Drake and some of his officers and that he removed some from their posts, and others say he executed them.' Wright, *Further Eng. Voyages*, p. 135.

[6] i.e. Fenner, captain of Drake's ship.

of the Captens where my master was likwise invited after dinner Captain Winter having moued the generall for a private parley betwixt him and my master¹ So the generall called my master and captain Winter into a chamber a part, where many matters were ript vp but not withstanding the generall vsed souch protestations of the [fol. 63v (MS 32v)] love he bare my master and that yf he wolde take the oathe that there was no man he meant to vse more than my master and besides he shuld be reeradmerall² and that he shuld have the chardge of his men by land yff he wolde. my master gave him great thankes and toulde him the chiefest thinge he allwayes desired was his love and good opinion & there was no place of chardge neyther by sea [nor]³ by lande he desired more then that, and touching the oathe, yf that [reply] he had offered before him wold satisfy him he shuld be very glad of it, and seeing he had no chardge by land, he tould the generall he thought that might suffyse. the generall saide it mought suffice him but not others. my master saide he came to satisfy him only and no others, *yet this wold I say to others, that I wold not desire to have any chardge by land but first I wolde have them to offer me the oathe.*⁴ but in fine this was there concluded, that yf my master wold take the oathe he shuld have any chardge he most desyred eyther by sea [or] land; if not he shuld remayne in his [Drake's] fauour and the good opinion of all men. so he departed, gyving my master tyme to determine with himsealfe. My master gave him thankes especially for his last proffer.⁵

¹ Edward Wynter, whose connections with the Court were known, may because of them have interceded on Knollys's behalf. Because the text of the MS has no punctuation here, it is not clear whether Knollys dined with the captains or came in afterwards for his talk with Drake.

² This probably means reinstatement to the post from which he had been removed because of his refusal to take the oaths. Since the *Summarie* is the only other record that refers to Knollys as rear admiral, and its list represents some appointments that were made during the voyage (see p. 215, n. 1), it is possible that Drake was now offering a special concession in order to regain Knollys's support. Cf. p. 22.

³ In the MS, *and.*

⁴ Italics inserted by the editor for a direct quotation.

⁵ Knollys may eventually have agreed to the oath, for in later action at Cartagena certain minor responsibilities were placed in charge of the rear admiral (see pp. 154,

The 11*th* day there was nothing donne but seeking and 11
bringing of gould, silver, and souch lick com*m*odetyes.

The 12*th day* the Capten of the towne came in, who brought 12
with him 200 beeves and certayne muttons. he remayned all
this night with the g*e*nerall discoursing but especially entreating
for the sauing of the towne. But [what] he offered [was] so
short of the second demaund that he had but smal*l*e hope of
agreement.[1] This man did enuy[2] much agaynst [fol. 64 (MS 24)]
Lawiers & bookmen,[3] saying they were the losse and destruction *Saint*
of many a florishing common welth for they did so enchant Domingo
the eares of princes, especially theyres of Spa*i*ne that no souldier Ianuarij
might be heard though the distresse were neuer so great, euen
in matters conserninge the kinges keeping and loosing of his
country. for when they come to speake [the custom was that]
they shuld be posted from one to another in somuch that they
were as good be silent for they shalbe neuer a whitt the better
for there speaking.

The 13*th* daye the Capten departed, being nothing contented 13
in that he could not compounde for the towne. Whilles he
remayned in the towne his cloake was gone, and the g*e*nerall
bestowed his [on][4] him w*h*ich he tooke ver*y*e kindly. the
G*e*nerall tould him likwise that before his departure he wold
send for him agayne, because he shuld see his shipp wheare he
was able to entertayne him better then in the best howse of
S*a*int Domingo. the C*a*ptain reioysed greatly with that, saying,
he wolde be all wayes ready at his commandement.[5] this daye

170). As late as 26–28 January, however, on the very eve of departure from Santo
Domingo, he was still under threat of being sent back to England (see p. 156).

[1] The first emissary whom the President of the *Audiencia* sent to treat with Drake
was Captain Juan Melgarejo, high sheriff of the city, but he left promptly when
negotiations failed. Wright, *Further Eng. Voyages*, p. 223; Castellanos, *Discurso*, p. 295.
See also p. 195, n. 6. On the amount finally agreed upon see p. 244.

[2] i.e. *envey*, or *inveigh*.

[3] Cf. the statement on p. 260 about the number of lawyers among the inhabitants,
because here was the court for highest appeals in the region.

[4] In the MS, *of*.

[5] The Spanish factor, in his later report on the ransom talks, wrote: 'They [the
English] said that although Captain Juan Melgarejo had asked to visit their fleet and
they had not wished to show it to him, they did desire to let me see it and to entertain

there was brought in by the Captens meanes a souldior that was lunetike, whose name was Harry Sorowe.¹ He ranted to the Euening, but yf he had been a man of any worth he shuld neuer have had that fortune.

This day towardes the Euening Captain Morgan was appoynted to take 200 men and to go to a Chappell which was a mile out of the towne northward² & to burne it because the Spaniards did vsually kepe watch and ward there, with whome my master and Captain Winter went.³ and when they weare come to the chappell they sent skoutes to the toupe⁴ of yt who did discouer to the number of 200 and more Spaniards a horsback & Foot who weare in troupe within 11 score [yards?] to vs in the woodes. and when they sawe the chappell fyer they beganne to besture them selves, making a bravado as yf [fol. 64v (MS 24v)] they wold have sett vppon vs.⁵ We seeing that made oure selues ready to march homewarde & burnt not only the Chappell but divers other howses, the which the Spaniards perceaving putt spures to there horses and gat betwixt vs and home as If they wolde have done sum thing. but it was but a brage. my master was appoynted to lead a troupe of shoott in the vanwarde & Master Stanton⁶ had the reerward but the Spaniards prickt before vs so longe as that one of them was striken by one of my masters troupe and his horse was taken, but because yt was a Iadde, he was panched thorow with a

Saint Domingo Ianuary

---

me aboard the flagship.' He however declined the offer. Wright, *Further Eng. Voyages*, p. 224.

¹ *Young* was written, but crossed out.

² This may be the place marked on the larger Boazio map for Santo Domingo (Plate V(B)) as *H.H.* See Note on Maps, p. 315.

³ Knollys seems to have taken advantage of Drake's compromise offer, but without having taken the oath (see below). Wynter may have been with him in some supervisory capacity; he was always eager for action (see p. 253). The diarist himself may have accompanied Knollys here.

⁴ i.e. *top.*

⁵ President Ovalle and other officials, after scattering in the countryside, came together at a sugar estate on the Hayna River, west of the town, and they sent men out occasionally to observe or to annoy the enemy. Wright, *Further Eng. Voyages*, p. xxxviii, n. 5; Castellanos, *Discurso*, p. 295. See also below p. 156, n. 1.

⁶ Stanton was Knollys's lieutenant (see above, p. 135).

*part*isan. at our comming to the townes end we burnt an Abbey in which ley an old fryer dead, who was kilde by sum of the souldiors *w*hich weare dysorderly. We did burne divers other howses./[1]

The 14*th* day there was more burninge. this day at dynner 14 the *generall* dranke to my m*aste*r, protesting great kindne*ss* vnto him. he was allso desirous to knowe his resolution touching there laste taulke, the which my m*aste*r tould him he shuld knowe after dynner in privatt. so after dynner my m*aste*r came to him and tould him his opyneon of the o*a*the, and that [what] he had done was with [such] good consideration as he was not [willing] to alter his mynde from y^t [which] he sett downe [earlier]. And se*e*inge that might not suffice, he did most thanckfully accept of the *Generalls* last offer which was that he shuld [go] forwarde in the good favor of all men, especially of himsealfe, who*m* he wolde gladly please by all the meanes he might, desyringe rather in lyuing a priva*t*e liffe to be in quiet then in hauing chardge to be an offence to any./

The 15*th* they burnt agayne and carried hiddes to the 15 wharfe.[2]

The 16*th* & 17*th* dayes ther was likwise burning and carrying 16 17 of hides. these dayes was carried abourd the shippes good store of wine and oyle & meale, and most of the smalle shippes did ride at receyt by the key, & the great shipes did ride in the range or rode.[3]

The 18*th* there was howses fyerd. this day our men went out 18 of the west gate of the towne wheare they made a [rode][4]

---

[1] Drake was systematically burning sections of the city as he pressed for a ransom agreement. The Spanish documents report that two-thirds or three-fourths of the town were destroyed, including all of the religious houses, with only the shell of the cathedral left. Among the religious houses were the Franciscan monastery, two nunneries (Regina Angelorum and Santa Clara), and the houses of the Dominicans and the Mercedorians. Wright, *Further Eng. Voyages*, pp. xl, 28, 55, 179.

[2] Cf. pp. 197, 246. Richard Hakluyt noted in 1587 that hides were among 'the chief merchandise' of the island. Taylor, *Writings . . . Hakluyts*, p. 374.

[3] The Spaniards had blocked the harbour. Cf. p. 195.

[4] i.e. *raid*.

because we sawe certayne troupes of horsmen braving in the playnes.[1]

[Once more two folios are missing, with the record lost until 26 January. The record resumes in the midst of a conference or councill on 26 January.]

Sainte
Domingo
Ianuary
[26]

[fol. 65 (MS 27)] my master was not minded to disquiet the generall, as he saide. but it was thought that the generall seeinge Master Thorowgood in the next roome, he suspected him to have sitten there of purpose to take advantage of his wordes, which since draue him into a franzy. But finally the awarde of the court delivered by the lifftenant generall was that my master shuld prepare to go aborde the Bark Hawkins,[2] that he shuld have yᵗ daye and the nexte to carry his thinges abourde her, that he shuld not faile to be a bourde her the next night, that he shuld be in company with Thorowgood, Chamberlain and Willis, which shulde in convenient tyme be sent into Englande, with which he was contented.[3]

27

My master went aborde the Bark Hawkins according to the order aforesaide, where the only prouision was wine & meale, as well for gentlemen as mariners./

28

The generall sent aborde a mutton & a quarter of beeffe for my master & a 1000 poor Iohns./[4]

This day the Spaniards brought in there first payment for the ransome of the towne which was in goulde and Syluer & perle. the daye before they sent beefes & muttons./

30

The last payment was brought in where in was little coine but most in perle & plate./[5]

[1] A Spanish report dated 14 February 1586 stated that 'A troop of horse under Don Diego Osorio [captain of the royal galley] has hung persistently on its [the city's] outskirts and upon what occasions have offered have killed some of the enemy. We remained masters of the countryside although we never had the means to attack.' Wright, *Further Eng. Voyages*, p. 34.

[2] The wording suggests that Knollys was present for a time at the conference on his affairs and then withdrew to await the decision.

[3] The terms are the same as those of 9 January.

[4] Salted and dried hake. *OED*.

[5] On the ransom negotiations see pp. 243-4. The payments were gotten together

This night folowinge, the galley we fownde at Domingo was towed out and burnt by *Captain* Vaughan.[1] Besides there were burnt an olde shippe of 600 or 700 tonnes & a great many smale barkes. the number of all was no lesse then 20.

In the morninge we sett saile from *Saint* Domingo,[2] beinge [31 Jan.] in number 24,[3] smale & great, havinge lefte the Hope, the Beniamin & the Scoute & for them we had the New Years Gifte[4] & the new Hope, the one 400, the other 200 tonnes, & three other smalle Barkes.[5] Oure course was all this day & night South by East./[6]

This daye we caped s and by E, the winde at E, & sumwhat February 1 to the northe, a very stiffe gale./ The New Yeares Gifte but especially the new Hope were so light for want of Balast that they could beare but smalle saile so that the *generall* was compelled to spare sailes & to stay for them. The New Years

---

with difficulty (President Ovalle's report in the Archivo del Instituto de Valencia, pr. in Castellanos, *Discurso*, App. III).

Besides the valuables collected for the official ransom, and the bells and ordnance, there was other rich booty. Cf. *Primrose* journal (p. 197). A Spanish official lamented that 50,000 ducats in the royal treasury could not be saved (Wright, *Further Eng. Voyages*, p. 17); and Drake's Italian captive thought the booty amounted to 200,000 ducats (Wright, op. cit., p. 55). It was rumoured afterwards in Europe that several ship-loads of captured treasures were sent back to England (*C.S.P.Ven. 1581–1591*, pp. 164, 165). The English accounts of the voyage, however, do not support that report.

[1] President Ovalle's order for the galley to be burned had not been carried out. Wright, *Further Eng. Voyages*, p. 40.

[2] A Spanish document dates the ransom settlement on Sunday, 30 January/ 9 February, with departure the following day. Another dates the departure on that Sunday (Wright, *Further Eng. Voyages*, pp. 35, 40). According to Cheney (*Handbook of Dates*), 31 January 1586 was a Monday. The dates of 1 February (Map Text, p. 69) and 2 February (*Tiger* journal, p. 103, and newsletter, p. 112) are late.

[3] In the MS, the word *saile* was written but crossed out, as if the writer had not been sure of his count.

[4] The *New Year's Gift* was a large ship belonging to Antonio Corço, of Seville. Castellanos, *Discurso*, pp. xxxviii, 86; Wright, *Further Eng. Voyages*, p. xlii, n.

[5] Cf. pp. 112, 197. The *Leicester* journal's figure agrees with a Spanish report that the English took five ships from the harbour and burned others. Wright, *Further Eng. Voyages*, pp. xxxvi, 40.

[6] Except for a reference in Greepe's ballad (see p. 247, n. 4), this is the only account that has been found for the voyage from Hispaniola to the Main. If Drake had earlier thought of attacking Margarita (Lansdowne MS 100, fol. 98, pr. in Corbett, *Sp. War*, pp. 70–1), that plan had been abandoned. It would have required turning back toward the east, and his voyage was already behind schedule.

Gyfte splitt her foresaile which made the flett to ly at Hull awhile./

2   We caped south & sometymes to the W wardes, the winde at E and by N, a stiffe gale.

3   We caped s & sumtymes to the W wardes, the winde at E, a stiffe gale. The generall put out his topsailes in hope to see lande but could not, so that towardes the Euening he bated them & stayed for the fleett, bearing all night but his 2 Corses.

Cape de Vela February [4]   [fol. 65v (MS 27v)] We caped s & to the W wardes, the winde at E, a stiffe gale, We founde smooth water which was a signe that lande was not farre of, yet was it so late ere the generall wolde dyscover [it] that he was driuer to take[1] a bout to the offinge and to staye for his fleett, for sum of them were 5 leagues asterne. but when we were come togeather we all tackte to the Shorewarde, bearinge all this night but our forecorse./

5   In the morninge the Admirall was hard aborde the shore so he tackte to the offerd[2] agayne, shoutinge of a pece of Ordenance for a warning to the rest not to go too neare the shore for feare of shoale water & beinge put of the shoer he bare alongest the shoreside. the lande very low, without woode. our course was s w. about 3 of the cloke in the afternone we doubled the point of Cape de Vela, within which poynt the generall & all the fleett came to an anker, the winde blowinge stiffly and the rode very open.[3] The cape taketh his name of a rocke which lieth to W wardes of the pointe hard by the maine, which rocke is couered with foule.[4] But whether it be the doing of the foule or the color of the rocke or sumthinge else I cannot tell, but this rocke afarre of showeth so licke the saile of a shipp especially towardes the W wardes, that thereof it seemeth to take the name of Vela. The shippes beinge at anker, the generall put out a Saile to consult touchinge the lande./ The new Hope, for wante of Balast not beinge deepe yenough in the water, brake a cable & an anker & drave a great waye, but came to Anker agayne.

---

[1] i.e. driven to tack.
[2] i.e. offing.
[3] Cf. Map Text for 5 February.
[4] i.e. fowl.

At six a cloke in the morninge we waied anker, bearing 6
alongest the coast S S W, the winde at E, a smalle gale. the
fleett went S W & by W meaninge to have borne hard
abourde the shore. We founde shoal water all allongest the
way to the west ende of Cape de Vela./

The generall was enformed of a howse 6 leagues of in which
was pearl, & thether he sent Captain Forbusher with his pinasse
to take the same yf he coulde,[1] but it wolde not be. neyther
coulde the generall (as he desyred) bringe his shippes neare the
place because of the shoale waters. so y*t* there was nothinge
done but that Captain Forbusher dyscouered the coaste towardes
the Eueninge. about 6 of the cloke the generall bore in agayne
with the shore, but because it grew darke, he put out 2 lightes
and came to anker. but sum of the Fleet, sypposinge he laye at
hull, came not to anker, so that by the morninge they were
cast so farre to Leeward that we coulde not see them.

About 7 of the cloke we waied anker bearinge to the 7
westwards & in halfe an ower we saw our lost shippes cast to
Leewarde, and being come togeather we bare alongest with
the shore as close as we coulde.

[fol. 66 (MS 28)] Our shippes caped S.S.W. the winde at E. Cartha-
and by N, a stiffe gale. our smalle pinasses & boates went hard gena
by the shore where they founde shoale water still, so that our February
shippes could not cume neare the lande, which was very low [7]
sauinge that in the maine we might see here & there a hill.
about 2 of the cloke this day, passinge allongest the waste we
saw exceding high lande within the maine,[2] by coniecture
almost as high as Teneriffe, which was 16 leagues to the W wards
of Cape de Vela.[3] the generall at 3 a cloke put out his toppesailes,

---

[1] Probably this was near Rio de la Hacha, a town which had been considered for a
possible raid (see Corbett, *Sp. War*, p. 71), and to which Drake had offered to take
Maldonado from Santo Domingo (Wright, *Further Eng. Voyages*, p. 30). A captive in
Drake's company stated afterward that the plan to go in there was given up when
pilots advised against it because 'it was an open beach and there was a heavy sea'.
Wright, op. cit., p. 213.

[2] i.e. mainland, often referred to at the time as *Tierra firme*.

[3] Probably this refers to the mountains near Santa Marta, a day's sail from Rio de la
Hacha (Corbett, *Sp. War*, p. 71). Drake's Florentine captive stated that the English

to double a pointe w*hi*ch he sawe ahead him, bear*i*nge W N W.
This night the Talbote shott of 2 peces of Ordinance for that
she had broken her mainyard, but it was mended and fished[1]
agayne by the morninge.

8   We bare alongste the waste, stille vnder our foresailes. our
co*u*rse was W & by north. we founde 4 leag*u*es of the shore
4 or 5 fadom water, & 10 fadom the deepest, all this night the
fleet laye at hull, the winde blowinge stiffely./

9   All the Fleet set saile towardes Carthagena, caping S & by
W, the winde E N E, a small*e* gale. About 2 of the cloke we
dyscouered Carthagena, but few of the M*a*st*er*s of the Fleet
knew it.[2] Our small*e* barkes went into the bay sumwhat ne*a*re
the towne & they of the towne shott 6 or 7 peces of Ordinance
at them,[3] but they were w*i*thout danger. the ge*n*erall bore into
the harbor, the entrance whereof was 2 leag*u*es to the s W
wardes of the towne.[4] There are dange*r*ous flates, before the

---

steered from Santo Domingo 'for the mountain range at Santa Marta' and thence to
Cartagena. Wright, *Further Eng. Voyages*, p. 194.

[1] Repaired by use of a piece called a *fish*. *OED*.

[2] The date agrees with that given in the Spanish records, i.e., Ash Wednesday,
9/19 February (Wright, *Further Eng. Voyages*, pp. xlvii, 47, 73, 118). Drake himself had
been at Cartagena in 1572.

[3] The Spaniards made a military display along the beach as the fleet passed, and fired
some of their ordnance (Wright, *Further Eng. Voyages*, pp. xlviii, 106, 153). Their
accounts note that Drake sent one small ship cruising along the beach to inspect it
(Castellanos, *Discurso*, pp. xliv–xlv, 173), and that from it one man, a Portuguese,
swam ashore to spread alarm about the strength of the English forces (Wright, op. cit.,
p. 173). The citizens were already prepared by the exaggerated reports brought from
Santo Domingo by Francisco Maldonado to believe that the ships they saw entering
the harbour were only part of Drake's fleet (Wright, op. cit., pp. 47, 53, 131;
Castellanos, *Discurso*, pp. xliii, 156–7, 303).

[4] Cf. p. 248 and the Boazio map (Plates VI(A), (B)). One entrance, Boca Grande, lay
between a spit of land stretching westward from the town and the Isle of Cares.
Farther west, beyond the island, was another channel, Boca Chica, or 'little mouth',
which was more hazardous, requiring a good pilot (see the description by Baptista
Antonio, surveyor in 1587, printed in Hakluyt, *Prin. Nav.* (x, 137); and Wright,
Further Eng. Voyages, pp. xliv, xlviii). Neither of the entrances was protected by a fort,
possibly because entering at either required a favourable wind, and because the narrow
passage to the inner harbour had a fort and a chain (see below, p. 198, n. 6).

Although Oppenheim thought that Drake used the more distant channel (*Naval
Tracts . . . Munson*, p. 130), the statement of the captain general of the royal galleys,
Don Pedro Vique y Manrique (Wright, *Further Eng. Voyages*, p. 106) establishes that
the nearer one was used: 'The enemy with his fleet passed on and entered the port and

towne especially at the entrance of the harbor before the mouth of the channell. For in sailinge 2 leagues we found 4 fadome water, but the nearer we came to the lande & entrance of the harbor, the Deeper water we founde, & beinge entred the channell we had 8 or 9 fadom water, & after we were come within the mouth of the harbor which is sumwhat narrowe not much more then a muskett shott ower,[1] we founde very deepe water & the goodliest harbor that euer I sawe & safest for all windes, able by estimation to contayne all the shippes of Englande. it Beareth East. there is 2 leagues farther to the west wardes a nother entrance into this harbor.[2] Our shippes beinge come in we lett faule our ankers in the middest of the harbor, from which went 4 branches like ryuers, one N wardes towardes the towne of Carthagena, another East into the maine, the 3rd south, which goeth to the other entrey of the harbor. there is no fresh water nor riuer that runneth to any of these/ we came to an anker about 3 a cloke in the after noone, where we rode in 15 fathom water. not long after the generall put out a flagge of counsell[3] & after consultation it was determined that our men shuld be [fol. 66v (MS 28v)] landed about 2 a cloke at night, the which was done. our men were landed at the westernmost end of the point 2 leagues of the towne,[4] & did march vpon the sande alongest the sea side[5] where were sett an

Cartha-
gena
February

---

anchored in the port at Bocha Grande at three or four o'clock in the afternoon.' See also Wright, op. cit., p. 153. The *Leicester* journal confirms that the entrance nearer the town was used.

[1] Against the advice of some military men, the city officials had decided not to place guns there (Hicacos Point). Wright, *Further Eng. Voyages*, pp. xlvi, 71–2, 125.

[2] i.e. Boca Chica.

[3] In his poem Castellanos states that the English seized two negro fishermen in the bay and learned from them about approaches to the city and about the poisoned stakes along the sea shore (*Discurso*, pp. xlv, 175). Decisions about the night march from the unprotected Hicacos Point were doubtless made at the council.

No reference to black flags on Drake's ships, mentioned also by Castellanos (*Discurso*, p. 173), appears in either Spanish official accounts or English narratives.

[4] Led by Carleill, the lieutenant general. Cf. pp. 104, 248.

[5] According to some accounts, in order to avoid the stakes, they marched in the water itself (up to the navel, as the French narrative put it (Lacour, p. 24); see also Castellanos, *Discurso*, pp. xlvi, 183–5; and below, p. 251). Since the tide was low (see

infinitt number of prickes, poisened & sent in the sande of length a foote & an halfe & so thick that a man coulde not sett clere yf he came amongest them. yet by God's providence our men escaped them most miraculously, the weather beinge darke & by chance they happened one another way. If they had lighted one them, skarse one coulde have eskaped prickinge, and none pricked coulde have eskaped death, the poison is so stronge/ it groweth on trees & is a fruite, whereof I myselfe sawe some.[1] But to returne to our discourse. our men marchinge towards the towne were encontred with a few light horsmen skouts, who fled vpon the shottinge of a few peeces at them by vs,[2] we marchinge one till we came to a streyghte, havinge at our left hande the maine sea, on the other the water of the harbor in which, harde by the shore, were 2 galleys & a galleaqe with 9 peces of Ordinance & 300 good shoott, as the Spaniards confest, moste of which were come out of Flaunders, which did play vpon our men with great shott & smalle, as thicke as haile.[3] so that had it not[4] been for the lownesse of the water, beinge at an ebbe whereby they gott the advantage of a little Banke betwixt them and the shott, fewe of them had escaped aliue.[5] for the passage they were to passe by was but 30 paces brode from one water to the other, moreouer [ly]ing Before them vpon this strayt was a forte or rather a Barecatho, walled almoste the heyght of a man & a trench before yt, which walle

---

below, and Wright, *Further Eng. Voyages*, pp. 107, 133, 155), this may not have been necessary all the way.

[1] On the stakes see pp. 199, 252, and Wright, *Further Eng. Voyages*, pp. li, 154. They were probably branches from the box-thorn, a shrub whose thorns are poisonous. See Bravo's deposition (Wright, op. cit., pp. 116-17). Castellanos (*Discurso*, pp. xliii, 153) said the stakes were placed by the Indians.

[2] Cf. p. 199 and n. 6. The writer uses the first person here as if he had participated in this landing operation. If so, this may account for his failure to mention the naval attack led by Frobisher on the fort (see pp. 198, 249).

[3] Cf. pp. 104, 197.

[4] In the MS, *non*.

[5] A Spanish report stated that 'It is supposed that the artillery was aimed too high and so missed them.' The night was so dark that the English were not seen by the defenders until the light from the artillery fire exposed them. Wright, *Further Eng. Voyages*, p. 132. Cf. below, p. 251.

& trench went almost thwart the passage savinge about a 30 foote [strip] nexte to the sea, which was only fortefyed with pipes filled with earth.[1] in this place were 5 great peces of ordenance and 500 men who discharged there shott.[2] but the weather being darke we coulde not discerne them well, nor they vs. Nevertheless our men went forwarde vpon them, of whome some stayed the pushe of the pike, the most parte fled.[3] Our men, hauinge taken this Barecatho, hasted towardes the towne, some alongest the sea side by a trench, others ouer a faire sandy plaine, havinge the Spaniards in chase, of whome were many more killed & one Alonso Bravo Hithalgo taken prysoner, an auncient gentlemen & a valiant souldior.[4] he was Captain of the Barecatho & though his [men] all fledde from him, yet he stayed the last man fightinge valiantly and, beinge hurt in the heade & legge, was taken by Captain Goringe and his ansient also.[5] but because there [fol. 67 (MS 29)] was controuersy betwixt divers for the takinge of him, I omitt to

Carthagena February

[1] According to the investigating Spanish judge, the narrow stretch on the Caleta measured 150 paces across, and 65 feet on the seaward side had no protection. This part was hastily barred with wine butts filled with sand. Wright, *Further Eng. Voyages*, pp. xlviii–xli, 97, 118; also pp. 62, 72, 103, 130). Cf. below, pp. 199, 250; and Castellanos, *Discurso*, p. 302.

[2] Cf. pp. 104, 199. Don Pedro Vique stated that there were at the wall four of pieces artillery, and 600 men (300 harquebuses, 100 pikes, and 200 Indian bowmen). Wright, *Further Eng. Voyages*, p. 62. Other estimates were somewhat lower (ibid., pp. 48, 107). The strength of the forces had been reduced by the dispersion of some to guard other places at which the English might try to enter. Wright, *Further Eng. Voyages*, pp. xlvii, 47, 91–2, 130, 132.

[3] The English had longer pikes and their bodies were better protected (see p. 251). Some of the Spanish pikes had been made in haste, and many of those at the trench were unskilled in using them (Wright, *Further Eng. Voyages*, pp. lii, 65, 67, 69, 117).

[4] Captain Alonso Bravo Hidalgo de Montemayor, a nephew of Alvaro de Mendoza, was himself a leading resident. He was in command at the unfinished barricade, and his English captors referred to him as the 'chief commander of the city' (see the French narrative (Lacour, p. 24) and also p. 253). Although he was criticized by some for going beyond the improvised line of defence, the governor commended him for doing his duty, as did his own brother, Diego Hidalgo Montemayor, who came from Santa Marta as the investigating judge (Wright, *Further Eng. Voyages*, pp. xliii, li, 98, 133, 141; Castellanos, *Discurso*, pp. xlii, 148, 194, 304). Alonso Bravo's own deposition is in Wright, *Further Eng. Voyages*, pp. 115–24. On Drake's dealings with him see below, pp. 167, 173, 175.

[5] The ensign, Juan Cosme de las Sal, or Sala, however, was killed in the fighting. Wright, *Further Eng. Voyages*, pp. li, 98, 119. See also pp. 104, 251.

speake thereof.[1] our men winninge to the towne founde made
at euery entrance a Barecatho to hinder them of there passadge
& sum Ordinance in them, but the Spaniards neuer stayed to
defende them sufferinge our men to enter peaceably.[2] but after
theyre entrance we had a great annoyance by the Indian
arrowes comminge very thick out of the howses aboute theyre
eares with which many of vs were hurte & the arrows beinge
poysoned, sum dyed & sum recovered with much adoe.[3] the
Spaniards that there of them 1500 well appoynted horsemen &
footmen for the defence of the towne,[4] all [of] which helped
themselves with theyre horses or theyre heeles. Few were taken, &
none of reckoninge but Alonso Bravo, the greatest man of estimation in all the towne but the Governor, who was neyther good
souldior nor welbeloved. If eyther, we shuld never have taken
the towne. But Alonso & the Governor were at dissention./[5]

The manner of Entringe was this. Lieftenant Kettill, Captain
Winter's Lieftenant, was appoynted to lead certayne loose shott,
3 out of every company, of the best, which went as a forlourne

[1] There was confusion among both the Spanish and the English at this time. Alonso
Bravo declared that he was taken prisoner without any formal surrender by 'an English
captain and four men' while he was wounded (Wright, *Further Eng. Voyages*, p. 119).
Goring seems to have captured Bravo, and it was Carleill who killed his ensign-bearer
(see p. 104). Sampson, who was in the vanguard with Goring, received a sword wound,
possibly in a hand-to-hand encounter with the old camp-master, Alvaro de Mendoza
(*Summarie*, p. 253 below; and Wright, *Further Eng. Voyages*, pp. 1, 133).

[2] Cf. below, p. 252; also, Wright, *Further Eng. Voyages*, pp. xlv, 70–1, 91.

[3] Action by the Indians is mentioned in the *Summarie* (p. 252) and in Wright,
Further Eng. Voyages, p. liv and n. One Spanish force, returning from an outpost in the
swamps, attempted some brief resistance (Castellanos, *Discurso*, p. 305; Wright,
Further Eng. Voyages, pp. 50–1, 110–11, 133).

[4] One Spanish record listed 874 armed defenders (C. Fernández Duro, *Armada
Española*, II, 396, cited in Corbett, *Sp. War*, p. 19, n.). The figures in the depositions
of the Spanish officials vary from about 500, exclusive of Indians, freed blacks, and
galley crews (Castellanos, *Discurso*, p. 302; Wright, *Further Eng. Voyages*, p. 131) to
Vique's total of 979, which included 400 Indians, 25 free blacks, and 54 horse (Wright,
op. cit., p. 104). Alonso Bravo's list of some 520 men included 120 from outlying
villages (Wright, op. cit., p. 117).

[5] There had been much criticism of the governor's plans for defending the city,
of his special reliance upon Don Pedro Vique, commander of the royal galleys, and
of the arrangement for Vique to assume land responsibilities instead of staying with
the galleys. See Wright, *Further Eng. Voyages*, pp. xlv–xlvi, 63, 71–3, 101, 105, 116,
123, 127. Both Busto and Vique were prisoners in Spain before the end of 1587.
Wright, op. cit., p. liv, n.; Kraus, *Sir Francis Drake*, pp. 128, 189–91.

hope. *Captain* Gorynge had the leadinge of the vanward, & *Captain* Winter[1] & Captain Bixe[2] were with theyre companyes apoynted to secund him. the Lieftenant generall [Carleill] followed with the maine battell,[3] & *Captain* Platts company had the rereward.[4] but what with the darkness & with the shottinge of from the galleys & from the fort, our men were so farre out of order as some Captens had lost theyre companyes, but moste of the companyes theyre leaders, so that had not God him sealfe fought for vs, blindinge them with darkness & dauntinge theyr hearts with feare, it had not ben possible for vs to take Carthagena.[5] The towne beinge in our possession, this day was [10 Feb.] spent in consideringe courses most necessary for the preservation of it in saffety. the first night we laye all in armes ready to make resistance yf need shuld be./[6]

This day our men begune to hunte both above & vnder ground for goulde, siluer & other kindes of Pilladge & we begane to entrench our selues in a lesser roome, making Barecathes in euery quarter so that the one halfe of the towne was turned into suburbes./

These days was busied in the same affaires./   11. 12.
13. 14.
The 15th *day* the Governor, called Don Piedro Hernando [15] Iauguste,[7] & the Bishop, Don Frey Iohn de Montano,[8] &

---

[1] The *Summarie* states that Goring, Sampson, and Wynter were with the vanguard, Powell with the main battle, and Morgan with the rear. Carleill probably moved to the fore when he sensed the confusion among the advanced troops, and rallied them by his call. Wynter, though a ship captain, had requested the land assignment (see below, p. 253).

[2] i.e. Walter Bigges.

[3] In the MS, *battaile* was crossed out and *battell* substituted.

[4] Platt's company from the *Leicester* may have been placed under Morgan.

[5] Cf. p. 104.

[6] By the end of the day the Spanish evacuated their small fort (Wright, *Further Eng. Voyages*, pp. 141, 157). Then the English began to fortify the town, spending five or six days in the process. They occupied the main square, planted the Spaniards' guns for their own defence, and moved the fleet closer to the town. See p. 200, and Wright, *Further Eng. Voyages*, pp. liv, 134, 140, 157.

[7] Pedro Fernández de Busto. 'When the enemy had been in town six days he [Drake] sent a trumpeter to bid us come to ransom the place,' and refused to deal with anyone but the chief officials. Wright, *Further Eng. Voyages*, p. 142; Castellanos, *Discurso*, p. 316.

[8] The bishop was Fray Don Juan de Montalvo. Wright, *Further Eng. Voyages*, pp. liv, 134. Cf. Castellanos, *Discurso*, pp. 306, 331.

Tristando Doricte Merchadante,[1] Don Piedro de Marathis,[2]
Piedro Messe, capten of the castell,[3] [and] Piedro Loupes,[4] with
divers [fol. 67v (MS 29v)] others came to the *Generall* with
theyre flagge of truce to parley for the towne. the *generall*
demaunded 400,000 ducketts & they offered 5000. so, beinge
so great oddes betweene them, they departed, *re infecta*.[5] Only
our *generall* assured them that he wolde consume theyre towne
with fyer yf they did not speedely agree for the ransome of it,
so they departed.

Parte of the church roofe fell downe vpon the shootinge of,
of a culveringe at the discharge of the watch.[6]

We fortefyed the towne & made our selues stronge,
determininge to staye so longe there that the Spa*niards* beinge in
the Feldes & woodes shulde be glad to ransome theyre towne
for very hunger and want of such necessaryes as they had in
theyre howses, particular*ly* in respect of theyre wyues & Ladyes.

Cartha-
gena

February
[15]

16

17.18.19.
20.21.

[1] Tristan de Orive Salazar, merchant, who was to become one of the principal
negotiators. Wright, *Further Eng. Voyages*, pp. liv, 41, 67.

[2] Probably Don Pedro Marradas, nephew of the galley commander, Vique. The
latter refused to participate in ransom negotiations, but his nephew informed him of
the discussions. Wright, *Further Eng. Voyages*, pp. 113-14.

[3] The captain of the fort was Don Pedro Mexia Mirabal. Wright, *Further Eng.
Voyages*, pp. liii, 80.

[4] 'Piedro Loupes' was doubtless Pedro López Triviño, who suffered heavy losses.
Castellanos, *Discurso*, pp. 334, 340. The *Summarie* (p. 258) mentions the coming of the
governor and bishop with other gentlemen, but gives no names.

[5] The 5,000 should probably be 25,000. Tristan de Orive wrote later that Drake
began with a demand for 500,000 pesos in gold, and the city offered 25,000 ducats.
Drake's demand, according to one Spanish report was the equivalent of 750,000
Castillian ducats (Wright, *Further Eng. Voyages*, pp. 43, 158). Others quoted the first
demand as 400,000 ducats (Wright, op. cit., pp. 54, 61); in another account, it was
700,000 ducats (Castellanos, *Discurso*, pp. xlviii, 210). See note on money values,
p. 259 below.

The city's first offer of 25,000 (see Busto's letter of 25 May 1586 to the king (Wright,
Further Eng. Voyages, p. 142), quoted also in Castellanos, *Discurso* (p. 317), where the
figure is given as 20,000), was made on the ground that their city was smaller than
Santo Domingo, whose ransom had been 25,000 ducats. Drake's reply was that he
had collected pillage there also, whereas in Cartagena no booty had been taken because
the citizens had had time to remove their valuables before he arrived. Cf. the *Tiger*
journal, p. 105.

[6] The guns at the changing of the watch, according to the Greepe ballad, 'So shooke
theyr Church, the roof fell downe' (st. 49). The building was under construction,
nearly completed. The Spaniards regarded the destruction as intentional. See below,
p. 201; and Wright, *Further Eng. Voyages*, pp. lvi, 143; Castellanos, *Discurso*, p. 211.

There were certayne howses fiered,[1] which were the 22
vttermost & farthest howses from the towne, which beinge of
woode & canes & dried with the heate of the sune made so great
a flame as that more were burned then we meant. This day
2 canons of brasse were waighed out of the galleyes, which were
burnte & sunk by the Spaniards at our first cominge to the
towne,[2] and after[wards] 6 smaller peces allso. A Fregate
the day before came into the harbor loden with Cassavia,
which Captain Fenner[3] tooke, & havinge vnladen sett her
afier./

Alonso Bravo's wife sent vnto the generall, which he him 23
self presented, a very rich suite of Buttons of gold & pearle, &
a very faire Iewell sett with Emerauldes & a ringe with an
Emerald & a nother Emeralde sett in a pendent. the Lifftenant
generall likwise was presented with a faire Iewell sett with
Emeralde & a faire ringe with an Emeralde, likwise the
Vicadmirall a faire ringe with an Emeralde. All this he presented
as from his wyfe. the generall at that tyme receued them not
but they were sett aparte & reaceued afterwarde more
conveniently.[4]

This daye there was espied from the church which was our

---

[1] Drake was using pressure since the ransom negotiations were dragging. The
citizens raised their offer successively to 30,000 ducats, 80,000 ducats, and then
100,000 ducats. Wright, *Further Eng. Voyages*, pp. 142–3, 158.

[2] The two royal galleys had been kept in the lagoon instead of going out to meet
Drake's fleet (see above, p. 162). Having been used ineffectually to protect the land
approach at the Caleta, they tried to move closer to the fort and out into the larger
harbour. They were hampered by low water and possibly by mutiny aboard, and then
by a gunpowder explosion on one of them. Abandoned by their slaves and crews, both
were burned the next night by Vique's order to prevent their use by the English. The
latter were able, however, to remove their guns. Wright, *Further Eng. Voyages*,
pp. liii, 58–9, 76–8, 110–11, 127, 133–4, etc.; Castellanos, *Discurso*, pp. 195–6, 305–6.

[3] Captain of Drake's ship.

[4] Although this passage indicates suspicion about Drake's handling of these gifts,
the transaction related to Alonso Bravo's personal ransom. Because he was a prisoner
Drake set the figure of 6,000 ducats for his person and for real estate belonging to
him and a nephew. Of this 1,000 was remitted because Drake was using his house as
headquarters and had received certain jewels. The 5,000 ducats were paid, Bravo's
deposition stated, in gold, jewels, and pearls, for which Drake issued a receipt. Wright,
Further Eng. Voyages, pp. lvii, 89, 96, 124, 235; Castellanos, *Discurso*, pp. xlviii, 214.
This ransom was separate from that required from the city.

watch tower a saile bearinge in with the harbor.[1] [John] Grante, the Master of the Tigar, took a pinasse & went out towards her. Captain Moone & Captain Varney [took] another and Capten Fenner the thirde, very well appoynted. John Grante with his pinasse was the first that aborded the Frigate. He chased him [fol. 68 (MS 30)] hard ashore to a smale Iland ioining to the continent. Captains Moone & Varney were the 2 that came to her with theyre pinasse. But Grante, beinge abourd, wold not suffer them to enter & whiles they were reasoninge, there came a shott or two about there eares, beinge within 40 paces of the shore. Captain Varney havinge a pece [of ordinance] desired his brother Moone to stande before with targat of proofe,[2] & he wolde bestowe a shott one them; for the targat saide he wilbe a defence for vs both. thus standinge in this manner, there came out of the bushes a shoot with 2 bullets. the one of them strake Captain Varney in the head, whereof he fell downe presently & died. the other strake Captain Moone in the right thighe close vnder the belly, which caused him to live not longe after.[3]

This vnfortunate shott strake such a terror into our men that Grante & his men gott them into theyre pinasse agayne without firing the Frigate, and Captain Moones pinasses likwyse haste awaye, Captain Fenners pinasse was rune a grounde so that he coulde not goe to the Fregate but he called to [the] others & wolde have had them staye, but they wolde not or could not heare him. so after he had discharged two or three pieces of Ordinance into the bushes amongest them for company, he came awaye & lefte the Fregate vnburnt. Theire was no body in the Fregate, for as sone as she came a grounde they rane a shoore. there was not above 5 men seene one the lande, but Captain Fennerd saide there were more men comminge in

Cartha-
gena
February

[1] '... a couple of small barkes or boates', according to the *Summarie* (p. 257); a caravel, according to a Spanish report. Wright, *Further Eng. Voyages*, p. 121.

[2] A light round shield or buckler. *OED.* Targets of proof were issued, along with swords and rapiers for Drake's voyage of 1595. Andrews, *Last Voyage*, p. 61.

[3] Moone died some days later (see pp. 176, 258). The vessel put in to an inlet, where Indian bowmen and a few soldiers on a nearby estate came to its aid. They killed 'two English captains who were among the best who came over, and two or three soldiers'. Wright, *Further Eng. Voyages*, pp. 60, 121.

boates. This Fregate was loden with Cassava bread & other vittayles./[1]

This day the Generall caulled a courte where there were divers causes hearde & determinations for divers matters, namely order was taken for the vittaylinge of the soldiors in the towne with provision of meale and there thinges [fol. 68v (MS 30v)] from the shippes. Likwise it was sett downe that none vnder the degree of ansient[2] shulde keepe a Negro or other stranger.

Cartha-
gena
February

There was allso a generall commandement gyven for the well vsage of Strangers, namely Frenchmen, Turks & Negros.[3] There were divers Captens appoynted to make a generall view thorow euery quarter of all such comodyties & marchandize as wolde yelde money, & [it was decided] that the Spaniards shuld buy it yf they wolde, the which was done by my master & others, who deliuered the note of all to the generall.[4] The cheefe substance consisted most in soape from Cordes,[5] paper and such like./[6]

There was likwise a commandement gyven that all men which possess Spanish money shuld bringe it to certayne commissioners appoynted for the purpose & yf they coulde gyve a good account & reason how they came by it, they shuld have English money for it. yf any shulde conceale & not bringe it in, then not only [were they] to be punished, it beinge

---

[1] Castellanos, who described the ship as a frigate carrying provisions from Jamaica, told of the elaborate funeral for one of the English captains. *Discurso*, pp. xlviii–xlix, 216–17.

[2] i.e. ensign.

[3] Many Europeans, as well as negroes, had joined Drake's company during the stay (see p. 202), making up for some of his manpower losses. Most of them were probably released galley slaves. 'Most of the slaves and many of the convicts from the galleys went off with the English as did some of the negroes belonging to private owners.' Regarding the latter, Drake accepted ransom payments from their owners only if the slaves themselves wished to be returned. Wright, *Further Eng. Voyages*, p. 159.

[4] This is the first reference to Knollys in action at Cartagena. He was permitted to perform some non-military functions. See also below.

[5] This refers possibly to Cadiz, in Castile.

[6] Private individuals arranged to pay ransom for soap, wine, oil, and other merchandise. These commodities, along with some iron, were about all that had been left in the town. Wright, *Further Eng. Voyages*, p. 140.

knowne, but also [they were] to loose the benefitt of the voiadge./[1]

The *generall* gave order lickwise for the wateringe of shippes & that there shulde by made welles in the sande of purpose for it, because it was suspected that most of the welles in the towne were poisoned[2] & this was to be done with expedition & the charge thereof was given to the Rere admirall./[3]

The *generall* made an offer & wisht the Captens to thinke vpon it, that the golde and siluer allready gotten might be put in chestes fitt for it & committed to the charge of sum such as they thought meeteste for it, for he had no desire to kepe it him selfe. but this motion fell dead, beinge coldly offered, without farther proceedinge sauinge that the liftenant generall who had lickwise the keepinge of sum, said it was a very good motion./[4]

The *generall* appoynted Captain Fenner to bringe in a note of all the ordinance of Brasse & Iron which we had taken since the beginninge of the action,[5] for that most of the Captains misliked that so much good ordinance which was the chiefest credite of our voyadge shulde be bestowed in so leakey a shippe as the New Years Gyfte was at this [time].[6]

[There is another gap of two numbered pages, representing 23 to 27 February. The next page begins in the middle of the copy of the captains' resolutions of 27 February, calling for the expedition to turn homeward. The version in this document agrees closely with that printed in Hakluyt's edition of the

---

[1] i.e. their share in the total profit of the expedition.

[2] In 1594 Antonio de Barros made a statement that Drake had desired his capture or death for having poisoned the water at Cartagena (A. de I., 72–5–21, Santa Fé 92, cited in Wright, *Further Eng. Voyages*, p. lvii, n.), but such alarm seems not to be supported by other documents. The continuing loss of men by sickness may have prompted this measure.

[3] i.e. Francis Knollys. Cf. p. 152.

[4] Here is further indication of the writer's distrust of Drake and Carleill.

[5] As captain of Drake's ship Fenner was at times assigned special responsibilities. Cf. pp. 84, 167.

[6] It was this ship's serious leak after the departure from Cartagena that brought the whole fleet back to the city again. See pp. 105, 262.

Summarie, but begins with the second item, relating to disappointment about profit, it being far below the expectation,]

[fol. 69 (MS 33)]

which by the generalety of the enter prises was first conceaved,[1] Cartagena
& being farther advysed of the sclenderness of our strength, February
where vnto we are now reduced,[2] as well in the respect of the
smal*l*e nomber of able bodyes as also not littell in regarde of
the slake dysposition of the greatest parte of those w*h*ich
remayne, very many of the better mindes & men beinge eyther[3]
consumed by death or weak*e*ned by sickness or hurts; and
lastly, since that as yet there is not layd downe to our
knowledge any souch enterprises as may s*e*eme conuenient to
be vndertaken, w*i*th souch force as we are presently able to
make, and w*i*thall of souch certayne licklihood as w*i*th God's
good successe w*h*ich it may please him to bestowe vppon vs,
the same may promise to yelde vnto vs any souch sufficient
contentment, we do therefore conclude heare vppon, that it is
better to hould sure as we may the honor allready gotten, and
w*i*th the same to returne towardes our gratious Souerayne and
Country, from whence yf it shall please God and her Ma*i*esty
to sett vs out[4] agayne w*i*th her orderly meanes and entertayn-
ment we are most ready and willing to go thorow w*i*th any
thinge that the vttermost of our streng*t*h and endevours shalbe
able to reach vnto. But heare w*i*thall we do advyse[5] and protest
that yt is farr from our thoughtes eyther to refuse or so much
as s*e*eme to be we*a*ry of any thinge w*h*ich for the present
shalbe farther required or directed to be done by vs from our
gen*e*rall./

3   The 3*rd* and last poynt is conserning the ransom of this cytie

---

[1] These paragraphs from the captains' resolutions are printed here in full, since they
did not appear with the *Summarie* until Hakluyt's edition (see p. 255, n. 4). Here, as
with his version, they must have been copied from a document that was distributed
among the company.

[2] In the MS, *reduceded*.

[3] In the MS, *cyther*.

[4] In Hakluyt's version (see p. 255, n. 4), *forth* instead of *out*.

[5] In the MS, *adwyve*.

of Cartagena, for the which before it was touched with any fyer there was made an offer of sum 7 or 8000 *li*. sterling.[1]

This much we vtter as our opynions agreeing, so it be done in good sorte to accept the offer aforesaide rather then to break of by standing still vpon our demaundes of a [   ] 1000 *li*.,[2] which seemes a matter vnpossible to be performed by them for the present. & to say the truth we may now with much more[3] honor and reputation be better satisfyed with that offer of theires at the first (yf they will now be content to do it) then we might at that tyme with a great deal[4] more, in somuch as we have taken our full pleasure both in the vttermost sacking and spoyling of all theire howses, goods[5] and marchandice as allso in that we have consumed and ruined a great parte of the towne with fyer. and this much farther is considered of vs, that as there be in the voyadge a great many of poore men who haue willingly aduentured theire liues and travels[6] and divers among them having spent theire apparell and such other like

Cartagena February provisions as theire smalle [fol. 69v (MS 33v)] meanes might gyve them leave to prepare, which beinge donne vpon so good and allowable intention as this action hath allways carried with yt, meaning against the Spaniards, our greatest and most dangerous enemys, for which certainly we cannot but have[7] an inwarde regard so farr as may lye in vs, to healp in all good sorte towards the satisfaction of this theire expectation, and by procuring them some littell benefitt to encourage them and to nurrishe this willing and ready dysposition of theirs, both by them and in others by their example agaynst any other tyme

[1] In Hakluyt's version, 'some xxvii or xxviij thousand pounds.' The original offer of the Spaniards of 25,000 ducats (see above, p. 166, n. 5), at 5s. 6d. per ducat, represents £6,875.

[2] In the MS the figure is written thus: '10 1000 li.', as if the scribe was uncertain about the exact figure. In the Hakluyt version, the figure appears as 'one hundred thousand pounds', again (see note 1) confusing ducats and pounds and representing a sum far greater than any of Drake's demands.

[3] The word *more* does not appear in the Hakluyt version.

[4] In the MS, *greadell*.

[5] In Hakluyt's version, *their householde goods*.

[6] i.e. *travails*.

[7] In Hakluyt's version, after *enemy*, the wording is: *so surely wee cannot but have*. . . .

of like occasion. but because it may be supposed that here in we forgett not the privatt benefitt of our selues [   ]¹ to this composition, we do therefore thinke good for the claering² of our selues of all souch suspition do³ declare heareby that what part or portion yt be in this ransom or composition for Cartagen*a* w*hi*ch shuld cum vnto vs we do gyve⁴ and bestowe the same wholy vppon the poore men who hath traua*i*led⁵ w*i*th vs in the voyadge, meaning as well the Saylor as the Souldiour, wishing w*i*th all our h*e*artes yt wear souch or as much as might se*e*me a sufficient reward for the*i*r paynfull inde*a*uours. and for the firme confermation heareof, we have thought me*e*te to subscribe these presents w*i*th our handes in the place and tyme aforesaide.⁶

The 28*th* and last of February Alonso Bravo vvpon his owne worde was lett goe into the country to see his wyffe who was very si*c*ke.⁷ he returned that night at the hower appoynted. 28

The 1*st* of March came in many flagges of truce but none of any accompte.⁸ 1 of March

The 2*nd* day about a 11 a cloke came in a flagg of truce from the Gouernor. the messengers were Tristando Dorive, mercadante, [and] Piedro Messie, capten of the castell. These brought a letter from the gouernor to awtoricc the*i*r doinges for they came to entreat for the towne. after Dinner the g*e*ner*a*ll and certayne of his private counsell had conference with them, 2

---

¹ A line has been omitted here, as the copyist's eye moved to the second *ourselves*. From the Hakluyt version the missing words can be supplied: *and are thereby the rather mooved to incline our selves.*

² i.e. *clearing.*

³ i.e. *to.*

⁴ In Hakluyt's version, *freely give.*

⁵ In Hakluyt's version, *remained* instead of *travailed.*

⁶ The MS does not list the signers. In the Hakluyt version they are Carleill, Goring, Sampson, Powell, '&c.'

⁷ Alonso's wife, Doña Elvira de Azevedo, like the other women, was staying in the country (Wright, *Further Eng. Voyages*, p. 124). See also below.

⁸ This refers to attempts of individual citizens to reach terms regarding their property. One poorer citizen thought that private individuals might have furnished Drake with more than 200,000 ducats beyond the official ransom (Wright, *Further Eng. Voyages*, p. 197). One of Drake's hostages attempted to ransom some slaves (Wright, op. cit., p. 51). See also Castellanos, *Discurso*, pp. xlviii, 213.

but they offered [an amount] so shorte of the *generall's* de*m*aund as they were farr from agre*e*ing and so dep*a*rted./¹

3   The 3*rd* Tristando Dorive came agayne with Algozin Mayor² and divers others of mea*ner* sorte, who did entreat agayne for the*i*re towne, offering sum what more the*n* before. The*i*re offer was 1000 peces,³ but yt wold not be accepted. so they dep*a*rted, promising to come agayne the next day. this night Alonso Bravo had leave of the *generall* to go fourth with them.

4   The 4*th* day Alonso Bravo went a letter to the *generall* to excuse him selfe for that day for his wyffe was like to dye. this day the *generall* burnt [the] most p*a*rte of the howses w*i*thout the Barricados. this day there came certayne marchants who were desir*o*us to deale for the*i*r privatt*e* howses p*a*rticularly but the *generall* awnswered them, yf they wold among them make the some⁴ as much as he demanded he was content to deale with them, otherwise he desired them to spend no more tyme in the matter.

This day Cap*tain* Forteskue dyed abourd the barke Bonner, who was long sicke of the infection of Sai*n*t Iacamo and, being onc*e* recouered fell sicke agayne at Cartagena, and was throwne ouer bourd w*i*thout any other solemnety.⁵

Cartagena   [fol. 70 (MS 34)] This day Liff*t*enant Stanton⁶ was made
March   Capten of a company w*h*ich [the] Sergeant maior had the leading before of, the chardg*e* was delyvered him by the

¹ Cf. above, p. 166. According to the Spanish documents, the chief negotiators were Tristan de Orive, the merchant, and Diego Daça, lieutenant governor of the town (Wright, *Further Eng. Voyages*, pp. 68, 143). The former described some of the proceedings in a letter to correspondents in Panama, 1/11 March 1586 (ibid., pp. 41–6).

² Mayor became one of the hostages for the city (see p. 175).

³ In the MS, *pecos* or *peces*, probably referring to pesos, or 'pieces of gold', representing the Spanish ducat (see p. 259, n. 2). The figure given here, however, is inaccurate, since by this time the city's offer was increasing (see above, p. 167, n. 1).

⁴ i.e. *sum*.

⁵ George Fortescue, captain of the *Bonner*. On the recurrence of the sickness see p. 254.

⁶ Stanton had been lieutenant for the soldiers under Knollys (see p. 135). This promotion must explain the inclusion of his name at the end of the list of land captains printed in the *Summarie* (see p. 215), as well as its absence from the 'Furnishing List' of 1585 (Document 1).

generall publickly in the markett place. this night came in
6 or 7 Caveleroys[1] and lay all night in the towne.

The *5th* day Alonso Bravo came into the towne, who after 5
he had had conference with the Spaniards they agreed [on the
ransom] for theire towne. The some[2] was 200 and 20000 peses,[3]
[the city] hauing 10 dayes respet for the payment thereof so
that presently they did put in sufficient pledges,[4] the which they
agreed vnto, promising to bring them in the next day & so
they departed.

The *6th* day came in 2 gentlemen souldiors, one of which had 6
served a long tyme in Flanders. these were malecontents and
with smalle intreaty wold have gone with vs. This night came
in two pledges, the one called Algozin Mayor, and the other
Don Andres Senior dell Iudea.[5]

The *7th* day there was a court kept at the Vuead, where 7
divers matters were heard but none of any Importance.[6] this
day Alonso [wrote][7] vnto the *generall* of the death of his wyffe
with the request that she might be peaceabley buryed in the
priory of Saint Frauncisco,[8] the which the *generall* graunted.

The *8th* day Alonso Bravo brought his wyfe to the foresaid 8
pryory where she was buried after their owne manner with

[1] i.e. *caballeros*, or *cavaliers*, gentlemen above the 'mean' sort referred to on 3 March.
[2] i.e. *sum*.
[3] i.e. 220,000 pesos. The writer may have had in mind the less valuable silver peso, or plate, since the ransom figure finally reached was 110,000 (gold) ducats. Alonso Bravo was given credit by the Spaniards for persuading Drake to settle for this figure and for the form in which it would be paid. See Wright, *Further Eng. Voyages*, pp. lvi, 123.
[4] i.e. provided that hostages should be furnished immediately.
[5] On Algonzin Mayor see above, p. 174. Don Andres Señor dell Judea has not been identified. The Spanish documents do not give the names of the hostages (Wright, *Further Eng. Voyages*, p. xlii). One of the two wrote an account of 'The sack of the city of Cartagena, done by Francis Drake, Englishman,' which is printed in Wright, op. cit., pp. 46–52. He was evidently a man of some wealth, since he mentioned paying ransom for some of his own slaves.
[6] Again Drake was following customary procedure, possibly for minor cases of discipline.
[7] In the MS, *wroght*.
[8] The priory was located south of the town (see the town map). It was spared from burning and separately ransomed (Wright, *Further Eng. Voyages*, pp. lvii, 124). Bravo's wife had died at their estate at Turbaco (ibid., p. 59).

smalle solemnety, sauing that the generall bestowed a volley of shott of [for] her for Alonso's sake, of smalle and great shott because he was a souldier, the which he tooke it most thankfully. he sent this day to the generall by his man Ionas[1] a strange beast called a periculous Ezo.[2] This day about one of the cloke after dinner Captain Moone dyed, who was hurt with a shott the same tyme that Captain Varney was killed.[3] he was buryed the same night at 5 a cloke in the great church of Cartagena. The generall and all the Captains weare at the funerall. There was likwyse a volley of shott bestowed one him./

9   The 9th day Tristando Dorive came into the generall who shewed that the gouernour wold bargayne for the marchandice that was in the towne; wherevppon the generall caused many thinges to be brought from the shippes, but in fine they durst buy nothinge. this day Alonso came in greatly greving for the death of his wyfe. this night the generall shewed a letter to the Spaniards which was founde in the towne, in which was a Declaration of the warres betwene England and Spayne in the most severest manner that might be, in which was no mercy but fyer and sworde./[4]

10   This 10th day there came in divers of smalle accompte who brought word of the coming of the money the next day for the first paiment. this night at supper the generall spake very bitterly before the Spaniards of the Pope, describing the Dyssolute lyving of him and and his Cardenals at Roome, at which wordes

[1] Jonas, Drake's interpreter (see pp. 178, 295), assisted with the ransom arrangements. He was later mentioned by the investigating justice as the source of some of his information. Castellanos, Discurso, pp. xlvii, 204, 275, 307.

[2] Possibly intended for erizo, Spanish for hedgehog or porcupine. If the adjective was intended to be pediculous, then the creature may have been 'a lousy hedgehog'. I am indebted to D. B. Quinn for this suggestion.

[3] See above, p. 168.

[4] In his haste to leave the city the governor had neglected to take with him the warning despatches which had arrived from Spain. King Philip's reference to Drake as a corsair (pirate) so enraged him that he protested about it at the ransom negotiations, the Spaniards reported, and he declared his hope to be in Spain some day to demand satisfaction. Castellanos, Discurso, pp. xlvii, 208-9; Wright, Further Eng. Voyages, pp. lv, 114, 127, 134; Oppenheim, Naval Tracts . . . Monson, I, 131 and n.

one of the Spaniards, namely Don Andres, one[1] of the pledges, was sumwhat offended with the *generalls* speeches, desiringe him not to do them that wronge, beinge as his prisoners, as to vse speeches so much offensive to theire consciences, the freedome of which he could not take from them. but the *generall* wolde not leave them, so that agaynst theire willes they were enforced to heare the truth./

This 11*th* day in the morning[2] Tristando Dorive came to the 11 *generall*, who tould him that this night the money shuld come and so departed. About a 11 a cloke there came a nother with the like message. About 4 a cloke Piedro Messie, capten of the castell,[3] with 2 other Caveliers came to the bridge and sayde the plate[4] was hard by. then ran Tristando agayne, who desired the bridge might be let downe, for the Carriages were at hand, the which was done.[5] The Sergeant Maior and most of the land Captens *were* there ready to receaue them. so there came in 20 mules loaden with siluer wedges; 8 of them weare a loade, 4 one eache side. there was likwyse sum gould and Iewells brought. the most of the wedges wayed 50 li starlinge. All these mules weare brought to the *generalls* howse and there

[1] In the MS, *of*.

[2] Payment of the city's ransom was to be completed by Monday 14/24 March; or by 13/23 March, according to Spanish records (Wright, *Further Eng. Voyages*, pp. 59, 159). The *Leicester* journal notes the final payment on the morning of 15 March (see below). Various statements by individual citizens assenting to the ransom negotiations are in Appendix VII, Castellanos, *Discurso*, pp. 332–8.

[3] Don Pedro Mexia Mirabal (see p. 166).

[4] The figure of 110,000 ducats had been agreed upon for the city's ransom, but Drake consented to reduce it to 107,000 in bullion rather than taking 12,000 in jewels. Some 12,000 ducats came from certain public funds that Alonso Bravo had had in his custody, but for most of the payment the governor decided to 'borrow' two hundred silver bars belonging to the Crown which had recently been brought into the city by ship (worth 79,000 to 80,000 ducats), with repayment to be made by Christmas by the citizens, rated according to the value of their properties. Wright, *Further Eng. Voyages*, pp. 51, 61, 64, 89, 96, 123, 143, 149, 159. In the citizens' letter of 4 June 1586 (N.S.), the ransom figure was given as 108,000 ducats, of which 80,000 were 'borrowed'. Wright, op. cit., pp. 161–2. See also Castellanos, *Discurso*, p. 307. On the value of the ransom see below p. 259, n. 2.

[5] According to the deposition of Francisco Dalva (or de Alba), chief ensign of the city cavalry and clerk of the municipal council, who was present and kept a record, the transactions were completed by Tristan de Orive and Pedro Lopez Treviño. Wright, *Further Eng. Voyages*, pp. 65, 68.

dischardged, which lay all night vnwayde. There came in with
this siluer 7 Caveliers who were lodged sum with a nother.

12   The 12*th* day in the morning the weyghts were put vp and
3 of the *generalls* gentl*emen* by his appoynment [were ordered]
to se*e* the weight of the siluer, namely Ionas, Annes, and Ardle.
there was brought in the whole a 100 and 16 wedges.[1]

Cartagena   [fol. 70v (MS 34v)] The Spaniards did most ernestly desire
March   that they might pay the odde 1000 peses in Iewells, for they
protested and sware they weare not able to pay yt in platte, but
the*i*re wyves Iewells must be pawned for it. the *generall* was
contented to accept so much in Iewells at re*a*sonable prises.
so presently they shewed the*i*re Iewells which weare all of
Emeralds, sauing some pearle, which they held at such prises as
the *Generall* wold not agre*e* with them, at that tyme offeringe
to rebate them 300 peses to pay all in plate.[2] but they refused yt,
pleading disability. they shewed neuer a rare Iewill. they had
not many pearle, but those they had weare Orient, but the most
p*a*rte ragges for embro*i*derers, and some [ran][3] at 5 or 6 duketts
a pearle. The g*e*nerall went to deale with them, but fo*r* y*t* time
they were lycensed to departe./

This daye came in dyvers Spaniards to viewe the*i*re howses
and souch thinges as they lefte besydes. they made a shewe as
yf they wold buy yt, but yt proued otherwise, [and] those were
sent out agayne at night. they wear at the*i*re goinge out
appoynted, as many as wolde [be willing to] buy the*i*re stuffe,[4]
to come in the next day at the sound of the Drome an ower
after the Caveliers went out of the towne./

13   The 13*th* came in many Spaniards but none of any account,
or from the gouernour or Bishop.

14   The 14*th* came in many to see the*i*re howses and stuff, who
brought word that the next payment shuld be brought in the

[1] If each mule carried eight wedges, the total should be 160, not 116. If so, the weight
of silver was 8,000 pounds (50 pounds per wedge). These must be the 'blocks of silver'
listed in Drake's fiscal accounts. Corbett, *Sp. War*, p. 90.

[2] i.e. *plate*. Cf. above, p. 177, n. 4, where, however, the figures are 12,000 ducats
(or *peses*) and 3,000 ducats, instead of the 1,000 and 300 mentioned here.

[3] In the MS, *ronne*.

[4] Cf. note 8, p. 173.

next day. this night the ge*n*erall caused many fyer workes to be made.[1]

The 15*th* daye about 8 of the cloke came in vittell to the 15 ge*n*erall, and many Spaniards came to see the*i*re howses. about a 11 a cloke was brought in the last payment for the towne, of w*h*ich sum was in gould, som*e* in siluer, and some in Iewells. this daye the Spanyeards made a shewe as yf they wold agre*e* w*i*th the ge*n*erall for the marchandize, but it was but wordes, for nothinge was done, sauing y[t] sum souldiors made privat*e* com*m*odety of souch thinges as they had by the generalls appoyntment; namely Capten Morgan and Capten Sampson who had very great commedety of cardes and souch other thinges as was lefte i*n* the*i*re howses; likwise Ca*ptain* Heriza and Ca*ptain* Fennerd[2] . . . [end of the Harley fragment].

Document 10

The Discourse and Description of the Voyage of Sir Frawncis Drake & Master Frobisher, set forward the 14 Daie of September 1585/ (British Library Royal MS. 7 C. xvi, fols. 166–173).[3]

[fol. 166] The 14 Daie of September Wee set saile from

---

[1] This must refer to more burning of houses or else to use of the small brass bombs which Drake had brought in (see Wright, *Further Eng. Voyages*, pp. lvi and n., and 54; and Castellanos, *Discurso*, p. 327). It was probably done as a warning to hasten the payments, which were to have been completed by this date (see p. 177, n. 2).

[2] It is unfortunate that this MS, so richly detailed for the Cartagena stay, is incomplete. On the departure (31 March) and the second brief stop there see Documents 6, 7, and 10.

[3] This document, which bears the title as given here, was printed in full, but in modern English, by J. S. Corbett in 1898 (*Sp. War*, pp. 12–27). Commonly referred to since then as 'The *Primrose* Log', because its author travelled aboard that ship under Frobisher as captain, it has contributed much valuable information about the voyage. Corbett's editing was careful. It has been the task of the present editor to make a fresh transcription from the original text, correcting a very few errors in Corbett's reading, and to add further documentation from sources he did not use. The document is referred to in this volume as the *Primrose* journal.

The author of the narrative is still not known, although it is probably his name,

Plinmouthe in Devon with 29 Shippes & pinnisses,[1] directing our course for to touche at the Ilandes of Bayon & then alongst the Coast to Cape de Verde & so to the West Indies.

The 18 Daie of September wee met with a French man of 60 tunne, with whom wee talked, & fownde he came from New Fownd Lande & so wee let him departe/

The 19 Daie ther were ij shippes w[hich] sett chase to somme of vs & after they perceaved the whole fleet they tooke them to flighte[2]

The 22 & 23 daies an other ship gave chase to vs whom we[e let][3] passe, the same Daie wee tooke a Bisken[4] of a 150 tunne a [very] good new shipp laden with fisshe, Wee tooke her alonge with v[s and] made good prize of her shee was of *Saint Sebastians* in Spaine.

The 24 Daie wee fell with *Galizia* a place called the Moor[es][5] & presentlie the Spaniardes made greate fires & raised the coun[try]. Wee founde there 5 saile of Frenchmen, fowre, wee let goe & [one] wee tooke with vs becawse wee fownde no bodie in her,[6] their [men] weare runne ashore for feare, They were all loaden with salte. The same Daie wee mett verie neere with 20 saile of Inglisshmen. [Some we]re of London, some of Bristow,[7] Hampton &c:/ they tolde vs tha[t they] had burned a towne called *Viana*/[8] & lost 25 men there, & [they] woulde goe with vs to burne *Baion* & *Vigo*/

Henley or Henly, which appears at the bottom of the final page of the MS (see below, p. 210, n. 6). His record shows that he was a careful observer, and suggests that he was a soldier rather than a seaman.

[1] Corbett, in *Drake and the Tudor Navy* (II, 12, n.) quotes Tanner MS 79 for the figure of 21 ships and 8 pinnaces, a total of 29. See Table of Ships and the *Summarie* (p. 213).

[2] For incidents of 18 and 19 September see also pp. 73–4.

[3] The edge of the MS is torn. Words inserted within brackets are usually those supplied by Corbett (*Sp. War*, p. 2).

[4] i.e. Biscayne. Cf. pp. 75–6.

[5] i.e. Muros. Cf. p. 77, n. 2.

[6] This was the ship which was renamed *Drake*. See Table of Ships and p. 77.

[7] i.e. Bristol. Cf. p. 77, n. 1. Sparrowe's letter (Lansdowne MS 100, fol. 81) mentions meeting with four English men of war, two of which were pressed into Drake's fleet. One was doubtless the armed merchantman, *George Bonaventure*, which was with the fleet at Tysus but returned to England on 8 October. See pp. 86, 89.

[8] i.e. Viana do Castelo, a port in northern Portugal.

[The] 27 Daie wee tooke a Spanishe fissher boate in the morning,[1] [then] wee went into *Baion* & ankered in the harbour, which the [inhabita]ntes perceavinge made greate fires & raised the countrie, [very] greate numbers as well horsmen as footemen shewed themselues vnto vs with there Drummes & Ensignes/

The same Daie after noone wee landed about 700[2] men close before the towne vppon a little Iland, & there came to vs bothe Spaniardes & Inglishmen from the towne that Dwelled therin to know what wee woulde have,[3] Wee tolde them that wee weare comme for those Inglisshmen that they had in Prison & for our merchauntes goodes which they kepte & that wee lacked victualles & they gave vs faire woordes & tolde vs that wee should have wine & victuall & anie thinge thei had for monie.

The same Daie the Spaniardes sent vnto our governour grapes, apples, Orenges & such like,

There was vppon this Iland a little chapple with a howse adioining to hit, but the people were fledd, there was 3 or fowre Images in that chapple which wee brake & burned[4] & fownde nothinge else [on] this Ilande but an olde chest, with a cope in hit & other suc[h] reliques/ Wee kepte this Ile till midnight & then Departed/

The same Daie in the morninge wee tooke a fissher boate & abow[t] x of the clocke at nighte, wee tooke a boate carr[y]inge 6 hogges to those that were Incamped againste vs/

[fol. 166v] The 28 Daie wee had suche Tempestes that wee weare forced to strike [our] top & top mastes & tackle/ ij of

---

[1] See the Map Text. The Sparrowe letter notes that Drake took a French and an English bark on the 26th, and that on the 27th, before the fleet came to anchor, Drake and Frobisher went ashore in a fishing boat. Lansdowne MS 100, fol. 81v. Cf. p. 78 and n. 3.

[2] The figure was printed as 200 by Corbett (*Sp. War*, p. 2). According to other accounts it was 1,000 (see note on p. 78). A thousand men were landed at 'a small Round island', according to Cotton MS Titus B. VIII, fol. 251.

[3] The English messenger was the merchant, Short (or Sharp). See pp. 78–81 and 219.

[4] The English merchant negotiator wrote that Drake's men landed in the island of Our Lady of the Borge; and 'they were so bold as to take the clothes from her, and when they had so done, they took both her and all the rest of her company of the church that she was wont to have'. *C.S.P.For. 1585–1586*, p. 63.

our Shyppes were Driven to cut ther mastes & cast them over borde & some to forsake the harbour, And the same Daie wee loste the Barke Talbot for certaine daie[s].[1]

The 31 Daie[2] the Tempest beganne to cease & wee removed our shippes & came to an anker before *Vigo* & there wee fownde beddes & other howsholde stuffe carried into boates & lyinge on the shore, there we lefte 4 men which had bin behedded by the Spaniardes the night before,[3] thither came a Frenchman from the *Tarseros*[4] laden with wine & sugars, this shipp beinge loaden with Spaniardes goodes wee made [goo]d prize & tooke her into our custodie & shared the sugars emongst [the] fleete.

[The] night before there was taken a boate with certaine gentlewomen[5] [in] hit with monie, plate & Iewels & ij crosses verie riche, [li]kewise there was taken a boate loden with leather, one of [which] said ij crosses was as muche as one coulde lifte & was [val]wed to be woorthe 3000 Duckates. the other crosse, monie, [je]wels plate & leather was valewed at 3000 Duckates more.[6]

The 2 Daie of October the Spaniardes came Downe to the [w]ater side & Desired parley with vs[7] & then was Master Captaine Frobisher sent vnto them whoo tolde them that wee Desired to [take] water there & likewise to have our Inglisshmen which they had in prison & there goodes. & they awnswered wee shoulde vppon cond[ition th]at wee woulde Deliver them those goodes which wee had [taken] since wee came thither which they valewed as is before said [at] 6000 Duckates & presentlie after this parley there came Dow[n some] 8 Ensignes to the water side & shewed them selues to [vs].[8]

---

[1] Cf. pp. 81, 221.

[2] The date of 31 [September] was intended for 1 October. See pp. 64, 85.

[3] Only one young man is mentioned in the *Tiger* journal.

[4] i.e. Terceiras in the Azores, the rendezvous for fleets coming from the Indies, either East or West.

[5] The word was printed as *gentlemen* in Corbett, *Sp. War*, p. 4.

[6] Valued at 7s. or 8s. 6d. per ducat, 6,000 gold ducats would be worth 2,100 l. or 2,550 l. The Spaniards estimated their total loss as amounting to over 30,000 ducats. See the *Summarie*, p. 222 and n. 3. See also p. 259, n. 2.

[7] Cf. pp. 86, 222.

[8] Cf. pp. 85, n. 3 , 87.

The next Daie the 3 of October there came Spaniard*es*
ab[oard] o*ur* Admyrall to Banket[1] *with* vs & then Captaine
Crosse [and] Captaine [Erisey],[2] were sent to *Baion* & ij
Spaniard*es* we[re] lefte pledges for them. the*n* the Spaniard*es*
came thicke abowte o*ur* shipp*es*/

The 4 daie wee went a shore & watered & wasshed o*ur*
clothes & kepte o*ur* men in Garrison/

the 6 Daie wee came to an anker before *Vigo* againe/ & sent
on a shore to fetche o*ur* captaines aborde but they delaid the
time [and the]y sent more Spaniard*es* aboorde of vs & there were
speeches emongst the Spaniard*es* that if wee tarried there 16
Daies they woulde wasshe there hand*es* in Inglisshe mens blood/

In this harbour wee fownde a Carvell loden *with* fisshe. so
soone [a]s wee cam*me* the men forsooke her so that wee carried
her awa[y wi]th vs/[3]

The 7 Daie wee waied anker & came to an anker againe more
neere *Baion*. there wee tooke the fisshe owte of the Bisken
which wee tooke firste/ & brake the ship in peeces,[4] the othe*r*
Carvell that wee tooke owte of *Vigo* roade wee made a hole in
her & suncke her & her fisshe.

[fol. 167] The 8 Daie[5] wee manned iiij pinnesses & o*ur* galley
& the George & sent them to *Baion* where after muche parley
wee receaved o*ur* Captaines & Delivered there men/

The 9 Daie the winde began to wex greate & wee waied
anker & wente vnto the sea, the nighte before wee tooke a
Frencheman loden *with* fisshe *which* wee let goe & the same
daie the barke Talbot came & fownde vs in the same harbour
where shee left vs.

[1] i.e. banquet.

[2] The name is supplied from other accounts.

[3] The anonymous journal (Cotton MS Titus B. VIII, fol. 251v) notes for 5 October:
'Before Vigoe was a Portingall Shipe Lauden with Neve Found Land fish where the
Portingalls wher gone all ashore....' On the disposal of this vessel see below
(7 October).

[4] This was the Biscayan ship taken on 22–3 September. See pp. 75, 88.

[5] The dates (8–11 October) differ from those in Carleill's records and are probably
less accurate. According to Carleill's accounts, the *Talbot* got back on 7 October, the
hostages were returned on the 9th, the fleet sailed on the 11th, and the *Primrose* was
separated from the fleet the night of the 13th. See pp. 88–91.

The eleventh Daie wee in the Primrose beinge vizadmyrall lost all our Shippes by a Tempest savinge the Frenche ship wee tooke last.[1]

The 16 Daie we Descried the Iles of Matheros,[2] but wee went not in.

the 17 Daie wee met with our fleet againe but the Tiger had lost her pynnasses[3] & the Admirall had lost her pinnase with 6 men in her/

The 22 Daie wee gave chase to ij shippes but what they weare wee know not[4]

The 24 Daie wee fell with the *Canaries*.

The 26 Daie wee had sight of the Towne of Reff[5] & so coa[sted] alonge towardes the grawnd *Canaries*/

The 28 Daie we gave chase to a Frenche man & spoke to him, h[e] tolde vs that hee was bownde for *Peru*, or to meete with the k[ing] of Spaines fleete from the Indies & tolde vs that they mett with 40 saile of Spaniardes at *Cape Saint Vincentes*/[6] & said that hee had lost the companie of iij shippes that hee was Admirall of, he plied vp and Downe the Ilandes to meete with them againe & he was verie gladd of our companie/

On the iij[7] Daie of November wee put our Shippes into the Ilande of *Palme*[7] before the Towne called *Palme*/ thinkinge to have ankered ther but they presentlie shott there great ordinaunce at vs abowte xx[ti] shott & stroke the Admyrall quite thorowghe in ij severall places & shot the Barke Talbot thorowghe the sailes but thankes be to God our men had no hurte/ They had iij platt formes that they Did Discharge at vs & florisshed[8] with there Insignes/ wee had a faire leadinge

---

[1] The French ship, referred to in the *Tiger* journal as 'the Burton barke', afterwards known as *Drake*. See p. 91.

[2] i.e. Madeiras.

[3] The date was 19 October, according to the *Tiger* journal (p. 91).

[4] Cf. p. 92. The *Primrose* dates are in agreement once more with those of the *Tiger* journal.

[5] Possibly the town of Arrecifa (now Port Naos) on Lanzarote (Corbett, *Sp. War*, p. 6, n.).

[6] Cf. pp. 93, 128, n. 1.

[7] Cf. pp. 93, 128, 223.

[8] In the MS, *florishinge* had been written and crossed through.

gale of winde & put into the sea not meaninge to leave them soe.[1]

The 4 Daie wee went a shore on an other Ilande[2] harde by for water but ther was none to bee had, There wee fownde an Inglisshe boie, hee came Downe with the Iustice of the Ile with xx^ti or xxx^ti men with them. They asked vs what wee woulde have. wee tolde them oyle, wine & water. Wee got the boie into our boate with muche adoo. Wee asked the boie how he came there. he tolde vs that hee was borne at *Plimton* in Devon & that he was left there to sell wheate & kersies for a brother he had & he had bin there halfe a yeare. wee enquired the state of the countrie of him but he Durste not tell vs & then wee gott ij Spaniardes into our boate & they tolde vs what was in the Ilande so wee set them a shore & bad them bringe vs sheepe or goates, butter or cheese or oyle or anie thinge & they shoulde have monie for hit. The boie & these ij men went to the Iustice & tolde him & hee sent them to vs againe & promised to geeve vs a Doossen goates but none came/

[fol. 167v] Wee landed above 600 men there with there furniture[3] & marched & cast ringes. perceavinge they woulde send vs nothinge, we wente aborde thinkinge the next Daie to overrune the whole Ilande.

But the winde came faire the next Daie, & the same nyght wee Descried 4 of our shippes which had lost our companie before,[4] soe wee tooke the faire winde & went to sea, where otherwise wee had gonne to *Palme* & sacked hit if wee mighte/[5]

The 10 of November we Descried the land of *Barbarie* & sailinge alongst the coaste in sight of lande wee fell with Cape Blanke.

[1] The *Summarie* (p. 223) suggests that only conditions of the sea prevented a landing attempt. See also p. 94 and below.

[2] The landing at Ferro (Hierro), where they met the English boy, was on 5 November, according to the Map Text and the *Tiger* journal (see pp. 64, 95).

[3] On the numbers, see pp. 95, 224.

[4] The ships were *Hawkins*, *Hope*, *Francis*, and *Scout*. See p. 95.

[5] Corbett (*Sp. War*, p. 7 and n.) suggests that Drake's interest in Palma had been for replenishing his supplies, rather than for booty, since it was not mentioned in the plans as outlined in the document of April 1586.

The 14 Daie wee mett at that cape with 4 saile of Frenchmen ridinge at an Anker & so soone as they descried vs they waied [a]nker & got them to sea. Wee gave them chase & spoke with them. [The]y thoughte that wee had bin a fleete of Spaniardes.[1] And in [gi]vinge them chase they threw of a little pinnase which pinnase with [the] men in her went with vs/

The 16 Daie wee fell with *Bonafista*[2] an Iland/ & the next morne [w]e fell with an other Ile called *Maioy*[3] & the same night we [ank]red at an other Iland called *Santa Augo*,[4] where we presentlie [la]nded 600 men[5] & thought the next morninge to take them suddenlie. [b]ut they had descried vs the same night wee landed & in the morne when wee came into the towne they were all gon owte, neither man, woman nor childe lefte/ & they had taken with them all the best of ther goodes as golde, silver, plate & apparell. This towne had abowte 6 or 700 howses in hit.[6] They shott abowte a dossen greate shott at our shippes in the night & so lefte off/[7]

Wee fownde betweene 50 & 60 peeces of ordinaunce there in the fortes. They had iiij fortes & all of brasse. they were valewed with these peeces,[8] at a thowsand powndes. likewise wee fownde there xij barrels of Powder & brought all awaie with vs, so that wee lefte them not 1 peec[e]. Wee fownde in

[1] Cf. p. 224. The encounter was on 11 November, according to the *Leicester* journal (p. 133), but 13 November, according to the Map Text (p. 65) and the newsletter (p. 110).

[2] i.e. Buena Vista, in the Cape Verde Islands.

[3] i.e. Maia.

[4] i.e. Santiago. Although the dates of this journal are not always reliable, there is agreement here that the arrival was on 17 November, with the entry into the town occurring on the 18th. Cf. pp. 65, 97, 225, n. 1.

[5] The number is lower than that in other accounts. See pp. 135, 225.

[6] The town had a population of 1,500 at the 1572 census. Duncan, *Atlantic Islands*, p. 173.

[7] The French narrative (Lacour, p. 21) stated that there was some cannon fire on the evening of the landing.

[8] The *Summarie* list of captured ordnance (p. 276) specifies 53 pieces; the French narrative (Lacour, p. 21), says 'about sixty pieces of brass cannon'. According to earlier plans (as listed in April 1586) Drake expected to find sixty pieces here (*lx*, Lansdowne MS 100, fol. 98; printed in Corbett, *Sp. War*, p. 70, however, as only *10*). The value placed by the English on the captured guns and the powder is hardly consistent with the story of the noisy celebration that is given in the *Summarie* (see p. 227).

this towne good store of wine neere 100 tun*ne*/ with sweet oyle & olives, Bred & meale & dried goates[1] with greate store of cotton & everie howse so full of chest*es* made of sweet woode as of Cipres[2] &c that it was wonderful to see/

This towne had iij churches in hit but ther best Images were carried awaie wi*th* them, it is a verie frewtfull place & hathe greate abundance of sylke & cotton growinge all over the Ilande.[3] There is greate store of Orenges, sugar canes, & cokaies trees bearinge a frewte called Ginnye nuttes.[4] ther is greate abundance of these growinge therin wi*th* lemmons, figges & Dates, Quinces & potatos wi*th* greate store of small fisshe at the sea side w*hich* maie bee taken wi*th* little labour.

Also they have a fine river run*n*inge thoroughe the towne & monsterous highe rock*es* rownde abowte the same of suche heighte & so vpright that scarse anie man is able to attaine the toppes therof,[5] There ar in these rock*es* munkies & suche a n*um*ber of Newt*es* in everie howse, street*es* &c that it woulde amase a man to see them/

They have goodlie Ioiynde work*es*[6] in there churches & howses of greate coste & workmanshipp.

[fol. 168] There was adioiyninge to their greatest churche an Hospitall wi*th* as brave roomes in hit & in as goodlie order as anie man can Devise. Wee fownde abowt 20 sicke persons all *Nigros*, lyinge of verie fowle & fylthie[7] Diseases. In this Hospitall wee toke all the Belles owte of the steeple & browght them awaie wi*th* vs.[8]

This Iland is full of Beares, Deere, goat*es* & hennes, verie manie of them wilde. w*hich* never come to howse.

---

[1] Goats were an important product at this period. Duncan, *Atlantic Islands*, pp. 159–60, 215.

[2] i.e. cypress.

[3] In the sixteenth century the Cape Verde Islands produced textiles in which oriental silk was combined with the abundant native cotton. Duncan, *Atlantic Islands*, p. 219.

[4] i.e. cocoa trees and guinea nuts, or cocoanuts. Corbett, *Sp. War*, p. 9, n. Cf. p. 229.

[5] Cf. pp. 137, 229.

[6] i.e. joined work, or wainscoting. Corbett, *Sp. War*, p. 9, n.

[7] Corbett (*Sp. War*, p. 9), reads: *frightful*.

[8] Cf. p. 235.

There are Asses & goodlie horses,[1] All ther buildinges are of stone.

Besides all this there was fownde a greate deale of trasshe which woulde aske muche time to rehearse/

This towne standes in the Illandes of *Gynnye*[2] & thinhabitantes bee some Spaniardes & some Portingalles who have Divers bond slaves bothe blacke men & women.[3]

Wee kepte this town ix Daies & no person came to resist vs, When we had bin ther vj Daies there came an Italian downe, whome we toke to bee a spie & searched him & fownde 50 peeces of golde in his buskins, he was the master governor of the towne. Wee kepte him in prison & vsed a certaine kinde of torment to make him confesse/[4]

The next Daie wee tooke a nother & vsed him in like order. then the first tolde vs that in the Byshops howse wa[s] greate store of Treasure hyd/ Which wee presentlie serche[d] but fownde none/ Then hee tolde vs that they had car[ried] all there treasure into the mowntaines/

The other confessed that ther was certaine ordinaunce & powder hid in yᵉ grownde at an other towne not paste 6 leages of which wee fownde trewe[5]

---

[1] Livestock raised here at this period included horses, donkeys, goats, and cattle. Duncan, *Atlantic Islands*, pp. 159-60.

[2] The writer is referring to the general region. The location of this island group made it a centre for collecting and distributing the products and needs of the Guinea area, as well as European goods and products coming from Spanish America. Duncan, *Atlantic Islands*, pp. 215-19. See also n. 2, p. 228.

[3] Drake may have used a former slave as his guide for his inland march (see below, p. 189).

[4] The *Leicester* journal (p. 149) tells of the capture on the return from the inland march of the *master gunner*, a Spaniard, who told of ordnance buried at Praya. The term *master-governor* is an anachronism; nor was it Drake's custom to submit to torture men of genuinely official rank.

The keeper of the *Primrose* journal may have been reporting from hearsay evidence. The captured Italian, however, was probably the Florentine, Octavius Toscano, who escaped from Drake's custody at Cartagena. He had gone to the Canaries for work on a wharf at La Palma, and then, with a German captain, to Santiago to trade for slaves. He told the Cartagena officials that, after his capture by Drake (for which his date of 7 December (N.S.) must be incorrect), he had been made to serve at table, etc., for a captain 'named Carassa' (Carleill, perhaps, or Careless), who ordered him to teach him Italian. Deposition printed in Wright, *Further Eng. Voyages*, pp. 194-5.

[5] i.e. at Praya. See pp. 190, 232.

Duringe our abode there, there was a Gibbet set vp where was executed on of our men beinge steward of the Ayde for committinge Buggerie with ij boies in the shippe/[1]

The 6. daie after we had bin there, Came a horse man to the top of on of the rockes that stoode over the towne & there was sente on to parle with him, & he promised that the next Daie the rewlers of the Iland shoulde come & speake with vs, but they did not.[2]

Then we made owt a 700 men & tooke a *Nigro* to bee our guide which we brought owte of Inglande with vs that dwelte before in this Ilande & the generall promised this *Nigro* that if wee coulde take the Spaniarde that the *Nigro* before was slave vnto, that then the Spaniarde shoulde bee slave vnto the *Nigro*.[3]

Thus wee went 12 miles further into the countrie to a towne called *Saint Domingo*, but the people seinge vs a far of (for they had skowtes) were afraide & fledd, & misdowbtinge our comminge longe before had hid all there treasure, which wee seeinge set fire on the Towne & presentlie Departed thence/

[fol. 168v] The People seinge the towne on fyre made a greate crye Emongst the Busshes & weedes which wee might verie well heere.

At this place wee lost on of our men that wente stragglinge to gett pyllage, with whom the Spaniardes meetinge cut of hys head & ryppinge hys bellie tooke owt his hart & carried them awaie but let his boddie lie[4]

And as wee were comminge[5] backe abowte ij miles, Wee espied a number of horsmen so neere as wee coulde gesse a bowte ij hundred/ they began to make a shew against vs, Then

---

[1] See the *Leicester* journal (p. 148), where he is called steward of the *Talbot*. See also p. 243.

[2] Cf. *Summarie*, p. 230.

[3] No other account refers to a negro guide; the *Leicester* journal says that some Moors were guides. On incidents of the march, and its date, see pp. 97–8, 148, 230.

[4] Cf. pp. 98, 148. The account of this incident in the *Primrose* journal is more explicitly anti-Spanish in wording than is the MS variant of the *Summarie*. The description in the printed English editions of the *Summarie* (see p. 235) resembles the one given here.

[5] Transcribed in Corbett (*Sp. War*, p. 11) as *riding*.

wee began to bende our selves towardes them, which so soone as they perceaved put owte there flagge of trewse, but at anie hande they woulde not come neere vs, soe wee came backe againe to *Saint Domingo*[1] with the losse of on man.

Duringe our beinge there, there came 3 or 4 nigros whom wee succored & gave vittels vnto. wee fownde in the road 7 carvels & on a buildinge on the stockes, These shippes had in them Breade, wine, Oyle, Sugar, marmelade & succatts with such like thinges but wee fownde no boddie in them. they were made fast vnto the rockes, from whence wee losed them takinge there goodes & sendinge them to the seas to goe whither they woulde withoute anie boddie in them, the other new on we tooke in peeces & carried with vs.[2] Also ther was certaine plate of Lemman hid that wee tooke awaie with vs.

The Bisshop of this towne is of greate wealthe. he is carried to the churche vppon a barr[3] of silver with a verie riche Canopey over his heade borne by 8 or 12 men.

This Silver barr is a thinge of greate valew, the Bisshop is verie fearefull of his lyfe for it is but 3 yeeres since the towne was spoiled by the Frenche men & they killed man, woman, & childe.[4] The Bisshop was at that time taken & by faire promises that hee woulde fetche them greate treasure hee escaped thoughe not without great feare wherin hee hathe lived ever since.

The French men had from them at that time 50 peeces of Brasse Ordinaunce/

Thus when wee sau wee coulde gett no more, wee set the towne on fyre & Departed thence to an other towne about 6 leages of called *Prey*,[5] But the people were all fled, so likewise wee fyred that towne & wente to the sea.

The 28 of November, all which moneth is extreame hote

---

[1] It should be, *from Santo Domingo to Santiago.*
[2] On these caravels see also p. 149.
[3] i.e. bier.
[4] In the *Summarie* the inhabitants' fears were attributed to the raid by William Hawkins the elder in 1582 (see p. 234).
[5] i.e. Praya, or Porto Praya.

with them as the hottest time of summer is with vs in Inglande, they never have raigne somtime in iij yeeres togather, we sailed forwardes/[1]

There is an other Ile within 8 leages of them called *Fogo*,[2] of an excedinge greate heighte that dothe burne continuallie that no man dare go to the top of hit, There dwell both Portengalls & Spaniardes in hit but the most there ar *Nigros*/

[fol. 169] The 29 of November wee set saile. Then had wee 550 leages to fall with the next lande & wee had not bin ij Daies at the sea but there fell a greate sicknes emongst our men not in on ship alone but in all the whole fleete so that in the Admyrall there were sicke above an hundred men at on time & there were above 60 men sicke in the Vizadmirall at the same time & so in other shippes accordinge to ther number/[3]

There Died Divers of this Desease bothe in our ship & others, some times j sometime 2 & 3 in a Daie.

The 21 of Dece[m]ber wee fell with an Iland called [Dominica].[4] the people ar all as redd as Scarlet, Wee ankered there to refresshe our men. wee fownde verie goodlie rivers there, & there wee tooke in water for our neede. wee woulde have tarried there longer for to have refresshed our men but wee coulde finde no convenient place to keepe them in from the people of the countrie, for they ar greate devowrers & eaters of men/ And the Ile is all woodes.

Wee withe our boate met with 8 of these men at sea who as soone as they espied vs waved vs vnto them & put forthe a flagg of truce beinge a cake of *Cassado*[5] bread, Wee borded them presentlie, there boate was a *Cannow*[6] that is made like a hogges

---

[1] The actual departure occurred on 29 November (see below). That date is confirmed in the Map Text and the *Tiger* journal (see pp. 65, 99, n. 1).

[2] Fogo, or del Fogo.

[3] On the epidemic of fever see p. 99 and n. 3, and p. 235.

[4] Blank in the MS. See *Summarie*, p. 236. The anticipated arrival date, according to the plan dated in April 1586, had been 28 or 29 November (Lansdowne MS 100, fol. 98, pr. in Corbett, *Sp. War*, p. 70). 18 December was the date, according to the Map Text and the *Tiger* journal (see pp. 66, 100).

[5] i.e. cassava, although in the MS the word is regularly written as *cassado*.

[6] i.e. canoe.

trowghe, all of on tree. These people go naked withowte anie manner of clothe abowte them, There manner is when they kill anie of there enemies they knocke owte the[ir] teethe & were them abowte there neckes like a chaine & eate [the] flesshe for meate/

When wee had borded them as before they gave vs a kinde of Bottle full of water & *Cassado* bread that is made of a tree & wee gave them Bisket & a can of Beare, which they did presentlie bothe eate & drinke & then wee Departed from them & went rowinge close aborde the shore where the people of the countrie came runninge to the water side wounderinge greatlie at vs. Then we came to a goodlie river of fresshe water & thither came 6 men of the countrie vnto vs & emongst them ther was on that commaunded the reste. On broughte a cocke & a henne a nother browght Potatos, an other, Plantaine fruite. They did swime over the River to vs & came to our boate & the Captaine cawsed a combe to bee geven them, which was Doonne & the cocke required for hit, but they woulde not, Then the Captaine gave a loking glasse to be geeven them, for which they gave ther cocke & the Captaine Intised them to comme into the boate, which on of them did & woulde have gonne with vs but that his companions called him & would not suffer him, so hee lepte into the sea with his bow & arrowes in On hande & swame to shore with thother. Then we departed from them for that time/[1]

The next Daie wee wente to serche further into the lande & the people ranne alonge the sea side before vs. then the Captaine commanded a trumpet to be sownded which Doonne, the People hier[2] in the land gave a greate showte & kept a whistlinge & blew a thinge like a horne, then they came to the sea side & shott at vs. Wee sowght for some good place but fownde none to serve our turne & so departed.

[fol. 169v] Thys Ile is full of woodes & busshes, Wee saw manie of there howses. We fownde snakes of greate bigness

---

[1] On this bartering see also p. 111.

[2] *Higher* is the reading given by Corbett (*Sp. War*, p. 14).

with Newtes & other venemous worms. Also we sawe there manie Pellycans, ther ar Potatos, Orenges, Cokinos,[1] Plantaine, Cassado & manie kindes of frewtes which wee knew not.

On Christmas Even wee fell with an other Iland called [St. Christopher's][2] & landed there, refresshinge our selves with fresshe water & there staied iij Daies & saw no man but our companie, of whom Divers weare sicke. Wee buried 20 men whilest wee staied there. This Ile is verie full of goodlie trees of sweete woode & there ar greate store of Pellicans & manie birdes flyinge in the nighte, ther ar great snakes & crabbes verie bigge that live in the grownde & other kinde of thinges like serpentes verie strawnge/

The Last Daie of December wee tooke ij barkes[3] at sea bownde for *Saint Dominico*/[4] on was loden with Suger chest bordes thother with beefe & bacon, pease, Tabacco, ryse, hydes & other stuffe, ther were ij Spanisshe merchauntes in them & a woman *Nigro* with a boie & a Greeke. This Greeke was our Pylote[5] for landinge of our men at *Saint Dominico*.

The first of Ianuarij in the morninge our men beinge landed 7 or 8 miles from the towne & comminge towardes hit the Spaniardes horsmen made towardes vs but the[y] fledd quicklie vnto the woodes,[6] & perceavinge our men to marche towardes *Saint Dominico*, they had planted 3 peeces of Ordinaunce hard vnder the gate where our men showlde enter & shott of on of them killing 3 or our men,[7] but before they could discharge

[1] Read as *cocoas* in Corbett, *Sp. War*, p. 14.

[2] Blank in the MS. See *Summarie*, p. 237. The Map Text and the newsletter (p. 111) date the stay at St Christopher's as 21–5 December.

[3] Cf. *Summarie* (p. 238), which mentions only 'a small Frigot'.

[4] Santo Domingo in Hispaniola.

[5] Greeks were frequently used by the Spaniards as pilots at this period. Corbett, *Sp. War*, p. 15, n. Cf. p. 238.

[6] 'Flying in hopeless disorder,' according to one Spanish account; but in another 'in good order we returned to the city gate'. Wright, *Further Eng. Voyages*, pp. 21, 34.

[7] Carleill's men entered by the gate farther from the sea (see pp. 102, n. 1, 240; and Wright, *Further Eng. Voyages*, pp. 18, 34, 39). Corbett (*Sp. War*, p. 15) suggests that the description here supports the view that the diarist was a soldier rather than a naval man.

the rest[1] wee ranne so feerclie vppon them that we drave them from ther ordinawnce & they fled further into the towne. All this time *our* shipp*es* laie still batteringe the towne on the other side, & they shootinge at *our* shipp*es* shott the Admyrall quite thorowghe but hurte never a man. We lent them alwaies ij for on.[2] Thus Did this Indure by the space of 3 howers & after the shipp*es* perceaved *our* men had entred the towne, they lefte shootinge for feare of spoylinge of vs, When Owre men had entred the towne the Spaniard*es* fled into the Castle wh*i*ch is with highe walles & hit was allmost nighte.[3]

In the morninge when wee thoughte to have had the Spaniard*es* in the Castle, they weare all gone & fledd by night by certa*i*ne boates wh*i*ch they had, for on p*ar*te of that Castle laie to a river wh*i*ch runnethe into the lande & of that side they escap*e*d.[4]

Thus the Spaniard*es* gave vs the towne for a Newyeers gifte. They carried owt there treasure & a greate Image of silver owt of ther churche wh*i*ch was of great valew.[5]

[fol. 170] In this Towne we had greate Store of wine, meale, Oyle, Cassado, Cock*es*, henn*es* & chickens, that the verie henn*es* weare valewed at a 1000 *li*/ greate store of Apparell,

---

[1] *Recharge* is the wording in the MS variant of *Summarie* and the 1588 editions (see p. 240 and n. 6).

[2] This action by the fleet at anchor before the town was reported afterwards in Spain (S.P. 12/189: 27, pr. in Corbett, *Sp. War*, p. 79). Other reports that told of deceptive moves by the fleet for three days (S.P. 12/189: 42, pr. in Corbett, *Sp. War*, pp. 80-2) are exaggerated. Defensive firing from the city was limited, since their shots could not reach the English ships, even when, late in the action, they 'came up and stood off the streets ending on the waterfront'. Wright, *Further Eng. Voyages*, p. 33 (see also ibid., pp. 21, 24, 40).

[3] About 4 or 5 p.m. See pp. 102, n. 3, 241.

[4] See pp. 112, 241 and the Boazio map (Plates V(A), (B)). The Spanish reports show that no serious attempt was made to save the fortress. Wright, *Further Eng. Voyages*, pp. xxxviii, 21, 26. The English narratives do not mention prisoners held there or elsewhere within the city, but there were later rumours in Europe that at least 1,200 Europeans, only part of whom were in the galleys, had been prisoners there. S.P. 12/189: 42 (pr. in Corbett, *Sp. War*, p. 81).

[5] This item is not mentioned specifically in the printed Spanish documents, although they report the stripping of treasures from all the religious buildings (Wright, *Further Eng. Voyages*, p. xl and notes). Much of the cathedral plate was sacrificed for the ransom (ibid., p. xli). See also the comment of the French narrator (p. 244, n. 1).

Spices, Succates, Brasse, Pewter, Iron & all manner of things that doo belonge to a cittie. But that they had taken awaie ther golde & silver & the best of there apparell, all things else was lefte.

The Spaniardes sunke 3 shippes vppon the shallowest place of the harbour,[1] for at the entrie in of there harbor is but xiiij-foote water so that none of our shippes coulde enter at all. Wee fownde in the harbor a verie faire Gallye,[2] shee had belonginge vnto her 4 hundred slaves, Turkes Moores, Nigros, Frenchemen & Greekes. shee shott at vs at our firste comminge in. (her Ende was) wee Tawed her to the sea & set her on fier & all her slaves wee tooke with vs.[3]

After we had bin there x daies they came to vs with a flagge of trewse.[4] the cawse was, for that wee had in everie street at the owtside of the towne rownde abowte made rampyres & planted Ordinawnce & garded them with men; the cawse whi wee set somme of the howses on fire, was for that they weare owte of the cowtres of our gard[5] & rampires/ Then they came In & profered monie for redeminge of ther town[e] but it was longe ere they coulde agree of price so for xxti D[aies] space, they came in everie Daie with flagges of trewse.[6]

[1] See Wright, *Further Eng. Voyages*, p. 18.

[2] Two galleys had been sent in 1582 for the better defence of Hispaniola, but one had been wrecked and the other badly damaged in 1583. When Drake arrived, the latter was in Santo Domingo harbour being careened, and still unfit to go out against the English. On the advice of her commander, Don Diego Osorio, she was positioned across the harbour entrance so that her guns might be used, but she did little damage. Richard Boulind, 'Shipwreck and Mutiny . . . 1583,' *Mariner's Mirror*, LVIII (1972), 297–375.

[3] Some of the galley slaves who had been unchained so that they might assist in the defence helped the English ruin the city, and 'did more looting than the English'. Wright, *Further Eng. Voyages*, pp. xl and n., 35. Among them were eighteen or nineteen Frenchmen, according to the French narrative (Lacour, p. 23). Many negroes who had belonged to private persons also left with Drake. Wright, op. cit., p. 35. See also below, p. 197.

[4] The first emissary from the Audiencia came on 12 January and departed the next day. See p. 153.

[5] 'Courts of guard' refers to guard-houses connected with keeping of watch. See Corbett, *Sp. War*, p. 16, n.

[6] Further negotiators, including Don Francisco Maldonado, stayed for three days. They offered 20,000 ducats, and Drake demanded 200,000. Wright, *Further Eng. Voyages*, p. 30.

Now hit chawnced that a Spaniard cam*m*e in neere o*u*r
cowrt*es* [of] garde w*i*th his flagge of trewse on horsbacke, &
the Capt[ain] sent a *Nigro* boie to talke w*i*th him & after they
had talked togath[er] hee tooke his staffe & ranne the boie
thorowghe & rode awaie in hast for he was w*i*thowte o*u*r
cowrt*es* of garde.[1]

The next Daie when the Spaniard*es* came in w*i*th ther flagges
of trewse they weare tolde of hit & they saide hee showlde be
hanged if they mighte know him, but it was not doonne.
When the Towne was taken first wee tooke ij fryers & certaine
Spaniard*es* & they weare kepte in prison for to bee rawnsomed,[2]
& wee by consent made a paire of Gallowes w*i*thowte the
towne where the Spaniard*es* came Dailie/ & hanged the 2 friers
in lew of slainge the Nigro boie/

The same Daie the Spaniard*es* came & carried awaie the
fryers & 3 daies after, they hanged the same man that killed the
Nigro boie where they[r] friers weare hanged/

Wee hanged an Irisshe man of o*u*r owne Companie for
murderinge of one of his fellowes privelie.[3] Wee tarried in this
towne a monethe. they woulde never com*m*e past 20 or 40
against vs & that woulde bee in the nyghte.[4] the Time that
wee were there they woulde bringe vs in beefe, somtime
xx^ti sometimes forti oxen, & sheepe somtime an 100 &

[1] This report on the incident of the negro boy, which does not appear in the MS variant of the *Summarie*, is very similar to that printed in the English editions (see below, p. 242 and n. 2). Wright (*Further Eng. Voyages*, p. xxxvii, n.) notes that the Spanish documents mention neither the negro boy incident nor the execution of a Spanish officer in retribution for it.

[2] The cathedral was used as the centre of business by the English, and two of its chapels served as jails (Wright, *Further Eng. Voyages*, p. 28). The official Spanish reports from the city do not mention the execution of the friars, but other Spanish accounts mention, without explanation, the execution of two Dominicans (see Wright, *Further Eng. Voyages*, p. xxxvii, n.; and Castellanos, *Discurso*, pp. xxxviii, 90). According to Simón's *Noticias Historiales*, two old monks were hanged for protesting the defiling of churches. *E.H.R.*, XVI (1901), 57. See also the references in Documents 7 and 9 (pp. 112, 155), although they may not be related to this incident.

[3] On this and other actions of Drake's 'court' see pp. 151, 243. See also Wright, *Further Eng. Voyages*, p. 31. The ransom negotiator for the Spaniards, García Fernández de Torrequemada, observed that, 'He commands and governs imperiously. He is feared and obeyed by his men. He punishes resolutely'. Wright, op. cit., p. 225.

[4] Cf. p. 156, n. 1; and Wright, *Further Eng. Voyages*, p. 34.

more & lesse,[1] our men would fetche in Oxen & sheepe at pleasure.

Ther were so manie Drie hides in this towne that it was wonderfull, great store also of sugar which wee estemed not, hit was so plentifull.[2]

[fol. 170v] Ther was in this Towne great store of Copper monie more than x tunne weight in somme on howse. I Iudge also ther was in that towne of blacke monie an 100 tunne, Wee tooke 2 or 3 tunnes of hit with vs to the sea.[3] Also we tooke greate store of hides awaie with vs. Wee tooke also ther belles owte of there churches & 3 shippes owte of ther harbor & lefte 2 of our olde shippes there for them.[4] Wee had from thence 80 slaues, Turkes, Frenchmen, Greekes & Nigros.[5] Wee had manie peeces of Brasse ordinawnce thence, & lefte not on peece behinde vs.[6] Wee set parte of ther castle on fire & burned all ther Images of woode, brake & distroied all there fairest worke within ther churches. Wee had in this towne muche Plate, monie & pearle hidden in welles & other places.[7]

This Towne standethe verie pleasawntlie & is of a verie huge buildinge, All the walles of ther howses ar like the Walles of our churches but higher, & such greate Doores far greater then our churche Doores with such cost of Iron wourke that it is woonderfull.

There groweth great abundaunce of Ginger, Pepper, Lucoste[8] & strawnge frewtes.

---

[1] This was contrary to the hope of some of those who had fled to the country and wished to 'remove supplies in order that hunger may compel these people to depart'. Wright, *Further Eng. Voyages*, p. 21.

[2] The ransom negotiator for the Spaniards wrote that, at the end of their talks, Drake proffered to him 'all the sugar and hides that he had taken with the city', but that he accepted the offer only 'in the name of the people' and not for himself. Wright, *Further Eng. Voyages*, p. 225.

[3] Cf. p. 246. A Spanish report states that the English melted much of the copper coin. Wright, *Further Eng. Voyages*, p. 35.

[4] See the map of Santo Domingo (Plates V(A), (B)). On ships taken and left see p. 157, and also Corbett, *Sp. War*, pp. 75, 81.

[5] Cf. above, p. 195.   [6] Cf. pp. 102, 276.

[7] See above, p. 156, n. 5; and Wright, *Further Eng. Voyages*, pp. xl and n., xli; and Castellanos, *Discurso*, p. 301.

[8] i.e. locusts.

All this Ile is full of woodes; also ther ar Orenges, leimons, Pomegranetes & dates.

The Spaniardes dare not goe past x miles compasse for feare of the Indians.[1]

This is the cheefest towne in all *Hispaniola* & was first Inhabited by the Spaniardes. There they keepe Parlament for the kinge & doo the greatest busines for Spaine.[2]

The eleventhe Daie.[3] Wee came to an Anker at *Carthagina* & x daies ere wee came thither they had warninge of vs[4] & had carried awaie the most parte of ther goodes havinge fortefied & made souch rampires that it was Impossible by mans reason for vs to winne.[5] But God fowghte for vs, for our Shippes coulde not comme neere the towne for lacke of water to batter it & where our pinnasses showlde goe Inn, was but the lenght of ij shippes & hit was chained over from the Castle with xvj peeces of Ordinawnce in this narrow gutter.[6] Yet wee did attempte hit [so] that wee had the rowther[7] of our pinnasse stroke awaie & mens hattes from there headdes & the topp of

---

[1] See also *Summarie*, p. 246 and n. 5. A Spanish report noted that 800 Indians were in the government forces; it was negro slaves who turned especially to the aid of the English. Wright, *Further Eng. Voyages*, p. 31.

[2] Cf. p. 260. Several official reports express the humiliation felt at the loss of 'this key to the Indies'. Wright, *Further Eng. Voyages*, pp. 21, 23.

[3] The arrival was on Wednesday, 9/19 February. See pp. 103, n. 2, 160.

[4] Warnings from Spain had reached the city by 26 December/5 January, and despatches from officials in Hispaniola had come after the fall of Santo Domingo (Wright, *Further Eng. Voyages*, pp. xlv, 25, 47, 71); Francisco Maldonado arrived from there on 6/16 February with his eye witness account (ibid., pp. 47, 72).

[5] Earliest steps by the city authorities included sending their families and valuables into the country, organizing manpower for the defence, including a call-up of Indians, and planning fortifications. When the Santo Domingo news arrived, they placed artillery toward the swamps at the east and barricades at streets leading to the beach. They planned but did not complete a masonry wall and ditch across the land spit (the Caleta). They decided to keep the royal galleys in the inner lagoon, positioned for firing on troops moving along that spit, but they did not place a battery on its farther end. Wright, *Further Eng. Voyages*, pp. xlv–xlvi, 71–3, etc. See also pp. 162, 250.

[6] A small blockhouse stood at the Boquerón channel, guarding the entrance to the inner lagoon, and a chain was extended from it to the opposite side in such a way as to prevent the passage of even small boats (Wright, *Further Eng. Voyages*, pp. 51, 107). Several galley officers protested against the chain, because it also barred their vessels from passing into the outer harbour either to meet the enemy or to escape. See Wright, op. cit., pp. 74, 76, 93, 102, 110, 157; and see the map (Plates VI (A), (B)).

[7] i.e. rudder.

o*u*r meane maste[1] beaten in peeces, the Oares striken owte of
o*u*r menes handes as they rowed & o*u*r Captaine like to have
bin slaine.[2] They had planted xvj peeces againste vs in the castle.
Also they had planted ij galleis & a Galleasse w*i*th ordinaunce
& a nother forte w*i*th 6 peeces, that wee had not the lenghte of
a Pike lefte vs for passage to enter, & ther were 400 horsmen &
footemen in armes still bent against vs,[3]

[fol. 171] The ij Gallyes & Galliasse[4] Weare Well furnisshed
w*i*th men & Ordinawnce & this was then there sainge, as
afterwarde they did confesse, that wee shoulde all die but xx[ti]
of the beste & they shoulde bee made gallie slaves, they d[id]
so presume of there forte & strenghte.

In deede hyt was not likelie that anie man of vs shoulde
escape, but what God will have shalbee doonne, who put hit
into o*u*r mindes that wee shoulde enter vppon them in the
morne before Daie. Yet they weare reddie to resiste vs & had
set in the grownde thowsandes of poysoned arrowes. Yet verie
few of o*u*r men receaved hurte therbie.[5]

The Spanisshe horsmen met vs w*i*thowte the forte verie
couragiouslie[6] but o*u*r Pikemen made them soone retire & wee
followed so feerslie vppon them that wee made them forsake
ther forte.

[1] i.e. mainmast.

[2] This is the attack led by Frobisher (see p. 249). The captain of the fort declared that
seven launches, four pinnaces, and two small shallops attacked, and that shots from the
fort sank a pinnace, brought down the mast of another, and damaged others, forcing
them to withdraw. There was a renewed attack, under Drake himself, he thought,
since he flew a 'quartered flag', but Spanish fire badly damaged the launch of the
vice admiral, as well as another, and killed four or five men. Wright, *Further Eng.
Voyages*, p. 82.

Guns of the ships in the harbour afterwards fired upon the fort, and, following the
English penetration of the city from the other side, there was firing on it from the land.
Having too few men to hold out longer, it was evacuated at night (Thursday).
Wright, *Further Eng. Voyages*, pp. liii, 54, 59, 78, 83.

[3] Carleill's land operation is described here. Cf. pp. 103, 161–3, 249–51.

[4] Cf. p. 104. See also Wright, *Further Eng. Voyages*, pp. 84, 102–5, 109, etc.; and
Castellanos, *Discurso*, pp. 302, 305.

[5] Cf. p. 162.

[6] This was as the last defenders were withdrawing (Wright, *Further Eng. Voyages*,
p. 133). A few horsemen had been used as scouts along the land spit, and a few had
fought at the Caleta trench. The governor himself escaped on horseback (ibid.,
pp. xlvii, 48, 66, 108, 120, 155). See also pp. 163, 248.

The ij Gallies & Galliasse with the other forte did so plie ther Ordinawnce againste vs that hit was woonderfull.[1] ther Calivers, musketes & hargabusses did plaie ther partes. But God is all in all, by whose good helpe wee made them flie into the Towne like sheepe, but they galled manie of our men in the towne.[2]

Wee lost in this skirmisshe 28 men besides those that weare hurte yet constrained the Spaniardes to flie like sheepe into the mountaines/[3]

Thus we Inioyed the Towne but fownde little Store of Victuall therin, the most wee fownde was wine & Oyle. They had hid man[ie] thinges in the grownde which wee fownde not withstandinge/

We fortifyed this towne of our Fasshion and planted there owne Ordianwnce against them/[4]

Nowe when our men had got the Towne The Spaniardes set fyre on bothe the Gallyes becawse wee shoulde not enioy them, And the slaves & Spaniardes in the Gallies fell togather by the eares so that the Spaniardes killed manie of there slaues, and some they tooke with them, & verie manie of them did swimme to vs. the Spaniardes kepte there castle still, yet at last on a sudden fled awai.[5] Then wee browght our Shippes so neere the Towne as we coulde & the smallest of them went in & rode before the Towne. Wee kepte this Towne 5 weekes & 3 daies & afterwardes begunne to burne the owtsides of hit & then the

---

[1] See the deposition by the galley commander, Vique, in Wright, *Further Eng. Voyages*, pp. 110-11; also, ibid., pp. 76-8, 84, 134, 157.

[2] Cf. pp. 164, 252.

[3] The French narrative (Lacour, p. 24) states that forty or fifty English were killed, and about twelve or fifteen Spaniards. One of the Spanish hostages held during ransom negotiations learned that 78 Englishmen were killed, as opposed to a dozen or more Spaniards. Other Spanish estimates of English losses varied from about thirty to close to one hundred. Wright, *Further Eng. Voyages*, pp. 52, 95, 115, 121. Later English losses resulted from illness.

[4] They 'entrenched and fortified themselves there, closing every access and street by which they supposed they might be offended'. Wright, *Further Eng. Voyages*, p. 157. They moved some of the guns from the Caleta to the wharf for use against the fort (ibid., p. 83).

[5] See note 2 on p. 199 above.

Spaniardes came in with there flagges of Trewce to redeeme ther Towne.[1]

They weare buildinge a greate new churche in thys Towne & by our shootinge of a greate peece of Ordinaunce that stoode neere the churche, a greate parte therof was shaken downe.[2]

When the Spaniardes saw there churche downe they saide they woulde geeve no monie for there towne for they esteemed ther churche more then ther towne. Then wee began to burne more so that at last they compownded & Rawnsomed the same/[3]

When the Time was come that wee must avoide the Towne all our men wente aborde savinge 200 & they went in to a Fryerie that stoode a little withoute the Towne & kepte hit certaine Daies to see yf they woulde Raunsome hit, & even as we had laide wood to hit & were reddie to geeve fyre, The Prior came in & Ransomed the same.[4] then wee set the Galiasse on fire[5] & so departed to our shippes/

[fol. 171v] Wee had in thys Towne manie peeces of Brasse ordinawnce.[6] We[e] lefte them not on peece behinde, & the reporte wente that the Spaniar[des] woulde have geeven the weight in sylver for x or xij of them.

Also we browghte awaie all ther belles & all other metalles wee coulde finde.

Thys is a verie prettie Towne with 6 or 7 churches in hit. There is growinge abowte this Towne, Orenges, Leimons, Pomegranetes, Cytherons,[7] oliffe, Pepper, locoustes with manie other frewtes.

[1] Cf. p. 104. On the opening of ransom negotiations see the *Leicester* journal (p. 165).

[2] Cf. p. 166 above; also, Wright, *Further Eng. Voyages*, p. 143.

[3] Conferences about a ransom continued for about four weeks, with final payment not being made until mid-March.

[4] Drake argued that the Franciscan monastery was outside of the town, and demanded 3,000 ducats, threatening to burn it if the ransom was not paid. He finally yielded to the persuasions of the prior and of Alonso Bravo, whose wife had recently been buried there, and spared the property upon the payment of 600 or 1,000 ducats. Wright, *Further Eng. Voyages*, pp. lvii, 124, 159.

[5] The galleass *Napolitana* was the ship which gave support to the royal galleys during the night assault (see p. 104 and n. 1). On the destruction of the galleys see p. 167, n. 2.

[6] According to the French narrative (Lacour, p. 25), six or seven score; according to the totals in the *Summarie* (p. 277), 63 pieces. Cf. p. 105 above.

[7] i.e. citrons.

Ther is also greate store of Fisshe & hit is verie trewe that ther are growinge Oysters & Mussels on trees by the Sea side. I have both gathered & eaten of them/

Wee lefte ij small Shippes of owres behinde vs settinge them on fire & we took ij of there shippes for them.[1] Duringe the Tyme of our abode there wee loste a hundred men by sicknes.[2] Wee had manie Turkes,[3] Frenchmen, *Nigros, Moores, Greekes* & Spaniardes went with vs from This towne/

All the while wee weare in this Towne the Spaniardes gave vs no fyghte but they threatned vs shewinge them selves somtim[e] an hundred or 200 in a troupe & shott at vs, but soone would runne awa[y].[4]

After that wee were gone from the Towne wee remained x Daies abowte ij miles from the saide towne to take in water, so that wee were there in all seaven weekes.

The last of Marche we set saile from *Carthagina*,[5] and when wee had bin ij Daies at sea there fell suche a leake in on of our shippes that wee were Driven to goe backe againe to *Carthagina* & there to take owte all our Ordinawnce, goodes & other furniture & so set her on fyre.[6] There wee continewed 14 daies more.

---

[1] Similar substitutions had been made at Santo Domingo. Cf. p. 157. One Spanish document states that they carried away the galley's tender, but burned all other craft in the harbour. Wright, *Further Eng. Voyages*, p. 159.

[2] Cf. pp. 174, 254. Drake told his prisoner, Alonso Bravo, of the continuing sickness, and said he had lost 500 men by this means since the start of the voyage (Wright, *Further Eng. Voyages*, p. 121). See also the reference to attrition in the Cartagena resolutions (p. 255, n. 4).

[3] Drake was reported to have with him after leaving Cartagena some 200 Turks and 'Moors' (freed galley slaves), and additional numbers of negroes (Wright, *Further Eng. Voyages*, pp. 173, 212). After his return to England, the Privy Council wrote on 4 August 1586 to the 'Companie trading into Turkey', directing them to take charge of the two hundred Turks and make plans for sending them back to Turkey, possibly in exchange for favours to be granted by the Grand Seigneur. P.R.O., P.C. 2/14: 169.

[4] Don Pedro Vique especially had urged a night attack from outside the town. One feeble effort was made, but most of the citizens feared to provoke more damage to their property. Wright, *Further Eng. Voyages*, pp. lv, 112–13.

[5] Ransom payments were completed about 15 March (see p. 179), and the fleet sailed on Thursday, 31 March (see p. 105).

[6] This was the *New Year's Gift*. See p. 262 and Wright, *Further Eng. Voyages*, pp. lvii, 51–2, 167. A Spanish seaman who was captured by Drake during this stay told Cuban

THE *Primrose* JOURNAL

Now when wee came again The Spaniardes did Marvaile & fledd owt of the Towne. Then the Generall sent them woorde what the cawse was, & desired the Governour of the Towne that they mighte bake bredd there, & gave his woord to the Governoure that none shoulde come on shore but Bakers, for our shippes were five or 6 miles from the Towne.[1] And they Spaniardes for feare grawnted vs all the Ovens in the Towne. Wee weare bakinge of Bisket there 6 or 7 Daies, & the governour of the Towne receaved vs with greate courtesie & made proclamation vppon paine of deathe that no man shoulde molest vs but to helpe vs with woode water & all other necessaries, & to let vs goe when & where wee woulde & further commaunded ij Spaniardes in everie howse where wee did bake to suffer none to come vnto vs but those that wee did lyke/

There was more then 2000 Spaniardes in the Towne. The Iustices[2] woulde comme to vs at all howers in the nighte & daie, to see that no man did vs wronge; for they thowght that wee came a shore to pike a quarrell against them.

The 18 of Aprill[3] wee set saile the seconde time from *Carthagina* & the xxij of Aprill wee fell with an Ile that had no people in hit.[4] There wee fownde strawnge kindes of beastes &

---

officials afterwards that Drake also burned five of his own larger ships because they were leaking badly and took away another Spanish vessel (Wright, *Further Eng. Voyages*, p. 213). This report seems scarcely credible; the number of ships observed later off Cuba seems to have been close to thirty, of which sixteen were large (ibid., pp. 168, 171).

[1] The second stay lasted from 3/13 April to 14/24 April. See Wright, *Further Eng. Voyages*, pp. lvii; and Castellanos, *Discurso*, pp. 223–5.

[2] Corbett (*Sp. War*, p. 22) reads, *Justice*. Diego Hidalgo Montemayor, the judge who was sent to investigate matters at Cartagena, reported that he arrived during Drake's second stay, and learned much by talking with Drake's interpreter, Jonas. See the version of his report in App. IV, Castellanos, *Discurso*, p. 307. It differs somewhat from that printed in Wright, *Further Eng. Voyages*, pp. 129–36.

[3] The date is incorrect. It should be 14/24 April. See note 1 above, and also p. 106 and n. 3.

[4] The Grand Cayman, which was reached on 20 April, according to the Map Text and newsletter (see pp. 68, 113). The French narrative (Lacour, p. 25) notes that they passed the island of *Cayamans*, uninhabited, where there were great serpents called *cayamans*, similar to large lizards, which one can eat.

killed more than xx^{ti} *Alligatos*.¹ Those bee suche serpentes as have bin in London to be seene. There weare *Crocadiles* which did Incounter & fighte with vs, they live bothe in the sea & on lande. Wee tooke divers & made verie good meate of them; some of the same weare ten foote in lenghte.

[fol. 172] Also wee killed other little beastes like cattes & other little serpentes abowte 2 foote longe called *Guanos*, with a great number of Turtles of huge bignes which served vs for verie good meate;

This Ilande is a verie Deserte & wildernesse & so full of woodes as hit can growe. Wee thought to have watered there but could finde none. wee staid there ij Daies & set the woodes on fire & soe departed.

[The] 25 & 26 of Aprill wee sailed in sight of Lande & came [to] anker at *Cape Saint Anthonie*,² where wee thowght to have water/ [There] wee fownde ij frigottes which wee set on fyre³ & so departed [becau]se there was little store of water.

[The l]ast of Aprill we gave chase to a small Shipp, but what [it] was wee knowe not.⁴

¹ i.e. alligators.

² According to the newsletter (p. 113), they left the Caymans on 23 April, and arrived at Cape San Antonio on the 27th (see also, pp. 68, 263). Words have been supplied in square brackets because the MS is torn at the edge.

³ One frigate was burned, according to a Spanish report. Wright, *Further Eng. Voyages*, p. 167.

⁴ The English accounts give few details about incidents at Cuba, but additional facts are supplied by Spanish records, including depositions taken from men who escaped there from the English. A brief summary, based mainly on those reports, follows.

After finding little water at Cape San Antonio, Drake sailed eastward toward Havana and Matanzas. Because the winds were unfavourable, or for other reasons (see p. 263 and n. 6), after two weeks of sailing they returned to the cape. There they set about collecting rain water and held a council to decide on their next course. At this time a former galley-slave from Santo Domingo, as well as some captives from Cartagena, escaped. The fleet started eastward again on 13/23 May (see pp. 68, 264). Possibly Drake had intended to attack Havana (see Corbett, *Sp. War*, pp. 23, n.; 73), but his actions near the city show that he had decided against it, knowing that the city had had ample warning, and that his own strength was much depleted. His ships were sighted close to Havana on 20/30 May and he overtook a ship, from which the crew escaped. Two shots were fired from the castle, but he made no effort to go in. About 23 or 24 May (O.S.) he left, going in the direction of Matanzas, and was not seen again. Wright, *Further Eng. Voyages*, pp. lviii–lx, 166, 172, 173, 176–8, 213.

The French narrative (Lacour, p. 25) reports the Cuban incidents very briefly. It mentions the watering at the cape, the passing of Havana, where they did not wish to

[The] 14 of Maie we came backe againe to *Cape Saint Anthonies* & then fownde more store of water & staied ther 5 daies to refresshe vs/[1]

The 19 daie we waied Anker & sealed alongst the coaste thinkinge to goe to the Matances[2] & there to take a towne, & by the waie wee tooke a carvell, the men forsooke her & ranne to shore. shee was loden with salte. Wee came in sight of the harbour that wee showlde have entered, but wee coulde not for contrarie windes.[3]

The 23 of Maie wee put of into the sea for the *Cape of Florida*,[4] and the xxv^th Daie wee gott sight therof, & sealinge alonge the coast, the 27 Daie wee fell with a Towne called *Saint Awgustine*.[5] There wee went on shore in the morninge, but coulde not enter the Towne for they had warninge of our comminge, and made a castle[6] of pur[pose] for there Defence against vs in suche order that wee must f[irst] winne the castle before wee coulde get the Towne, and our s[hips] could not come neere the Towne to batter hit; the water w[as] shallowe excepte it weare a v or 6 miles from hit. Yet there wa[s] a goodlie River runninge close by the Towne into the countrie.[7]

---

stop because their own numbers were too weak, and then proceeding to the Florida coast, and St Augustine. There is no reference to the early weeks of May.

[1] Again there is disagreement about the dates. According to the Map Text and the *Summarie*, the fleet returned to the cape fourteen days after their first leaving it (i.e. about 10 May), and the second departure was on 13 May (see pp. 68, 264). One Spanish document (Wright, *Further Eng. Voyages*, p. 171) states that this departure occurred on 15/25 May, with good weather.

[2] i.e. Matanzas.

[3] The events here described occurred as the fleet passed along the northern coast of Cuba; the salt ship was taken just outside of Havana (see note 4 on p. 204 above; and Wright, *Further Eng. Voyages*, pp. 168–72, etc.). That ship was destroyed at St Augustine (see below, p. 207).

[4] From this point (23 May) until the end, this narrative has been printed also in Quinn, *Roanoke Voyages*, I, 303–8. The date refers to the departure from the Havana area. Cf. Wright, *Further Eng. Voyages*, p. 172.

[5] The fleet was sighted by the Spaniards on Friday, the 27th, and the landing was made on the 28th. Wright, *Further Eng. Voyages*, p. 163.

[6] i.e. the fort called St John's.

[7] The French narrative (Lacour, p. 25) mentions arriving at the river Matanée. This probably refers to the Matanzas Inlet, south of St Augustine. Quinn, *Roanoke Voyages*, p. 310, n.

The 28 Daie wee tooke ordinawnce on shore to batter the Castle which stoode on the one side of the river & wee were on the other. Yet when wee had shott ij peeces at them, like fainte harted Cowardes they ranne awaie. This was abowte midnight.¹ Then came over the river to vs a Frenche man & a Dutchman who tolde vs they were all fledd.²

Then the Admyrall & Vizadmirall³ went over with xxᵗⁱ men & Entringe there Castle fownde there woordes trew. Then on the other side where our men laie the savages & others came owte of the woodes & with a verie strawnge crie, assawlted our men.⁴ But they weare soone Driven backe, and our men followinge them into the woodes, by mischawnce on Master Waterhowse the Captaines lieftenaunte⁵ Of our shipp was slaine.

The 29 Daie of Maie wee entered the Towne & the Spaniardes gave vs 3 or 4 small shott & Ranne awaie & in followinge of them Captaine Powell was slaine by a horsman & ij footmen Spaniardes.⁶

The 30 Daie after wee had taken the spoile of this Towne

¹ This account omits much. See pp. 114–5, 265–7; and Wright, *Further Eng. Voyages*, pp. 181–3, 198–9.
² The Frenchman was Nicholas Burgoignon (Quinn, *Roanoke Voyages*, pp. 296–7, 763–6). The Spanish reports add a Fleming (the Dutchman?) and a Spaniard (Morales?). Wright, *Further Eng. Voyages*, pp. 182, 186; and Quinn, *Roanoke Voyages*, pp. 297, n., 304, n., 720). See also pp. 115, 266.
³ Drake and Frobisher. This was early on Sunday, 29 May. Wright, *Further Eng. Voyages*, pp. 182, 183, 200.
⁴ The attack by the 'savages' does not appear in the *Summarie*; but see Wright, *Further Eng. Voyages*, (p. 199): 'That afternoon the general [of the fort] ordered ... [the] Indian interpreter for the district around the city, to make a night attack. Since he could not find Indians to accompany him, with only ten of them he attacked the enemy that night and they say that they killed four Englishmen but could do no more because of the enemy's much superior force.'
⁵ In the MS, after *lieutenant*, the words *Vizml Frobusher* were written and then crossed out. Corbett (*Sp. War*, p. 24, n.) suggested that Waterhouse was a naval lieutenant, but he has elsewhere been identified as lieutenant to Captain Goring (see pp. 115, 151). Since Goring had been assigned command of the soldiers on Frobisher's ship (see p. 139), the association of Waterhouse with him is understandable.
⁶ See also pp. 115, 269. A Spanish record which tells of the death of 'a captain who was much esteemed by the English commander', suggests that this occurred near the fort. Wright, *Further Eng. Voyages*, p. 187. Spanish accounts indicate that there was no resistance at the town, since it had been evacuated (ibid., pp. 184–5).

wee set it on fire¹ & soe wente to the Castle where wee rested 3 daies.

In This Castle wee fownde a Cheste with the kinges Treasure, and hard by the Castle wee fownde a small carvell with certaine treasure in her and somme letters from the kinge of Spaine.²

[fol. 172v] For Shee was newlie come [from thence] and further Wee fownde a lit[tle] Childe in her which the Span[iards] had lefte behinde them for has[te]. Wee sent them the childe and they tooke her but woulde not c[ome] to vs for anie thinge wee coulde doe.³

There was 9 of the savages set vp a flagge of Truce abo[wt] ij miles from the Towne, which our men fownde and carried them another.⁴

The seconde daie of Iune wee set fire on the Castle, a[nd the] same night set saile fron Thence.⁵

Also In that nighte wee set fire on the Carvell [which we] had taken by the Matacosse⁶ laden with salte and tooke th[e other] Carvell alonge with vs.

This Towne Saint Awgustine/ standethe in *Florydaie*, [where is] as goodlie a soyle as maie bee, with so greate abundaunce [of] sweete woodes &c as is woonderfull, with goodlie meadowes, [great] store of fisshe, Oysters & mussels with Deere & goodlie feeldes of Corne after there manner,

¹ The Spaniards reported the complete destruction by the English, with everything (fields as well as buildings) destroyed, and all that could be carried taken away, food, tools, furniture, money belonging to private persons (possibly 3,000–5,000 ducats), and small boats. Wright, *Further Eng. Voyages*, pp. 164, 181, 183–5, 188–9, 204. On these matters the *Summarie* is silent, but the confiscated artillery was reported (see p. 277). No ransom demands were made.

² According to the Spaniards, the chest contained 5,000–6,000 ducats. Wright, *Further Eng. Voyages*, pp. 181, 188.

³ The published Spanish documents do not refer to this child.

⁴ Quinn noted (*Roanoke Voyages*, p. 305, n. 2) that the Spanish non-combatants were at the mercy of the 'only nominally friendly Indians'; the English were hoping to have the Indians join them against the Spanish, and so did not damage their village. See also Quinn, op. cit., p. 804, and Wright, *Further Eng. Voyages*, pp. lxii, 183–4, 187.

⁵ The Spanish documents differ as to whether it was 2/12 or 3/13 June. Wright, *Further Eng. Voyages*, pp. 188, 190.

⁶ i.e. Matanzas. On the capture of this ship see above, p. 205. The English careened one vessel during the St Augustine stay. Wright, *Further Eng. Voyages*, p. 181.

There was abowte 250 howses in this Towne,¹ but wee left not one of them standinge.

Wee fownde 40 pipes of meale in this place & much ba[rley] but wee fownde neither wine nor Oyle nor anie other vict[ual] to make accowmpte of.²

Wee had in this towne xij great peeces of Brasse Ordinawnce.³

This Towne had v weekes warninge before, of our comminge, and had builded this castle onlie for vs keeping 90 sowldiers there in garrison,⁴ And There wee vnderstoode that the *Hyabans*⁵ had burn[ed] there towne themselves, and had gotten 1200 men to helpe the[m] thinkinge that wee woulde come to them.⁶

The wilde people at firste comminge of our men Died verie fast and saide emongest themselues, It was the Inglisshe God that made them die so faste.⁷

There ar Divers kinges emongest them, and these kinges ar Distaunte on from an other & they haue manie wifes. They tolde our men of on kinge not far from thence that had 140 wives.

Owre men killed the kinge of that place wee were In for that hee with hys people in on nighte had Determined to murther all the Inglishmen/ And an Indian did Bewraie the[ir] cowncell, Soe we gave the kinge that for his paines which hee woulde haue geeven vs.⁸

¹ This figure is too large, since the Spanish documents mention only 70–80 soldiers and 200–250 non-combatants. Wright, *Further Eng. Voyages*, pp. 164, 183, 200.

² The poverty of the settlement is indicated here. A few barrels of flour had been removed when the town was evacuated. See Wright, *Further Eng. Voyages*, pp. 164, 181; and Quinn, *Roanoke Voyages*, p. 306, n.

³ The fourteen pieces reported in the *Summarie* (p. 277) probably include those from the town as well as from the fort (see p. 268 and n. 3).

⁴ The *Summarie* (p. 268) mentions 150 men, but the Spanish records speak of only 70 or 80. Wright, *Further Eng. Voyages*, pp. lxii, 164, 183.

⁵ i.e. habitants. One Spanish text states that the Indians began to burn the town as soon as the English took the fort (Wright, *Further Eng. Voyages*, pp. 184–5); others attribute the destruction to the English alone.

⁶ Quinn (*Roanoke Voyages*, p. 306, n.) suggests that this may imply that the Spaniards enrolled 1,200 Indians to meet an English attack.

⁷ The deaths may have been from measles or smallpox. Hariot commented on Indian deaths. Quinn, *Roanoke Voyages*, pp. 306, n. 5; 378.

⁸ This incident does not appear in other accounts. Quinn (*Roanoke Voyages*,

The[y] have a churche w*i*th 3 Images in hit, And the[y] speake w*i*th the Divell once everie yeere vppon an highe Mowntaine. Also they ar cladd in Skins and they have a Copper Myne emongest them, And for the tagge of a pointe, a bell, a cownter, a pinne or suche like, They will geeve you anie thinge they haue/¹

Then wee sailed alonge the coast of this Lande vntill wee Came to the place where those men did lyve that *Sir* Walter Raleghe had sente thither to Inhabitt The yeere before/²

[fol. 173] [Those gentlem]en³ & others as soone as they saw [vs thin]kinge wee had bin a new supplie/ [came from the] shore & tarried certaine Daies,⁴ & a[terwards we browght]e thence all those men w*i*th vs except iij⁵ [who had gone furt]her into the countrie and the winde grew [so that] wee coulde not staie foor them/

[The 13] of Iune⁶ iiij of o*u*r Shippes weere forced to [put to sea]; the weather was so sore & the Storme so [great th]at o*u*r Ankers woulde not holde, and no shipp [of them all] but eyther brake or lost ther Ankers. And o*u*r [ship th]e Prymrose Brake

---

p. 306, n.) suggests that these relations with the Indians must refer to contacts farther along the coast. The Spanish records tell of a stop (7/17 June) to search for Santa Elena, another at Cruz harbour (the Savannah River?), and then at Oristan (presently South Carolina). At the latter point they took on water and firewood, and replaced a ship's mast. Wright, *Further Eng. Voyages*, pp. 190–1.

¹ On the bartering habits of the Indians see Quinn, *Roanoke Voyages*, p. 307, n. 4. The existence of the copper mines is doubtful (ibid., pp. 269, 307, n.).

² Cf. the statement in the *Summarie*. The fleet made contact with the colonists on 9 June, according to the *Summarie* (p. 270). Ralph Lane's account states that the fleet of 23 sails was sighted from Lord Admiral's Island by Captain Stafford on 8 June, and that the fleet reached the colony on the 10th (Hakluyt, *Prin. Nav.*, VIII, 342).

³ Here the MS is badly mutilated, all of the margins being torn. These words are supplied from the catch words at the bottom of the preceding page. In most of the later cases the words suggested by Corbett (*Sp. War*, pp. 26–7) are used.

⁴ On this conference see p. 271–2; and Lane's statement (Hakluyt, *Prin. Nav.*, VIII, 342–4). Quinn points out (*Roanoke Voyages*, p. 307, n.) that Stafford waited to get Drake's letter before going to tell Lane.

⁵ The number is read as *two* in Corbett (*Sp. War*, p. 26). This is the only reference to the abandoning of three settlers (Quinn, *Roanoke Voyages*, p. 307, n.).

⁶ Lane dates the storm, which occurred after his first conference with Drake, as continuing from 13 to 16 June (Hakluyt, *Prin. Nav.*, VIII, 344). This is the only account specifying how many of the ships, unable to join the fleet went instead for England (cf. p. 274). See Table of Ships.

an Anker of 150 *li* waighte.¹ [All the] Time wee weare in thys countrie, Wee had thunder, [lightning] and raigne with hailstones as Bigge as Hennes egges. [There were] greate Spowtes at the seas as thoughe heaven & [earth] woulde have mett.

[This c]owntrie is Indifferent frewtfull and hathe good [store of] fisshe with Land Turtles & Mice Frewtes & saxafrage² [which are] the best thinges in all the lande that wee know of: [the rest] after the reporte of the people³ woulde bee to longe. [let thi]s suffice/

[The 18th] Daie of Iune 1586⁴ wee set saile Directinge our course [to Ne]wfound Lande⁵ & so homewardes/

[At bottom] Henley⁶

Document 11

A SUMMARIE AND TRUE DISCOURSE OF SIR FRANCES DRAKES WEST INDIAN VOYAGE. Wherein were taken, the Townes of *Saint Iago, Sancto Domingo, Cartagena & Saint Augustine.* Imprinted at London by Richard Field, dwelling in the Blacke-Friars by Ludgate. 1589.⁷

¹ Quinn (*Roanoke Voyages,* p. 307) read the weight as 250 li. ² i.e. sassafras.

³ This may refer to reports by colonists after they had returned. Cf. Hariot's reference (in *A Brief and True Report*) to their speeches and reports. Quinn, *Roanoke Voyages,* pp. 308, n.; 324.

⁴ The date may have been 19 June (Lane's narrative, in Hakluyt, *Prin. Nav.,* VIII, 345); it is given as the 18th in the *Summarie* and the corresponding Map Text. The accuracy of some of Lane's dates has been questioned by Quinn (*Roanoke Voyages,* pp. 288, 308, n.). The *Summarie,* however, is not infallible (see below, p. 274, n. 7).

⁵ Drake's plan to return by way of the Newfoundland Banks was reported to Spanish officials at Havana. Wright, *Further Eng. Voyages,* p. 169.

⁶ The surname Henley, or Henly, probably the name of the diarist, is written at the bottom of the page. It was not noted by Corbett. Quinn (*Roanoke Voyages,* p. 308, n.) thought it might be read as *Henrey.* As written here, the name does not appear to be that of the master of the *Primrose,* Hampton (see p. 294). No identification has been found.

⁷ The wording is from the title page of the first issue of Richard Field's edition, which has been chosen as the basic text of this major narrative (see Bibliographical

A Summarie and True Discourse

TO THE RIGHT HONORABLE ROBERT D'EVREUX,
EARLE OF ESSEX AND EWE, VISCOUNT of Hereford
and Bourchier, Lord Ferrers of Chartley, Bourchier and
Louaine, Maister of the Queens Maiesties horse, and knight of
the most honorable order of the Garter, T.C. wisheth increase
of all honour and happinesse.[1]

Right Honorable, hauing by chaunce recouered of late into
my handes (after I had once lost the same) a copie of the
Discourse of our late West Indian voyage, vvhich vvas begun
by Captaine Bigges,[2] vvho ended his life in the said voyage
after our departure from Cartagena, the same being aftervvardes
finished (as I thinke) by his Lieutenant Maister Croftes,[3] or
some other, I knovve not vvell vvho. Novve finding therein

Note on *A Summarie and True Discourse* for a report on the various printed editions
of the narrative, and on the MS variant at the British Library, Harley MS 6221,
fols. 93–8v). The Grenville copy at the British Library (G 6510) has been used for the
text which follows, but the wording above has been taken from the Bodleian Library's
copy as reproduced in facsimile by Theatrum Orbis Terrarum Ltd. (Amsterdam,
1969). On the MS variant (Harl. 6221, fol. 94) the title appears simply as 'Sir Frauncys
Drakes voyage', and the date 'anno 1585' is written at the upper left-hand corner.

The Field edition is *S.T.C.* No. 3056, under which it is noted that on 26 November
[1588] a licence was granted to Master [William] Ponsonbye to publish 'A Booke
intytuled, The voyadge into the West Indyes made by Sir Frauncis Drake Knighte.'

On the title page of Roger Ward's edition (1589), attention is called also to the
town plans 'diligently made by BAPTISTA BOAZIO' (see Note on Maps), and on
the back of the title page are printed directions for the placing of the maps (see B.L.
copy, C.32.f.25). In Hakluyt's edition, which is best known, are the following
additions to the title: after *voyadge*, the words, *begun in the yeare 1585*; and after
Augustine, the words, *in Florida*. Hakluyt omitted the dedicatory epistle, and added
simply, *Published by M. Thomas Cates*. No title page mentions an author; only in the
dedicatory epistle that was printed with the earlier London editions (see below) is the
narrative attributed mainly to Walter Bigges.

On the back of the title page of the Field, Ward, and Ponsonby (1596) editions is
the following note that explains the delay in publication: 'The Reader must
vnderstand, that this Discourse was dedicated, and intended to haue bene imprinted
somewhat before the comming of the Spanish Flette vpon our coast of England; but
by casualtie of the same was forgotten and slacked for a time of some better leasure.'
(The wording is from the facsimile edition mentioned above.)

[1] The text of the dedicatory epistle has been taken from the facsimile edition. The
words are the same in the Ward edition, although the latter is set in different type and
uses some variations in spelling.

[2] i.e. Walter Bigges. This statement is the basis for all designations of Bigges as the
author of the *Summarie*.

[3] Nothing more is known of Lieutenant Croftes.

a most true report of the seruices and other matters vvhich happened in the sayd voyage, the sight vvhereof is vvonderfully desired by manie honest and vvell disposed persons. I haue presumed to recommend the publishing thereof, vnto your Lordships protection and fauour, for these tvvo causes. The one, for that your Lordships Honourable disposition is in the knovvledge of all men that knovv your selfe, most thirstingly affected to embrace in your ovvne person, the brauest enterprises, if the time vvould once affoord anie such fit occasion as might be agreeable to her Maiesties resolution: vvho vvisely (and long may she do it) gouerneth all things to the greatest aduantage of her selfe and people. The other, because my selfe hauing bene a member in the sayd actions, and vvas Lieutenant of Maister Carleils ovvne companie, vvhereby I can vvell assure the truth of this report:[1] I thought it my bounden duetie, hauing professed my seruice to your Lordship before all men, to dedicate the same rather vnto your Lordship then to anie other. And although it be novve a yeare and a halfe sithence the voyage ended, vvhereby some man vvill say, that it is novve no nevve matter:[2] yet the present time considered, hovv doubtfull some of our meaner sort of people are of the Spanish preparations, I thinke this Discourse a very fit thing to be published, that they may see vvhat great victories a fevve English men haue made vpon great numbers of the Spaniardes, euen at home in their ovvne countreyes. The beholding vvhereof vvill much encourage those, vvho by fame and bare vvordes are made to doubt much more then there is cause vvhy they should. Vpon vvhich point, as there may be

[1] Thomas Cates has not been identified further. His name does not occur in the narrative or in other accounts of the voyage. Perhaps his statement of his reasons for publishing should be taken at face value; but possibly, since he had had associations with Carleill, he may have been assigned his role as editor by others who desired a full report on the voyage to be printed (see Bibliographical Note).

[2] Since the fleet returned near the end of July 1586, a year and a half later would be approximately January 1588. This statement implies that simultaneous editions in England and on the continent were planned for early in 1588, but that concern about the Armada delayed action in London until November (see Bibliographical Note and Note on Maps). The value of the narrative for propaganda against the Spanish, as Cates suggests, was important in 1588, whether early in the year or late.

much sayd: so my selfe being no Discourser, do desire to be
held excused therein: and therefore doe onely commend the
trueth of this report vnto your Lordship: vvhich vvill be also
auovved by diuers Captaines that vvere in the sayd voyage.
And so in all humblenesse do take my leaue, readie to do your
Lordship all faithfull seruice.

Your Lordships souldier
and humble seruant.
THOMAS CATES.

A SVMMARIE AND TRVE DISCOVRSE....[1]

This worthie knight for the seruice of his Prince and countrie,
hauing prepared his whole fleete, and gotten them downe to
Plimouth in Deuonshire, to the number of fiue & twenty saile

---

[1] The title is repeated on the first page of the printed text. Internal evidence suggests
strongly that the manuscript variant of the *Summarie* (B.L. MS Harl. 6221, fols. 93–8v)
is closer to an original account than are the printed versions, and that the successive
English editions, beginning with that of Field (1589) represent a report considerably
revised and expanded – whether for the purpose of anti-Spanish propaganda, or to
promote interest in colonial ventures, or to aggrandize the English leaders. Because,
however, supportive evidence from other sources, both English and Spanish, indicates
that many of the insertions regarding events and observations are valid, it has seemed
best to use for the text of this volume the printed version of the *Summarie* rather than
the shorter manuscript variant. Editorial marks and notes are used to indicate where
changes or additions occurred: longer passages identified as insertions are marked by
double asterisks and square brackets [** ... **], and significant variations in wording
are pointed out in notes. Variations in spelling, whether in the MS variant or in later
editions of the printed text, have usually not been noted, although attention has been
called to any significant changes made by later English editors, particularly by Ward
and Hakluyt.

Occasionally, because close textual comparison indicates that the Latin and French
editions (Leyden, 1588) include only some of the changes that appear in the English
printed form, and that they otherwise resemble the earlier MS text, passages from
those editions are included in the notes. Also included in notes are references to
Thomas Greepe's ballad, *The True and Perfecte Newes ... 1587* (1587). Although it
differs from the *Summarie* in certain details, its author appears to have had at hand
either the original or a copy of it, upon which he drew for portions of his account.
(See pp. 1, 7.)

Excerpts from two other sources also have been included in various notes. One is a
fragment of an anonymous journal (B.L. Cotton MS Titus B. VIII, fols. 251–251v).
The other is the printed French narrative 'Voiage du Sievr Drack', edited by L. Lacour
(Paris, 1855) from a MS now in the Bibliothèque Nationale. It seems farther removed
from the *Summarie* than any of the printed versions, but it follows the narrative so
closely as to suggest that its author used it in preparing his own briefer account (see
Quinn, *Roanoke Voyages*, p. 309, n., and also p. 7, n. 4 above).

of ships & pinnaces,[1] & hauing assembled of souldiers and mariners to the number of two thousand and three hundred in the whole, embarqued them and him selfe at Plimouth aforesayd the twelfth day of September 1585.[2] being accompanied with these men of name and charge, which hereafter followe.

Maister Christopher Carleill Lieutenant Generall, a man of long experience in the warre as well by sea as land, & had formerly carried high offices in both kindes in many fights, which he discharged alwaies verie happily, and with great good reputation.[3]

Anthonie Powell Sergeant Maior.

Captaine Matthew Morgan, and Captaine Iohn Sampson Corporals of the field.

These principall officers had commandement ouer the rest of the lande Captaines, whose names hereafter follow.[4]

[1] Twenty-five ships and fifteen pinnaces, according to the Greepe ballad (st. 5); twenty-two ships, a galley, and eight pinnaces, according to Cotton MS Titus B. VIII, fol. 251. The French narrative (Lacour, p. 19) mentions 22 ships and one bark. Cf. p. 14 above, and Table of Ships.

[2] The MS variant (Harl. 6221, fol. 94) begins differently. Under the heading, 'Anno 1585. Sir Frauncys Drakes voyage', is the following paragraph: 'Thys worthy knight, for the service of this prince, the advauncment of his honor, he benefitt of his contry and comon wealthe, with the gentlemen and Capitayns vndarnamed, As also with .2300. men aswell souldiours as mariners and saylors took shippinge at Plimowth the xij day of Septembar. 1585. Concerninge whose prosperows successe, honorable acts, martiall and valiant exployts performed aswell by sea, as by land, with the politiqwe advise, counseyll and conducte of Captayne Christopher Carleill Esqwiere his lievtenaunt Generall, I thowght best to set downe the Coppie of a letter sent by a gentleman of good accompte to a frind of his, In which the same is without favour, feare, or mallice truly and exactly set downe, agreable also to the reporte of sondry credible persons with whom I have conferred towchinge the same /' [With a slightly indented paragraph, the account continues]: 'The names of the Captains, which went with Ser Fraunces Drake aswell those which took charge of the soldiors by land, as also of those who had charge of the shippes by sea/ The land Captens were thus, with theyr principall officers, viz.'

[3] The MS variant (Harl. 6221, fol. 94) differs, reading: 'Christopher Carleill Esquier Lieveteaunt generall, a man of longe and greate experience in the warres aswell by land in all sortes, As also by sea in sondry greate fyghtes. Greate offices had bene layde on hym in the warres of forreyne Contries which he discharged alwayes verye happely with greate good reputacion/'

[4] Harl. 6221 (fol. 94) reads, after Powell as sergeant major: 'Mathewe Morgan Corporall of feild, John Sampson Corporall of field. All these principall officers had commaundement over the rest of the Captaynes which were these, viz.'

Captaine Anthonie Plat.[1]
Captaine Iohn Merchant.
Captaine Edward VVinter.
Captaine Iohn Goring.
Captaine Robert Pew.
Captaine George Barton.
Captaine VVilliam Cecill.
Captaine VValter Bigs.
Captaine Iohn Hannam.
Captaine Richard Stanton.
Captaine Martine Frobusher Vizeadmirall,[2] a man of great
experience in sea faring action, and had carried chief charge

---

[1] The arrangement of the names of land captains varies slightly among the different
English editions, but the same names appear in all. Both the Latin and the French
editions omit Cecil as a land officer, but the Latin version names him as a ship
captain.

Harl. 6221 (fol. 94) arranges the land captains with some additional comments, as
follows:

Capten Anthony Platt ⎤ Capten John*n* Merchant ⎟ Capten Edward Wynter ⎟ Capten John*n* Goringe ⎟ Capten Robert Piewe ⎦	⎡Capten George Barton Capten William Cicell dead Capten Walter Biggs dead ~~Capten Richard Stanton~~ Capten John*n* Hannam dead ⎣Capten Richard Stanton

All these Captens aforesayde, Master Wynter only excepted whose yonge and formar
yeres had bene spent at schole, and Cowrte, and now beinge heire to Sir William
Wynter his fathar, began to goe abrode. The resydewe were men of good experyens
and for the moaste parte had taken charge in the warrs abrode/' (The location of
Stanton at the end probably represents his late appointment to a captaincy. See
pp. 47, n. 4, 135, 174.)

[2] For fuller details on the ships see Document 1 and Table of Ships. The list in
Harl. 6221 (fol. 94), where the ships are numbered from 1 to 22, differs slightly from
the printed one. The chief officers appear thus:

'1. The sea Captaynes with theyr officers were Ser Fraunces Drake Generall aswell
by land as sea but cheflye intended to the sea charge in the Elizabeth
Bonaventure/

2. Mastar Martyn Frobussher Vice admirall, a man of greate and longe experience
and had caried chefe charge of many shippes hym selfe, now Captayne also of
the Primerose/
Mastar Thomas Fenner Vice Admyrall by office, and Capten in the
Bonadventure/ [The number 3 was written and crossed out.]

3. Mastar Fraunces Knollis Capten in the Gallion Leyster/'

There is no reference here to the post of rear admiral. The Latin and French versions,
which include no ship names, do not designate any special rank for Knollys.

of many ships himselfe, in sundry voyages before, being
nowe shipped in the Primerose.[1]
Captaine Francis Knolles, Rieradmirall in the Gallion Leicester.
Master Thomas Venner Captaine in the Elizabeth Bonaduenture
vnder the Generall.
Maister Edward VVinter Captaine in the Aide.
Maister Christopher Carleill the Lieutenant generall, Captaine
in the Tigar.
Henrie VVhite Captaine of the sea Dragon.
Thomas Drake Captaine of the Thomas.
Thomas Seelie Captaine of the Minion.
Bailie Captaine of the Barke Talbot.
Robert Crosse Captaine of the Barke Bond.
George Fortescute Captaine of the Barke Bonner.[2]
Edward Carelesse Captaine of the Hope.
[William Hawkyns Captayne of the barke Hawkyns][3]
Iames Erizo Captaine of the white Lion.[4]
Thomas Moone Captaine of the Francis.
Iohn Riuers Captaine of the Vantage.
Iohn Vaughan Captaine of the Drake.[5]
Iohn Varney Captaine of the George.[6]
Iohn Martin Captaine of the Beniamin.

[1] The Greepe ballad (st. 8): 'The Primrose next, Vize-Admirall/ appointed by
theyre best devise/ Captayne Frobisher Vize-Generall/ A valiant Captayne ware
and wyse.'
[2] Hakluyt's edition corrected the spelling to *Fortescue*.
[3] In Harl. 6221 (fol. 94) the list of captains and ships, numbered in sequence with
slight variations in the spelling of names, is the same from Winter (4) through
Fortescue (11). The name of the ship for 'Edward Carlesse' was written first as *barke
Hawkyns*, but then crossed out and replaced with *Hoape*. For neither Seely nor Baily
is a Christian name given in the MS.
   No. 13 in the Harl. 6221 list (supplied above in square brackets) is 'William Hawkyns
Capten of the barke Hawkyns'. This ship is mentioned in the voyage narratives, but
its name is missing from all of the printed editions of the *Summarie*. It was listed in the
1585 'Furnishing Lists'. See Document I and Table of Ships.
[4] No Christian name for 'Erizey' appears in the MS variant (Harl. 6221).
[5] The *Drake*, however, was not with the fleet until she was taken as a prize (see
Table of Ships). In Harl. 6221 (fol. 94) the entry for ship No. 17 reads: 'John Vaughan
Capten of the ~~Elizabeth~~ Drake/'
[6] Varney's ship, No. 18 according to Harl. 6221 (fol. 94), was the *Elizabeth*. No ship
George is in the MS list. See Table of Ships.

Edward Gilman Captaine of the Skout.

Richard Hawkins Captaine of the Galliot called the Ducke.

Bitfield Captaine of the Swallow.[1]

After our going hence, which[2] was the fourteenth of September, in the yeare of our Lord, one thowsand fiue hundred eighty and fiue:[3] [** and taking our course towards Spaine,[4] we had the winde for a few daies somewhat skant, and sometimes calme.[5] And being ariued neere that part of the coast of Spaine,[6] which is called the Mores, we happened to espie diuerse sailes, which kept their course close by the shore, the weather being faire and calme. The Generall caused the Vizeadmirall to go with the Pinnaces well manned to see what they were, who vpon sight of the said pinnaces approching nere vnto them, abandonned for the most parte all their shippes (being Frenchmen) laden all with salt, and bounde homewardes into France, amongst which ships (being all but of small burden) there was one so well liked, which also had no man in her, as being brought vnto the Generall, he thought good to make stay of her for the seruice, meaning to pay for her, as was accordingly performed at our returne, which barke was called

---

[1] *Swallow* is No. 22 in the Harl. 6221 (fol. 94) list, and her captain's name appears simply as '[   ] Byttfyeld.'

[2] After the ship list, before starting with the narrative, the scribe of Harl. 6221 (fol. 94v) inserted the following paragraph: 'Ser I know yow expect earnestly the newes of our passed voyage, and trwe it is that I owe a greater travayle then the writing of a large dyscowrse, but as my fortune hathe not aforded me the benefitt of the skole to prove anye thynge able in this facultie of discowrsynge, so yet to yow as one of my best frinds, I will not refuse to delyver the relation of the substaunce and trewthe of that which is passed, as neare as my knowledge may vndartake, desyringe that my good will to do yow any further service may be well accepted/'

[3] In Harl. 6221 (fol. 94v) the opening sentence of the account reads: 'Aftar owr goinge hence which was the .xiiij. of Septembar. 1585. wee put in with the Iles of Bayon in Spayne.' This MS does not include the remainder of the paragraph as it is printed here, nor incidents of the voyage to Spain, but goes directly to events at Bayona (see p. 219). The Latin and French editions follow the wording of the Harl. 6221 MS, omitting the same material, and the Greepe ballad omits it also.

[4] The account between the signs [** . . . **], though not in the MS variant, can be accepted as authentic, except that the editor reversed the time order for the occurrences. The incidents are reported in other sources. See pp. 77, n. 3 and 180.

[5] For events of 14–21 September, and weather conditions, see the *Tiger* journal (pp. 70–5).

[6] The Hakluyt edition omits *of the coast.*

the Drake.[1] The rest of these ships being eight or nine, were dismissed without any thing at all taken from them. VVe being afterwards put somewhat further off from the shore, by the contrarietie of winde, we happened to meete with some other French ships, full laden with Newland fish, being vpon their returne homeward from the said New found land: whom the Generall after some speech had with them, and seeing plainly that they were Frenchmen, dismissed without once suffering any man to go aboorde of them.

The day following standing in with the shore againe, we discried an other tall ship of twelue score tunnes or thereabouts, vpon whom Maister Carleill the Lieutnant generall being in the Tiger, vndertooke the chase, whom also anone after the Admirall followed, and the Tiger hauing caused the said strange ship to strike her sailes, kept her there without suffering any bodie to go aboord vntill the Admirall was come vp: who foorthwith sending for the Maister, and diuerse others of their principall men, and causing them to be seuerally examined, founde the ship and goodes to be belonging to the inhabitants of S. Sebastian in Spaine, but the marriners to be for the most parte belonging to S. Iohn de Lvce[2] & the Passage.[3] In this ship was great store of drie Newland fish, commonly called with vs Poore Iohn,[4] whereof afterwards being thus found a lawfull prize, there was distribution made into all the ships of the Fleete, the same being so newe and good, as it did very greatly bestead vs in the whole course of our voyage. A day or two

[1] This incident of the salt ships, as recorded by others, did not occur until 24 or 25 September (see p. 77 and n. 3, and p. 180). According to the journal fragment (Cotton MS Titus B. VIII, fol. 251), which gives the less reliable date of 27 September, the vessels were '5 Birtons' laden with salt and wine, homeward bound from Lisbon. The 'men of one Rane awaye & Lefte ther Baurke which the generall tooke & the Rest where Discharged'.

This was after the encounter with the fishing ships from Newfoundland (see below).

[2] In Hakluyt, S. John de Luz.

[3] The capture of the Biscayan or San Sebastián vessel occurred on 22-3 September (see pp. 75-6, 180). The anonymous fragment (Cotton MS Titus B. VIII, fol. 251) states that it occurred about 70 or 80 leagues of the English coast, and that the 40 men and boys aboard proclaimed themselves to be 'of Bayon in Fraunce nere unto Byske'. Cf. p. 76 and notes.

[4] Cf. p. 108.

after the taking of this ship **] we[1] put in with the Isles of
BAYON, for lacke of fauourable wind,[2] where we had no
sooner anckered some part of the Fleete, but the Generall
commaunded all the Pinnaces with the ship boates to be
manned, and euerie man to be furnished with such armes as
was needefull for that present seruice, which being done, the
Generall put him selfe into his Galley,[3] which was also well
furnished, and rowing towards the Citie of BAYON, with
intent, & the fauour of the Almighty to surprise it.[4] Before we
had aduaunced one halfe league of our way, there came a
messenger being an English Marchant from the Gouernour,[5]
to see what straunge Fleete we were,[6] who came to our
Generall, and conferred a while with him, and after a small
time spent, our Generall called for Captaine Sampson, and
willed him to go to the Gouernour of the Citie, to resolue him
of two pointes. The first, to knowe if there were any warres
betweene Spaine and England. The second why our Marchants

---

[1] At this point (**) the account in Harl. 6221 (fol. 94v) resumes with: 'wee put in
with the Isles of Bayon in Spayne. . . .' The Latin and French editions agree, as does
the Greepe ballad. The date was 27 September (see pp. 78, 181), although the
anonymous fragment (Cotton MS Titus B. VIII, fol. 251), again in error by two days,
dates the arrival on the 29th.

[2] Omitted in this printed version, perhaps because it was considered to reflect upon
Drake's inadequate preparations, is a reference also to lack of water. According to the
Harl. 6221 (fol. 94v) text, the fleet entered here, 'as well for lacke of favorable wynd,
As also in suche tempestious wethar, to take the benefite of freshe watterynge.' The
need for water was mentioned also in the Latin and French editions.

The *Primrose* journal (p. 181) states that food was needed also. Carleill, in his
despatch to Walsingham from here, explained the stop first, because of stormy
weather, and secondly, for 'the refurnishing ourselves with water, [and] the giving
to many of our ships their needful wants out of the store . . .', for which there had not
been time in the hasty sailing from Plymouth. He added as a third reason the need to
set down proper Articles of Order for the fleet. (Carleill's despatch of 10 October, as
pr. in Corbett, *Sp.War*, pp. 41–2.)

[3] Presumably not the 'galliot' *Duck*. The *Tiger* journal (p. 78) speaks of pinnaces and
long boats.

[4] In Harl. 6221 (fol. 94v), the wording is: '. . . surprise it, but before we had
advansed . . .'. The encounter was at a small island (see p. 181, n. 2), described in
Cotton MS Titus B. VIII (fol. 251) as 'a small Round Iland'. Cf. Plate II.

[5] The merchant, Short or Sharp (see pp. 78–81). Harl. 6221 (fol. 94v) is less explicit,
reading: '. . . there came a messengar from the governor to see. . . .' Both the Latin and
French editions identify the messenger was an English merchant.

[6] Instead of *we were*, Harl. 6221 (fol. 94v) reads: *was in the river.*

DRAKE'S WEST INDIAN VOYAGE, 1585-86

with their goods were imbarred or arrested.¹ Thus departed
Captaine Sampson with the said messenger to the citie, where
he found the Gouernour and people much amazed of such a
sudden accident.²

The Generall with aduise and counsell of Maister Carleill his
Lieutenant generall, who was in the galley with him, thought
not good to make any stand, till such time as they were within
shot of the Citie, where they might be readie vpon the returne
of Captaine Sampson, to make a sudden attempt if cause did
require³ before it was darke.

Captaine Sampson returned with his message in this sort.
First, touching peace or warres,⁴ the Gouernour sayd he knew
of no warres, and that it lay not in him to make any, he being
so meane a subiect as he was. And as for the stay of the
Marchants with their goods, it was the kings pleasure, but not
with intent to endommage any man. And that the kings conter
commandement was (which had bene receaued in that place
some seauennight before) that English Marchants with their
goods should be discharged: for the more verifying whereof,
he sent such Marchants as were in the towne of our Nation,
who traffiqued those parts:⁵ which being at large declared to
our Generall by them, counsell was taken what might best be
done.⁶ And for that the night approached, it was thought

¹ On the report of the governor, Pedro Bermudez, regarding this meeting see
p. 79, n. 2. See also p. 181.

² By *accident* is meant an unusual occurrence. It was translated into the Latin as
novelty. The Greepe ballad, which devotes only one stanza to the Bayona events,
asserts that Drake did not intend to attack the town.

³ The punctuation in Harl. 6221 (fol. 94v) gives a slightly different meaning. The
sentence ends with the word *require*, and the clause, *before it was darke*, begins the next
sentence concerning Sampson's return, thus: 'Before it was darke Captayne Sampson
came to vs and returned his message. . . .'

⁴ In Harl. 6221 (fol. 94v), after the words *peace or warres*, the following words were
written and then crossed out: '*That it lay not in hym to make any and*'. This seems to be
a copyist's error, for the words occur in the next line.

⁵ Instead of *who traffiqued those parts*, Harl. 6221 (fol. 94v) reads: *who testified as afore
sayde*. The Latin and French editions appear to have followed the former reading,
referring to those who *trade*. Carleill's despatch to Walsingham (see Corbett, *Sp.War*,
p. 44) describes them simply as 'other marchants who came with him [Short]'.

⁶ For fuller accounts of these conferences see above, pp. 79-81, and Corbett, *Sp. War*
pp. 42-4.

needefull to land our force, which was done in the shutting vp of the day, & hauing quartered our selues to our most aduantage, with sufficient gard vpon euery straight, we thought to rest our selues for that night there.[1] The Gouernour sent vs some refreshing, as bread, wine, oyle, apples, grapes, marmalad[2] and such like. About midnight the weather beginnes to ouercast,[3] insomuch that it was thought meeter to repaire aboord, then to make any longer abode on land, and before we could recouer the Fleete, a great tempest arose, which caused many of our ships to driue from their ancker hold, and some were forced to sea in great perill, as the barke Talbot, the barke Hawkins and the Speedewell, which Speedewell onely was driuen into England,[4] the others recouered vs again, the extremity of the storme lasted three daies, which no sooner beganne to asswage,[5] but Maister Carleill our Lieutenant generall, was sent[6] with his owne ship and three others: as also with the galley and with diuers Pinnaces, to see what he might do aboue VIGO, where he toke many boates and some Caruels, diuersly laden with things of small value, but chiefly with houshold stuffe, running into the high countrey, and amongst the rest he found one boate laden with the principall Church stuffe of the high Church of VIGO, where also was their great Crosse of siluer, of very faire embossed worke, and

---

[1] In Harl. 6221 (fol. 94v), *there* is omitted. Concerning other events on the island where the English landed see p. 181.

[2] In the Latin edition, and in the German translation which is derived from it, paranthetical explanations were inserted to define marmalade as a food made of honey.

[3] The storm, beginning on the night of 27 September, lasted through the 30th (see pp. 82–3). Stormy weather continued for seven days, according to Cotton MS Titus B. VIII, fol. 251v.

[4] The *Talbot* and the *Hawkins* returned to the fleet, but the *Speedwell* went back to England (see p. 81 and n. 6). The statement here, and also in the MS variant (Harl. 6221), that she actually reached England, a matter about which Drake's fleet could scarcely have been informed during the voyage, indicates that this comment was not written until after 27 July 1586.

[5] The third day of the storm, 30 September, according to Carleill's account (see p. 83). See also the Map Text.

[6] Harl. 6221 (fol. 94v) is more brief: '. . . but Captayne Carliele by our Generall was sent. . . .' The French edition translated it this way. In the Latin edition, his rank is given, *Vicarius Generalis*.

double¹ gilt all ouer, hauing cost them a great masse of money.²
They complained to haue lost in all kind of goods aboue thirtie
thowsand Duckets in this place.³

[** The⁴ next day the General with his whole Fleete went vp
from the Iles of BAYON, to a very good harbour aboue
VIGO, where Maister Carleill stayd his comming, aswell for
the more quiet riding of his ships, as also for the good
commoditie of fresh watering, which the place there did afoord
full well.⁵ In the meane time the Gouernour of GALLISIA
had reared such forces as he might, his numbers by estimate
were some two thowsand foot, and three hundred horse, &
marched from BAYON to this part of the countrey, which
lay in sight of our Fleete,⁶ where making stand, he sent to parle
with our Generall, which was graunted by our Generall, so it
might be in boates vpon the water: and for safetie of their
persons, there were pledges deliuered on both sides, which
done, the Gouernor of GALLISIA put him selfe with two
others into our Vize-Admirals Skiffe, the same hauing bene
sent to the shore, for him: And in like sort our Generall in his
own skiffe, where by them it was agreed, we should furnish our
selues with fresh water, to be taken by our own people quietly

¹ The word *double* is not in Harl. 6221.
² The two crosses, with certain other valuables, were worth 6,000 ducats, according
to the *Primrose* journal (p. 182).
³ So also in Harl. 6221. The figure appears as forty thousand in both the Latin and
French editions. In the separate French narrative (Lacour, p. 20) it is stated that the
English did no damage at the Isles of Bayon, except to burn one or two houses, before
the governor's parley with Drake (see below), and that they 'plundered not a thing'
after the parley. See the *Tiger* journal (p. 84 and n. 7).
⁴ This paragraph (**), with the first six words of the next, does not appear in the
MS variant (Harl. 6221), but is included in the Latin and French editions. If it was
missing from the original account, the sources for its inclusion here might have been
Carleill's record from his ship *Tiger*, or his despatch to Walsingham from Vigo (see
Corbett, *Sp.War*, pp. 46–7).
⁵ Drake moved the rest of his fleet up the river on 1 October (see pp. 64, 83), and
the ensuing parley was on 2 October.
⁶ The Latin and French editions change the meaning slightly. After *country*, they
state the governor's purpose (trans.): 'where he could best keep our fleet in sight.'
The governor's *bravado*, according to the journal fragment (Cotton MS Titus B.
VIII, fol. 251v), occurred on the day before the next parley, but that record errs about
the dates, giving them as 4 and 5 October (see p. 86, n. 3).

on the land, and haue all other such necessaries, paying for the same, as the place would afforde.[1]

VVhen all our businesse was ended, **] we departed,[2] & toke our way by the Islands of CANARIA, which are esteemed some three hundred leagues from this part of Spain, & falling purposely with PALMA,[3] with intention to haue taken our pleasure of that place, for the full digesting of many things into order,[4] and the better furnishing our store with such seuerall good things as that affoordeth very abundantly, we were forced by the vile sea gate, which at the present fell out, and by the naughtinesse of the landing place, being but one, and that vnder the fauor of many Platformes, well furnished with great ordinance,[5] to depart with the receipt of many their Canon shot, some into our ships,[6] and some besides, some of them being in very deede full Canon high. But the onely or chiefe mischiefe, was the daungerous sea surge, which at shore all alongest, plainly threatned the ouerthrow of as many Pinnaces and boates, as for that time should haue attempted any landing at all.[7]

Now seeing the expectation of this attempt frustrated by the

---

[1] For fuller descriptions of this conference see above, pp. 86–7, 182, and also Carleill's despatch to Walsingham (Corbett, *Sp. War,* p. 47).

[2] The MS variant (Harl. 6221, fol. 94v) here continues the narrative: 'Departynge from the[nce] we toke owr way. . . .' The fleet moved to Bayona on 7 October. Having been ready to leave there by the 10th, the fair wind at NNW the next day enabled them to start. See pp. 64, 88, 89 and Carleill's despatch (Corbett, *Sp. War,* p. 49).

[3] For events during this part of the voyage see pp. 90–3, 120–8, 183–4. Although plans made in England may have called for a stop only at Ferro (Lansdowne MS 100, fol. 98, pr. in Corbett, *Sp. War,* p. 72), the decision to try for Palma was made at a council on 24 October (see p. 93). The fleet arrived there on 3 November. See pp. 128–9, 184 for reports on the action there.

[4] The set of orders distributed here is given in full in the *Leicester* journal (see pp. 130–1).

[5] The words *with great ordinance* are not in Harl. 6221 (fol. 95).

[6] The French narrative (Lacour, p. 20) stated that the English did not set foot on land in the Canaries because they did not feel strong enough; and at Palma they received a number of cannon shot from the fortress, (tr.) 'of which one passed between the legs of the said Sir Drake'. Cf. p. 128.

[7] According to the *Primrose* journal (p. 185), the fleet put to sea because of the wind, intending to return later. See also p. 94. The Greepe ballad (st. 14) reports the Palma incident: 'Twas not theyre Gunnes nor force that could/ Once make our English harts to daunte./ If wynde and waves had not so wrought:/ Full deerely they theyr pride had bought'.

causes aforesaid, we thought it meeter[1] to fal with the Isle of FERRO,[2] to see if we could find any better fortune,[3] and comming to the Island, we landed a thousand men[4] in a valley vnder a high mountaine, where we stayed some two or three houres, in which time the inhabitants, [**[5] accompanied with a yong fellow borne in England, who dwelt there with them, **] came vnto vs, shewing their state to be so poore, that they were all readie to starue, which was not vntrue: and therefore without any thing gotten,[6] we were all commaunded presently[7] to imbarke, so as that night we put off to sea South Southeast along[8] towards the coast of Barbarie.

Vpon Saterday in[9] the morning, being the thirteenth of Nouember, we fell with Cape Blancke, which is a low land & shallow water, where we catched store of fish, & doubling the Cape, we put into the Bay, where we found certain French ships [** of war,[10] whom we entertained with great curtesie, and

[1] In Harl. 6221 (fol. 95), *mete* instead of *meeter*.

[2] 'Theyle of Ferro' in Harl. 6221 (fol. 95). The Latin edition offers an explanation: (tr.) 'commonly called del Ferro (some used to call it Pluitalia)' [i.e. rainy]. Hakluyt changed the spelling to *Hierro*.
The date of arrival here was 4 or 5 November (see pp. 94, 131, 185).

[3] In Harl. 6221 (fol. 95): *hazard* instead of *fortune*.

[4] The number was six or seven hundred, according to other records (see pp. 95, 185).

[5] The incident of the English boy is not in the MS variant (Harl. 6221), which continues here: '. . . we stayed a tyme, and duringe ower stay the inhabitaunts came to vs, and tolde vs ther state to be. . . .' Both the Latin and the French editions, however, mention the English boy, as do all of the other principal narratives.

[6] After the word *gotten*, in Harl. 6221 (fol. 95) is added: 'vnlesse it were some little freshe watar, not so moche as would fill a hogshed out of a depe pitt.'

[7] Harl. 6221 (fol. 95) omits *presently*.

[8] The French edition states the course direction as given here and in the MS variant. The Latin translator erred: (tr.) 'toward the shore of Africa, while the south and southeast winds were blowing'. The German edition avoided the problem by stating simply, 'with favorable wind.' Cf. p. 65.

[9] 13 November 1585 was a Saturday. The French edition printed the date as the 14th. For several days the fleet had been becalmed, and had spent the time in fishing. See pp. 96–7, 132.

[10] In Harl. 6221 (fol. 95) the words after *shippes* [** — **] are omitted, the text continuing to the next sentence, *the aftarnone.* . . . The *Leicester* journal (p. 133) reported meeting a French 'man of war' (probably meaning an armed merchantman) on the 11th. The newsletter reported an encounter with several French ships on the 13th (see p. 110). The *Primrose* journal (p. 186) told of meeting four French ships on the 14th, but noted no exchange of courtesies.
Although the reported exchange of courtesies with the French commander is

there left them. **] The after noone the whole Fleete assembled,
which was a litle scattered about their fishing, & put from
thence to the Isles of Cape Verde, sayling till the sixteenth of
the same moneth in the morning,[1] on which day we descried
the Island of S. IAGO,[2] and in the euening we anckered the
Fleet betwene the towne called the PLAY OR PRAY[3] and
S. IAGO,[4] where we put on shore a thousand men or more,[5]
vnder the leading of Maister Christopher Carleill Lieutenant
Generall, who directed the seruice most like a wise com-
maunder.[6] The place where we had first to march did affoord

---

missing from the MS variant, it appears in both the Latin and the French editions
of the *Summarie*. To include such a note may have been considered useful for propaganda purposes. The separate French narrative (Lacour), however, does not mention
it.

[1] A variation as to date occurs here. The Harl. 6221 (fol. 95) text reads: '. . . the .17.
of the same monthe, and in the morninge the same day we discryed the Iland . . . , and
in the evenynge late we ankered the flete betwene the Play and Seint Iago. . . .' On the
next page, written and then crossed out, is an abbreviated summary of events here (see
below, p. 233, n. 5), in which the date was written, obviously in error, as xxvij of
Novembar.

Agreeing with the arrival date of 17 November are the Map Text, and the journals
from the *Tiger*, the *Leicester*, and the *Primrose* (see pp. 65, 97, 134, 186). Even the
Greepe ballad, which was printed in 1587, states that the landing occurred on that date
(st. 15). The date when the town was occupied was 18 November, therefore, and not
the anniversary of the queen's coronation (see below). By moving the arrival date
back one day, to 16 November, the editor was able to fit in a bit of patriotic
propaganda in connection with the entry into the town. This change was included
also in the Latin and French editions.

[2] The separate French narrative (Lacour, pp. 20–1) added the observation that the
island of Santiago is forty leagues from the mainland, and some forty leagues in
circumference. It mentions the arrival and landing on 17 November, which, it notes,
was coronation day, but it says nothing about a victory celebration. Although this
narrative does not alter the date of arrival, the reference to an English anniversary
suggests that the writer may have had the printed narratives at hand.

[3] In Hakluyt's edition, *Playa or Praya*.

[4] In the Latin edition, and also in the French, an explanatory clause was added, thus:
(tr.) '. . . S. Iago, which is the metropolis of the whole island and gives it its name.'
Cf. the wording in p. 233, n. 5.

[5] On the number of men and details about the officers see pp. 134–5, 186.

[6] The description in Harl. 6221 (fol. 95) differs slightly, with this sentence
continuing: '. . . a wyse comander: for first the place where we marched ded afforde
no good ordar, for the grownd was mountayny and full of dalles marveylous thike
and stony, whiche passage or marche I thinke yf it had bene day, we had hardly
vndartaken, yet with great travayle we waded thrwghe, and comynge vpon the
playne we made stonde. . . .'

no good order, for the ground was mountaines and full of dales, being a maruellous stonie[1] & troublesome passage, [** but[2] such was his industrious disposition, as he would neuer leue, vntil we had gotten vp to a faire plaine, where **] we made stand for the assembling of the Army. And when we were all gathered together [** vpon[3] the plaine, some two litle miles from the towne, **] the Lieutenant generall thought good not to make attempt till day light: [** because[4] there was not one that could serue for guide or giuing knowledge at all of the place. And therefore after hauing well rested, **] euen halfe an houre before day, he commanded the Armie[5] to be deuided into three special parts, such as he appointed,[6] whereas before we had marched by seuerall companies, being thereunto forced by the naughtinesse[7] of the way as is aforesayd.

Now by the time we were thus raunged into a very braue order day light began to appeare,[8] and being aduaunced hard to the wall, we sawe no enemie to resist, whereupon [** the Leiutenant generall **][9] appointed Captaine Sampson with

---

[1] Hakluyt change *mountaines* to *mountainous*, and *marvellous stonie* to *very stony*.

[2] The words [** — **], in which Carleill's leadership is praised, do not appear in Harl. 6221. See note 6, p. 225 above.

[3] Harl. 6221 (fol. 95) omits the words [** — **]. The Latin and French versions include the statement, giving the distance from the town as half a league in the Latin, and one league in the French. Hakluyt dropped the word *litle*.

[4] Harl. 6221 (fol. 95), in which the words [** — **] do not appear, reads: '. . . tyll daylyght. And even halfe an howre. . . .'

[5] In Harl. 6221, *trowpps* instead of *Armie*.

[6] The description of the military arrangements differs in Harl. 6221 (fol. 95). It omits the word *special* before *parts*, and continues after the word *appointed*, thus: 'and for the first battalion, it was put owt of two companys and comitted to be lead by Captayne Sampson corporall of the field, Captayne Powell beinge sargant maior had the leadinge of two othar companyes, in an othar battalion on the othar syde of the battayle, and with the battayle digested into very brave ordar, came the lievtenaunt generall, Captayn Morgan and the rest of the Captaynes. Now by the tyme we were thus ordared, day lyght began to appeare. . . .'

These details, which suggest the observations of a soldier, and the similar ones in the *Leicester* journal (p. 134), are depicted on the Santiago map (Plates III(B), (C)). They may have been abbreviated for the printed edition, with civilian readers in mind.

[7] Hakluyt substituted *badnesse* for *naughtiness*.

[8] With the words, *daylight began*, agreement with the wording of the Harl. 6221 variant resumes.

[9] The Harl. 6221 (fol. 95) account differs slightly, omitting at the start the direct reference to Carleill [** — **], and reading: '. . . where vpon Captayne Sampson . . .

thirtie shot, & Captaine Barton with other thirtie, to goe
downe into the towne, which stood in the valey vnder vs, and
might verie plainely be viewed all ouer from that place where
the whole Army was now arriued & presently after these
Captaines was sent the great Ensigne, which had nothing in it
but the plaine English Crosse, to be placed towardes the sea,
that our fleet might see Saint Georges Crosse florish in the
enemies fortresse. [** Order[1] was giuen that all the ordinance
throughout the towne and vpon all the platformes, which was
aboue fifty peeces all ready charged, should be shot of in honor
of the Queenes Maiesties coronation day, being the seuenteenth
of Nouember, after the yearly custome of England, which was
so answered againe by the ordinance out of all the ships in the
fleete which now was come neere, as it was straunge to heare
such a thondering noise last so long to gether.[2] In this meane
while the Leiutenaunt generall held still **][3] the most part of
his force on the hill top, till such time as the towne was
quartered out for the lodging of the whole armie,[4] which being
done euerie Captaine toke his owne quarter, and in the euening

---

and Captayne Barton . . . were appoynted to enter the towe. Captaynen Sampson
takynge a bulwarke for his place of stand, and Captayne Barton the market place, the
livetenaunte generall sent presently certayne ensigns to be placed, that owr flete might
see Seint Georges Crosse florishe in thenemyes fortresses, holdynge the moaste parte
of his force on the hill toppe tyll such tyme as the towne was quartered. . . .' Cf. the
Leicester journal (p. 134–6) for the report by men who went in with Sampson.

[1] The anecdote included in the lines [** — **], and printed also in the two Leyden
editions of 1588, illustrates an embellishment for propaganda purposes. None of the
MS journals reports such a celebration, and even the patriotic Greepe ballad does not
mention it (see note 2). Without the change of date to make the entry into the town
fall on 17 November (see above, p. 225, n. 1), the double function of the celebration
in honour of queen and victory would have been impossible.
Possibly the loaded guns of the town were fired, since the English planned to
confiscate all of them, but it seems improbable that Drake would squander his own
ships' supply of powder before an evacuated town. The *Primrose* journal (p. 186), notes
particularly the number of guns and barrels of powder taken here. See also p. 136.

[2] The Greepe ballad, instead of describing a thunderous celebration, notes (st. 17)
that the English found some coins and food in the town and 'Then quietly praise God
therefore/ They made a worthy victors feast'.

[3] With the words, *the most part*, agreement between the MS variant (Harl. 6221)
and the printed versions resumes.

[4] Cf. p. 138.

was placed such sufficient gard vpon euerie part of the towne that we had no cause to feare any present enemie.

Thus we continued in the citie the space of fourteene daies,[1] taking such spoiles as the place yelded, which were for the most part, wine, oile, meale, and some other such like things for victuall, as vineger, oliues & some other trash, as marchandise for their Indian trades.[2] But there was not found any treasure at all, or any thing else of worth besides.

[** The[3] scituation of Sainct IAGO[4] is somewhat strange in forme like to a triangle, hauing on the East and VVest sides two mountaines of Rocke and cliffie, as it were hanging ouer it, vpon the top of which two mountains was builded certaine fortifications to preserue the towne from any harme that might be offered.[5] From thence on the South side of the towne is the maine sea, and on the North side, the valley lying betweene the foresayd mountaines, wherein the towne standeth: the saide

[1] The Greepe ballad (st. 18) mentions the stay of fourteen days, but the time was shorter, 17–29 November. On the date of departure see pp. 65, 99.

[2] In Harl. 6221 (fol. 95) the reading is: '. . . some other trashe as marchandyze for theyr Guyney trades was found but not any treasure at all. . . .' Mention of the trade with the *Indies*, appearing in the Latin edition as well as in those printed in England, was possibly intended to emphasize the relationship of the Cape Verdes with Spain's overseas empire.

As to the 'Guinea trade' of this area see p. 188 and n. 2, and the cartouche on the left-hand side of the Santiago map (Plate III(c)).

[3] The next four paragraphs of descriptive material [** — **] do not appear in the Harl. 6221 MS, nor are they in the Latin and French editions. Either they were not a part of the original narrative, or they were omitted because of their length or because, in the case of the Leyden editions, they were thought to be of less interest to non-English readers. To the present editor the first explanation seems probable. Such a description seems more likely to have been written by an observer who was more highly educated than a soldier like Captain Bigges, and undoubtedly Drake had in his company men who could make such reports (cf. the similar observations in the *Leicester* journal, pp. 137–8). If the printed *Summarie* is indeed a much edited narrative of the voyage, intended to encourage English trading interests as well as national pride, insertion of this kind of matter could be expected.

[4] The French narrative (Lacour, p. 21) describes the town as follows: (tr.) '. . . large like Saint-Malo; it is large and narrow . . . [and] produces much cotton and sugar.' See also the maps (Plates III(a), (b), (c)).

[5] The Ward edition refers here to the map, inserting after *offered*, the words, *as in this Plot is plainly shewed*. This is one of the best indications that the town maps were placed in that edition in accordance with the instructions printed at the beginning of the volume. The Hakluyt edition, which follows that of Ward closely, changed the wording here to: *as in a plot*. See Bibliographical Note, Appendix III.

valley and towne both do grow very narrow, insomuch that the space betweene the two cliffes of this ende of the towne is estimated not to be aboue tenne or twelue score ouer.

In the middest of the valley cometh downe a riueret, rill or brooke of fresh water, which hard by the sea side maketh a pond or poole, whereout our ships were watered with very great ease and pleasure. Somewhat aboue the towne on the North side betweene the two mountaines, the valley wageth somewhat larger then at the townes end, which valley is wholie conuerted into gardens and orchards well replenished with diuers sorts of fruicts, herbes & trees, as lymmons, orenges, suger canes, cochars or cochos nuts, plantens, potato roots, cocombers,[1] small and round onions, garlicke, and some other things not now remembred, amongst which the cochos[2] nuts and plantens are very pleasant fruicts, the sayd cochos hauing a hard shell and a greene huske ouer it, as hath our walnut, but it farre exceedeth in greatnesse, for this cochos in this greene huske is bigger then[3] any mans two fistes, of the hard shell many drinking cups are made here in England, and set in siluer as I haue often seene.

Next within this hard shell is a white rine resembling in shew very much euen as any thing may do, to the white of an egge when it is hard boyled. And within this white of the nut lyeth a water, which is whitish and very cleere, to the quantitie of halfe a pint or thereabouts, which water and white rine before spoken of, are both of a very coole fresh taste, and as pleasing as any thing may be. I haue heard some hold opinion, that it is very restoratiue.

The Planten groweth in cods, somewhat like to beanes, but is bigger and longer, and much more thicke together on the stalke, and when it waxeth ripe, the meate which filleth the rine of the cod becommeth yellow, and is exceeding sweet and pleasant. **]

---

[1] In the Ponsonby (1596) and Hakluyt editions, the spelling is *cucumbers*.
[2] i.e. cocoanuts, referred to in the *Primrose* journal (p. 187) as 'Ginnye nuts'.
[3] Hakluyt substituted *than* for *then*.

In this time of our being there, hapned to come a Portingall to the VVestermost fort, with a flag of truce,[1] to whom Captaine Sampson was sent with Captain Goring, who comming to the sayd Messenger, he first asked them what nation they were, they aunswered Englishmen, he then required[2] to know if warres were betweene England & Spaine to which they answered that they knew not, but if he would go to their Generall he could best resolue him of such particulars, and for his assurance of passage and repassage, these Captaines made offer to ingage their credits, which he refused for that he was not sent from his Gouernor. Then they tolde him, if his Gouernor did desire to take a course for the common benefit of the people and contrie,[3] his best way were to come & present himselfe vnto [** our Noble and merciful Gouernor Sir Frances Drake: **] whereby he might be assured to finde fauour, both for him selfe and the inhabitants. Otherwise within three daies we should march ouer the land, and consume with fire all inhabited places, and put to the sworde all such liuing soules[4] as we should chaunce vpon: so this much he tooke for the conclusion of his answer, and departing, he promised to returne the next day, but we neuer heard more of him.

Vpon the foure and twentieth day of Nouember,[5] [** the

[1] On this incident, with which the correspondence between the MS variant and the printed *Summarie* reappears, the wording in Harl. 6221 (fol. 95) differs slightly. It reads: 'In this tyme aforesayde many things chaunsed, as the cominge downe to the westermoste forte, a flagg of trwse, to whom Captayne Sampson. . . .' Neither the Latin nor the French edition identifies the man as a Portuguese. On this messenger see p. 189.

[2] The parley, according to Harl. 6221 (fols. 95–95v) continued thus: '. . . he then required at theyr hands to know . . . , they knew not, but yf it would please hym to goe to theyr generall he could best resolue. . . . The Captaynes aforesayde ingaged theyr credits. . . .'

[3] The reading of the MS variant (Harl. 6221, fol. 95v) is more brusque; and the reference to Drake [** — **] is less personal: '. . . yf his governor would follow theyr cownseyle that his best way was to surrendar hym selfe to the misericordea of theyr generall where by he might. . . .' The Latin edition includes the suggestion that the governor should consider the safety of his people and refers to 'our Generall' and 'his mercy and humanity'. The French edition omits reference to these latter qualities.

[4] A massacre of the people is mentioned in Harl. 6221, but the two Leyden editions give a more general reading, simply that the English intended 'to see everything laid waste by fire and sword'.

[5] On the date of this march, probably 27 November, see pp. 97, n. 7, 111, 148.

Generall accompanied with the Lieutenant generall and **]
six hundred men, marched foorth to a village twelue miles
within the lande, called S. DOMINGO, [** where[1] the
Gouernor and the Bishop with all the better sort were
lodged, **] and by eight of the clocke we came to it, finding
the place abandoned, & the people fled into mountaines:[2] so we
made stande a while to ease[3] our selues, and partly to see if any
would come to speake to vs. After we had well rested our
selues, the Generall commaunded the troupes to march away
homewardes,[4] in which retreat[5] the enemy shewed them selues,
both horse & foote, though not such force as durst encounter
vs:[6] [** and so in passing some time at the gase with them, **]
it waxed late and towards night, before we could recouer
home to S. IAGO.[7]

On Munday the six & twentieth of Nouember,[8] the Generall

[1] The Harl. 6221 (fol. 95v) differs and omits the words [** — **]. It does not
mention the English officers, stating merely, after *November*: 'we marched forth with
syx hundred men to a towne which in theyre langwage is Called Seint Domingo beinge
distant of.3. leagwes, and by eyght. . . .'

Some further details about the inland march, including references to the Spanish
officials, were inserted in the MS variant at a later point, as if to compensate for this
omission, and the Latin and French editions follow the arrangement of the MS (see
below, p. 234 and n. 3).

It seems probable that, before the Field edition was published, the editor decided to
combine the material from these two related passages into a single paragraph,
presenting it here in the proper time sequence, thus avoiding the awkward repetition
or afterthought that occurs in the MS.

[2] The Greepe ballad (sts. 19–20) includes a detail that does not show up elsewhere,
that of some friars being left behind, expecting the town to be defended. 'But they so
sore did fear the Drake/ They let theyr Fryars stand to stake.'

[3] In Harl. 6221, the word is *rest* instead of *ease*.

[4] According to other accounts (see pp. 98, 148, 189), the English fired the town
before leaving it.

[5] Instead of *in which retreat*, Harl. 6221 (fol. 95v) reads: *and beinge vpon owr marche*.

[6] In Harl. 6221 (fol. 95v) *but* is used instead of *though*, and *myght* instead of *durst*.
The words [** — **] do not appear, and the concluding portion reads: '. . . it beinge
late the same day before we recovered home, restinge owr selvs the next day.' See also
p. 234, n. 3 below.

The reference to a silent and watchful encounter appears in the Latin and French
editions. See also pp. 98, 189.

[7] The English brought back with them on this occasion at least one prisoner. See the
Leicester journal (p. 149) and below.

[8] The date, which appears also in the MS variant, is incorrect; 26 November was
a Friday. Probably intended was Monday, 29 November, which is the date given in
the Map Text (p. 65), the *Tiger* journal (p. 98) and the newsletter (p. 111).

commanded all the Pinnaces with the boates, to vse all dilligence to imbarke the Armie into such ships as euery man belonged. [** The¹ Lieutenant generall in like sort commaunded Captaine Goring and Lieutenant Tucker, with one hundred shot² to make a stand in the market place, vntill our forces were wholly imbarked, the Vizeadmirall making stay with his Pinnace and certaine boates in the harbour, to bring the sayd last company aboord the ships. **] Also the Generall³ willed foorthwith the Gallie⁴ with two Pinnaces to take into them the company of Captaine Barton, and the company of Captaine Bigs,⁵ vnder the leading of Captaine Sampson, to seeke out such munition as was hidden in the ground, at the towne of PRAY or PLAY, hauing beene promised to be shewed it by a prisoner,⁶ which was taken the day before. The Captaines aforesaid comming to the PLAY, landed their men, and hauing placed the troupe in their best strength,⁷ Captaine Sampson tooke the prisoner, and willed him to shewe that he had promised, the which he could not, or at least would not: but they searching⁸ all suspected places, found two pieces of ordinance one of yron, an other of brasse. In the after noone the Generall anckered the

---

¹ The sentence [** — **] is not in the Harl. 6221 variant, but it appears in the foreign editions. A brief reference to the manner of embarkation is in the *Tiger* journal's note for 28 November.

² The French translator here and regularly afterwards translated *shot* as *harquebousiers*. The Latinist, who had more difficulty with sixteenth-century military terms, usually translated *shot* as *sclopetarii*.

³ The MS variant, in which the preceding sentence does not appear, begins here with *he* instead of *the Generall*.

⁴ In the Latin edition, and also in the German derivative of it, there is a parenthetical explanation after galley (*galeram*), that it is a modern term for a type of large ship.

⁵ i.e. Captain Walter Bigges, to whom a major portion of the *Summarie* is attributed. It is spelled *Bygge* in Harl. 6221.

⁶ The wording varies slightly in Harl. 6221 (fol. 95v), thus: '. . . Sampson, and go to the towne of Playe to seke for suche munition as was there hydden in the ground, being promised to be. . . .' On the prisoner who was the guide here see pp. 149, 188.

⁷ A few words in the MS variant do not appear in the printed version, possibly because they place the actions of the English in a less favourable light. After noting the landing of the men, Harl. 6221 (fol. 95v) continues: '. . . and placed them selvs in the church for theyr assuraunce', and then Sampson proceeded with the prisoner. The Leyden editions agree with printed version here.

⁸ In Harl. 6221, *lokynge*, instead of *searching*.

rest of the Fleete before the PLAY, comming him selfe a shore, willing vs to burne the towne and make all haste a boorde, the which was done by six of the clocke the same day, and our selues imbarked againe[1] the same night, and so we put off to sea Southwest.

But before our departure from the towne of S. IAGO,[2] we established orders for the better gouernment of the armie, euery man mustered[3] to his Captaine, and othes ministred to acknowledge her Maiestie supreame Gouernour, as also euery man to do his vttermost endeuour to aduaunce the seruice of the action, and to yeeld due obedience vnto the directions of the Generall and his officers.[4] [** By this prouident counsell, and laying downe this good foundation before hand, all things went forward in a due course, to the atchiuing of our happie enterprise. **]

In[5] all the time[6] of our being there, neither the Gouernor

---

[1] The Harl. 6221 variant ends the sentence with the word *agayne*. The following sentence reads: 'The same nyght we put to sea sowthe west.'

[2] This sentence begins differently in Harl. 6221 (fol. 95v): 'Furthermore I will not omyt to let it be knowne how that in the yle of Seint Iago we establyshed. . . .' However, the words between *Furthermore* and *in the yle* were crossed out.

[3] In Harl. 6221, 'every man was mustered. . . .'

[4] In Harl. 6221 (fol. 95v) the wording varies slightly, with no use of the words *due obedience*. After *endeavor*, the passage reads: 'to aduaunce the action and also to follow the direction of the generall and his officers.' For the full wording of these regulations, and an account of the circumstances of their establishment that disagrees with the tone of the final printed sentence see pp. 140-2. That sentence [** — **], missing from the MS variant and also from the Latin and French editions, seems to be an editorial insertion that pays respect to good administration. It avoids any suggestion that there was resistance to the oaths or to the Knollys quarrel.

[5] Inserted before the words *in all* in the MS variant is a brief summary of the Santiago stay, written in nine lines and underlined, but then completely crossed through as if it should be ignored. That summary reads: 'Takynge owr cowrse towards the llands of Cape Verde, wee put owr selves on shore vnder the conducte and chefe charge of Captayne Christopher Carleill levetenaunt generall the xxvij of Novembar in the Ilands of Saint Iago the chefe towne where of is called by the same name, and was very well builded and well peopled, but the Inhabitaunts afeard abandoned the towne and gave vs qwiet leave to enter wherein we spent some xiiij dayes, we fownd here no treasure at all of no kynd, but howses well furnished of many good necessaries for the refresshinge of the trowpes, meale in some quantytie, and wyne of Spayne, there was muche where of we shipped some to serve to make beverage of/'

[6] The word *Besydes* is inserted in the MS variant before *In all the time*, probably to provide the necessary continuity after the summary passage was discarded.

for the king of Spaine, which is a Portingall,¹ neither the
Bishop, whose authoritie is great, neither any of the inhabitants
of the towne or Island² euer came at vs (which we expected
they should haue done) to intreate vs to leaue them some part
of their needefull prouisions, or at the least, to spare the ruining
of their towne at the going away.³ The cause of this their
vnreasonable distrust (as I do⁴ take it) was the fresh remembrance
of the great wrongs they had done to olde Maister VViliam
Hawkins of Plimouth,⁵ the voyage he made fower or fiue
yeares before, [**⁶ when as they did both breake their promise,
and murdered many of his men **] whereof I iudge you have
vnderstood, and therefore needelesse to be here repeated.⁷ But

¹ In Harl. 6221 (fol. 95v) *Spaniard* was written and crossed out, with *Portingale*
substituted. Both the Latin and the French editions omit the clause, *which is a
Portingale*.

² Harl. 6221 (fol. 95v) omits the words *any of*; and it inserts *thus* after *Island*. The
refusal of the inhabitants to come to parley is mentioned in the Greepe ballad (st. 21).

³ After *away* in Harl. 6221 is inserted an addition to the account of the inland march,
reading: 'We trauayled, as I sayde, into the yland some dozen miles to a principall
village called Seint Domingo, where we vnderstode the governor and the bysshope
shuld be, but they fled, And on owr retorne homeward they would now and then
show them selvs in the filde farr from vs, but would neyther come at any few of vs,
nor yet send any to vs/'

The corresponding passage in the Latin edition is (tr.): 'And though we penetrated
into their land the distance of twelve English leagues (as we said above) where we
heard that the Governor and the Bishop were, they fleeing from us as we advanced;
and as we returned from there, we awaited these men, because they had shown
themselves to us from a distance; nevertheless they were never willing to approach us
any nearer, although we sent a few men to the town to invite them to a council.'
The French edition is similar, but in the latter sentence states that we sent 'only a small
number, up to four persons in a group', to draw them to talk with us.

The editor of the Field edition appears to have chosen to combine this passage with
the earlier report of the march instead of repeating it here (see above, p. 231 and n. 6).

⁴ The word *do* is not in the Harl. 6221 variant.

⁵ In Harl. 6221 (fol. 96): 'to olde Hawkyns of Plimowthe.' The Latin and French
editions give the name as 'William Hawkins of Plymouth'. Hakluyt changed the
Maister to *Mr.* for his edition.

⁶ The wording in Harl. 6221 (fol. 96) is: '. . . in the voyage he made a fewe yeres
synce, where of I Iudge yow have vnderstode, and therefore nedeless to be here
repeted/ but sens they came not at vs. . . .' The passage is more correct as to date
(i.e. 1582) than is the printed version, and it does not have the words [** — **],
which have an anti-Spanish flavour. Both the Latin and the French editions give the
date correctly by using the words, 'some three years before'; they include the
reference, as in the printed version, to broken promises, but do not speak of murders.
Cf. p. 190.

⁷ In the German edition (1589), which up to this point had followed the Latin text

234

since they came not at vs, we left written in sundry places, as also in the Spitle house[1] (which building was onely appointed to be spared) the great discontentment and scorne we tooke [** at[2] this their refraining to come vnto vs, **] as also at the rude maner of killing, and a sauage kind of handling the dead body of one of our boyes, found by them stragling all alone[3] [** from whom they had taken his head and his heart, and had stragled the other bowels about the place, in a most brutish and most beastly maner. **]

In reuenge whereof at our departing we consumed with fire all the houses, aswell in the countrey which we sawe, as in the towne of S. IAGO.

From hence putting ouer to the VVest Indies, we were not many dayes at sea, but there begannne amongst our people such[4] mortalitie, as in few daies there were dead aboue two or three hundred men.[5] And vntil some seuen or eight dayes after our comming from[6] S. IAGO, there had not died anie one man

---

closely, the editor interrupted the narrative to introduce the descriptive material for the Santiago map which was inserted here. The items of the description, using numerals rather than letters to correspond with the numbers shown on the smaller version of the map, are somewhat abbreviated from the textual keys (see Note on Maps).

[1] The hospital was spared except for its bells (see p. 187). The Latin and French editions omit the first part of this sentence, going directly to the incident of the straggler.

[2] Harl. 6221 (fol. 96) uses the words *there of* instead of the phrase [** — **].

[3] This incident is more simply told in the MS variant (Harl. 6221), which does not include the words after alone [** — **] but goes directly to the words, *In revenge*. The French narrative gives a literal translation of the wording shown in the MS. The Latin edition, however, includes part of the more savage detail, thus (tr.): '. . . because they had deformed most cruelly the body of one of our boys, found rashly [wandering] along the way, cutting off the head and taking out the intestines, we burned. . . .'

The description [** — **], which may have been inserted editorially for its propaganda value, has some foundation. It corresponds closely with the report in the *Primrose* journal (see p. 189). See also pp. 98, 148.

[4] In Harl. 6221 (fol. 96) the word *generally* follows *people*.

[5] Cf. p. 191. The Latin and French editions give the figure as 'more than three hundred men'. In the separate French narrative (Lacour, p. 21), it appears as 'three or four hundred'. For other high estimates of the losses see p. 99 and n. 3. This period of sickness is not mentioned in the Greepe ballad.

[6] In Harl. 6221 (fol. 96) the word is *to* instead of *from*. No narrative indicates the appearance of the illness before the fleet put to sea.

of sickenesse in all the Fleete: the sickenesse shewed not his infection wherewith so many were stroken, vntill we were departed thence, and then seazed our people with extreme hote burning and continuall ague, whereof some verie fevve escaped vvith life, and yet those for the most part not vvithout great alteration and decay of their vvittes and strength for a long time after.[1] In some that dyed vvere plainely shevved the small spottes, vvich are found vpon those that[2] be infected vvith the plague, we were not aboue eighteene daies in passage betweene the sight of Sainct IAGO aforesaid, and the Island of DOMINICA,[3] being the first Island of the VVest Indies that we fell withall,[4] [** the same being inhabited with sauage people, which goe all naked, their skin couloured with some painting of a reddish tawney, verie personable and handsome strong men who doe admit little conuersation with the Spaniards:[5] for as some of our people might vnderstand them, they had a Spaniard or twaine prisoners with them, neither doe I thinke that there is any safety for any of our nation or any other to be within the limits of their commaundement, albeit they vsed vs very kindely for those fewe houres of time which we spent with them, helping our folkes to fill and carie on their bare shoulders fresh water from the riuer to our ships boats, and fetching from their houses, great store of Tobacco, as also

---

[1] Cf. p. 254.

[2] In Harl. 6221 (fol. 96) the word *often* is inserted before *found*; and *which* instead of *that*.

[3] The Map Text dates this arrival on 18 December (see p. 66), agreeing with the dating in the *Tiger* journal (p. 100). The *Primrose* journal (p. 191), however, places the arrival on the 21st.

[4] The wording in Harl. 6221 (fol. 96) differs slightly. It reads: '. . . Dominica, beinge the first Iland we fell within the West Indies.' The subsequent descriptive passage [** — **] does not appear in the MS, and it is missing also from the Latin and French editions. The Greepe ballad, however (st. 23) tells of the island's savage inhabitants, 'Wyld and nakte,' who were willing to trade for trifles. This is among the rare instances in which the ballad gives a detail that is not in the MS variant.

[5] For a fuller account of incidents here see the *Primrose* journal, pp. 191-3. The French narrative (Lacour, p. 21) noted that this island is (tr.) 'inhabited by people whom they call cannibals, who are large men entirely naked. The island is some fifty leagues in circumference and well peopled, and it is said there are some fifty thousand Indians there'.

a kind of bread, which they fed on, called Cassado,[1] verie white and sauerie, made of the rootes of Cassania.[2] In recompense whereof, we bestowed liberall rewardes of glasse, coloured beades and other things, which we had found at Sainct IAGO, wherewith (as it seemed) they rested very greatly satisfied, and shewing some sorowfull countenance when they perceaued that we would depart.

From hence we went to **][3] another Island VVestward of it, called Sainct CHRISTOPHERS Island, wherein we spent some dayes of Christmas, to refresh our sicke people, and to cleanse and aire our ships.[4] [** In which Island were not any people at all that we could heare of. **]

[**[5] In which time by the General it was aduised and resolued, with the consent of the Lieutenant general, the Vizeadmirall, and all the rest of the Captaines to proceede to the great Island of HISPANIOLA,[6] as well for that we knewe our selues then

---

[1] The word is written as *Cassado* also in the MS of the *Primrose* journal, (see p. 191). The English editions retained that spelling until Hakluyt changed it to *Cassavi*.

[2] The French narrative (Lacour, p. 22) reported (tr.): 'The English took fresh water there and the savages gave them many hens, parrots, and other (*autres*) good fruits.'

[3] The narrative in Harl. 6221 (fol. 96) resumes here with: 'In another Iland to the westwarde of it called Seint Christovall Iland we spent. . . .' The Latin and French editions are similar.

[4] The stay at St Christopher's, according to the Map Text and the newsletter (see pp. 66, 111) was 21–25 December. The *Primrose* journal (p. 193) placed the arrival on Christmas Eve, and departure after three days. It noted also that the English 'saw no man but our owne companie', an observation resembling the comment [** — **] in the printed *Summarie* which does not appear in the MS variant, or in the Latin and French editions.

The French narrative (Lacour, p. 22) noted the arrival on Christmas Day at 'l'isle a Montour' and that it was uninhabited.

[5] This paragraph and the next one [** — **] are not included in Harl. 6221. Instead, the MS variant goes directly from the stop at St Christopher's to events at Hispaniola, opening a new paragraph thus: 'Aftarwards we proceded to the greate Iland of Hispaniola and on New Yeres Daye in the morning. . . .' (See note 5, p. 238.)

At this point, the Latin and French versions agree with the printed *Summarie*. It seems probable that the passage, valuable for propaganda purposes for both English and continental readers, was inserted to emphasize the significance of Drake's easy success here. Certainly the fall of Santo Domingo was a humiliation to Spain.

The decision to proceed directly to Hispaniola meant giving up a stop at Margarita, which, according to the voyage plan dated April 1586, had been proposed for early December (see Corbett, *Sp. War*, pp. 70–1).

[6] For places passed on the way to Hispaniola see pp. 100, 111. The French narrative

to be in our best strength as also the rather allured therunto, by the glorious fame of the Citie of S. DOMINGO, being the auncientest and chiefe inhabited place in all that tract of country thereabouts. And so proceeding in this determination, by the way we met with a small Frigot, bound for the same place, the which the Vizeadmirall tooke,[1] and hauing duly examined the men that were in her, there was one found by whom we were aduertised, the hauen to be a barred hauen, and the shore or lande thereof to be well fortified, hauing a Castle therevpon furnished with great store of artillerie, without the daunger whereof, was no conuenient landing place with[in][2] ten English miles of the Citie, to which the sayd Pilote tooke on him to conduct vs.

All things being thus considered on, the whole forces were commaunded in the euening to imbarke them selues into Pinnaces, boates, and other small barkes appointed for this seruice. Our souldiers being thus imbarked, the Generall put him selfe into the barke Fraunces as Admirall, and all this night we lay on the sea, bearing small saile vntil our arriuall to the landing place,[3] which was about the breaking of the day, and so we landed,[4] being New yeares day, nine or tenne miles **][5]

(Lacour, p. 22) mentions also the town of 'Saint Jehan-Porto-Richo-des Poules', distant about thirty leagues from Santo Domingo.

[1] According to the *Primrose* journal (p. 193) two barks were taken on 31 December, and the pilot was a Greek. At some time Drake may have intercepted a Spanish ship that was carrying King Philip's warning to the city (see p. 101, and n. 2, and also Wright, *Further Eng. Voyages*, p. 151).

[2] In the second issue of the Field edition the list of *errata* noted that the word should be *within* instead of *with*. The Ward edition printed the word as *within*.

[3] The Latin and French editions contain this material although it is not in the MS variant. The Spaniards observed the small vessels passing the harbour, but did not understand their intent. Wright, *Further Eng. Voyages*, p. 39.

[4] i.e. at the mouth of the Hayna River, with a thickly wooded region lying between it and the town. Wright, *Further Eng. Voyages*, p. 39.

[5] Harl. 6221 (fol. 96) here resumes the narrative (see p. 237, n. 5 above) thus: '. . . on New Yeres Day in the mornynge vnder the leadinge and chefe conducte of owr lievetenaunt generall we put foote on shore by breake of daye myles or ten to the west ward of that brave Citie of Seint Domyngo. For at that tyme nor yet is knowne to vs any landinge place nearer, where the sea surge doth not threaten to overthrowe a pinnace or boate'.

The repetition of parts of this passage for the printed version, when a fuller

to the VVestwardes of that braue Citie of S. DOMINGO:
for at that time nor yet is known to vs, any landing place,
where the sea surge doth not threaten to ouerset a Pinnace or
boate. [** Our¹ Generall hauing seene vs all landed in safetie,
returned to his Fleete, bequeathing vs to God, and the good
conduct of Maister Carleill our Lieutenant generall,² at which
time, being about **] eight of the clocke, we began to march,
and about noone time, or towards one of the clock we
approched the towne, where the Gentlemen and those of the
better sorte, being some hundred and fiftie braue horses³ or
rather more, began to present them selues, but our small shot⁴
played vpon them,⁵ which were so sustained with good
proportion of pikes in all partes, as they finding no part of our
troope vnprepared to receaue them (for you must vnderstand
they viewed all round about) they were thus driuen⁶ to giue vs

---

explanation had already been inserted (see above), represents an awkward bit of
editing.

¹ The words [** — **] are not in Harl. 6221. Without mentioning Drake and
Carleill, it continues (from the wording in note 6, p. 238): '. . . by eyght of the cloke we
were all landed and began to marche, and. . . .'

² The Greepe ballad (st. 31), again giving a detail that differs from the MS variant,
states that the 'general' returned to his ships, where, anchored before the town, they
battered both town and fort. See also p. 194.

³ The MS variant reads: 'some hundreth brave horses.' The French account (Lacour,
p. 22) gives the figures as some five hundred horsemen, another five hundred on foot,
and three or four thousand negroes, of whom some were armed. These figures are
exaggerated. All of the Spanish documents show very limited forces available (Wright,
Further Eng. Voyages, pp. 18, 39). Cf. p. 101, n. 4.

⁴ The word *shot* is translated for the French version here as *harqueboussiers &
mousquettiers*. The Latin edition, instead of the customary *sclopetarii*, here uses also:
Musquetteriis atque Hacquebuseriis. This suggests that the Latinist may have had the
French translation at hand.

⁵ Harl. 6221 (fol. 96) differs slightly, reading: '. . . small shott playenge vpon
them, and so sustayned . . . in all partes, so as they findinge. . . .'
The Greepe ballad (st. 27) tells of the defenders being forced to retire by the small
shot fired by 'our fore wings'.

⁶ The French narrative (Lacour, p. 22), describing the flight of the defenders, adds
a detail (tr.): 'The Spaniards, thinking to defeat the English, drove [out] about seven
or eight hundred cattle, hoping that they would divide the English, whereby they
might defeat them more easily.' However, Drake [*sic*] turned forty or fifty toward
the woods, and the rest followed them. 'Thus the five hundred Spaniards lost heart,'
and the English entered the town at 2 p.m., finding only forty or fifty Spaniards there.
None of the English narratives, and none of the printed Spanish records, mentions the

leaue to proceede towardes the two gates of the towne,¹ which
were the next to the seaward. They had manned them both,
and planted their ordinance for that present² and sudden alarum
without the gates, and also some troopes of small shot in
Ambuscado vpon the high way side. VVe deuided our whole
force, being some thousand or twelue hundred men into two
partes,³ to enterprise both the gates at one instant, [** the
Lieutenant generall hauing openly vowed to Captaine Powell
(who led the troope that entred by the other gate) that **] with
Gods good fauour he would not rest vntill our meeting in the
market place.

Their ordinance had no sooner discharged vpon our neere
approche, and made some execution amongest vs, though not
much,⁴ but the Leiutenant generall beganne forthwith to
aduaunce both his voice of encoragment and⁵ pase of marching,
the first man that was slaine with the ordinaunce being verie
neere vnto him selfe, and thereupon hasted all that he might to
keepe them from reaching [i.e., recharging]⁶ of the ordinaunce.

cattle drive. The Boazio map, however, shows the cattle (see Plates V(A), (B)). See also
p. 246, n. 7.
¹ The wording in Harl. 6221 (fol. 96) here is: '. . . toward the towne gates, which
were two gates the nexte to the seaward'.
²² The description in Harl. 6221 (fol. 96) differs somewhat, with the words [** — **]
missing. It reads: '. . . present hastie and sodayne Allarome without the gates, As also
some litle troopes of smale shott in an ambuscado vpon the highe waye syde. We
devyded our whole force beinge some Thowsand or .xij. hundrethe men into two
partes to enterprise bothe the gates at one instaunt determininge with Gods favor not
to rest vntill owr metynge in the market place'.
Both the Latin and the French editions lack the passage [** — **]. Although
Carleill's name is not mentioned in these versions, his actions are reported in the
Tiger journal (p. 102) and the newsletter (pp. 111-2). See also p. 193 and the text for the
Santo Domingo map (Plate V(B)).
³ The Spaniards stated that the English 'deployed along the whole front of the city'
and, with the firing by the ships in the harbour, were able to sweep the approaches
'both from within and from without'. Wright, Further Eng. Voyages, p. 40.
⁴ Two or three of the English were killed by these shots (see pp. 102, 193). The Greepe
ballad (st. 28) tells of the ordnance planted at the gate, and 'Their foes discharge a
peece or twayne/ Yet as God would but two were slayne'.
⁵ The word and is omitted in Harl. 6221.
⁶ Printed as reaching in both English editions of 1589, the note that the word should
be recharging appeared in the errata list of Field's second issue and also that of Ward's

And notwithstanding their Ambuscadoes,[1] we marched or rather ranne soe roundly into them, as pell mell we entered the gates with them, and gaue them more care euerie man to saue himselfe by flight, then reason to stand any longer to their broken fight, we forthwith repaired to the market place, but to be more truely vnderstood a place of very faire spatious square ground[2] before the great Church, [** whither[3] also came as had been agreed, Captaine Powell with the other troope, which place **] with some part next vnto it we strengthened with Barricados, & there as the most conuenient place assured our selues, the Citie being farre too spatious for so small and wearie a troope to vndertake to gard.[4] [** Somwhat[5] after midnight they who had the gard of the Castle, hearing vs busie about the gates of the said Castle, abandoned the same, some being taken prisoners, and some flying away by the helpe of boates, to the other side of the hauen, and soe into the countrey. **]

The next day we quartered a litle more at large, but not in the

edition. The editions of Ponsonby (1596) and Hakluyt show the corrected text. The word was written as *reacharginge* in Harl. 6221 (fol. 96) and was translated in the foreign language editions with that meaning.

[1] Cf. pp. 112, 193. The Spanish accounts suggest no ambuscades at all, the approach on this side being completely defenceless except for the three or four pieces hastily planted at one gate. Wright, *Further Eng. Voyages*, pp. 18, 21, 34.

[2] This open space at the cathedral was near the centre of the town. The market place was to the northeast, nearer the river and harbour, and facing the church of Santa Barbara (see Plate V(B)). By late afternoon the English flag had been raised over Santa Barbara as well as over the royal palace (Castellanos, *Discurso*, App., p. 294). Hakluyt, possibly aware that the cathedral square was not the market place, omitted from his edition the words, *before the great Church*.

[3] The words [** — **] are missing in Harl. 6221 (fol. 96), where the passage reads: '. . . great church which with some parte. . . .' The passage is missing also from the Latin and French editions.

The statement must have been added for the English editions to correspond with the inserted comment above regarding Powell's command.

[4] The conflict had lasted about three hours, until 4 or 5 p.m. See p. 194, n, 3, and Wright, *Further Eng. Voyages*, p. 25.

[5] The comment about the castle [** — **] is not in the MS variant, nor is it in the Latin and French editions. For other English accounts about the castle see the newsletter (p. 112) and especially the *Primrose* journal (p. 194).

The Spanish officials reported that the castle could not be held against any attack from the town side. Even the town officials fled up the river in the late afternoon. Wright, *Further Eng. Voyages*, pp. 21, 26, 34; Ovalle's letter pr. in Castellanos, *Discurso*, p. 294.

halfe part of the towne, and so making substantiall trenches, and planting all the ordinaunce, that each parte was correspondent to other, we held this towne the space of one moneth.[1]

[**[2] In the which time hapned some accidents more then are well remembred for the present, but amongest other things it chaunced that the Generall sent on his message to the Spaniardes a negro boy with a flagge of white, signifying truce as is the Spaniards ordinarie maner to do there, when they approch to speake with vs, which boy vnhappily was first met withal, by some of those who had bene belonging as officers for the king in the Spanish galley,[3] which with the towne was lately fallen into our hands, who without all order or reason, & contrary to that good vsage wherewith we had entertained their messengers, furiouslie stroke the poore boy through the body with one of their horsemens staues, with which wound the boy returned to the Generall, and after he had declared the maner of this wrongfull crueltie, died forthwith in his presence, wherewith the Generall being greatly passioned, commanded the Prouost martiall, to cause a couple of Friers, then prisoners, to be caried to the same place where the boy was stroken, accompanied with sufficient gard of our souldiers, and there presently to be hanged,[4] dispatching at the same instant another poore prisoner, with this reason wherefore this execution was done, and with this message further, that vntill the partie who had thus murthered the Generals messenger, were deliuered

[1] In Harl. 6221 (fol. 96): *a monthe.*
[2] The next three paragraphs [** — **], which tell the story of the negro boy and report disciplinary actions during the stay, are missing from the Harl. 6221 variant. They are missing also from the Latin and French editions, and from the Greepe ballad.

Wright (*Further Eng. Voyages*, p. xxxvii), noting that the Spanish official reports also failed to mention this incident, raised a question about the authenticity of the story, although she did not consider it completely impossible.

The *Primrose* journal (see p. 196 and n. 1), however, provides an account of the incident, although with fewer details. Probably the editor or editors, knowing something of the affair, possibly from the *Primrose* record itself, decided to make the most of it for propaganda value by inserting it for the English audience.
[3] On the royal galley, which had been used to protect the harbour, see p. 195.
[4] According to the *Primrose* journal (p. 196) 'wee by consent' set up the gallows and hanged the two friars. The newsletter (p. 112) and also the French narrative (Lacour, p. 23) mention that the two clerics were hanged, but give no reasons.

into our hands, to receaue condigne punishment, there should no day passe, wherein there should not two prisoners be hanged, vntill they were all consumed which were in our hands.

VVhereupon the day folowing, he that had bene Captaine of the kings galley,[1] brought the offendor to the townes ende, offring to deliuer him into our hands, but it was thought a more honourable reuenge, to make them there in our sight, to performe the execution them selues, which was done accordingly.

During our being in this towne, as formerly also at S. IAGO, there had passed iustice vpon the life of one of our owne companie for an odious matter:[2] so here likewise was there an Irish man hanged, for the murthering of his Corporall.[3] **]

In this time[4] also passed many treaties betweene their commissioners and vs, for ransome of their Citie,[5] but vpon disagreements, we still spent the early mornings in firing the outmost houses: but they being built very magnificently of stone, with high loftes, gaue vs no small trauell to ruine them. And albeit for diuers dayes together, we ordained eche morning by day breake, vntill the heate began at nine of the clocke, that two hundred mariners did nought else but labour to fier and burne the sayd houses without our trenches, whilest the souldiers in a like proportion stood foorth for their gard: yet did we not or could not in this time consume so much as one

---

[1] This officer was Don Diego Osorio, who afterwards served as Governor of Venezuela and, 1596–1600, as President of the *Audiencia* of Santo Domngio. R. Boulind, 'Shipwreck and Mutiny . . . , 1583,' *Mariner's Mirror*, LVIII (1972), 315. The English editions of the *Summarie* appear to be the only evidence of his involvement in this affair (see above, p. 242, n. 2).

[2] The Ogle case. See above, pp. 148, 189.

[3] On matters dealt with by Drake's procedures of justice see also pp. 112, 151, 156, 196 and n. 3.

[4] With this sentence agreement of the printed *Summarie* with the MS variant and the Latin and French editions resumes. The opening sentence of the paragraph in Harl. 6221 (fol. 96), referring to its immediately preceding comment about the stay for a month (see p. 242), begins: 'In which tyme passed. . . .'

[5] The negotiations, begun on the tenth day of occupation, dragged out for twenty days, according to the *Primrose* journal (p. 195). See also the *Leicester* journal (pp. 153–6) and below. Details about the negotiations, as reported by the Spaniards, are in Wright, *Further Eng. Voyages*, pp. 30, 35, 40, 223–5.

third part[1] of the towne.[2] And so in the end, what wearied with firing, and what hastened by some other respects, we were content to accept of fiue and twentie thousand Duckets,[3] [** of fiue shillings sixe pence the peece, **] for the raunsome of the rest[4] [** of the towne.[5] Amongst other things which

[1] Harl. 6221 (fol. 96v) reads: *consume above a thirde parte.* The fraction is 'a fourth part' in the Latin and French editions.

The French narrative (Lacour, p. 23) provides the following account of events at Santo Domingo (tr.): 'The English remained . . . two months. They took . . . much wealth, as well church ornaments, vessels of gold and silver, and also some silk cloths. It is as large as Bordeaux, but not so populous. The plunder which they took, including the ransom required of the citizens, which was 70,000 ducats, could be valued at 200,000 ducats; in all there were at least a hundred pieces of ordnance, great and small, which were taken. The town was half burned, two friars were hanged, and two were burned in the church. There was in the harbour a galley which was burned, and the slaves who were in it, of whom there were eighteen or nineteen Frenchmen, were set free'.

[2] At this point in the Ward edition these words are added: 'which Towne is here plainly described and set forth in this Map'. The reference to the map appears in the Hakluyt edition, thus: 'a certaine Map'.

[3] The figure is given in Harl. 6221 (fol. 96v) as 'xxv thousand crowns', without the statement equating Spanish money with English values [** — **]. An English crown (5 s.) was somewhat less valuable than a Spanish ducat (5 s. 6 d.). (See p. 259, n. 2 on money values.)

In the foreign editions of the *Summarie* the amount was stated here in terms of gold pieces familiar to the region and without reference to the equivalent value in English money. The French edition used the word *escuz*; in the Latin it was *aureorum* (gold pieces), and in the German, *gulden*.

[4] After the failure of early discussions by Spanish representatives, including Captain Juan Melgarejo, high sheriff of the city, and Don Francisco Maldonado, of Rio de la Hacha (see p. 153, n. 1; Wright, *Further Eng. Voyages,* pp. xlvi–xlvii, 224; and Castellanos, *Discurso,* pp. 295, 297), the royal factor, García Fernández de Torrequemada, agreed to negotiate on behalf of the city, though not in the name of the king. By persistent bargaining he brought Drake's demand for a million ducats down to 100,000, then to 40,000, and finally to 25,000. This figure was reached only after an actual survey was made of the houses still unburned, and represented an amount which would be paid largely by individual citizens. The report of these negotiations, written in February 1586, is printed in Wright, *Further Eng. Voyages,* pp. 220–5.

The negotiations were carried on through interpreters in Latin, French, and Italian, with some Spanish, since 'Drake knows no language but English'. Drake 'is a man of medium stature, blonde, rather heavy than slender, . . . sharp, restless, well-spoken, inclined to liberality and to ambition, vainglorious, boastful, not very cruel.' Wright (op. cit., pp. 223–5).

The ransom money was paid on Sunday, 31 January/9 February (ibid., p. 40). On the ordnance and other valuables, in addition to the ransom money, see pp. 156, 197 and n. 1 above.

[5] The last words of the sentence, *of the towne,* are not in Harl. 6221. On the following passage of the printed *Summarie* [** — **] see note 1, p. 245.

happened and were found at S. DOMINGO, I may not omit
to let the world know one very notable marke and token of
the vnsatiable ambition of the Spanish King and his nation,
which was found in the kings house, wherein the chiefe
Gouernour of that Citie and countrey is appointed alwayes to
lodge, which was this. In comming to the hall or other roomes
of this house, you must first ascend vp by a faire large paire of
staires, at the head of which staires is a handsome spatious place
to walke in somewhat like vnto a gallerie, wherein vpon one of
the walles, right ouer against you as you enter the sayd place,
so as your eye can not escape the sight of it, there is described &
painted in a very large Scutchion,[1] the armes of the king of
Spaine & in the lower part of the said Scutchion, there is
likewise described a globe, containing in it the whole circuite
of the sea and the earth, whereupon is a horse standing on his
hinder part within the globe, and the other fore part without
the globe, lifted vp as it were to leape, with a scroll painted in
his mouth, wherein was written these wordes in Latin NON
SVFFICIT ORBIS: which is as much to say, as the world
sufficeth not, whereof the meaning was required to be knowne
of some of those of the better sort, that came in commission to
treate vpon the ransome of the towne, who would shake their
heads, and turn aside their countenance in some smiling sort,

---

[1] This anecdote about the escutcheon is another example of material apparently
inserted by the editor for its anti-Spanish propaganda value. It is not in the Harl. 6221
variant, nor is it in the Greepe ballad of 1587, where something of this nature might
have been expected. It was printed in both of the 1588 Leyden editions, however;
and on what seems to be the more finished version of the Santo Domingo map an
elaborate representation of the escutcheon, as here described, was placed (see Plate V(b)
and Note on Maps).

Although the other English narratives do not mention the escutcheon, evidence
regarding Drake's taking it into his possession comes from Spanish sources. Officials
at Cartagena heard, perhaps from Francisco Maldonado, that Drake declined to
ransom the 'dosel' with the royal arms which he had taken from the Santo Domingo
Audiencia, regarding it as more valuable as a trophy in England. See Wright, *Further
Eng. Voyages*, pp. xxxvii, n., 30; and documents appended to Castellanos, *Discurso*,
pp. 297, 301. In his poem (Canto II, p. 96) Castellanos mentioned it: 'Tomó de la
Real Chançillería/ el sérico dosel y armas reales . . . porque notoria/ fuese, donde las
viese, su victoria.' The captured escutcheon, which Drake may have regarded as a
personal prize, is not mentioned in his fiscal reports.

without aunsering any thing as greatly ashamed thereof.[1] For by some of our companie it was told them, that if the Queene of England would resolutely prosecute the warres against the king of Spaine, he should be forced to lay aside that proude and vnreasonable reaching vaine of his, for he should finde more then inough to do, to keepe that which he had alreadie, as by the present example of their lost towne they might for a beginning perceaue well inough.[2]

Now to the satisfying of some men who maruell greatly that such a famous & goodly builded Citie so wel inhabited of gallant people,[3] very brauely apparelled[4] (whereof our souldiers found good store for their reliefe) should afoord no greater riches then was found there, wherein it is to be vnderstood that the Indian people, which were the naturals of this whole Island of HISPANIOLA (the same being neare hand as great as England) were many yeares since cleane consumed by the tyrannie of the Spaniards,[5] which was cause, for lacke of people to worke in the Mines, the gold and siluer Mines of this Island are wholie giuen ouer, and thereby they are faine in this Island to vse copper money, whereof was found verie great quantitie.[6] The chiefe trade of this place consisteth of suger & ginger, which groweth in the Island,[7] and of hides of oxen and kine, which in this wast[8] countrey of the Island are bred in

[1] The foreign-language editions mention shame, but not smiles. The Latin reads (tr.): 'They did not answer anything to us but now looking away, now covered with blushes, with heads lowered toward the ground, they kept silent.'

[2] This passage and the critical comment about Spanish-Indian relations in the next paragraph must have had political value in 1588–89.

[3] Compare the observations in the *Primrose* journal, pp. 195, 197.

[4] Hakluyt changed *bravely apparelled* to *very brave in their apparell*.

[5] The Spaniards had fears about the Indians in the countryside (see p. 198), but the records do not suggest that the Indians took special advantage of Drake's capture of the city.

[6] Cf. p. 197.

[7] The economic welfare of the city depended upon sugar plantations and cattle ranges inland and westward. Livestock were sometimes kept even in the city's fort. Wright, *Further Eng. Voyages*, p. xxvii. During the English occupation various officials of the city stayed at sugar plantations and other locations in the country. Wright, op. cit., pp. 19, 21, 223.

[8] The word *wast* puzzled various editors. It was translated in the French edition as

A Summarie and True Discourse

infinite numbers, the soile being very fertile: and the said beasts are fed vp to a very large growth, & so killed for nothing so much, as for their hides aforesaid. VVe found here great store of strong wine, sweete oyle, vineger, oliues and other such like prouisions, as excellent wheate meale packed vp in wine pipes and other caske, and other commodities likewise, as wollen and linnen cloth, and some silkes, all which prouisions are brought out of Spain and serued vs for great releefe. There was but litle plate or vessell of siluer, in comparison of the great pride in other things of this towne, because in these hote countreyes they vse much of these earthen dishes finely painted or varnished, which they call Parsellina,[1] and is had out of the East India, and for their drinking, they vse glasses altogether, whereof they make excellent good and faire in the same place. But yet some plate[2] we found, and many other good things, as their houshold garniture very gallant and rich, which had cost them deare, although vnto vs they were of small importance. **][3]

From S. DOMINGO we put ouer to the maine or firme land, and going all alongest the coast we came at the last in sight of CARTAGENA,[4] standing vpon the sea side, so neare as some of our barkes in passing alongest, approched within the reach of their culuerin shot,[5] which they had planted vpon

---

west (*Occidentaux*), in the Latin as eastern (*Orientali*), and was omitted from the German. Hakluyt decided to print it as *waste*.

[1] Printed in the French edition as *Porcelina*. Hakluyt edited it as *Porcellana*.

[2] *Plate* was translated in the Latin and French editions as 'silver vessels'.

[3] With the next paragraph the similarity between the two versions reappears, the opening words in Harl. 6221 (fol. 96v) being: 'From hence we put....'

[4] According to the French narrative (Lacour, p. 24), this voyage required only eight days, with arrival on the first day of Lent. The arrival date agrees with that given in the *Leicester* journal and the Spanish documents, i.e. 9/19 February, Ash Wednesday. See pp. 103, n. 2, 160.

For incidents on this leg of the voyage see pp. 157–60. A few details appear also in the Greepe ballad (st. 39): 'Then presently they sayled thence/ to one ritch Iland they were bent:/ But winde and storme turned their pretence/ And other course then they invent/ With Carthagena they set at last/ Where all theyr fleete their Anchors cast.' This may be a reference to Santa Marta, since stops both there and at Rio de la Hacha had been mentioned in the voyage plan (Lansdowne MS 100, fol. 98; Corbett, *Sp. War*, p. 71).

[5] Cf. p. 160 above, and Wright, *Further Eng. Voyages*, pp. xlviii, 106, 153.

certaine platformes. The harbour mouth lay some fiue miles to the VVestward of the towne,[1] wherinto we entred about three or foure of the clocke in the after noone without any resistance, or [i.e., of][2] ordinance or other impeachment planted vpon the same. In the euening we put our selues on land towards the harbour mouth vnder the leading of Maister Carleill our Lieutenant generall, who after he had digested vs to march forward about the midnight,[3] as easily as foot might fall, [**[4] expressely commanding **] to keepe close by the sea wash of the shore for our best and surest way, whereby we were like to go through, and not to misse any more of the way, which once we had lost[5] within an hower after our first beginning to march, through the slender knowledge of him that toke vpon him to be our guide, wherby the night spent on, which otherwise must haue bene done by resting. But as we came within two miles of the town, their horsemen which were some hundred,[6] met vs, and taking the Alarum, retired to their

---

[1] The distance to the entrance by the Boca Grande was four miles, according to the *Tiger* journal (p. 103); two leagues (six miles) according to the *Leicester* journal (p. 160).

[2] The list of *errata* in the later editions (Field II and Ward) calls for changing *or* to *of*, and both the Ponsonby and Hakluyt editions use *of*. The MS variant is clearer; after *resistance*, it reads: *no ordinaunce or other ympechement beinge planted*. The Latin and French translations resemble this version.

On the lack of defences here see p. 198 and n. 5.

[3] The wording in Harl. 6221 (fol. 96v) is: 'In the eveninge nyght we . . . leadynge of Captayne Carlile owr lyvetenaunt Generall, and aftar we had dygested owr selvs in full ordar to aunsweare all accidents, we marched. . . .'

The French translation follows the MS version closely (tr.): 'And after we were in order so as to be able to avoid all accidents, we marched. . . .'

The Latin translator carried the idea of accident still further (tr.): 'With our line arranged for resistance, if by chance some one should wish to attack us on the way, or to rise up from ambush . . . we proceeded. . . .'

On this march see also pp. 103, 161-3

[4] The words [** — **] which relate to Carleill's leadership are not in the MS variant, the wording being simply: '. . . fall, kepinge the sea washe of the shore. . . .' Here, as in the passage quoted in n. 3, less credit is given to Carleill for the successful march. On the march along or in the water see p. 161 and n. 5.

[5] In Harl. 6221, the word is *done* instead of *lost*, which changes the meaning slightly. In the Latin edition the wording is (tr.): '. . . lest again, as a little before, by the mistake of one who was leading us, we should stray from the road.' The French is similar.

[6] One Spanish officer stated that there were only 54 horse available (Wright, *Further Eng. Voyages*, p. 104). Only a small number were used at this location (ibid., pp. 48, 108, 120, 155; and also pp. 163, 199 above).

towneward againe vpon the first volley of our shot[1] that was giuen them: for the place where we encountred[2] being woodie and bushie euen to the waterside, was vnmeete for their seruice.

[**3 At this instant we might heare some peeces of artillerie discharged, with diuers small shot towards the harbour, which gaue vs to vnderstand, according to the order set downe in the euening before by our Generall,[4] that the Vizeadmirall accompanied with Captaine Venner, Captaine VVhite, and Captaine Crosse,[5] with other sea Captaines, and with diuers Pinnaces and boates should giue some attempt vnto the litle fort standing on the entrie of the inner hauen, neare adioyning to the towne, though to small purpose, for that the place was strong, and the entrie very narrow was chained ouer: so as there could be nothing gotten by that attempt, more then the giuing them an Alarum on that other side of the hauen, being a mile or two from the place where we nowe were.[6] In which attempt the Vizeadmirall had the rudder of his Skiffe stroken through with a Saker shot, and litle or no harme receaued elsewhere.[7]

The troopes being nowe in their march **][8] halfe a mile behither the towne or lesse, the ground we were on grewe to be straight, and not aboue fiftie pases ouer, hauing the maine sea on the one side of it, and the harbour water or inner sea (as you

[1] A slightly different word order is in Harl. 6221 (fol. 96v), thus: '. . . retired vpon owr first volley to theyr towne warde agayne.'

[2] In Harl. 6221, *recountered* instead of *encountered*.

[3] The paragraph describing the naval attack [** — **] is not included in the MS variant, nor is it reported in Greepe's ballad. It appears, however, in the Latin and French editions.

[4] The reference is probably to the council held shortly after the fleet anchored in the harbour. See p. 161.

[5] i.e. Martin Frobisher, the Vice Admiral, with Thomas Fenner, Henry White, and Robert Crosse.

[6] i.e. at the narrow portion of the Caleta, where the night march was being made. See the Cartagena map (Plate VI(B)).

[7] For a fuller account of the naval attack, which served partly as a diversionary action, see p. 198.

[8] The Harl. 6221 (fol. 96v) reading here, continuing immediately from the description of the march, is: 'Halfe a mile behethar the towne or lesse, . . . fifty pases ovar, the mayne sea beinge the one syde, and the harbor watar or Inwarde sea (as you may tearme it) beinge the othar syde/'

may tearme it) on the other side.¹ This straight was fortified cleane ouer with a stone wall and a ditch without it, the said wall being as orderly built with flanking in euery part, as can be set downe. There was onely so much of the straight unwalled, as might serue for the issuing of the horsemen, or the passing of cariage in time of neede: but this vnwalled part was not without a very good Barricado of wine buts or pipes, filled with earth, full and thick as they might stand [** on end one by another, some part of them standing **]² euen within the maine sea.

This place of strength was furnished of sixe great peeces,³ demi-Culuerins and Sakers, which shot directly in front vpon vs as vve approched. Novve without this wall vpon the inner side of the straight, they had brought likewise two great gallies with their prowesse to the shore, hauing planted in them eleuen peeces of ordinance which did beat all crosse the straight, and flanked our comming on.⁴ In these two galleyes were planted three or foure hundred⁵ small shot, and on the land [** in the gard onely of this place **]⁶ three hundred shot and pikes.

They in this⁷ their full readinesse to receaue vs, spared not their shot both great and small. But [** our Lieutenant

---

¹ Here the Ward edition inserts the words: 'which in this plot is plainly shewed.' Hakluyt followed Ward, but changed *this* to *the*.

² The words [** — **] are not in Harl. 6221 (fol. 96v). The Latin and French editions end the sentence with the mere reference to wine barrels filled with earth. On the defences here cf. pp. 162-3.

³ The French narrative (Lacour, p. 24) mentions ten pieces of artillery. See also pp. 104, n. 1, 199.

⁴ Cf. pp. 162-3.

⁵ In Harl. 6221 (fol. 96v) the figure is 'fowre or fyve hundreth'. There were only about 400 'shot' in the town altogether, according to the Spaniards. Wright, *Further Eng. Voyages*, p. 104. Gonzales, captain of one galley, said his ship had, besides soldiers and seamen, 74 petty officers and 150 rowers (Wright, op. cit., p. 78). The governor expected that 150 men would be spared from the galleys to aid him at the Caleta fort. Wright, op. cit., p. 139.

⁶ Harl. 6221 does not have the words [** — **], and reads: '. . . on the land some fowre hundreth shott and pikes.' The figures in the Latin and French editions in this passage agree with those of the printed *Summarie*. The Greepe ballad (sts. 40-2) mentions 400 Indians in readiness, a fort well manned, 5 sconces, 3 galleys with 15 guns, and 'poysoned prickes' along the way.

⁷ Harl. 6221 (fol. 96v) omits *this*.

generall **]¹ taking the aduantage of the darke (the day light
as yet not broken out)² approched by the lowest ground,
[** according to the expresse direction which him selfe had
formerly giuen, the same **] being the sea wash shore, where
the water was somewhat fallen,³ so as most of all their shot
was⁴ in vaine. Our Lieutenant generall commaunded our shot
to forbeare shooting vntill we were come to the wall side,⁵
& so with pikes roundly together we approched the place,
where we soone found out the Barricadoes [** of pipes or
buts, **] to be the meetest place for our assault,⁶ which notwithstanding it was well furnished with pikes and shot, was
without staying attempted by vs: downe went the buts of
earth, and pell mell came our swordes and pikes together, after
our shot had first giuen their volley, euen at the enemies nose.
Our pikes were somewhat longer then theirs, and our bodies
better armed, for very fewe of them were armed,⁷ with which
aduantage our swordes and pikes grew to hard for them, and
they driuen to giue place.⁸ In this furious entrie, the Lieutenant
generall slue with his owne hands, the chief ensigne bearer of
the Spaniards, who fought very manfully to his liues end.⁹

¹ The two specific references to Carleill [** — **] are omitted in Harl. 6221, which
reads: '. . . but we takynge . . . by the lowest grownde beinge the sea wasshe shore. . . .'

² See p. 104. It was 3 a.m. when the Spanish caught sight of the English, the night
being so dark that only the lighted matches of the harquebuses were visible. Wright,
Further Eng. Voyages, p. 140.

³ See p. 161, n. 5. In the Greepe ballad (st. 42): 'The water lowe as Gods will was/
Twixt strand and seas they safely passe.'

⁴ Harl. 6221 (fol. 96v) reads: '. . . so as muche of theyr shot. . . .'

⁵ They had earlier fired a few shots at mounted patrols (see p. 162). Alonso Bravo,
captain at the trench and wall, stated that the English were less than a hundred paces
away when his men fired on them. Most of the fighting actually was hand-to-hand
combat, with the English pikes being especially effective. Wright, *Further Eng. Voyages*,
pp. 118–19.

⁶ Harl. 6221 (fol. 96v) varies slightly. It omits the words [** — **] and reads:
'. . . assault, which beinge well garded with pikes and shot. . . .'

⁷ i.e. with body armour. Cf. p. 163 and n. 3.

⁸ The Spaniards resisted for about fifteen minutes. The governor declared:
'. . . friends and enemies came down together, without firing upon each other because
they did not recognize each other. Pell-mell they entered the town.' Wright, *Further
Eng. Voyages*, p. 53.

⁹ In Harl. 6221 (fol. 96v), *to the laste* instead of *to his lives end*. Carleill had dashed in
to rally his men and with his own hands he killed the ensign bearer, Juan Cosme de
la Sal(a). Cf. p. 104.

VVe followed into the towne with them, and giuing them
no leasure to breath, we wanne the market place, [** albeit they
made head, and fought a while before we got it, **] and so we
being once seazed and assured of that,¹ they were content to
suffer vs to lodge within [** their towne, **]² and them selues
to go to their wiues,³ [** whom they had caried into other
places of the countrey before our comming thither. **]⁴

At euerie streetes end they had raised very fine Barricadoes of
earth workes,⁵ with trenches without them, as well made as
euer we saw any worke done: at the entring whereof was some
litle resistance, but soone ouercome, it was⁶ with few slaine or
hurt. They had ioyned with them many Indians,⁷ whom they
had placed in corners of aduantage, all bowe men, with their
arrowes most villanously empoisoned, so as if they did but
breake the skinne, the partie so touched died without great
maruell: some they slue of our people with their arrowes, some
they likewise mischieued to death⁸ with certaine prickes or
small stickes sharply pointed, of a foote and a halfe long, the
one end put into the ground, the other empoisoned, sticking
[** fast vp, **]⁹ right against our comming in the way, as we

¹ Harl. 6221 (fol. 96v) omits [** — **] and reads: '. . . no leasure to breathe or to
tourne abowte wanne the market place, and so once assured of that. . . .' The Latin
and French editions resemble the printed form. The Greepe ballad boasts (st. 46):
'And so they fled straung newes they tell/ These be no men but fiendes of hell.' See
also pp. 164, 199.

² Harl. 6221 omits [** — **].

³ Instead of *their wives*, Harl. 6221 uses *the woods*. The wording is: '. . . and them
selvs to take the woods', and here the sentence ends, omitting [** — **]. The Latin
and French editions have similar wording, with no reference to wives but rather to
living in the country. The French narrative (Lacour, p. 24) also says the Spanish
retired to the woods.

⁴ They went actually to various country estates and villages to which their families
had previously been sent. The governor himself went to Turbaco. Wright, *Further
Eng. Voyages*, pp. xlv, liii, 142.

⁵ Harl. 6221 (fol. 96v) omits the word *workes*. See also Wright, *Further Eng. Voyages*,
pp. 65, 70–1, 137; and Castellanos, *Discurso*, p. 302.

⁶ In Harl. 6221 (fol. 97) the words *it was* were written but crossed out. ⁷ Cf. p. 164.

⁸ Harl. 6221 (fol. 97) places *the* between *to* and *death*.

⁹ Words are omitted [** — **] at two places here in Harl. 6221 (fol. 97), which
reads: '. . . stickynge right agaynst owr comynge in the waye as we shuld approche,
wherefore they had planted a wonderfull numbar in the orinarie way. . . .' On the
poisoned stakes see also p. 162, n. 1.

should approch [** from our landing towardes the towne, **] whereof they had planted a wonderfull number in the ordinarie way, but our keeping the sea wash shore, missed the greatest part of them very happily.

To ouerpasse many particular matters,[1] as the hurting of Captaine Sampson at sword blowes in the first entring,[2] vnto whom was committed the charge of the pikes of the Vantgard by his lot and turne, as also of the taking of Alonso Brauo the chiefe commander of that place by Captaine Goring, after the sayd Captaine had first hurt him with his sword, vnto which Captaine was committed the charge of the shot of the said Vantgard.

Captaine VVinter was likewise by his turne of the Vantgard in this attempt, where[3] also the Lieutenant generall marched him selfe,[4] [** the sayd Captaine VVinter through a great desire to serue by land, hauing now exchaunged his charge by sea with Captaine Cecill for his band of footemen. **][5]

Captaine Powell the Sergeant maior had by his turne, the charge of the foure companies which made the battaile.

Captaine Morgan, who at S. DOMINGO was of the Vantgard, had nowe by turne his charge vpon the companies of the Riergard.[6]

[1] Harl. 6221 (fol. 97) reads: 'I ovar passe many particular mattars for want of sufficient laysure, as the. . . .' The Latin and French editions are similar, with the Latin reading (tr.): 'Many other things happened at this time which, since there is not time for setting them down, I willingly pass over.' Hakluyt, though otherwise following the printed wording, changed the first word *To* to *I*.

[2] On Sampson, Goring, and this action see p. 164 and n. 1, and Wright, *Further Eng. Voyages*, pp. 120, 154.

[3] In Harl. 6221 (fol. 97), *in whose company* instead of *where*. The latter word, by which any implication of subordination of Carleill to Wynter is avoided, appears in the Latin and French editions. The *Leicester* journal (p. 165), however, states that Carleill led the 'battell', rather than being in the vanguard.

[4] Because pp. 35–6 of the first issue of Field (copy G. 6510), which has been used for the *Summarie* text are imperfect, the second issue (copy G. 6509) has been used to fill in the missing portions. These correspond with the pages of the Bodleian Library's copy that was used for the 1969 facsimile edition.

[5] The words after *him selfe* [** — **] are not in Harl. 6221 (fol. 97), and are missing also from the Latin and French editions. The editorial insertion to explain Wynter's role in a land operation was probably made for the English audience. The *Leicester* journal confirms that Wynter commanded a company here.

[6] Harl. 6221 (fol. 97) reads: 'Captayne Morgan . . . vpon the three companyes. . . .' One of these was Captain Platt's, from the *Leicester*. Cf. p. 165 and n. 4.

Euerie man aswell of one part as of another, came so willingly
on to the seruice, as the enemie was not able to endure the furie
of such hote assault. VVe stayed here six weekes,[1] & the
sickenesse with mortality before spoken of, still continuing[2]
among vs, though not with the same furie as at the first, and
such as were touched with the said sicknesse,[3] escaping death,
very few or none almost could recouer againe their strength,[4]
yea many of them were much decayed in their memorie,
insomuch that it was growen an ordinarie iudgement, when
one was heard to speake foolishly, to say he had bene sicke of
the Calentour,[5] which is the Spanish name of their burning
ague: for as I told you before,[6] it is a verie burning & pestilent
ague. The originall cause thereof, is imputed to the euening or
first night aire which they termed La serena, wherein they say
and hold very firme opinion, that who so is then abroad
[** in the open aire, **][7] shall certainly be infected to the death,
not being of the Indian or naturall race of those countrey
people: our people by holding their watch, were thus subiected
to the infections aire,[8] which at S. IAGO was most daungerous
and deadly [** of all other places. **]

With this inconuenience of continuall mortality,[9] we were
forced to giue ouer our intended enterprise, to go with

---

[1] The entire stay was slightly more than six weeks, 9 February to 31 March. See
p. 67, n. 7.

[2] In Harl. 6221 (fol. 97) *continuyng* was written, but changed to *continued*. Hakluyt
printed it as *continued*.

[3] The Greepe ballad again omits any reference to the illness.

[4] In the Ward edition, and in Hakluyt, the word order is: '. . . few or almost none
could recover their strength. . . .'

[5] In Hakluyt, *Calentura*.

[6] Harl. 6221 (fol. 97) reads: 'For as I told before. . . .'

[7] In Harl. 6221 (fol. 97) the words [** — **] are missing.

[8] Harl. 6221 (fol. 97) reads: 'Our people . . . theyr garde were . . . to this infectiouse
ayre. . . .' The sentence ends without the words [** — **]. In the Hakluyt edition the
word order at the start of the clause is reversed, thus: '. . . by holding their watch,
our men were. . . .'

[9] A hundred so died at Cartagena, according to the *Primrose* journal (see p. 202).
Among them was Captain Fortescue (see p. 174). Cf. pp. 99, n. 3, 236. One Spanish
document estimated that of some 500 English deaths here only 150 were from wounds.
Wright, *Further Eng. Voyages*, p. 145.

A Summarie and True Discourse

NOMBREDEDIOS,[1] and so ouerland to PANNANIA [PANNAMA],[2] where we shoulde haue stroken the stroke for the treasure,[3] and full recompence of our tediouse trauailes. And thus at CARTAGENA we toke our first resolution to returne homewards.[4]

[1] The Latin edition, but not the French, refers to Nombre de Dios as an island. The German derivative does likewise.

[2] This is one of the *errata* listed in the second Field issue and the Ward edition, with the spelling to be corrected to *Pannama*. In Harl. 6221 (fol. 97) it appears as 'Pan*n*ama'. The two Leyden editions spell it as *Pannania*. Ponsonby (1596) printed it in the text as 'Pannama', and Hakluyt, as 'Panama'.

[3] According to the plan dated April 1586, it was expected that, with the aid of 5,000 Cimarrons, a million ducats might be taken as ransom at Nombre de Dios; and that, after crossing to the South Sea, Drake might secure another million ducats at 'Panamaw'. Lansdowne MS 100, fol. 98v (see Corbett, *Sp. War*, p. 72).

[4] In Harl. 6221 (fol. 97), *homeward*. After this paragraph Hakluyt inserted in his edition the set of resolutions by the land captains, although they had appeared in no previous edition of the *Summarie*, and are not in the MS variant. Hakluyt probably secured this copy from one of the returning officers, but he introduced them into the text as though they had been copied there by the original narrator. Only one other surviving narrative, the *Leicester* journal, mentions or quotes these resolutions. Because the version given there is incomplete, owing to the loss of pages from that MS, the version printed in Hakluyt is given here in full (from *Prin. Nav.*, x, 120–4).

After the word *homewards*, the Hakluyt edition continues thus: 'The forme of which resolution I thought good to put downe under the principall Captaines hands, as followeth.

A resolution of the Land-captaines, what course they thinke most expedient to bee taken. Given at Cartagena the xxvij. of Februarie 1585.

WHereas it hath pleased the Generall to demaund the opinions of his Captaines what course they thinke most expedient to be now undertaken, the Land-captaines being assembled by themselves together, and having advised hereupon, doe in three points deliver the same.

The first, touching the keeping of the towne against the force of the enemie, either that which is present, or that which may come out of Spaine, is answered thus.

WE hold opinion, that with this troope of men which we have presently with us in land-service, being victualled and munitioned, wee may well keepe the Towne, albeit that of men able to answere present service, we have not above 700. The residue being some 150. men by reason of their hurts and sicknesse are altogether unable to stand us in any stead: wherefore hereupon the Sea-Captaines are likewise to give their resolution, how they will undertake the safetie and service of the Shippes upon the arrivall of any Spanish Fleete.

The second poynt we make to be this, whether it be meete to goe presently homeward, or els to continue further tryall of our fortune in undertaking such like enterprises as we have done already, and thereby to seeke after that bountifull masse of treasure for recompence of our travailes, which was generally expected at our comming forth of England: wherein we answere.

THat it is well knowen how both we and the souldiers are entred into this action as voluntarie men, without any imprest or gage from her Majestie or any body els: and

Footnote 4, page 255, continued

forasmuch as we have hitherto discharged the parts of honest men, so that now by the great blessing and favour of our good God there have bin taken three such notable townes, wherein by the estimation of all men would have bene found some very great treasures, knowing that S. Iago was the chiefe citie of all the Islands and traffique thereabouts, S. Domingo the chiefe citie of Hispaniola, and the head government not only of that Iland, but also of Cuba, and of all the Ilands about it, as also of such inhabitations of the firme land, as were next unto it, & a place that is both magnificently builded, and interteineth great trades of marchandise; and now lastly the citie of Cartagena, which cannot be denied to be one of the chiefe places of most especiall importance to the Spaniard of all the cities which be on this side of the West India: we doe therefore consider, that since all these cities, with their goodes & prisoners taken in them, and the ransoms of the said cities being all put together, are found farre short to satisfie that expectation which by the generality of the enterprisers was first conceived: And being further advised of the slendernesse of our strength, whereunto we be now reduced, as well in respect of the small number of able bodies, as also not a litle in regard of the slacke disposition of the greater part of those which remaine, very many of the better mindes and men being either consumed by death, or weakened by sicknes and hurts: And lastly, since that as yet there is not laid downe to our knowledge any such enterprise as may seeme convenient to be undertaken with such few men as we are presently able to make, and withall of such certaine likelihoode, as with Gods good successe which it may please him to bestowe upon us, ths same promise to yeeld us any sufficient contentment: We doe therefore conclude hereupon, that it is better to hold sure as we may the honour already gotten, and with the same to returne towards our gracious Soveraigne and Countrey, from whence if it shall please her Majestie to set us foorth againe with her orderly meanes and intertainment, we are most ready and willing to goe through with any thing that the uttermost of our strength and indevour shall be able to reach unto: but therewithall wee doe advise and protest that it is farre from our thoughts, either to refuse, or so much as to seeme to be wearie of any thing, which for the present shalbe further required or directed to be done by us from our Generall.

The third and last poynt is concerning the ransome of this citie of Cartagena, for the which, before it was touched with any fire, there was made an offer of some xxvij. or xxviij. thousand pounds sterling.

THus much we utter herein as our opinions agreeing (so it be done in good sort) to accept this offer aforesayde, rather then to breake off by standing still upon our damaunds of one hundred thousand poundes, which seems a matter impossible to bee performed for the present by them, and to say trueth, wee may now with much honour and reputation better be satisfied with that summe offered by them at the first (if they will now bee contented to give it) then we might at that time with a good deale more, inasmuch as we have taken our full pleasure both in the uttermost sacking and spoyling of all their householde goods and marchandize, as also in that we have consumed and ruined a great part of their Towne with fire. And thus much further is considered by us, that as there bee in the Voyage a great many poore men, who have willingly adventured their lives and travailes, and divers amongst them having spent their apparell and such other little provisions as their small meanes might have given them leave to prepare, which being done upon such good and allowable intention as this action hath always caried with it, meaning, against the Spanyard our greatest and most dangerous enemie: so surely wee cannot but have an inward regarde so farre as may lye in us, to helpe eyther in all good sort towards the satisfaction of this their expectation, and by procuring them some little benefite to incourage them and to

[** But[1] while we were yet there, it happened one day, that our watch called the Sentinell, vpon the Church steeple,[2] had discouered in the sea a couple of small barkes or boates, making in with the harbour of CARTAGENA, wherepon Captaine Moone[3] and Captaine Varney, with Iohn Grant the Maister of the Tyger, and some other seamen, embarqued them selues in a couple of small Pinnaces, to take them before they should come neare the shore, at the mouth of the harbour,[4] lest by some stragling Spaniards from the land, they might be warned by signes from comming in, which fell out accordingly, notwithstanding al the diligence that our men could vse: for the Spanish boates, vpon the sight of our Pinnaces comming to wards them, ran them selues a shore, and so their men presently hid them selues in the bushes hard by the sea side, amongest some others that had called them by signes thither. Our men presently without any due regard had to the qualitie of the place, and seeing no man of the Spaniards to shew them selues,

---

nourish this readie and willing disposition of theirs both in them and in others by their example against any other time of like occasion. But because it may bee supposed that herein wee forgette not the private benefite of our selves to this composition, wee doe therefore thinke good for the clearing of our selves of all such suspition, to declare heereby, that what part or portion soever it bee of this ransom and composition for Cartagena, which should come unto us, wee doe freely give and bestowe the same wholly upon the poore men who have remayned with us in the Voyage, meaning as well the Sayler as the Souldier, wishing with all our hearts it were such or so much as might seeme a sufficient rewarde for their painefull indevour. And for the firme confirmation thereof, we have thought meete to subsigne these presents with our owne hands in the place and time aforesayd.

Captaine Christopher Carleill Lieutenant Generall
Captaine Goring.   Captaine Sampson
Captaine Powell &c.

[1] This paragraph and the next one appear neither in the Harl. 6221 variant nor in the Latin and French editions. All of these continue the narrative directly from the sentence ending with the word *homeward* to the one which begins, *This towne of Cartagena* (see p. 258).

The occurrence here reported [** — **] is authenticated by other sources, as the notes below indicate.

[2] Although the Greepe ballad also fails to report this particular incident, it includes the detail about the collapse of this church steeple which is not in the *Summarie*. See pp. 166, 201.

[3] Thomas Moone, of the *Francis*, and John Varney, of the *George*.

[4] Cf. p. 167 above. See also Wright, *Further Eng. Voyages*, p. 12.

aboorded the Spanish barkes or boates, and so standing all open in them, were suddenly shot at by a troope of Spaniards out of the bushes, by which volley of shot there were slaine Captaine Varney, who died presently, and Captaine Moone, who died some fewe dayes after, besides some four or fiue others that were hurt: & so our folkes returned without their purpose, not hauing anie sufficient number of souldiers, with them to fight on shore. For those men they carried were all marriners to rowe, fewe of them armed, because they made accompt of their ordinance to haue taken the barks well inough at sea, which they might full easily haue done, without any losse at all, if they had come in time to the harbour mouth, before the Spaniards boates had gotten so neare the shore.

During our abode in this place, as also a S. DOMINGO, there passed diuerse curtesies betweene vs and the Spaniards, as feasting, and vsing them with all kindnesse and fauour: so as amongst others there came to see the Generall, the Gouernour of CARTAGENA, with the Bishop of the same, and diuerse other Gentlemen of the better sort. **]¹

This towne² of CARTAGENA we touched in the out parts, and consumed much with fire,³ as we had done S. DOMINGO⁴ vpon discontentments, and for want of agreeing with vs in their first treaties touching their ransome, which at the last was concluded betweene vs, should be a hundred and ten thousand

¹ Although Drake had been angry upon discovering King Philip's references to him as a pirate (*corsair*) in documents left behind in the governor's house (see p. 176 and n. 4), he treated his prisoner, Alonso Bravo, with great courtesy. While the governor and the bishop reluctantly yielded to Drake's demand for ransom conferences, others went in to negotiate individually for their properties (Wright, *Further Eng. Voyages*, pp. liv–lv, 121, 134, 197). The investigating judge noted such irregularities as bartering with the enemy, and communicating and eating with them (Castellanos, *Discurso*, p. 308); and word got back to Europe that, after the ransom had been arranged, there was much banqueting (*C.S.P.For. 1586–1588*, Pt. I, p. 57). See also Castellanos, *Discurso*, pp. 205–6, 213, 306, 316, 331–8.

² With this paragraph the Field edition resumes its agreement with the Harl. 6221 version and the Leyden editions.

³ One Spanish estimate was that 248 houses were burned, of which one-third were of wood. Wright, *Further Eng. Voyages*, pp. lvi, 146. See also Castellanos, *Discurso*, p. 317 and above, p. 167.

⁴ Harl. 6221 (fol. 97) reads: '... as we had done at Domingo. ...'

Duckets[1] for that which was yet standing, [** the Ducket valued at fiue shillings sixe pence sterlinge. **][2]

---

[1] The amount again is stated in Harl. 6221 (fol. 97) as in *crownes*, in the Latin as *aureorum*, and in the French as *escus*; and none of these adds the explanation [** — **], which must have been intended for English readers. The French narrative (Lacour, p. 25) gives the total as 120,000 ducats, paid in silver ingots. More details on the ransom negotiations are provided by the *Leicester* journal (see pp. 167, 173–8).

[2] Money values of the period varied considerably, but there appears to be general agreement that the silver ducat, or 'plate', having 11 *reales*, was worth 5s. 6d. in English money. (I(ohn) B(rown), *The Marchants Aviso* (1589), ed. by Patrick MacGrath (Boston, Mass.), [1957]). In Hawkins's naval accounts of 1586, the Spanish *reale* was valued at 6d. (P.R.O., A.O. 1/1586/21). This corresponds with the valuation of the ducat that is inserted in the printed edition of the *Summarie* here.

The gold ducat represented a higher value, however, and the various references to Drake's ransom demands indicate that it was value in gold that he was seeking. The words used vary according to the different accounts, even among the printed versions of the *Summarie*, but 'gold pieces', possibly the colonial *peso de oro*, seem to have been intended, whether the term used was *crown*, *ducat*, or *escu*. At one point in the Cartagena negotiations, Drake stated his demands according to the old Spanish gold *castellano* (Wright, *Further Eng. Voyages*, p. 51); and one official mentioned an early demand of 500,000 *pesos* in fine gold (ibid., p. 43).

The actual equivalent in English money represented by the gold ducat in this period is almost impossible to state. By a royal proclamation of 1554, the value of the Spanish ducat of fine gold had been declared to be 6s. 8d. (P. L. Hughes and J. F. Larkin, eds., *Tudor Royal Proclamations* (3 vols., New Haven, 1969), II, 39); but it is doubtful that the rate then declared would have been acceptable in money markets a generation later. It is possible to compare the amount of gold in various English and Spanish coins of the period, using the figures from the English royal mint (Sir John Craig, *The Mint* (Cambridge, 1953), p. 414; Rogers Ruding, *Annals of the Coinage of Britain* (5 vols., London, 1819), III, 50); and the coinage records of Spain (Earl Jefferson Hamilton, *American Treasure and the Price Revolution* (Camb., Mass., 1934), pp. 51, n., and 55, n.). Calculations by these records show the weight of fine gold which a gold ducat represented is close to seven times that represented by a shilling (about 3.5 grams per ducat, in contrast with 5 grams in a gold angel which had a value of 10s.); in other words, that a gold ducat's value would be approximately 7s. if the 'fine gold' used in each mint was of the same quality. Calculations based on the comparative money values tabulated by Henri Lapeyre (*Une Famille de Marchands: Les Ruiz* (Paris, 1955), pp. 468–71) suggest only a slightly lower value of the gold ducat, 1584–86, but the tables show also that there were many fluctuations among the currencies of western Europe at this period.

By some scholars the gold ducat has been calculated as having had a value of close to 8s. (See Quinn, *Roanoke Voyages*, pp. 220, n., and 473, n.). C. H. Haring, in *The Spanish Empire in America* (N.Y., 1947), pp. 287 ff., has pointed out that the West Indies gold coin, *peso de oro de minas*, which was similar to the old Spanish *castellano*, increased considerably in value over the corresponding silver coin because of the changing ratio of gold to silver. He states that its value in 1579 was as high as 556 maravedís, as opposed to a possible 425 maravedís value for the silver coin. This suggests a ratio of roughly 55 to 42. If that ratio is applied to comparing gold and silver ducats, and if the value of the

This towne (though not halfe so bigge as S. DOMINGO) giues as you see, a farre greater ransome, being in very deede of farre more importance, [** by reason of the excellencie of the harbour, and the fit situation thereof, to serue the trade of NOMBRE DE DIOS and other places, and is **][1] inhabited with farre more rich merchants. The other is chiefly inhabited with Lawyers and braue Gentlemen being the chiefe [** or highest **][2] appeale of their sutes in law of all the Islands about it, and of the maine land coast[3] next vnto it. [** And it is of no such accompt as CARTAGENA,[4] for these and **][5] some other like reasons, which I could giue you, ouer long to be now written.

The warning[6] which this towne receaued of our comming towards them, from S. DOMINGO, by the space of twentie dayes before our ariuall hither, was cause that they had both fortified & euery way prepared for their best defence.[7] As also that they had caried & conueyed away all their treasure and principall substance.

---

silver ducat is accepted as being 5s. 6d., then the higher value for the gold ducat would approximate 8s. 6d.

The Cartagena ransom of 110,000 ducats (gold) would come, at the 7s. value, to £38,500; at the 8s. 6d. value, to £47,300.

[1] The words [** — **] do not appear in the Harl. 6221 variant, and the word *rich*, before *merchants* is missing also. The statement about the excellent location was included, however, in the Latin and French editions. In the French, there is a slight expansion, thus (tr.): '. . . other places of the province of Be [incomplete word]. . . .' In the Ward and Hakluyt editions the word *fit* is omitted.

[2] In Harl. 6221 (fol. 97) the words *or highest* do not appear.

[3] Although the reference to the mainland occurs also in the MS variant, it is not in the foreign editions.

[4] When the Spaniards argued that Drake was demanding a much larger ransom than he had received from Santo Domingo, he replied that much more damage had been done there. Castellanos, *Discurso*, pp. 316–17; Wright, *Further Eng. Voyages*, p. 142.

[5] The words [** — **] are not in Harl. 6221 (fol. 97), which concludes the paragraph thus: '. . . next vnto it, some othar lyke reasons I cowlde gyve yow here of ovarlonge to be nowe written.' The final sentence does not appear in the Latin or French versions.

[6] The sentence in Harl. 6221 (fol. 97) reads: 'The warnynge which this towne receyved vpon owr wynnynge of Seint Domingo by the space of twenty dayes before owr comynge hethar was cawse that. . . .' The capture of Santo Domingo is mentioned also in the two Leyden editions.

[7] Cf. p. 198 and notes.

[**¹ The ransome of an hundred and ten thousand Duckets thus concluded on, as is aforesayd, the same being written, & expressing for nothing more then the towne of CARTAGENA, vpon the paiment of the sayd ransome, we left the sayd towne, and drewe some part of our souldiers into the Priorie or Abbey,² standing a quarter of an English mile belowe the towne vpon the harbour water side, the same being walled with a wall of stone, which we told the Spaniards was yet ours, and not redeemed by their composition: whereupon they finding the defect of their contract, were content to enter into onother raunsome for all places, but specially for the sayd house, as also the blocke house or Castle, which is vpon the mouth of the inner harbour. And when we asked as much for the one as for the other, they yeelded to giue a thousand crownes for the Abbey,³ leauing vs to take our pleasure vpon the blocke house, which they sayd they were not able to raunsome, hauing stretched them selues to the vttermost of their powers: and therefore the sayd blocke house was by vs vndermined, and so with gun pouder blowen vp in peeces.⁴

VVhile this latter contract was in making, our whole Fleete of ships fell downe towards the harbour mouth, where they ankered the third time, & employed their men in fetching of fresh water aboord the ships for our voyage homewardes, which water was had in a great well, that is in the Island by the harbour mouth,⁵ which Island is a verie pleasant place as hath

¹ The next two paragraphs [** — **] are not in the Harl. 6221 variant, nor are they in the Latin and French editions. The Greepe ballad, however, tells of the ransom of the friary and of the destruction of the 'castle' as the fleet departed (sts. 50–2).
² This was the Franciscan priory. Cf. p. 201 and n. 4. The other soldiers were withdrawn to the ships, staying in the outer harbour until the departure on 31 March/10 April. See below, and Castellanos, *Discurso*, p. 320. See also the Boazio map (Plate VI(B)).
³ The figure was given as 1,000 ducats in a Spanish report. Wright, *Further Eng. Voyages*, p. 159. See note 2, p. 259 above.
⁴ This was the small fort at the entrance to the inner harbour. One Spanish record stated that, 'Because the fort stands actually on water they could not blow it up, and so demolished it.' Wright, *Further Eng. Voyages*, pp. lvii, 159.
⁵ Cares Island. Wright, *Further Eng. Voyages*, pp. xliv, 124. See also the Cartagena map (Plate VI(B)), and the key for item *I*.
There had been some concern about poison in the drinking water in the town. Wright, op. cit., p. lvii, n.

bene seene, hauing in it manie sorts of goodly and very pleasant fruits, as the orenge[1] trees and others, being set orderly in walkes of great length together. Insomuch as the whole Island being some two or three miles about, is cast into groundes of gardening and orchards. **]

After sixe weekes abode in this place, we [**[2] put to sea the last of March,[3] where after two or three dayes a great ship which we had taken at S. DOMINGO, and thereupon was called the New yeares gift, fell into a great leake, being laden with ordinance, hides, and other spoiles, and in the night she lost the companie of our Fleete, which being missed the next morning by the Generall, he cast about with the whole Fleete, fearing some great mischaunce to be happened vnto her, as in verie deede it so fell out, for her leake was so great, and her men were all tyred with pomping. But at the last hauing found her and the Barke Talbot in her companie, which staying by great hap with her, was readie to take their men out of her, for the sauing of them. And so the Generall being fully aduertised of their great extremitie, made saile directly backe againe to CARTAGENA with the whole Fleete, where hauing stayed eight or tenne dayes more, about the vnlading of this ship, and the bestowing thereof and her men, into other ships, we departed once againe to sea,[4] directing our course **][5]

---

[1] In Hakluyt's edition, *Oreng*.

[2] The opening words of this paragraph are the same as those in the Harl. 6221 variant, but divergence soon develops. No reference to the mishap of the leaking ship and the return to Cartagena is in the variant, which reads simply: 'Aftar syx wekes aboade in this place we departed towards the Cape Seint Anthony beinge the Estarmost parte of Cuba. . . .' (See note 1, p. 263.)

The tale of the *New Year's Gift* appears, however, in the Latin and French editions, and is well authenticated by the *Primrose* journal (p. 202) and by Spanish reports. See Wright, *Further Eng. Voyages*, pp. 51–2, 167; Castellanos, *Discurso*, p. 307.

[3] The departure was on Thursday, 31 March. See note 7 on p. 105. No account supports the Greepe ballad's description of a triumphal departure with gunfire and drums (st. 53).

[4] In his poem Castellanos states that the English first announced that they had returned to await the royal fleet from Spain, instead of admittin g a mishap (*Discurso*, pp. 222–3). They left again on 14/24 April. See also above, pp. 106, 203.

[5] With the words, *towards the Cape*, the text once again agrees with the Harl. 6221

towards the Cape S. ANTHONIE being the Eastermost[1] part
of CVBA, whither we arriued the seuen & twentieth of Aprill.
But because fresh[2] water could not presently be found, we
weyed anker and departed,[3] thinking in fewe dayes to recouer
the MATTANCES, a place to the Eastward of HAVANA.[4]
After we had sailed some fourteene dayes, we were brought
to Cape S. ANTHONIE againe,[5] [** thorough lacke of
fauorable wind: **][6] but the*n* our scarsitie was growen such,
as neede made vs looke a litle better for water, which we found
in sufficient quantitie, being in deed, as I iudge, none other then
raine water newly fallen, and gathered vp by making pittes in
a plot of marrish ground,[7] some three hundred pases from the
sea side.

---

variant. The *Primrose* journal (p. 204) dates the arrival here on 25 or 26 April, but see pp. 68, 113. On events during the voyage see the Map Text and also p. 203. The Greepe ballad mentions only stops at a few islands before the arrival at St Augustine.

[1] This error in location is in Harl. 6221 (fol. 97) and in each of the English editions until Hakluyt corrected it to read *Westermost*. In the Map Text and in the foreign language editions, however, the cape is properly referred to as in the western part of Cuba. Corbett (*Sp. War*, p. 23, n.) points out the strategic importance of this location as commanding the passage for ships going to Havana, either from Mexico or from the Spanish Main with cargo from Peru.

[2] The word *fresh* is not in Harl. 6221 (fol. 97).

[3] Cf. p. 204 and notes.

[4] Harl. 6221 (fol. 97) spells Havana as *Hannana*. The French edition correctly translated the location of Matanzas as to the east, but in the Latin and German editions, it is said to be to the west of Havana.

[5] Cf. the Map Text (p. 68). The fleet stayed there from 14–19 May, according to the *Primrose* journal.

[6] The words [** — **] do not appear in the MS variant, although both the Latin and the French editions mention the lack of a favourable wind. The delay may, however, have had other causes. Corbett (*Sp. War*, p. 84, n.) suggests that Drake perhaps was hoping to intercept the new Indies treasure fleet. There were at least some rumours afterwards in England that Drake had lost his way. When William Barlow published *The Navigator's Supply* in 1597 (*S.T.C. 1445*), he noted that Drake sailed as if in a circle, arriving after sixteen days at his starting point, because he lacked proper navigational instruments. (For this reference I am indebted to Jackson Boswell.) On the difficulty of sailing eastward in this region, against trade winds and local currents, see S. E. Morison, *The European Discovery of America: The Southern Voyages* (N.Y., 1974), p. 129.
When Drake moved the second time from the Cape toward Havana, the weather was good. Wright, *Further Eng. Voyages*, p. 171.

[7] The wording in Harl. 6221 (fol. 97) is: '. . . and gathered togethar by vs in a plott of marishe grownde. . . .'

[**¹ I do wrong if I should forget the good example of the Generall at this place, who to encourage others, and to hasten the getting of fresh water aboord the ships, tooke no lesse paine him selfe then the meanest, as also at S. DOMINGO, CARTAGENA and all other places, hauing alwayes so vigilant a care and foresight in the good ordering of his fleet, accompanying them, as it is sayd, with such wonderfull trauell of bodie, as doubtlesse had he bene the meanest person, as he was the chiefest, he had yet deserued the first place of honour: and no less happie do we accompt him, for being associated with Maister Carleill, his Lieutenant generall, by whose experience, prudent counsell, and gallant performance, he atchiued so many and happie enterprises of the warre, by whom also he was verie greatly assisted, in setting downe the heedefull orders, lawes, and course of iustice, and for the due administration of the same vpon all occasions. **]

After three dayes spent in watering our ships,² we departed now the second time from this Cape of S. ANTHONIE the thirteenth of May,³ and proceeding about the Cape of FLORIDA, we neuer touched aniewhere, but coasting alongst FLORIDA, and keeping the shore still in sight,⁴ the eight and twentieth of May early in the morning,⁵ we descried on the shore⁶ a place built like a Beacon, which was in deede a scaffold vpon foure long mastes, raised on ende for men to discouer to

¹ The following paragraph [** — **], with its tribute to the leaders, is not in the Harl. 6221 variant, although it is included in the two Leyden editions. Drake's own work in loading water here was reported to Spanish officials by an escaped prisoner. Wright, *Further Eng. Voyages*, p. 214.
² The printed edition resumes agreement with Harl. 6221 (fol. 97v) with the words, 'After three dayes. . . .'
³ The Map Text also gives this date. On the events at the cape and along the Cuban coast see p. 204, n. 4.
⁴ Harl. 6221 (fol. 97v) is slightly shorter, reading: '. . . any where vntill coastinge alongst Florida the xxviij. of Maye. . . .'
⁵ On the date, cf. pp. 68, 205.
⁶ There is confusion in the Latin edition here. It mentions the watch tower as observed (tr.), 'far away, toward the north'; and it adds, after the word *masts*, 'to which there was an ascent of thirty steps'. The translator obviously misunderstood the notation on 'latitude of thirty degrees'. The German, following the Latin, repeated the error, mentioning '30 staffeln'. The French edition, however, gives the correct translation for degrees of latitude.

the seaward, being in the latitude of thirtie degrees,[1] or verie neare thereunto. Our Pinnaces manned, and comming to the shore we marched vp alongst the riuer side, to see what place the enemy held there: for none amongst vs had any knowledge thereof at all.[2]

Here the General tooke occasion to march with the companies him selfe in person, the Lieutenant generall hauing the Vantgard,[3] and going a mile vp or somewhat more [**[4] by the riuer side, **] we might discerne on the other side of the riuer ouer against vs, a fort,[5] which newly had bene built by the Spaniards, and some mile or there about aboue the fort, was a litle towne or village without walles, built of woodden houses;[6] we forthwith prepared to haue ordinance for the batterie, and one peece was a litle before the euening planted, and the first shot being made by the Lieutenant generall him selfe at their Ensigne, strake through the Ensigne, as we afterwards vnderstood by a French man,[7] which came vnto vs from them. One shot more was then made,[8] which strake the foote of the fort wall, which was all massiue timber of great trees like mastes. The Lieutenant generall was determined to

---

[1] The latitude of St Augustine is 29° 54′.

[2] The words *at all* are not in Harl. 6221 (fol. 97v). The Spaniards thought that Drake had a Portuguese pilot who knew the Florida coast. Wright, *Further Eng. Voyages*, p. 185.

[3] The wording in Harl. 6221 is: '. . . to marche with the Companye him selfe in person and the lyvetenaunte generall with hym in the vantegarde.' The Latin edition reads (tr.): 'Our Generall ordered the Lieutenant to lead the vanguard.'
On the two successive approaches made that day see p. 113, n. 10. The Spanish told of the first English landing force as marching with flags, and of the second, in which Drake was presumed to be present, as being accompanied with martial music. Wright, *Further Eng. Voyages*, pp. 182, 183, 199.

[4] The words [** — **] are not in the MS variant, nor are they in the Latin and French editions.

[5] i.e. St John's Fort, located on the western side of the inlet, where only small boats could go. See the St Augustine map (Plate VII(B)).

[6] After *houses*, in the Ward edition, is an insertion: 'as this Plot here doth plainlie shew.' In Hakluyt, this reads: 'as the Plot doeth plainely shew.'

[7] In the foreign-language editions there is here an explanation that this Frenchman had been held prisoner by the Spaniards, although that note does not appear until later in Harl. 6221 and in the printed English text (see p. 266, n. 6).

[8] The MS variant reads: 'One shott more there was made.' The *Primrose* journal (p. 206) mentions two shots by the English.

passe the riuer this night with foure companies, and there to
lodge him selfe intrenched as neare the fort, as that he might
play with his [** muskets and **]¹ smallest shot vpon anie
that should appeare: and so afterwards to bring and plant
the batterie with him, but the helpe of marriners for that
sudden to make trenches could not be had, which was the
cause that this determination was remitted vntill the next
night.

In the night the Lieutenant general tooke a litle rowing
Skiffe,² and halfe a dosen well armed, as Captaine Morgan,
and Captaine Sampson, with some others besides the rowers,³
and went to viewe what gard the enemie kept, as also to take
knowledge of the ground. And albeit he went as couertly as
might be, yet the enemy taking the Alarum, grew fearefull⁴
that the whole Force was approching to the assault, and
therefore with all speede abandoned the place after the shotting
of some of their peeces.⁵ They thus gone, and he being returned
vnto vs againe, but nothing knowing of their flight from their
fort, forthwith came a French man being a Phipher (who had
bene prisoner with them) in a litle boat,⁶ playing on his phiph
the tune of the Prince of Orenge his song, and being called vnto
by the gard, he tolde them before he put foote out of the boate,
what he was him selfe, and howe the Spaniards were gone from

---

¹ The words, *muskets and*, do not appear in Harl. 6221 (fol. 97v). The Latin version
refers only to 'small shot', and the French version mentions only one type of firearm,
l'harquebouserie.

² The reading in the Harl. 6221 variant is: '. . . a fyne litle rowynge lyght skyff.'

³ Captain Matthew Morgan and Captain John Sampson. The MS version and the
French edition agree, but the Latin edition, and also the German, specify 'with four
others'.
Cf. p. 118. This must be the reconnoitering operation referred to in the Spanish
documents. Wright, *Further Eng. Voyages*, pp. 183, 201.

⁴ In Harl. 6221 (fol. 97v) the word *throwgheley* is inserted after *Allarom*.

⁵ Harl. 6221 (fol. 97v) reads: '. . . shotynge of some pieces.' The Spanish accounts
report a more deliberate decision to leave, because of the small number of defenders.
However, they took with them only their arms, and left behind the royal treasure
chest. Wright, *Further Eng. Voyages*, pp. 163, 165, 181, 182–4, 201–2.

⁶ A Frenchman and a Dutchman are mentioned in the newsletter and the *Primrose*
journal (see pp. 115, 206). The Frenchman was identified by Hakluyt as 'Nicholas
Borgiognon'; he was probably a survivor of the San Mateo fight of 1580. The tune
was probably 'Wilhelmus van Nassouwe'. Quinn, *Roanoke Voyages*, p. 297, n. 1.

the fort, offering either to remaine in hands there, or else to returne to the place with them that would go.

[**¹ Vpon this intelligence the Generall, the Lieutenant generall, with some of the Captaines in one Skiffe, and the Vizeadmirall with some others in his Skiffe, and two or three Pinnaces furnished of souldiers with them, put **] presently ouer [** towards the fort, giuing order for the rest of the Pinnaces to follow. **] And in our approch, some [** of the enemie **]² bolder then the rest, hauing stayed behind their companie, shot off two peeces of ordinance at vs: but on shore³ we went, and entred the place without finding any man there.⁴

VVhen the day appeared, we found it built all of timber, the walles being none other then⁵ whole masts [**⁶ or bodies of trees **] set vpright [** and close together in maner of a pale, **] without anie ditch as yet made, but who intended⁷ with some more time, for they had not as yet finished all their worke, hauing begun the same some three or fower moneths before: so as to say the truth, they had no reason to keepe it, being subiect both to fier and easie assault.

The platforme whereon the ordinance lay, was whole bodies of long pine trees, whereof there is great plentie, layed a crosse

¹ In Harl. 6221 (fol. 97v) the first sentence of this paragraph is more brief, and at two points [** — **] words in the printed version are missing. The MS reads: 'Where vpon the pinaces manned we put presently ovar and in owre approche some bolder then the rest. . . .'
The Latin and French editions resemble the printed text here, in naming the general, lieutenant general, the vice admiral, etc. The *Primrose* journal (p. 206) mentions the admiral and the vice admiral who went with twenty men, but does not name Carleill.
² The insertion of the words in the printed text avoids the ambiguity of the MS wording.
³ In the Ponsonby edition (1596), *hard* appears instead of *shore*.
⁴ There were Indians, however, who attacked from the woods. See p. 206, n. 4.
⁵ In both Ward and Hakluyt editions, *but* appears in place of *then*.
⁶ Harl. 6221 (fol. 97v) reads here: '. . . then mastes set vp right without any dyche. . . .' The words [** — **] are missing. The Latin edition adds (tr.): '. . . in the fashion of Palisades (as today we call this kind of fortified place).'
⁷ The reading in Harl. 6221, instead of *who intended*, is *was intended*, which is more logical, as referring to the unfinished ditch. The Ponsonby edition changed *who* to *was*. Hakluyt changed the word to *wholy*.
One Spanish document indicates that the moat was still 'being built'. Wright, *Further Eng. Voyages*, p. 202. Construction had started after arrival of word about events at Santo Domingo. Wright, op. cit., p. 164.

one on another,[1] and some litle earth amongst. There was in it thirteene or [fourteene][2] great peeces of brasse ordinance,[3] and a chest vnbroken vp, hauing in it the value of some two thousand pounds sterling,[4] by estimation of the Kings treasure, to pay the souldiers of that place, who were a hundred and fiftie men.[5]

The fort thus wonne, which they called S. Johns fort,[6] and the day opened, we assayed to go to the towne, but could not by reason of some riuers and broken ground which was between the two places:[7] and therefore[8] enforced to imbarke againe into our Pinnaces, we went thither vpon the great maine riuer, which is called as also the towne by name of S. AUGVSTINE.

At our approching to land, there was some that began[9] to shew them selues, and to bestowe some fewe shot vpon vs, but

---

[1] The Latin edition offers a further descriptive note regarding the trees, as being 'connected in the fashion of a wheel'. Possibly the idea was derived from examination of the Boazio map (see Plate VII(B)).

[2] By a printer's error the figure was printed as *fourreene* in the Field text.

[3] Cf. p. 208. In the list at the end of the *Summarie* (see p. 277, n. 3), the ordnance taken here is referred to in Harl. 6221, and also in the Latin and French editions, as coming from Fort St John. The newsletter (see p. 115) mentions 8 or 9 pieces from the fort. The Spanish records, while not giving numbers, indicate that all of their pieces were taken, whether from the town or from the fort.

[4] The word *sterling* does not appear in Harl. 6221 (fol. 97v). The Latin and the German editions carry over the wording as 2,000 pounds *sterling*; the French edition, giving that figure, adds that this amounts to about 6,666 French *escuz*. The Spanish records mention the amount of 5,000 or 6,000 ducats (Wright, *Further Eng. Voyages*, pp. 165, 181, 188); at the value of 7s. or 8s. 6d. per ducat (see p. 259, n. 2) 6,000 gold ducats would be 2,100 *l.* or 2,550 *l.*
The French narrative (Lacour, p. 26) was probably in error in stating the value as fifteen (*quinze*) thousand ducats. The newsletter (p. 115) gives the value as 'at least 1,000 *li*. of silver'.

[5] The figure was written as *130*, but crossed out and replaced by *150* in the MS variant.

[6] San Juan, or San Juan de Pinos, as the Spaniards called it. Wright, *Further Eng. Voyages*, p. 202. Cf. p. 113. The Harl. 6221 variant reads: '. . . they had called Seint Johns forte.'

[7] Instead of *some rivers . . . was between*, Harl. 6221 (fol. 97v) reads: *a River which runs betwene*. Both of the Leyden editions use the singular, *a river*. The map, however, shows two streams flowing into the west bank of the St Augustine river.

[8] Hakluyt inserted *being* after *therefore*.

[9] Harl. 6221 (fol. 97v) reads: '. . . There was some a litle began. . . .' Hakluyt changed *was* to *were*.

A Summarie and True Discourse

presently withdrewe them selues. And in their running thus away, the Sergeant maior[1] finding one of their horses readie sadled and bridled, tooke the same to follow the chase, and so ouergoing all his companie, was (by one layed behind a bush), shot through the head, & falling downe therewith,[2] was by the same and two or three more, stabbed in three or foure places of his bodie with swords and daggers,[3] before anie could come neere to his reskue. His death was much lamented, being in verie deede an honest wise Gentleman, and a souldier of good experience, and of as great courage[4] as anie man might be.[5]

In this place called S. AUGVSTINE, we vnderstood the King did keepe as is before said, one hundred and fiftie souldiers, and at an other place some dozen leagues beyond to the Northwardes, called S. HELENA,[6] he did there likewise kepe an hundred and fiftie more, seruing there for no other purpose, then to keepe all other nations[7] from inhabiting any part of all that coast, the gouernement wherof was committed to one Pedro Melendez Marquesse,[8] nephew to that Melendez the Admiral, who had ouerthrown Maister Iohn Hawkins[9] in the Bay of MEXICO some fifteene or sixteene yeares agoe.[10] This Gouernour had charge of both the places, but was at this time in this place, and one of the first that left the same.

[1] Sergeant Major Anthony Powell. On this incident see also pp. 115, 206.

[2] In Harl. 6221 (fol. 97v), *he*, instead of *therewith*.

[3] The Latin edition reads (tr.): '. . . was stabbed by three or four of them . . .'; the French edition is similar.

[4] The word in Harl. 6221 (fol. 98) is written as *valewe* instead of *courage*. The original may have been *valor*. Both of the Leyden editions refer to *courage*.

[5] The Greepe ballad contains only a single stanza (57) on the capture of St Augustine, and gives no detail. The remainder is devoted to praise for Drake and celebration of his victorious voyage.

[6] The distance (to 32° 20′ N.) was greater, possibly sixty leagues. See Quinn, *Roanoke Voyages*, pp. 299, 723; Wright, *Further Eng. Voyages*, pp. 186–8, 203.

[7] The Latin translation was: 'all foreigners (as English and French).'

[8] Spelled *Marquez* in Harl. 6221 (fol. 98). This was Pedro Menéndez Marqués. Quinn, *Roanoke Voyages*, p. 310.

[9] In the French edition, *Captain* John Hawkins; in the Latin, *one* John Hawkins. The latters adds, 'contrary to a pledge given.'

[10] Hakluyt changed the figures to *seventeen or eighteen*, possibly to be nearer to the incident at San Juan de Ulua in 1568. There is confusion about the names, however, since the Spanish admiral, Pedro Menéndez de Avilés, was not the official (Don Martin Enrique) who tricked Hawkins in Mexico. See Quinn, *Roanoke Voyages*, p. 299, n. 3.

269

Here it was resolued in full assemblie of Captaines,[1] to vndertake the enterprise of S. HELENA, and from thence to seeke out the inhabitation of our English countrymen in VIRGINIA, distant from thence some sixe degrees Northward.[2]

VVhen we came thwart of S. HELENA,[3] the shols appearing daungerous, and we hauing no Pilot to vndertake the entrie, it was thought meetest to go hence alongst.[4] For the Admirall had bene the same night in foure fadome and halfe three leagues from the shore:[5] and yet we vnderstood, that by the helpe of a knowen Pilot,[6] there may and doth go in ships of greater burthen and draught then anie we had in our Fleete.

VVe passed thus alongest the coast hard abord the shore, which is shallow for a league or two from the shore, and the same[7] is lowe and broken land for the most part.

The ninth of Iune[8] vpon sight of one speciall great fire (which are verie ordinarie all alongst this coast, euen from the Cape FLORIDA hither)[9] the Generall sent his Skiffe to the

[1] Harl. 6221 (fol. 98) reads: '. . . captayns and masters. . . .' The *Primrose* journal (p. 207) dates the departure from St Augustine on 2 June, but does not mention Santa Elena.

[2] Quinn points out (*Roanoke Voyages*, p. 299, n. 4) that this is a fairly accurate statement on the latitude of the English settlement, but that it was probably added after the arrival there, since Drake had been so uncertain about its location. He suggests that it may have been unwise to publish so clear a note on the colony's position, both in Leyden and in English editions. The Spanish officials had surmised that Drake, with his freed slaves and captured utensils, planned to stop at the settlement. Wright, *Further Eng. Voyages*, pp. 188-9, 203. See also p. 202 and n. 3.

[3] In Harl. 6221 (fol. 98), *Seint Helena*. Hakluyt added in the margin *Santa Helena*.

[4] The Spanish, who thought Drake had a pilot, told of his stopping at a point south of Santa Elena, and of going out to sea to pass it at night. Wright, *Further Eng. Voyages*, pp. 185, 191, 203, 204-6. See also p. 208, n. 8.

[5] Thus also in Harl. 6221 and the French version. The Latin translation, however (and the German derivative), reads (tr.): '. . . had explored the depths of the sea four leagues from the mainland and discovered it to be only three and a half fathoms.'

[6] In the French, 'a good pilot'; in the Latin, 'a pilot experienced in the shallows.' Quinn (*Roanoke Voyages*, p. 300, n.) suggests that the informant was probably the Frenchman, Burgoignon (see above, p. 266).

[7] In Harl. 6221 (fol. 98), *shore* instead of *same*. The Latin edition reads (tr.): '. . . a shore marked by several islands . . .'; and the French edition also refers to islands.

[8] Cf. below, p. 271, n. 8.

[9] Commas, instead of brackets, are used in Harl. 6221, and the words *even* and *hither* are omitted. Hakluyt's edition changed the name to *Cape of Florida*. The French

shore,[1] where they found some of our English countrey men
[**[2] that had bene sent thither the yeare before by Sir VValter
Raleigh **] & brought one[3] aboord, by whose direction[4] we
proceeded along to the place, which they make their Port. But
[** some of **] our ships [** being of great draught **] vnable
to enter, we ankered all[5] without the harbour in a wild road
at sea, about two miles from shore.[6] [** From whence the
General wrote letters to Maister Rafe Lane, being Gouernour
of those English in VIRGINIA, and then at his fort about six
leagues from the rode in an Island, which they call
ROANOAC, wherein specially he shewed how readie he was
to supply his necessities and wants, which he vnderstood of,
by those he had first talked withall.[7]

The morrow[8] after Maister Lane him selfe and some of his
companie comming vnto him, with the consent of his

---

narrative (Lacour, p. 26) gives the distance from St Augustine to *Norambega* as 350
leagues, although the sailing distance to Roanoke was not more than 600 miles.
Quinn, *Roanoke Voyages*, p. 10, n.

[1] The Latin edition adds after *skiffe* (tr.): 'with some sailors.'

[2] The parenthetical statement [** — **], which was probably added later, is not in
Harl. 6221, nor is it in the two Leyden editions. The words resemble those of the
Primrose journal (see p. 209). In the French narrative (Lacour, p. 26) it was noted that
Lane (printed *Lames*) had been left by Frobisher on a voyage a year and a half before.
See also Quinn, *Roanoke Voyages*, p. 311, n.

[3] In Hakluyt's edition, *them* instead of *one*.

[4] In Harl. 6221 (fol. 98), *intellygence geven* instead of *direction*.

[5] Hakluyt omitted *all*.

[6] The sentence is shorter in Harl. 6221 (fol. 98), reading: '. . . but owr shipps vnable
to entar within the harbor ankered all without. . . .' This version is followed in the
Latin and French editions; in none of them are the words marked [** — **]. None of
them includes the material which is in the next two paragraphs and part of the third
[** — **], all going immediately to the incident of the storm (see below). The Greepe
ballad contains nothing about the Roanoke stop.

[7] Although this account of Drake's negotiations with Lane [** — **], is missing
from the MS variant, and also from the corresponding Latin and French editions, all
include later a summary of part of Drake's offer (see below, p. 273, n. 3). As to Lane's
own report of these matters see p. 272, n. 3.

[8] i.e. 10 or 11 June. According to Lane's account (Hakluyt, *Prin. Nav.*, VIII, 342), the
fleet was sighted by Stafford from Croatoan, 'my lord Admiral's island', on 8 June,
a letter from Drake was delivered by Stafford to Lane on 9 June, and the fleet reached
the location of the colony on the 10th. Lane went out to talk with Drake on the 11th.
Cf. Quinn, *Roanoke Voyages*, pp. 289, 310. The French narrative (in a sentence not
included in Lacour's edition) stated that Drake remained at Lane's colony 'eighteen
days because of a storm which separated them'.

Captaines, he gaue them the choise of two offers, that is to say:
Either he would leaue a ship, a Pinnace, and certaine boates
with sufficient Maisters and mariners, together furnished with
a moneths victuall to stay and make farther discouerie of the
country and coastes, and so much victuall likewise that[1] might
be sufficient for the bringing of them all (being an hundred and
three persons)[2] into England if they thought good after such
time, with anie other thing they would desire, & that he might
be able to spare.

Or else if they thought they had made sufficient discouerie
alreadie, and did desire to returne into England, he would giue
them passage. But they as it seemed, being desirous to stay,
accepted verie thankefully, and with great gladnesse that which
was offred first.[3] VVherupon the ship being appointed &
receaued into charge, by some of their owne companie sent
into her by Maister Lane, before they had receaued from the
rest of the Fleete, the prouision appointed them,[4] there arose a
great storme (which they sayde was extraordinarie and verie
straunge) that lasted three dayes altogether, and put all our
Fleete in great daunger, to be driuen from their ankering vpon
the coast.[5] For we brake manie Cables, and lost manie ankers.
And some of our Fleete which had lost all (of which number
was the ship appointed for Maister Lane and his companie)

[1] Hakluyt printed *as* instead of *that*.

[2] The number of colonists is given as 105 in the summary that appears later in
Harl. 6221 (fol. 98), and in the Latin and French editions (see below). The German
translation mistakenly gives the figure as 150.

Quinn (*Roanoke Voyages*, p. 228) notes that there had probably been 160 on the
outward voyage, of whom 108 were colonists.

[3] According to Lane (Hakluyt, *Prin. Nav.*, VIII, 342–4), he asked Drake to take back
to England some colonists who were ill, and to supply him with some able-bodied
men and tools, as well as vessels and food to make possible a return to England 'about
August'. After consultation with his captains Drake offered the *Francis* (of 70 tons),
with a hundred men and food for four months, as well as a few small boats. Two
experienced masters, Abraham Kendall and Griffith Herne, were assigned to help
with the return journey.

[4] Lane states that the promised supplies and men were put aboard the *Francis* and
another boat on 12 June, and that the storm began on the 13th and lasted until the 16th.
Hakluyt, *Prin. Nav.*, VIII, 344.

[5] Here ends the difference between the printed *Summarie* and the Harl. 6221 variant
on factual matters, but the difference in wording continues [** — **], until p. 274.

A Summarie and True Discourse

were driuen to put to sea in great danger,[1] in auoiding the coast
and could neuer see vs againe vntill we met in England.[2] Manie
also of our small Pinnaces and boates were lost in this storme.
Notwithstanding after all this, the Generall offered them[3]

[1] Among them was the *Francis*, with her two masters, crew, and provisions assigned
for Lane. Another was possibly the *Duck*; Richard Hawkins, who had been her captain,
reached England by 21 or 22 July. Having landed at Mount Edgcombe, he rode to
Exeter, arriving there about 3 p.m. on the 22nd, according to the letter sent on that date
to Burghley by two Exeter justices. Although he had been parted from Drake by a
'tempest at Virgenea', he sent on the good news of Drake's successes at 'St. Domingo,
St. Jacoma, Carthagena, and St. John's in Florida', and promised to tell more when he
reached London. H.M.C., *Salisbury MSS*, III, 152. A copy of the letter was sent also to
Walsingham; see H.M.C., *Rutland MSS*, I, 200.

[2] The briefer description of the storm, which appears in the Harl. 6221 variant, and
in the Latin and French editions, follows immediately after the statement on the fleet's
arrival (see above, p. 270). A translation of the Latin version was printed in Quinn,
Roanoke Voyages (p. 301). Because the similarity between the *Expeditio* text and the
Harl. 6221 variant is important (see Appendix III), both versions are given here:
(a) From Harl. 6221 (fol. 98): '. . . But our shippes vnable to . . . without, where
they weare not a litle tormented with storms, which began the next day aftar owr
comynge to that place, and grewe so greate as some of the flete not able to ryde were
put to sea, where of some returned to owr company in that place agayne and some
could not but came home by them selves/'
(b) From the Latin *Expeditio* (E. Ridington's translation): '. . . they cast anchor
outside. When a great storm seized them, on the day after we had put in; since most of
them were forced to raise their anchors and make sail, some of them came back to the
rest of the fleet, others went directly to England.'
The French version follows the English closely; the German translation follows
the Latin.

[3] An abbreviated report on this arrangement is in the Harl. 6221 variant and in the
foreign editions. Because the resemblance between those versions is striking, the
passages are given here in full:
(a) Harl. 6221 (fol. 98): 'The Generall with the consent of his Capteyns made offar
to Mystar Rauffe Lane, Generall of the Englyshe in Virginia, that he would furnishe
many [of] them wantes, and also to leave with hym a shippe and a barcke that in case
aftar one monithes staye more there came [not] in supplie for them out of England
that then they myght come home in them, being an hundrethe and fyve persons/ but
theyr povertie beinge suche as had wearied the greatar parte of them, they instantly
reqwired to be conveyed presently with vs dispersed into the whole fleete as we weare
then togethar which accordinglie was not refuse[d].' No date of departure is given.
(b) Latin (*Expeditio*, a literal translation by E. Ridington): 'Here our General [with]
all his captains, to Rudolph Lane, the General of the English who were in Virginia,
to him and to his men, offered to provide all things which were especially necessary,
and to leave there one larger ship from his own, with a pinnace, by which, if within
a month the number of soldiers should not be filled up, which at that time was one
hundred and five, he might be able to return to England. But they were so pressed and
broken by the lack of all things there, that they chose nothing rather than as soon as
possible to return with us to our country. And so, soone having been received into our
ships, they set sail with us from there.' No departure date is mentioned.
(c) The French edition differs slightly, although the wording of the offer to Lane,

273

(with consent of his Captaines) another ship with some prouision, although not such a one for their turnes, as might haue bene spared them before, this being vnable to be brought into their harbour.¹ Or else if they would, to giue them passage into England, although he knewe he² should performe it with greater difficultie then he might haue done before.

But Maister Lane with those of the chiefest of his companie he³ had then with him, considering what should be best for them to doe, made request vnto the Generall vnder their handes, that they might haue passage for England:⁴ the which being graunted, and the rest sent for out of the countrey and shipped, we departed from that coast the eighteenth of Iune. **]⁵

And so⁶ God be thanked, both they and we in good safetie arriued at Portesmouth the eight and twentieth of Iuly 1586.⁷

'General of the English,' is similar. The last part reads (tr.): 'But the poverty being so great that it wearied the greatest part of them, they asked to be taken away at once. This was not refused; and thus being dispersed through all the fleet, they returned with us.' Again, no departure date appears.

¹ Consultation with a council is stressed. The ship now assigned was the larger *Bonner*, which was to remain in the road outside the harbour. Lane's narrative in Hakluyt, *Prin. Nav.*, VIII, 344.

² Hakluyt substituted *we* for *he*.

³ Hakluyt inserted *which* after the word *company*.

⁴ The colonists' decision was based not only upon their own weakness but on their loss of the two especially chosen ship-masters who had gone out with the *Francis*, and on their discouragement about the delay of Grenville's supply ship, for which they had been waiting since Easter. Hakluyt, *Prin. Nav.*, VIII, 344-5.

⁵ At this point the divergence of the printed *Summarie* from the Harl. 6221 variant temporarily ends. Lane's narrative (Hakluyt, *Prin. Nav.*, VIII, 345) placed the departure on 19 June. His reckoning may, however, have been off by a day. Cf. p. 210, n. 4.

⁶ In Harl. 6221 (fol. 98), *thus* instead of *so*.

⁷ Harl. 6221 (fol. 98) gives the date as 'the .xxvij. of Iulie. 1586'. The 27th is the date also in each of the foreign-language editions, and in Lane's narrative (Hakluyt, *Prin. Nav.*, VIII, 345). This is probably correct, although in all of the English editions it is given as 28 July. Drake's letter of 26 July to Burghley (see above, p. 6, n. 2) was probably written on the eve of his fleet's arrival. If they had passed the Scilly Isles on 22 July (see the Map Text), reaching Portsmouth by the fifth day thereafter was not impossible. The more ponderous Armada moved from the Scilly Isles to the Isle of Wight in six days (19-25 June O.S.). G. Mattingly, *The Armada* (N.Y., 1959), pp. xx, 265-97.

Perhaps some propaganda advantage was sought in placing the arrival on 28 July, as has been suggested with regard to the date for the taking of Santiago (see above, p. 225, n. 1). By 1589, when the English edition appeared, 28 July had become a date to the great glorie of God, and to no small honour to our Prince, our country, and our selues.[1]

The totall value of that which was gotten in this voyage, is estimated at three score thousand pou*n*ds, whereof the companies which haue trauelled[2] in the voyage were to haue twentie thousand pounds,[3] the aduenturers the other fortie. [**4 Of which twenty thousand poundes **] (as I can iudge) will redound some sixe pounds to the single share.

VVe lost[5] some seven hundred and fiftie men in the voyage. The men of name that died and were slaine in this voyage,[6]

---

worth remembering, for on that day in 1588 (28 July/7 August) the fire ships, borne in upon the Armada off Calais, had brought the turning point of its threat to England (Mattingly, *Armada*, pp. 324–6). With this date the Map Text, also planned apparently for English readers (see Note on Maps), agrees.

[1] By 27 July Burghley was eagerly expecting Drake's arrival (Burghley to Walsingham, *C.S.P.D. 1581–1590*, p. 341). Rumours abroad had him arriving at points in Ireland or Scotland (Letter from Cologne, 11/21 August, in *The Fugger News-Letters*, 2nd series (1926), p. 116), and it was reported in Madrid that he had arrived in England on 8 August (N.S.) (ibid., p. 118). By 10 August Leicester was writing from the Netherlands about the ordnance Drake had brought back (*C.S.P.For. 1586–1587*, p. 119).

[2] In Harl. 6221 (fol. 98), *travayled*.

[3] i.e. the customary one-third for the men.

[4] Harl. 6221 (fol. 98) ends the statement differently, using *where of* after *fortie* instead of [** — **]. This makes the return per share apply to the return on investment rather than to what was due to the men. The insertion of the amount in pounds [** — **] by the editor may represent the correction of an ambiguity. Reference to the return for the adventurers does not appear in the foreign editions. The fiscal records (see Document 2) do not indicate such an apportionment.

[5] Harl. 6221 (fol. 98) reads: 'We have loste....'

[6] This sentence in Harl. 6221 is: 'The men of name that dyed in this voyadge as I presently call them to my remembraunce according to the tymes of theyr deathe/' A list of sixteen names follows, as compared with the seventeen names of the Field edition. The order is as follows: Master Nicholas Wynter, Master Alexander Carleill, Master Robert Alexander, Thomas Tucker a lifetenant, Alexander Starkey a lifetenaunt, Master Escott a lyvetenaunt, Master Vyncent a lyftenaunt, Master Waterhouse a leyftenaunt slayne, Captayne Powell, Captayne Varney, Captayne Mone [these last three bracketed as *slayne*], Captayne Forteskewe, Captayne Bryggs [i.e. Bigges], Captayne Cicill, Captayne Hannam, Captayne Greenfeld.

The list includes two names not shown in the Field edition (Alexander Carleill and Lieutenant Vincent), but lacks the three names at the end of the Field list (Scroope, Dier, and Duke). The attempt to list according to the order of death was not completely successful, for Varney, Moone, and Fortescue died at Cartagena, and Powell at St Augustine.

as I can presently call to my remembrance, are these.[1]

Captaine Powell.   Captaine Bigges.
Captaine Varney.   Captaine Cecill.
Captaine Moone.   Captaine Hannam.
Captaine Fortescute.   Captaine Greenefield.
Thomas Tucker a Lieutenaunt.
Alexander Starkey a Lieutenaunt.
Maister Escot a Lieutenaunt.
Maister VVaterhouse a Lieutenaunt.[2]
Maister Nicholas VVinter.
Maister Robert Alexander.
Maister Scroope.
Maister Iames Dier.
Maister Peter Duke.

VVith some other,[3] who for hast I can not so suddenly thinke on.

The Ordinance gotten of all sorts brasse and iron were about two hundred and fortie,[4] whereof the two hundred and some more were brasse, and were thus found and gotten.[5]

In S. IAGO some two or three & fiftie peeces.[6]

In S. DOMINGO about foure score, wherof was varie

[1] The Latin version reads: '. . . who perished either by violent death of sickness or otherwise,' but it omits, 'as I can . . . remembrance.' The French edition states simply, 'Here are the names of the most renowned (signalés) who died by blows or otherwise.' On variations in names see below.

[2] In the Latin, French, and German editions the names are listed according to rank, as they are in the Field edition. All, however, insert the name of Lieutenant Vincent before that of Waterhouse, and Alexander Carleill before Robert Alexander. Both of these names are in the Harl. 6221 variant (see above, p. 275, n. 6). The last three names of the Field edition list (Scroope, Dier, Duke), though not in the MS variant, are in the foreign editions.
The list in the Ward edition corresponds with that of the Field edition, but in the editions of both Ponsonby and Hakluyt the name of Alexander Carleill was inserted. Hakluyt also inserted 'Master George Candish' after Waterhouse. None of the printed English editions, however, gives the name of Vincent.

[3] In Harl. 6221 (fol. 98v), some others. The Latin and French editions likewise refer to others.

[4] Harl. 6221 (fol. 98v) inserted peces after fortye. The word peeces was added here also by Hakluyt. The Latin and French editions give the number as 240, but the German translator made it 242.

[5] In Harl. 6221 (fol. 98v): gotten viz. For the official report on the ordnance brought back see Drake's accounts (Document 2).

[6] Saint Iago, in Harl. 6221 (fol. 98v). Cf. p. 186.

276

A Summarie and True Discourse

much great ordinance,[1] as whole Cannon, Demi-Cannon, Culuerins and such like.

In CARTAGENA some sixtie and three peeces,[2] and good store likewise of the greater sort.

In the fort of S. AVGVSTINE were foureteene peeces.[3]

The rest was Iron ordinance,[4] of which the most part was gotten at S. DOMINGO, the rest at CARTAGENA.[5]

[1] Harl. 6221 (fol. 98v) reads: 'In Seint Domingo . . . , where of was muche very great ordinance. . . .' The number included 66 of brass, and over 70 pieces all told (see p. 102 and n. 5). The French edition reads (tr.): '. . . as Canons, Demi-Canons, Culverins, Demi-Culverins, with others of very fine length & great calibre.'

[2] In Harl. 6221 (fol. 98v) the figure is stated: 'three score and two or three.' The Latin and French editions give the number as sixty-two or sixty-three. The *Tiger* journal noted 62 brass pieces.

[3] Instead of *St. Augustine*, the place name in Harl. 6221 and in the Latin and French editions is given as *Fort of Seint John*. See also p. 268, n. 6.

[4] Harl. 6221 (fol. 98v) reads: 'The moaste of the Iron Ordinaunce was had at Seint Domingo, the rest at Cartagena.'

A concluding paragraph is added in the MS variant, thus: 'I remember not any othar particularitie for the present, and the berer makynge me beleve that he is forthwith to departe is cawse that I end and alwaies recommende my selfe vnto yow/'

The wording suggests that this paragraph was not from the manuscript which was being copied but, as in the sentences at the start (see p. 217, n. 2), was addressed to the person to whom the whole account was being sent.

[5] In the second issue of Field's edition a list of four *errata* appears, relating to pp. 21, 23, 30, and 36 of the first issue (see above, pp. 238, 240, 248, 255). Ward included a list of three errors, one of them having been corrected in the text. Ponsonby's edition, which follows Field's closely, has the emendations made in the text. Hakluyt, who seems to have used Ward's edition as his base, also corrected the text. He made a number of other changes, such as correcting geographical errors, or in the interest of clarity. The more significant ones have been noted previously.

DOMINGO.

FF Ships of the Spaniards in the inner harbour, which vpon our departure we consumed with fire.

GG Gardens which were very pleasant being very ful of many excellent forts of fruits, which belonged to the Indwellers of the citie.

HH A Fuerte on the top of a hill called Saint Barbara.

℞ The way which *Baptift* the Lieftenaunt Generals Page went as Messenger from the Generall vp into the countrey to the Lord President of Saint Domingo, being some 12. miles distant from the citie.

KK A place called the white Tower.

LL A strange beast drawne after the life, and is called by our English mariners Algarta, by the Spaniardes Caiman, which liueth both at sea and land, he watcheth the Tortoise when she laieth egges, and when the Tortoise is gone from them, he will hunt them out, and deuoure them all that he findeth. He hath bene seene by the Spaniards to take hold of an oxe or a cowe by the taile and so to draw them forcibly into the sea, and there deuour them: & so likewise a man whome hee hath surprised a sleepe or otherwise at vnawares: for if hee bee in time espied, a man may wel escape by flight, for he runneth not so fast as a man, but with peeces and pikes we have killed many in desolat Ilands and eat them, whose flesh is, like to veal in sight, but the old are somewhat rammish in tast: the yong of halfe grow'h are verie special good meat, his backe is well armed with a strong scale, but his belie soft, & betweene the forelegge and the bodie is the best place to strike him with a pike, they are of eight or nine foote long, and some lesse, his backe of a darkish gray colour, his bellie whitish yellow.

MM A Tortoise is a fish that liueth in the sea, but commeth to the land to lay his egs in breeding time, and going vppon her fins which are strong & rough, commeth to the sand some 40. or 50. paces from the sea, there wuh her forefinnes scrapeth a hole in the sand, and so turning her hinder part in the said hole laieth her egges, which at one time are about one hundred, and so scraping the sand ouer the egges againe to hide them, goeth her way to the sea and neuer commeth againe, the egges by the heat of the sunne are in a due time hatched, and the yong goe presently to the sea, one following of another, with whome the Aligarta doe meet, hee deuoureth them one after another as they come. This Tortoises flesh is good meate, and is like vnto beefe both in tast & shew, the egs are also verie good, sauing that they haue a little rammish tast (as to mee seemeth) but many others liked

la mer, & estoit ceinct d'une courtine de pierre de taille douce, & deffendu par les Espagnols qui le garderét 12. heures apres la ville, prins mais voyans les nostres les approcher le sauuerent a fuitte auec petiz bateaux a l'entrée du haure pour empescher nos nauires d'entrer dedans.

DD Nauires enfoncées a l'entree du haure pour empescher nos nauires d'entrer dedans.

EE Vne grande gallere que les Espaignols auoyent en leur haure, & qu'au fortir nous auons bruslée.

FF Autre s Nauires ennemi es, qui estant dedans le port, furent bruslées a nostre departement.

GG Tresbeaux, & tresfertiles Iardins des Citoyens.

HH Le monastere de Sainct: Barbe, de nonains, sur la poincte de montaigne.

II Le chemin par lequel *Baptifta Boazio* page de l'lieutenat general fur messagier, enuoyé par le general au gouuerneur de S. Domingo.

KK Vng lieu qu'ils appellent la tour blanche.

LL Vne grande beste, autant de la mer, que de la terre contrefaicte du naturel estant viue, appellée par noz Anglois, Algarta, & par les Espaignols Cayman.

MM Vne Tortue, qui vient faire ses œufs en terre, & y marche deffus, auec quatre pieds, lesquelz sont tres forts, & il y en à de longues trois pieds, & larges deux & demy.

Plate IX. Page from the 'Tiger Journal' showing two different hands
(B.L., Cotton MS Otho E. VIII, fol. 230v.)

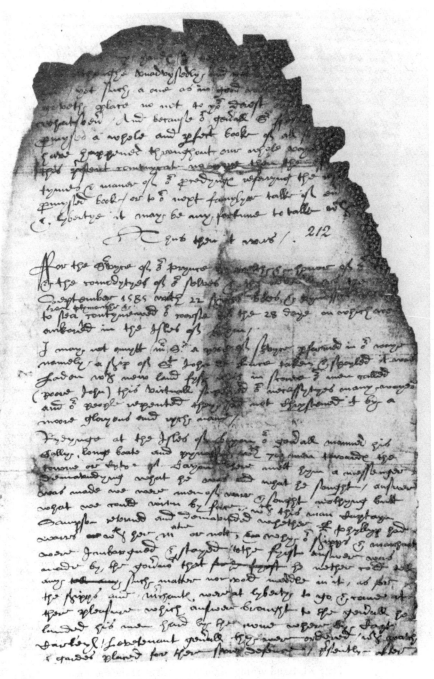

Plate X. Handwriting of the Newsletter, Document 7
(B.L., Cotton MS Otho E. VIII, fol. 235)

Plate XI. Handwriting of the MS variant of the *Summarie*
(B.L., Harl. MS 6221, fol. 94v.)

APPENDIX I
TABLE OF SHIPS

LIST OF SHIPS FOR DRAKE'S EXPEDITION, 1585-86*

Name	Tonnage		Number of Men		Officers
	Harl. MS 366	Corbett or other	Folger MS L.b. 344	Harl. MS 366	
1 Elizabeth Bonaventure	600	600	250 [270]	366 300	Admiral and General Sir Francis Drake Capt. Thomas Fenner
2 Primrose	400	[300]	180	200	Vice Admiral and Capt. Martin Frobisher Master, John Hampton
3 Galleon [Lettice] Leicester	400	400	180	200	Rear Admiral and Capt. Francis Knollys
4 Aid	200	250	120	130	Capt. Edward Wynter
5 Tiger	150	200	100	90	Capt. Christopher Carleill, Lieutenant General Master, John Grant
6 Sea Dragon	140	—	90	90	Capt. Henry Whyte
7 Thomas, alias Bark Hastings	100	200	100	100	Capt. Thomas Drake
8 Minion, of Plymouth	[100]	200	100	[100]	Capt. Thomas Cely, Master, Jo[hn] Newsome
9 Bark Talbot	150	200	85	90	Capt. [Walter?] Baily
10 White Lion	150	140	75	80	Capt. James Erisey
					Capt. Robert Cross

13 Bark Bonner	120	150	75	80	Capt. George Fortescue
14 Bark Hawkins	120	[150]	70	80	Capt. William Hawkins the younger
15 [Name unknown; Sir William Mohun's ship]	—	[120?]	75	—	[unknown]
16 Benjamin	—	[75?]	45	—	Capt. John Martin
17 Vantage	[50]	[65?]	40	[40]	Capt. John Rivers
18 Francis	60	[70]	35	40	Capt. Thomas Moone
19 Speedwell	[50]	[60]	30	[30]	Capt. [John] Wilson or Philip Sparrowe
20 George	—	[50]	30	—	[Capt. John Varney (printed *Summarie*)]
21 Scout	[30]	[30?]	20	[20]	Capt. Edward Gilman
22 Mathew	—	[40]	25	—	[unknown]
23 Galley [Duck]	20	—	10	22	Capt. Richard Hawkins
24 [Swallow (*Summarie* list)]	[20?]	[20?]	—	[15?]	Capt. —— Bitfield
25 [Elizabeth [Drake] (*Summarie* variant)]	—	[70?]	—	—	[Capt. John Varney (*Summarie* variant)]
26 [Drake (French prize)]	—	[80]	—	—	Capt. John Vaughan
27 [New Year's Gift (prize)]	—	[400–600]	—	—	[unknown]
28 Pinnaces (at least 8)	—	[20–60 each]	45	—	

Notes

* The list of ships in the printed *Summarie* (see pp. 216–7) and in Corbett (*Sp. War*, p. xii) is incomplete. Oppenheim's list (*Naval Tracts* . . . *Monson*, I, 124), for which he used also the 'furnishing list' in Harl. MS 366 (fol. 146), adds the *Hawkins* and also figures on tonnage and men, but it does not include the *Speedwell* or the *Elizabeth*.

For the present Table of Ships the Folger MS L.b. 344 has been used as the base, the listing being in the order of that MS, and its figures for men shown. The names of *Swallow* and *Elizabeth* have been added from the *Summarie* and its variant (Harl. MS 6221); the former appears to be in Harl. 366 also, since its captain's name is legible there. The *Drake* (no. 26), although listed in both versions of the *Summarie*, was not a part of the original fleet. The *New Year's Gift* (no. 27) was taken at Santo Domingo and later abandoned.

The figures for tonnage and complement of men from the Harl. MS 366 (fol. 146) list have been used in so far as the matching of names and sizes permits, although not all ship names therein are legible. The tonnage figures in the second column have been drawn chiefly from Corbett (*Sp. War*, p. xii); those in square brackets are from other sources, such as Laughton's *Armada*, Andrews, *Elizabethan Privateering*, Williamson, *Hawkins of Plymouth*, and Thomas Glasgow, Jnr, 'List of Ships . . . 1539–1588', *Mariner's Mirror*, LVI (1970), 299–307. In a few instances there are estimates based upon the navy's formula allowing 3 men for each 5 tons (Corbett, *Sp. War*, p. 265), since that ratio appears to have been followed roughly.

The table makes clear that there was considerable variation with regard to tonnage figures, and Laughton (*Armada*, II, 323) has warned that these are usually less reliable than figures for complements of men. As in most ship lists of the time, the 'furnishing lists' have arranged the vessels in order of size.

1. ELIZABETH BONAVENTURE, 600 tons, queen's ship, built in 1561 and rebuilt in 1581, was Drake's 'admiral' for the expedition. Captain Thomas Fenner. (Corbett, *Sp. War*, pp. 99, 224;

Williamson, *Hawkins of Plymouth*, pp. 259, 262.) *Bonaventure* underwent various repairs after her return in 1586 (Hawkins's accounts, P.R.O., A.O. 1/1685/20, 21). She was used in the Cadiz voyage of 1587, and in those of 1590, 1591, and 1595–96 (Laughton, *Armada*, II, 333).

2. PRIMROSE, 300–400 tons, a merchant ship, sometimes listed as 'of London', owned in part by John Hawkins, was the 'vice admiral' in 1585. Captain Martin Frobisher; master, John Hampton (see p. 151; *C.S.P.D. 1581–1590*, p. 449; Corbett, *Sp. War*, pp. xii, 257). Mendoza heard in early May that she was being fitted out for the voyage by the queen's order (*C.S.P.D. 1580–1586*, p. 537); and Spanish reports from Cartagena indicate that she belonged to Hawkins. (Wright, *Further Eng. Voyages*, p. 51.) She apparently was the *Primrose of London* (300 tons) which was on William Hawkins's voyage of 1582 (Williamson, *Hawkins of Plymouth*, pp. 219, 414; and E. G. R. Taylor, *The . . . Voyage of Captain Edward Fenton*, p. lv, n. 2); and possibly the one which escaped from the Spanish embargo in late May 1585 (Corbett, *Sp. War*, p. ix; Andrews, *Eliz. Privateering*, p. 3; Hakluyt, *Prin. Nav.*, VI, 413–16). One *Primrose of London* (200 tons, 100 men) was set forth by London in 1588 (Laughton, *Armada*, p. 100). Her 1585 complement of men (Folger MS figures) and her designation as vice admiral for the voyage suggest a size larger than 200 tons. Since John Hawkins's accounts for 1586 show the expense for repairs to a number of the ships, including *Primrose*, which had been on Drake's voyage (A.O. 1/1685/21), this may explain the 1587 accusation that he had worked in free repairs for the *Primrose*, 'his own ship' (Lansdowne MS 52/43, pr. in Corbett, *Sp. War*, p. 257).

3. GALLEON [LETTICE] LEICESTER, 400 tons, owned by the earl of Leicester. Captain Francis Knollys, 'rear admiral'. Built about 1580 as the Galleon *Ughtred*, but refitted and renamed the *Leicester*, she was Fenton's flagship in the 1582 voyage, and was repaired in the naval shipyard upon her return (Cotton MS Otho E. VIII, fol. 132v; Laughton, *Armada*, II, 326, 336; Corbett, *Sp. War*, pp. 242, 247). Used for the defence in the Armada year, she was sold upon the death of her owner at an official valuation of £1500 (L. Stone, *The Crisis of the Aristocracy*, p. 364; E. G. R. Taylor, op. cit., pp. 20–1, 234–5.)

4. AID, 200–250 tons, queen's ship, listed at 200 tons in 1579,

but at 250 after reconstruction in 1585 (Williamson, *Hawkins of Plymouth*, p. 262; Corbett, *Sp. War*, p. 241). Captain Edward Wynter. Built before 1571, she had been Frobisher's flagship in 1577 (Morison, *European Disc. Amer.*, pp. 516–18), being valued then, with her equipment, at 838 *l*. 16*s*. 8*d*. She underwent repairs in 1585 and 1586 (A.O. 1/1685/21; E 351/2223; Corbett, *Sp. War*, p. 227), and was used in 1588 (*C.S.P.D. 1581–1590*, p. 457).

5. TIGER, 150–200 tons, was evidently a London ship. Captain Christopher Carleill; master, John Grant (see p. 168). The royal ship of the same name (140–200 tons) was away with Grenville until October 1585 (Quinn, *Roanoke Voyages*, I, 178–93), and was listed in December 1585 as being in the West Country (Corbett, *Sp. War*, p. 313). Possibly Carleill's ship was the same *Tiger*, 'a warlike ship', meaning an armed merchantman, used by him when he escorted the embassy of English merchants to Russia in 1582 (Hakluyt, *Princ. Nav.*, III, 303). *Tiger* was among the ships of the 1585 expedition ordered to be repaired in the naval shipyard after their return in 1586 (A.O. 1/1685/21). A London ship *Tiger* (200 tons, 90 men) was equipped for the defence in 1588 (Laughton, *Armada*, II, 327). Tom Glasgow ('H.M.S. *Tiger*', *North Carolina Historical Review*, Spring 1966, pp. 115–21) has suggested that the old royal ship *Tiger* was on this voyage, having been exchanged for Wynter's ship *Sea Dragon* and that the *Tiger* with Grenville was actually the latter ship, renamed. However, the figures for tonnage and complement of men given in the Harl. 366 furnishing list for the Drake voyage indicate that both the *Tiger* (150 tons) and the *Sea Dragon* (140 tons) were smaller than the old naval vessel *Tiger* (*c*. 193 tons). The tonnage figure for Wynter's *Sea Dragon* is not far from the 149 ton listed for the 'new' *Tiger* in 1590, as Glasgow reports.

6. SEA DRAGON, 140 tons, owned by Sir William Wynter, Surveyor of Ships. Captain Henry Whyte, who replaced Drake's earlier appointee, William Hawkins, Senior (see p. 48). Some work in setting her forth had been done in the royal naval yard; an account of January 1588 shows that the charge for repairs of two royal ships (*Elizabeth Jonas* and *Revenge*) 'was borne by the venturers with Sir Francis [Drake] at the setting forth of the Bonaventure, Sea Dragon, and the Aid, the last of July 1585' (S.P. 12/208:18, pr. in Laughton, *Armada*, I, 44). She was lost from the fleet once on the outward voyage, and may have been blown away from it at

Hatteras, since new cables and anchors had to be supplied after the return (Corbett, *Sp. War*, p. 96). She was among the ships repaired in the naval yard later that year (Hawkins's Accounts, A.O. 1/1685/21) and was said shortly afterwards to have been assigned by Wynter to the navy, replacing the old royal ship *Tiger* (Corbett, *Sp. War*, pp. xi, n., 249 and n.). See also note on the *Tiger*.

7. THOMAS, 100–200 tons, formerly known as the bark *Hastings*, was sometimes referred to as the *Thomas Drake*, or the *Thomas of Plymouth*, and was owned by Sir Francis Drake. Captain Thomas Drake. As the *Hastings* (100 tons) she had been with William Hawkins in 1582 (Williamson, *Hawkins of Plymouth*, p. 414), but her complement of men in 1585 suggests a larger size (160–200 tons). She went to Cadiz in 1587, was listed at 200 tons in 1588, and was destroyed as a fire ship against the Armada. Drake was allowed £1000 for her loss (Laughton, *Armada*, II, 287, 326, 327; Corbett, *Sp. War*, p. 100).

8. MINION, of Plymouth, 100–200 tons, owned probably by a merchant or merchants of Plymouth, possibly some from Bristol. Captain Thomas Cely. Master, Jo[hn] Newsome (see p. 49). In the Harl. MS 366 list a ship that seems to correspond with the *Minion* is listed as of 100 tons, and her captain as [Gilbert?] Vaughan. As the *Minion of Plymouth*, but with some Bristol merchants interested, she had been held early in 1581 in Andalusia, on suspicion of piracy (*C.S.P.D. 1581–1590*, p. 11). Her captain in 1585 was a Bristol man (see p. 292). She was one of the Plymouth ships used for Cadiz in 1587 and against the Armada (Corbett, *Sp. War*, p. 100; Laughton, *Armada*, I, 31; II, 326, 337). She was probably not the *Minion of London* (200 tons) also listed for the Armada defence (Laughton, *Armada*, II, 200).

9. TALBOT, a bark of 150–200 tons, owned by George Talbot, earl of Shrewsbury. Captain [Walter?] Baily. The earl, who had owned her at least as early as 1574, had sent her on voyages to Newfoundland, had offered her in 1581 for the Fenton voyage, but sent her instead to the Azores for Don Antonio, and had sent her out as a privateer in 1583 and 1584 (Cotton MS Otho E. VIII, fol. 107; L. Stone, *The Crisis of the Aristocracy*, pp. 363–4; and p. 49 above). She was separated temporarily from the 1585 fleet by the Bayona storm (see p. 221), and may have been driven out also from Hatteras; a new cable and anchor were needed upon her return (Corbett,

Sp. War, pp. 96, 257). Used by Drake for a fire ship in 1588, her owner was allowed £900 in compensation (Laughton, *Armada*, I, 31; II, 287, 326, 337).

10. WHITE LION, 140-150 tons, one of the several private men-of-war owned by Charles Lord Howard of Effingham, the Lord Admiral. Captain James Erisey. She may have been used in some privateering (Andrews, *Eliz. Privateering*, p. 89). In the West Indies voyage she lost an anchor and cable at Roanoke; she was used on the Cadiz voyage and in the Armada year served as virtually one of the queen's ships (Corbett, *Sp. War*, pp. xviii, xx, 96; Laughton, *Armada*, I, 68; II, 328, 338).

11. BARK BOND, 120-150 tons, owned by John Hawkins, Treasurer of the Navy (Andrews, *Eliz. Privateering*, p. 90), although George Bond, mayor of Plymouth, may have had an interest (Laughton, *Armada*, I, 31 n.). Captain Robert Crosse. She was with Drake in 1588 and was used as a fire ship, with £600 being allowed to her owner (Corbett, *Sp. War*, pp. 236, 237; Laughton, *Armada*, II, 287, 326, 337). Cf. p. 145.

12. HOPE, a bark of 120 tons, probably owned by John Hawkins, possibly in partnership with William Hart (Corbett, *Sp. War*, p. 237 n.; Laughton, *Armada*, II, 237). Captain Edward Careless, although Fulke Greville had been listed for that post in August 1585 (see p. 50). One of the older ships in the fleet, she was replaced at Santo Domingo by 'a new Hope' (about 200 tons, see p. 157). The *Hope Hawkins* (180-200 tons) became one of the fire ships against the Armada, with her owner of that time, William Hart, being allowed £600 (Laughton, *Armada*, II, 287, 326, 337). She is not to be confused with the royal ship *Hope* (Hawkins's accounts A.O. 1/1685/20).

13. BARK BONNER, 120-150 tons, a merchant ship owned probably by William Hawkins. Captain George Fortescue. She had leaked badly when on the voyage with William Hawkins in 1582 (Williamson, *Hawkins of Plymouth*, p. 224). Drake offered her to Knollys in 1586 (see p. 145), and afterwards to Lane at Roanoke (Lane's narrative, Hakluyt, *Princ. Nav.*, VIII, 344). She was available for defence against the Armada in 1587 (Corbett, *Sp. War*, p. 236; Laughton, *Armada*, I, 31; II, 326, 337; E. G. R. Taylor, *The* . . . *Voyage of Captain Edward Fenton*, p. lv, n. 2).

14. BARK HAWKINS, 120-150 tons, a merchant ship owned

by John Hawkins. Captain William Hawkins, Junior. Drake used her in the 1585 voyage as a messenger ship several times, and once proposed her for taking Knollys back to England (see p. 156). She was with Drake on the Cadiz voyage, and again in 1588. She was described variously as of 130, 140, or 150 tons (Corbett, *Sp. War,* pp. 98, n., 100; Laughton, *Armada,* I, 31; II, 326).

15. [UNNAMED SHIP], possibly 120 tons, owned by Sir William Mohun of Cornwall (Document 1, p. 46); size suggested by the 3:5 ratio of men to tonnage. Captain's name unknown. Possibly this was the *Benjamin* or the *Vantage*, although these appear to have been smaller than Mohun's in capacity. The ship appears only in the Folger MS list.

16. BENJAMIN, a bark of possibly 75 tons, probably owned by Drake, or a West Country associate. Captain John Martin (Document 1, p. 50; Corbett, *Sp. War,* pp. xi, xii). She was left at Santo Domingo, being replaced by a prize taken there. (See p. 157.)

17. VANTAGE, *c.* 50–65 tons. Owner unknown, but probably one of Drake's associates. The size is suggested by the 3:5 ratio of men to tonnage; she may be the ship (unnamed) listed at 50 tons in Harl. MS 366. Captain John Rivers.

18. FRANCIS [FRANCES], 60–70 tons, a bark owned by Drake. Captain Thomas Moone. She had been commanded by Drake's nephew John on the Fenton voyage of 1582 (Cotton MS Otho E. VIII, fol. 133; Williamson, *Hawkins of Plymouth,* p. 217). She was suggested once for taking Knollys back to England (see p. 145), and was also the first ship assigned for the Roanoke colonists. Driven out to sea by the June storm, she made her way separately to England (Corbett, *Sp. War,* pp. 95–6). A smaller ship of the same name was with Drake in 1595–96 (Andrews, *Last Voyage,* p. 38).

19. SPEEDWELL, *c.* 50–60 tons, a merchant ship possibly owned by John Wilson but fitted out by the earl of Leicester. Captain John Wilson, or Philip Sparrowe. Wilson is listed as captain in the Folger MS list (see p. 50), but Sparrowe, evidently in command of the ship, addressed his account of her experiences to Captain Wilson upon her return to Weymouth on 11 October (Lansdowne MS 100, fols. 81–2). Her name is missing from the list in *Summarie.* Driven out of the fleet by the Bayona storm, she made her way back to England, but never rejoined Drake, and he listed

expenses of £115 for her repairs after his return. She was ready for the Cadiz voyage, however, and also in the Armada year (Corbett, *Sp. War*, pp. 96, 99; Laughton, *Armada*, II, 326).

20. GEORGE, *c.* 50 tons, owner unknown. Captain John Varney (?). The burden is suggested by the 3:5 formula, reckoned from the complement of 30 men (see p. 46). The *George* is listed in the printed *Summarie*, though not in the MS variant; in the printed edition, Varney is named as her captain; but in the variant, Varney is listed as captain of the *Elizabeth*. No ship identifiable by the name of *George* appears in the Harl. MS 366, but the *George* was mentioned as with the fleet on 18 October (see pp. 91, 122).

21. SCOUT, 30 tons, owner probably John Hawkins or one of his partners. The tonnage figure is that given for an unidentified ship in the Harl. MS 366 list. Captain Edward Gilman. She may have been one of five barks fitted out for privateering in 1584, but is not to be confused with the larger queen's ship of the same name (*C.S.P.D. 1581–1590*, pp. 218, 243, 552; Corbett, *Sp. War*, pp. 262, 271; P.R.O., A.O. 1/1685/20 and E 351/2223). She is mentioned in the narratives of the West Indies voyage, and was replaced by one of the prizes taken at Santo Domingo (see pp. 95, 127, 157).

22. MATHEW, *c.* 40 tons, owned by Drake. Captain unknown. This ship name appears in the Folger MS, with a complement of 25 (though written as 55 men; see p. 46). The estimate of size is based upon the 3:5 formula. The only other reference to this ship is in Sparrowe's letter, where he mentions her along with the galley and the pinnaces (Lansdowne MS 100, fol. 81). She had been on the Hawkins voyage in 1582. E. G. R. Taylor, *The . . . Voyage of Captain Edward Fenton*, p. lv, n. 2.

23. DUCK, a galley or galliot, 20 tons, probably owned by Hawkins or Drake. Captain Richard Hawkins. Corbett suggests (*Sp. War*, p. 5 n.) that she was probably a large pinnace or a small galleon fitted with oars. Her size made her useful for reconnoitering along a coast, as at Vigo (see p. 84).

24. SWALLOW [20 tons?], owner unknown. Captain Bitfield. This ship is not in the Folger MS, but the name of both ship and captain appear in the *Summarie*. Her location in the list suggests a small vessel, and she may be the one in the Harl. MS 366 (name of ship and captain both illegible), as of 20 tons, with 15 men. She is not mentioned in the voyage journals. She should not, however, be

confused with the 300-ton queen's ship of the same name (Corbett, *Sp. War*, pp. xii, 227, 271, 361; Laughton, *Armada*, I, 16, 79; P.R.O. A.O. 1/1685/21).

25. ELIZABETH or ELIZABETH DRAKE, 70 tons, probably owned by Drake. Captain possibly John Varney. Missing from both of the MS furnishing lists, and also from the printed *Summarie*, she is no. 17 (renumbered as 18) in the MS variant of *Summarie* (Harl. 6221), with Varney as her captain (see p. 216, n. 6). The 'little Elizabeth' is mentioned in the *Tiger* journal as being placed more directly under Frobisher's eye (p. 89), so-called perhaps to distinguish her from the larger *Elizabeth Bonaventure*. She apparently went with Drake to Cadiz and was with him also in 1588, along with another vessel, the *Elizabeth Fownes* (Corbett, *Sp. War*, pp. xx, 100 and n.; Laughton, *Armada*, I, 31; II, 326; Andrews, *Eliz. Privateering*, p. 90).

26. [DRAKE], 50 tons, a French salt ship *La Magdelaine*, sometimes called 'the Burton Bark', taken as prize by Drake, and kept throughout the expedition (see pp. 77, n. 3, 91). Captain John Vaughan, who must have transferred from another ship, possibly the *Elizabeth*. Although listed in both the printed *Summarie* and the MS variant, this ship is in neither of the 'furnishing' lists prepared before sailing. Possibly she was the *Drake of London*, owned by John Watts, which sailed for Cadiz in 1587 (Andrews, *Eliz. Privateering*, p. 85; Corbett, *Sp. War*, pp. 40, 99).

27. [NEW YEAR'S GIFT], a large prize taken at Santo Domingo, property of a Seville merchant, Antonio Corço (Wright, *Further Eng. Voyages*, pp. xlii, 145). She was used until a serious leak caused Drake to abandon her at Cartagena (see pp. 157, 262).

28. Pinnaces, eight in number, 20–60 tons each, owned by London and Plymouth men (see above, p. 46; Corbett, *Sp. War*, p. I, n.). They are mentioned frequently in action during the voyage.

APPENDIX II

PERSONNEL

BAILY [Baylye], [WALTER]. Captain of the *Talbot*, employed by the earl of Shrewsbury. He had been with that ship earlier, in the service of Don Antonio in the Azores (see p. 49). Probably he was the Walter Baylye who was in the royal service at Portsmouth in 1587 (P.R.O., E 351/2224).

BARTON, GEORGE. Captain in the land forces. An experienced soldier, he was sent to the Low Countries in June 1587 (*Acts P.C. 1588*, p. 47).

BIGGES, WALTER. Captain in the land forces under Carleill, and credited by Thomas Cates as the principal author of the *Summarie*. He died, probably of the fever, after the stay at Cartagena (see p. 211).

BITFIELD, ——. Captain of the *Swallow*.

BOAZIO, BAPTISTA. A 'page' or gentleman travelling with Christopher Carleill; probably the artist who drew the four town plans and the 'general' map of the voyage (see Note on Maps). His associations with Carleill, who returned to Ireland in 1587, may have continued through the drawing of a map of Ireland (1586–88). R. V. Tooley, *Maps and Map-Makers* (London, 1949), p. 92.

CARELESS, EDWARD. Captain of the *Hope*. Identified also as "*alias*" Wright, the mathematician, narrator of Cumberland's Azores voyage (1589), in Hakluyt, *Prin. Nav.*, VII, 1. Cf. *DNB*.

CARLEILL, CHRISTOPHER (1551?–93). Captain of the *Tiger* and lieutenant generall, or chief military officer. Son of a London vintner, Alexander Carleill, he became through his mother's remarriage a stepson of Sir Francis Walsingham. For some years after 1572 he served in naval and military commands under the Prince of Orange, but early in the next decade he became interested in projects for commercial expansion, influenced by his maternal grandfather, Alderman Barne of the Muscovy Company, and by Walsingham and the younger Hakluyt. In 1582 it was proposed that he go on Fenton's voyage (Cotton MS Otho E. VIII, fols.

127, 251), but in the same year and the next he was promoting plans to plant an English colony north of Spain's holdings in America, and he set forth his arguments in *A briefe and summary discourse upon the intended voyage* . . . (Hakluyt, *Prin. Nav.,* VIII, 134–47). He set out on neither project, but went instead in the *Tiger,* either an armed merchantman or a naval ship of that name, as convoy for the English commercial embassy to Russia (Hakluyt, *Prin. Nav.,* III, 303, 463). Another American venture, possibly with Raleigh and one of the Hawkins brothers, was being considered in 1583–84 and he took three ships as far as Cork (Quinn, *Gilbert,* pp. 94–5, 725–6; *Roanoke Voyages,* pp. 77–8). From October 1584 until the summer of 1585 he was stationed with the English forces in Ireland, but he was involved in frequent disputes with Lord Deputy Perrot, who insinuated that Carleill was engaging in piracy (*C.S.P. Ireland 1584–1585,* pp. 530, 540, 559, 560, 568), and he was called back, probably by Walsingham, to join in the Drake venture of 1585. He took with him John Sampson, who had served under him (*C.S.P. Ireland 1574–1591,* p. 585); and Baptista Boazio seems to have been attached to him as a 'page'.

Although not previously acquainted with Drake, Carleill early developed good working relations with him, and became his leading official adviser during the voyage (see Documents 6 and 9). He was, in a sense, Walsingham's representative, as his detailed report on the Vigo stay suggests (see p. 69, n.4), and he may have been helpful in assembling materials for the report that is known as the *Summarie* (see Bibliographical Note and also pp. 69, n. 4 and 106, n. 5). He returned to military commands in Ireland in the spring of 1587, and served as governor of Ulster 1588–90. He died in London in November 1593. (*Acts P.C. 1587–1588,* pp. 58, 75–6; *DNB;* C. Read, *Walsingham,* I, 26; Taylor, *Writings . . . Hakluyts,* pp. 12, 18, 24, 26–7, 31–2; and a recent biography, Rachel Lloyd, *Elizabethan Adventurer: A Life of Captain Christopher Carleill* (London, 1974).)

CATES, THOMAS. Lieutenant in Carleill's company, and editor of the *Summarie,* as published in England (see p. 213).

CECIL, WILLIAM. Captain in the land forces. He was assigned command of the soldiers on the *Aid,* and at Cartagena exchanged commands with that ship's captain, Edward Wynter (see pp. 139,

253). He died during the voyage. He may have been a relative of Lord Burghley, but was not the grandson William, son of Thomas Cecil, Burghley's heir, since that grandson was travelling on the continent at the time of the voyage (H.M.C., *Salisbury MSS*, III, 130, 179; *C.S.P. For. 1585–1586*, p. 449).

CELY, THOMAS (b. *c.* 1526). Captain of the *Minion*. A Bristol man, he had been taken prisoner in Spain in 1572, where he was tortured and forced to spend some four years in the galleys. He was still a prisoner in December 1579, and in 1588 he described himself as 'but a patched carcase'. (Laughton, *Armada*, I, xxi–xxii; 262–7; II, 343–7). Cf. p. 49. He served as captain of the *Elizabeth Drake* in the Armada year; as a consistent foe of the Spaniards, he urged then 'a sharp war and short [one]'. (Laughton, *Armada*, I, 264; II, 326.)

COTTELL, ——. Drake's secretary. He helped to draw up the articles that were presented to Francis Knollys in November, but died during the voyage (see pp. 61, 145).

CROFTES, ——. Lieutenant under Captain Bigges. He is mentioned by Thomas Cates as probably the one who completed the narrative of the expedition after Bigges's death (see p. 211).

CROSSE, ROBERT (*fl.* 1585–1596). Captain of the *Bond*. Identified in 1585 as having had previous sea experience but being currently in the employ of Vice Chamberlain Sir Christopher Hatton (see p. 49). He volunteered to be a hostage at Vigo, and afterwards served under Drake at Cadiz and in the Armada year. In 1592 he was in Raleigh's ship off the Azores, and in 1596 he was knighted at Cadiz. He was a brother-in-law of the land captain, John Marchant (q.v.). (Corbett, *Sp. War*, pp. xii, 4, 47 n., 109, 142; Laughton, *Armada*, I, 17, 25, 171; II, 58, 340; Thomson, *Sir Francis Drake*, p. 299.)

DRAKE, SIR FRANCIS (*c.* 1545–1596). Commander-in-chief, or 'general' of the expedition. He had been one of the chief promoters, and active in its organization since the summer of 1584. He enjoyed the confidence of Secretary Walsingham and the earl of Leicester, and was ardent in his desire to weaken Spain as England's enemy in matters of trade and colonial development, and as the principal champion of Romanism. He invested heavily in the voyage, putting in three, possibly more, ships of his own, and he commanded the personal loyalty of various captains who had sailed with him before. He had had experience with most of the regions into which he took the fleet, except the American coast north of the Florida strait. (See *DNB*; Andrews, *Drake's Voyages*; Corbett, *Drake and the Tudor Navy*, and *Sp. War*; Thomson, *Sir Francis Drake*.)

DRAKE, THOMAS. Captain of the *Thomas*. He was the youngest brother of Sir Francis, and his heir. Having served on the global voyage, he was recognized in 1585/6 as an able captain, and on this voyage commanded one of Drake's own ships. He commanded the *Revenge* in 1589, was with Drake in the final voyage of 1595–96, and as his brother's executor settled Drake's accounts with the queen in November 1596 (P.R.O., E 351/2222). (Andrews, *Last Voyage*, pp. 35, 41; Corbett, *Sp. War*, pp. xi, 293, 299.)

ERISEY, JAMES. Captain of the *White Lion*. The son of Richard Erisey of Erisey, Cornwall, who had had some associations with Frobisher, he was related to the Grenvilles of Stowe. Although he had lacked sea experience (see p. 49), he took an active part in the expedition. In the Armada year he was captain of the galleon *Dudley*, and in 1589 was engaged in privateering on the western coast. (Andrews, *Eliz. Priv.*, p. 258; M. F. Keeler, *The Long Parliament*, 'Richard Erisey'; Laughton, *Armada*, I, 118; II, 340; R. G. Marsden, 'The Early Career of Sir Martin Frobisher', *E.H.R.*, XXI (1906), 539–40.)

FENNER [Vennor], THOMAS. Captain of the *Elizabeth Bonaventure*, Drake's flagship. A professional seaman from a Chichester family of privateering activity, he had made a voyage to Guinea in 1564, and was given numerous special assignments by Drake during the West Indies voyage. He served under Drake on the Cadiz expedition and in the Armada year, and was interested in more privateering in 1589. (Andrews, *Eliz. Priv.*, pp. 61–2, 90; and 'Thomas Fenner and the Guinea Trade', *Mariners Mirror*, XXXVIII (1952), 312–14; Corbett, *Sp. War*, pp. 103, 143, 298; Laughton, *Armada*, I, 16, 118.)

FORTESCUE, GEORGE (d. 1586). Captain of the *Bonner*. A West Country seaman who had been around the world with Drake, he now commanded a ship belonging to William Hawkins. He died of the fever at Cartagena (see p. 174).

FROBISHER, MARTIN (1535?–1594). Captain of the *Primrose*, and

vice admiral under Drake. He and Carleill (q.v.) constituted
Drake's inner council for the voyage, but his influence was less
strong. During the quarrel involving Knollys he interceded in the
latter's behalf (see p. 145). Distinguished in his own right for his
three north Atlantic voyages and his service on a royal ship in
Irish waters in 1580, he stated afterwards that he had joined Drake
in 1585 at the express command of the queen (see p. 62, n. 5).
His ship *Primrose* and the London pinnaces may have been in his
special charge as representing the London merchants. (See *DNB*;
Corbett, *Sp. War*, p. xi and n.; Morison, *European Disc. of Amer.*,
pp. 498-550.)

GILMAN, EDWARD. Captain of the *Scout*, a smaller vessel probably
owned by John Hawkins.

GORING, JOHN. Captain in the land forces. He may have been from
the Sussex family, Goring of Hurstpierpoint. He had evidently
had military experience abroad before 1585, and in the West
Indies expedition he commanded the soldiers of Frobisher's ship
(see p. 139), distinguishing himself several times. He was sent to
the armies in the Low Countries in June 1587 (*Acts P.C. 1588*,
p. 47).

GRANT, JOHN. Master of the *Tiger*, Carleill's ship. (See pp. 168,
257.)

GRENVILLE, [JOHN]. Captain in the land forces. He died on the
voyage (see p. 276). He is identified as the second son of Sir
Richard Grenville, the colonizer and naval commander, in
Visitation of Cornwall, 1620 (Harl. Soc. IX), p. 85, n.

GREVILLE, FULKE, afterwards Lord Brooke (1554-1628). Captain
designate of the *Hope*. He withdrew from the voyage with
Sidney (see pp. 50, 70), and was replaced by Careless.

HAMPTON, JOHN. Master of the *Primrose*. He was involved in some
officers' quarrels during the voyage (see p. 151). Later, John
Hampton, master of the *Primrose*, was sent for by messenger from
her Majesty's Chamber to be brought up in custody from
Plymouth (undated request of the messenger for payment
(probably 1586 rather than 1587), *C.S.P.D. 1581-1590*, p. 449).
He was master of the *Rainbow*, a royal ship, in the Cadiz
expedition, and master of the *Talbot* in the Armada action.
(Corbett, *Sp. War*, pp. 87, 162; Laughton, *Armada*, II, 326.)

HANNAM, JOHN. Captain of land forces. He died during the voyage.

HAWKINS, RICHARD (1560–1622). Captain of the *Duck*. Son of John Hawkins, he had sailed with his uncle, the elder William Hawkins, in 1582, and now had his first important command in the small galliot. Having been separated from Drake off Roanoke, his early arrival on 21 July 1586 made him the advance messenger of news from Drake (see pp. 40, n. 4, 273, n. 1). For his later career, see *DNB*; J. A. Williamson, *Hawkins of Plymouth*, pp. 219–20, 224, 291; and Williamson, ed., *The Observations of Sir Richard Hawkins* (London, 1933), p. xlvi.

HAWKINS, WILLIAM, SEN. (*c.* 1520–89). Captain designate of the *Sea Dragon*. He was replaced before the fleet sailed, and although Drake may have offered him a post on his own ship (see p. 48), there is no evidence that he went on the voyage. Older than his brother John, he had shared in the preparations for the voyage (see Document 2). (See *DNB*; Corbett, *Sp. War*, pp. 292, 298; and Williamson, *Hawkins of Plymouth*, pp. 218–24.)

HAWKINS, WILLIAM, JUN. (*fl.* 1577–95). Captain of the bark *Hawkins*. Eldest son of the elder William Hawkins, and nephew of John, the navy treasurer, he had been with Drake on the global voyage. As Fenton's second in command in 1582, he was influential in persuading Fenton to turn against Spain's holdings in America, but eventually came back to England in irons. In the Armada year he was captain of one of the merchant ships under Drake. (See *DNB*; Corbett, *Sp. War*, pp. 293, 299; Laughton, *Armada*, II, 328, 340; Williamson, *Hawkins of Plymouth*, pp. 217–18.)

HENLEY, ——. Probable author of the journal of the *Primrose*, Frobisher's ship (see p. 210). He has not otherwise been identified. Corbett suggests that he may have been a soldier (*Sp. War*, p. 15).

HERNE, GRIFFITH. Shipmaster, assigned by Drake to the *Francis* in 1586 to assist with the return of the Roanoke colonists. (See p. 272, n. 3.)

JONAS, ——. Drake's interpreter. He assisted with the weighing of the Cartagena ransom (see p. 178). According to the Spanish judge there, who stated that Jonas told him much about the English, Jonas had lived for a time in Spain, serving as page to a magistrate from Xérez (Castellanos, *Discurso*, App., p. 307).

KENDALL, ABRAHAM. Shipmaster, assigned to assist the Roanoke colonists in 1586. He had probably been with Frobisher in 1578.

He reached England before Drake because his ship was driven out to sea. (See Quinn, *Roanoke Voyages*, p. 291, n.)

KNOLLYS [KNOWLES], FRANCIS (*c.* 1550–1648). Captain of the galleon *Leicester*, and rear admiral during parts of the expedition. Sixth son of Sir Francis Knollys, Treasurer of the Household, kinsman of the queen, he had been educated at Oxford and Gray's Inn, and twice elected to Parliament (1575, 1584). With his older brother Henry he had been involved in the proposed voyage with Gilbert in 1578 and in some of Henry's privateering ventures afterwards (see p. 16). In the 1585/86 list of sea captains (S.P. 12/186/8), he was listed as 'Francis Knollys, gent.', and absent (not as *Sir* Francis, as Corbett (*Sp. War*, p. 292) read it). As brother-in-law of the earl of Leicester, and captain of the earl's large ship, Knollys sought more recognition than Drake was prepared to give him during the voyage, and his jealousy of Carleill, which contributed directly to the quarrel he had with Drake, is evident throughout the *Leicester* journal (Document 9). Although he was removed from his command and under threat of being sent home, Knollys was finally returned to his official post and stayed with the fleet until the end. The quarrel was said to have been resumed after their return, and Mendoza heard that Knollys was under arrest for some days, on the queen's orders (Mendoza's letter of 8 November 1586 (N.S.), *C.S.P. Span. 1580–1586*, p. 650), but no further record of it has been found. Knollys was elected to Parliament again in September 1586, and in the Armada year he organized troops for the defence. (See *Acts P.C. 1588*, pp. 19, 196; M. F. Keeler, *The Long Parliament*, pp. 243–4; Quinn, *Gilbert*, I, 42; II, 209, 233.)

MARCHANT, JOHN. Captain in the land forces. Spoken of as 'brother', or brother-in-law, of Robert Crosse (Laughton, *Armada*, II, 340), he served as sergeant major in the Cadiz expedition, and supported Drake in the quarrel with Borough. He acted as a sea captain under Drake in 1588, and was quartermaster for Drake's last voyage. (Andrews, *Last Voyage*, p. 45; Corbett, *Sp. War*, pp. xiii, xxiv, 150–1, 156–64; Laughton, *Armada*, I, 118; II, 326.)

MARTIN, JOHN. Captain of the *Benjamin*. He had been around the world with Drake and was among those examined afterwards regarding some of the booty (Harl. MS 280, fol. 89). He was

probably the John Martyn whose commissions for the new
voyage testify to the 1584 and 1585 royal commissions to Drake.
(Corbett, *Drake and the Tudor Navy*, II, 9, 12). One 'Mr.
Martyn' went home to England from Vigo in a merchant ship (see p. 90).
There are no indications, however, in the *Summarie* that the
Benjamin's captain did not finish the voyage. (Corbett, *Sp. War*,
p. xi.)

MOONE, THOMAS. Captain of the *Francis*. One of Drake's oldest
and most devoted followers, he had been with him in 1573 and
in the global voyage. He died of wounds at Cartagena in 1586,
and was buried there (see pp. 168, 258). (Corbett, *Sp. War*,
p. 45, n.; Thomson, *Sir Francis Drake*, pp. 72–3.)

MORGAN, MATTHEW. Captain in the land forces, and one of the
two corporals of the field. He was a grandson of William Morgan
of St George's and Pencarn, Glamorganshire, and nephew of the
soldier, Sir Thomas Morgan, who served with the English forces
in the Netherlands much of the time between 1572 and 1588. The
latter wrote in December 1585 to Walsingham, mentioning
concern about the lands of his nephew, 'your honor's servant and
now in the voyage of Sir Francis Drake' (*C.S.P. For. 1585–1586*,
p. 200); and when Sir Thomas died in 1595 he bequeathed his gilt
armour to his nephew, Sir Matthew Morgan. (*DNB*, 'Thomas
Morgan (d. 1595)'.)

NICHOLLS, PHILIP. Drake's chaplain. He had been presented to
the chapel of Kympton, diocese of Wells, by Sir Francis Knollys,
Treasurer of the Household (*DNB*). It is doubtful that he went on
Drake's third West Indies voyage, 1572–73, but he has been
credited with the compilation of the account of that voyage
(published in 1626, with Drake's notes of *circa* 1592, as *Sir Francis
Drake Revived* . . . , by Philip Nichols, Preacher). As chaplain in
1585 he drew up and administered the oaths of obedience at
Santiago (see pp. 139–43); and he argued on theological matters
with the Spaniards at Santo Domingo (Wright, *Further Eng.
Voyages*, p. 224). He was chaplain also on the Cadiz expedition
(Corbett, *Sp. War*, pp. xxiv, 143, 187). See also *DNB*, 'Philip
Nichols (*fl.* 1547–1559)'.

PEW [PIEWE], ROBERT. Captain in the land forces. Although named
in both the printed *Summarie* and the MS variant, his name is
missing from the list in Document 1. He was an experienced

soldier, and in June 1587 was among those being sent to the Low Countries (*Acts P.C. 1588*, p. 47).

PLATT, ANTHONY. Captain in the land forces, and assigned to command the company aboard the *Leicester* (see p. 139). He was sergeant major with the land forces on the Cadiz expedition, was listed as available as a sea captain in 1588, and in Drake's voyage of 1595–96 was a company commander. (Andrews, *Last Voyage*, p. 45; Corbett, *Sp. War*, pp. xiii, xxiv, 157, 183–4; Laughton, *Armada*, I, 118.)

POWELL, ANTHONY (d. 1586). Sergeant major and second in command of land forces under Carleill. He was an experienced soldier, having served in Flanders (Wright, *Further Eng. Voyages*, p. 49), but was impetuous. He was killed at St Augustine (see pp. 151, 269).

POWELL, EDWARD. Recorder of the journal of the *Tiger*. He was probably in Carleill's personal employment, rather than a ship officer (see p. 86). His handwriting indicates that he copied for Carleill or Walsingham the original narrative of the *Summarie* (see p. 69, n. 4).

RIVERS, JOHN. Captain of the *Vantage*. He afterwards went on the Cadiz voyage, and was one of the Plymouth men recruited for the Armada defence, serving as captain of the *Hope Hawkins*. (Corbett, *Sp. War*, pp. xii, 157, 159; Laughton, *Armada*, I, 118; II, 326.)

SAMPSON, JOHN. Captain in the land forces and one of the two corporals of the field. He had been with Carleill in Ireland, returning with him for the voyage, and was Drake's first intermediary in negotiating with officials at Bayona (see pp. 79, 219). He was sent to the Netherlands in June 1587 (*Acts P.C. 1588*, p. 47), was used briefly in a naval command in 1588, and was lieutenant colonel in Drake's expedition with Norreys in 1589. (Corbett, *Sp. War*, p. 43: Laughton, *Armada*, II, 169, 182, 184; Thomson, *Sir Francis Drake*, p. 285.)

SPARROWE, PHILIP. Sailor aboard the *Speedwell*, possibly as captain. His letter to Captain John Wilson, giving the account of the ship's adventures from 14 September until her return to England on 11 October is in Lansdowne MS 100, fols. 81–2 (see p. 5).

STANTON, RICHARD. Soldier. Although listed in the *Summarie* (p. 215) as one of the captains of land forces, he began the voyage as a lieutenant on the *Leicester*, under Knollys. He supported the latter in the quarrel with Drake, but took an active part in land operations and was promoted to a captaincy at Cartagena (see pp. 146, 174). He was a company commander in Drake's 1595–96 voyage (Andrews, *Last Voyage*, p. 45).

VARNEY, JOHN. Captain of the *George*, or possibly of the *Elizabeth* (see Table of Ships). He was killed at Cartagena (see p. 168).

VAUGHAN, JOHN. Sea captain, assigned to the captured prize *Drake*, after starting in command of a smaller ship, such as *Elizabeth* or *George* (see Table of Ships). He was among the ship captains listed in 1586 as absent (i.e., with Drake), and in the later quarrel (1588) between Drake and Frobisher was a witness to Frobisher's words. (Corbett, *Sp. War*, pp. 293, 299.)

WATERHOUSE, ——. Lieutenant in the land forces. He was in Goring's company, aboard Frobisher's ship *Primrose*, and was killed at St Augustine (see pp. 115, 151, 206).

WHYTE, HENRY. Captain of the *Sea Dragon*. He had probably had experience in royal ships (see his letter of August 1588 pr. in Laughton, *Armada*, II, 63–5), and he was assigned at the request of Sir Philip Sidney to replace the aging William Hawkins in 1585 (see p. 49). Although ill in 1588, possibly from effects of the West Indies voyage, he volunteered for the Armada defence, and served as captain of the *Talbot*. (Corbett, *Sp. War*, p. xii; Laughton, *Armada*, II, 63–5, 326.)

WILSON, JOHN. Possibly captain of the *Speedwell* (see pp. 50, 287), but he may have been replaced by Philip Sparrowe (q.v.) before sailing. He was one of the Plymouth captains being recruited for the Armada defence. (Laughton, *Armada*, I, 118.)

WYNTER [WINTER], EDWARD. Captain of the queen's ship *Aid*, but transferred to a land captaincy at Cartagena (see p. 253). The eldest son of Sir William Wynter, Master of Ordnance and Surveyor of Ships, he was less experienced than many other officers (see p. 215, n. 1), but his name was on the 1585/86 list of English sea captains. He may have owed his 1585 appointment to Walsingham, whom he thanked for favours in a letter from Vigo in October 1585 (see p. 85, n. 3, and Corbett, *Sp. War*, pp. 49–51), and the quarters assigned him at Santiago by Carleill were said to be fine (see p. 139). On his later career see *DNB*, articles on 'Sir William Winter (d. 1589)' and 'Sir John Winter (1600?– 1673?)'.

WYNTER, NICHOLAS. One of the men 'lost' on the voyage (see p. 276), probably serving as a gentleman volunteer. He was a brother of Edward Wynter (q.v.), being the second son of Sir William (*Vis. Gloucestershire, 1623* (Harl. Soc. XXI), p. 273).

ADDITIONAL PERSONNEL, not specifically identified, include: Robert Alexander (died); —— Annes and —— Ardle, among Drake's 'gentlemen'; Mr Burke, a soldier, ensign; Alexander Carleill (died; possibly kinsman of Christopher Carleill); George Cavendish (died); —— Chamberlain, a gentleman with Knollys; James Dier [Dyer] (died); Peter Duke (died); Lt Escot (died); —— Ketill, lieutenant to Captain Wynter; —— Longe, a gentleman with Knollys; Jo[hn] Newsome, master of *Minion;* Thomas Ogle, steward of the *Talbot* (hanged at Santiago); Mr Scroope (died); Lt Alexander Starkey (died); —— Thorowgood, a gentleman with Knollys; Lt Thomas Tucker, a soldier (died); Lt —— Vincent (died); —— Willis, a gentleman with Knollys.

APPENDIX III

BIBLIOGRAPHICAL NOTE ON
A SUMMARIE AND TRUE DISCOURSE

Questions have been raised at various times regarding the authorship of *A Summarie and True Discourse*, attributed by its English editor, Thomas Cates, chiefly to the land captain, Walter Bigges, about the circumstances of its publication, and about the relationship of the English editions of 1589 to those in Latin and French which appeared in 1588. Early brief collations of the several editions appeared in H. Huth, *Catalogue of the Famous Library of . . . Henry Huth* [1911–20] and in G. W. Cole's *Catalogue . . . Library of E. D. Church* (1907), but without detailed textual comparisons. A special study, summarizing the views of several scholars, was drawn together by R. G. Adams and J. C. Wheat of the Clements Library (Ann Arbor, Michigan) into an unpublished 'Trial Bibliography', relating both to the various editions and to the accompanying maps. This, with its supporting correspondence, is now in the John Carter Brown Library (Providence, R.I.), along with additional papers and notes made by Lawrence C. Wroth. Wroth's own summary was printed in the *Annual Report* of the John Carter Brown Library, 1942–43. Summaries, based largely upon these materials, have been printed in Quinn, *Roanoke Voyages*, I, 294; D. B. Waters's introduction to Greepe, *The True and Perfecte News* (pp. 53–70), and H. P. Kraus, *Sir Francis Drake*, pp. 198–9. In the latter volume (opp. p. 120) are illustrations of the title pages of the Latin edition (Leyden, 1588) and the two English editions of 1589.

Although it has been generally concluded that the original text was in English, with the foreign editions being translations, and that it had been planned originally that publication in London and Leyden should be at about the same time (see App. IV, Note on Maps), nothing has been learned about the manuscript of that text, lost perhaps while in the hands of one printer or another. However, the appearance of Thomas Greepe's newsballad, *The True and Perfecte News*, printed in England in 1587, before any of the prose texts, suggests that Greepe had seen and used an even earlier manuscript, either the original or a copy of it (see above, p. 7). Something of this sort may have been the basis also for the brief account in Latin that was sent by the French ambassador to Paris in 1586 (see p. 7, n. 3). Possibly several copies of the account were being circulated before publication plans were completed; and some statements, such as the reference to the *Speedwell*'s safe return to England, could have been written only after the fleet came home. What appears to be one copy of such a manuscript has been found by the present editor at the British Library (in Harley MS 6221), a copy done in the hand of an associate of Christopher Carleill (see p. 69, n. 4), under whose command both Walter Bigges and Thomas Cates had served. Close textual comparison of this manuscript with the various editions of the *Summarie* leads to the conclusion that it is a variant of the original document from which all of the others were derived. Before discussing this point more fully, it is in order to review the sequence of the several printed editions. The texts of these, as well as the manuscript, have been collated and checked for significant variations.

Earliest in print were those in Latin (*Expeditio Francisci Draki equitis Angli in Indias occidentales A. M. D. LXXXV*) and in French (*Le voyage de messire François Drake chevalier, aux Indes Occidentales*), both issuing from the same Leyden publishing house, Fr de Raphelengien, in 1588. A second issue of the Latin, with a different vignette, appeared in the same year. For my study of the Latin I have been assisted by a literal translation made and collated with the English text by Edith F. Ridington. The close resemblance of these two editions to each other and to the English texts of 1589 indicates a common original, each being a translation from an English source. Both are shorter than the English editions, with portions of the action and most of the geographical descriptions missing, the omissions being the same in each case, and these editions resemble at various points the text of the MS variant (see below). The wording chosen by the translators varies somewhat, with the French following the English more precisely, perhaps because the Latinist had difficulty in finding words for sixteenth-century military and navigational terms. He once allowed the French term *harquebuosiers* to slip in for his usual expression *sclopetarii* in translating *small shot*, and may have had the French translation at hand while preparing his own. At several points (e.g., Cuba and St Augustine) the French follows the English more accurately. A German edition, *Relation oder Beschreibung der Rheiss und Schiffahrt ausz Engellandt*, [Cologne], 1589, is clearly derived from the Latin, repeating various explanatory phrases and some of the mistakes (e.g., *steps*, instead of *degrees* in the St Augustine description; see p. 264, n. 6). In the matter of dates, however, the German used the contemporary system instead of following the Latinist's careful transposition of dates into the classical reckoning by Kalends and Ides; and occasionally, where possibly he noted disagreement between the Latin and the French or English, he chose to be less explicit regarding a geographical detail. Although the town plans by Boazio were prepared for both the Latin and the French editions (see Note on Maps), they are not mentioned in the text of either, but in the German edition the narrative is broken by the insertion on appropriate pages, next to the points at which the maps were tipped in, the descriptive passages relating to them, a procedure which may account for the irregular pagination of this edition. In all of the continental versions there are differences in the spelling of English names; and all add at least two names (Lieutenant Vincent and Alexander Carleill) to the list of officers who died on the voyage, names which appear in none of the English editions of 1589, although that of Alexander Carleill was included in the editions of 1596 and 1600.

Another edition in Latin, virtually a re-issue of the *Expeditio*, was printed as part of *Narrationes Duae . . . Quarum Prima Continet Diarium Expeditionis Francisci Draki in Indias Occidentales . . . MDXXXV* (Nuremberg, 1590). T. de Bry included a version (in Latin, and also in German) in his well-known collection of voyages, 'Americana', Part VIII, 1599. This, too, is a derivative of the earlier text (see the Wheat-Adams Trial Bibliography, and App. IV, Note on Maps).

The *Summarie* was printed first in England in 1589, with separate publication by two printers, Richard Field and Roger Ward. An explanatory note on the back of the title page (see p. 210, n. 7) suggests that the threat of the Armada had interfered with plans for an earlier date. Authorization for the printing of the narrative was secured on 26 November 1588 by William Ponsonby, a well-known stationer (*S.T.C.* 3056; *Stationers' Register* (ed. E. Arber, 5 vols., 1875), II, 508), and two issues from Richard Field's publishing house were made in 1589, with a dedication to Robert D'Evereux, Earl of Essex.

The second issue (British Library G 6509) included a list of *errata* (p. 52) and on the title page reference to the town maps. The second English edition in the same year, printed by Roger Ward (*S.T.C.* 3057) varies slightly from that of Field in matters of spelling and punctuation, and is set in different type, with a resulting difference in pagination. The town maps, with Boazio named as artist, are mentioned on its title page, and the text includes references to these at the points where they were to be tipped in. The *errata* list, however, with three items instead of four, suggests that Ward was following the second issue of Field. The so-called Ponsonby edition of 1596 (copies at the Johns Ryland Library, the John Carter Brown Library, and elsewhere), is virtually a re-issue of Field's, using the original type plates (identical as to type size and pagination), but with the four errors corrected, and with several other changes in spelling and punctuation. Since Ponsonby added the name of Alexander Carleill to the list of officers lost in the expedition, he may have used either the original source or else one of the Leyden editions in order to make his more valid. Possibly the correction was prompted by a relative of the dead man, although whether Alexander was a kinsman of Christopher Carleill and Walsingham is not known. Ponsonby's list does not include the name of the other officer, Lt Vincent, and his edition contributes no other new matter.

When Richard Hakluyt included the *Summarie* in the third volume (1600) of his enlarged *Principal Navigations*, he seems to have used Ward's rather than the Field or the Ponsonby edition, for he incorporated into his text, as did Ward, the references to the town maps (changed, so as to refer to 'a plot' rather than specifically to 'this plot'); his variations in spelling, while they represent a developing contemporary usage, bear more frequent resemblance to Ward than to Field; and in at least one statement on distance he followed Ward rather than Field. He made various editorial changes in the interest of clarity, and he added Alexander Carleill's name, as Ponsonby had done. The most noticeable change is his insertion, from a source which he did not disclose, of the text of the resolutions adopted at Cartagena by the land captains when they desired to turn homeward. Presumably he had picked up a copy of these from some member of the expedition, probably from one of the captains if not from one of the chief leaders. They had appeared in no previous edition of the narrative, omitted perhaps because they revealed Drake's weakness at that stage of the expedition. (A copy of these resolutions is in the *Leicester* journal.)

The manuscript variant mentioned above, and collated with Document 11 in this volume, is in Harley MS 6221, fols. 93–8v, with fols. 94–8 showing earlier numbers 2–6. It is bound in with materials relating to Drake's voyage of circumnavigation and the Doughty affair (used by W. S. W. Vaux for his edition of Fletcher's *The World Encompassed*, 1854). The opening sentence resembles that of the printed *Summarie*, but it is followed by a statement that this is a copy from a letter about the voyage. With the list of officers are comments that are not in the printed accounts, and it lists one ship, the *Hawkins*, which was omitted, probably by a copyist's or printer's error, from all of the English editions (see Document 11, p. 217 and note 3). The foreign-language editions give only incomplete lists of the officers' names, and no list of ships.

The narrative in the MS variant is more brief than that provided by the 1589 English editions, but it contains none of the errors which were noted in Field's second issue and in Ward's (e.g., it uses the word *recharging*, instead of *reaching*, *Pannama* instead of *Pannania*; another error noted in Field II but corrected in Ward did not occur because, in a briefer account, the erroneous word was not used; and in the fourth instance also a slight difference in wording gives a clearer account that avoids the error; see pp. 238, 240, 248, 255). In this respect Harl. 6221 bears more resemblance to the Latin and French editions, where at least one of the errors (*recharging*) did not occur. But there are even more striking points of similarity which suggest that this MS and those 1588 editions were all based on a common account that was somewhat shorter than the one which emerged as Cates's edition in England in 1589. The places at which passages are omitted are much alike (e.g., pp. 217, 228, n. 3, 242); Harl. 6221 includes both of the officers' names, Vincent and Alexander Carleill, that are in the Leyden editions but are missing from the 1589 editions; like the Leyden editions, Harl. 6221 refers to ordinance brought back from the Fort of St John rather than St Augustine (see p. 277, n. 3); and also, like each of the foreign-language editions, it places the date of the fleet's arrival at Portsmouth on 27 instead of 28 July 1586 (cf. p. 274, n. 7). There are fewer passages of an anti-Spanish nature in this MS than in the printed versions, somewhat fewer even than in the Latin and French texts, and also fewer laudatory comments regarding Drake and Christopher Carleill, but the MS contains details regarding military actions at various points (e.g., Santiago and Cartagena, pp. 226, n. 6, 253, n. 3) which correspond with those given in the *Leicester* journal. For a variety of reasons, therefore, it can be concluded that Harl. 6221 provides at least a variant of the original account which, with editorial changes, was published as Bigges's *Summarie*.

Within the MS itself are several possible clues as to its origin. On fol. 94, just after the statement on the departure from Plymouth and preceding the list of ships, is the following (see p. 214, n. 2):

'Concerninge whose prosperows successe . . . I thowght best to set downe the Coppie of a letter sent by a gentleman of good accompte to a frind of his, In which the same is without favour, feare, or mallice truly and exactly set downe, agreable also to the reports of sondry credible persons with whom I have conferred.'

The paragraph indicates clearly that Harl. 6221 is a copy from an earlier document. This fact might explain the omission of passages which the copyist thought less interesting, although no attempt at abbreviation is mentioned.

Another clue appears on fol. 94v where, following the listing of the ships, is this paragraph (see p. 217, n. 2):

'Ser I know yow expect earnestly the newes of our passed voyage, and trwe it is that I owe a greater travayle then the writinge of a large dyscowrse, but as my fortune hathe not aforded me the benefitt of the skole to prove any thynge able in this facultie of discowrsynge, so yet to yow as one of my best frinds, I will not refuse to delyver the relation of the substaunce and trewthe of that which is passed, as neare as my knowledge may vndartake, desyringe that my good will to do yow any further service may be well accepted/'

Although the writer does not identify either himself or the person addressed, he had apparently taken part in the expedition, and the copyist evidently found the narrative of sufficient interest to undertake the task. The wording tends to support the assertion by Cates that the account came from the hands of a professional soldier or soldiers, men who had not gone far in formal education. The name of Walter Bigges as one author of the *Summarie* need not therefore be discarded.

Further questions, however, and some possible answers, are raised by the handwriting of the copyist. Although Harl. 6221 is bound among the materials thought to have been in the possession of Ralph Starkey (see Cyril Ernest Wright, *Fontes Harleiana* (London, 1972), p. 314), and fol. 93 bears the initials 'R. St.' and the date '1615', the distinctive handwriting of fols. 94 to 98v is that of the scribe of the *Tiger* journal (Document 6), which was written under the direction of Christopher Carleill. Confirmation on this point has been provided by experts at the Department of Manuscripts of the British Library, and at the Folger Shakespeare Library. See also Plates IX and XI. On the basis of this fact, one may hypothesize that this copy of an interesting narrative of the expedition was made by Carleill's order, perhaps to fill out the 'book' of the voyage which he had planned to keep but had not finished (see p. 71). Was it perhaps intended for the eyes of Carleill's distinguished stepfather, Secretary Walsingham, as a kind of official report on the voyage? Since Walsingham had been active in the planning of the voyage and had been interested in reports concerning it at various stages, one might conjecture further that he or someone close to him decided to use this report as the basic text for whatever published account was to be issued in England and in friendly regions abroad. Thomas Cates, who became the editor of the text printed in London, and who stated that he had served on the voyage in Carleill's own company, might have worked, therefore, under instructions from Mr Secretary. If this was the case, the various editions of the *Summarie* in 1588 and 1589 could be considered as the 'official' account of the voyage, judiciously edited so that it would support the purposes for which the voyage had been planned.

The strongly anti-Spanish feeling which had been so evident in the preparations for the expedition seems indeed to have influenced the plans for publishing the record of its achievements. Cates's dedicatory note, calling attention of the need for all classes to be aware of Spain's enmity toward England, suggests this. The threat of Spain's impending attack in 1588 may have delayed the project in England, but even for the text that was translated for publication in Leyden, there was time to add some passages to round out and embellish a brief original. The delay before publication in London could have permitted still further editing, not merely for the sake of propaganda, but for the incorporation of factual matter from different sources, such as Carleill's despatch to Walsingham regarding early events, or even some of the records from Frobisher's ship, *Primrose*.

An examination of the editorial insertions, if this was indeed what occurred, can be made if the MS variant is considered as the basic text, the two Leyden editions as examples of a partially edited version, and those of London as the final one. The additions to the 'original' fall into three general categories. First, there are factual additions, drawn from the type of source indicated above, such as the incidents on the voyage from Plymouth to Bayona, although they were inserted in incorrect order (see pp. 217–9); the elaborate geographical descriptions of the places that were raided, probably written by men who had been sent out specifically to make observations and to report (cf. p. 228, n. 3); and the account of the negotiations with Lane at Roanoke. Some of these may have been left out of the foreign-language editions because they were thought to be of less interest to non-English readers, although they would be useful for arousing Englishmen's interest in colonial enterprises. Possibly the captains' resolutions at Cartagena, inserted years afterwards by Hakluyt, were not distributed in 1588 and 1589 because they revealed Drake's weakness.

A second kind of addition was the insertion here and there of a name, a phrase, or even a paragraph tending to emphasize the successful leadership of Drake and especially of Carleill (e.g. the stop at Cuba, p. 264). Just as Greepe's ballad ends with elaborate praise for Drake's accomplishments, so it might be expected that praise for the leaders would be added in this account, if only to counterbalance any rumours that the voyage had been less than successful.

The third type of editing is related to bits of anti-Spanish propaganda and appeals to English pride, and these show most clearly in the London editions. Only these tell of the noisy celebration upon the entry into Santiago in the Cape Verdes, for example, with a possible change of date to make it coincide with the queen's coronation anniversary (see p. 227). The desecration of the body of the English straggler there is more vividly described than in the MS variant and the foreign editions (see p. 235); and the famous tale of the Spaniards' brutality toward Drake's negro boy at Santo Domingo, though partially substantiated by the *Primrose* journal, is missing from the MS and from the continental editions (see p. 242). Perhaps the best known example of anti-Spanish propaganda, one which Drake himself recognized as important, is the description of the escutcheon found at Santo Domingo. It was not mentioned in the MS variant, but was included in the Latin and French translations, following closely the wording of the printed English editions (see p. 245). Care seems to have been taken also to see that this item should be set forth dramatically in the Boazio maps (see Note on Maps).

To sum up these evaluations of the texts of the *Summarie and True Discourse*, it seems probable that a narrative, of which Walter Bigges may indeed have been the original author, was considerably edited before any publication occurred. There is the possibility, of course, that his was the longer account, printed without great change by Cates in 1589, but condensed by both the copyist of the Harl. 6221 MS and by the editors or translators for a non-English audience. On the other hand, for a time when the value of propaganda was well recognized, it seems to the present editor that the *Summarie* as it has been known since 1589 may well represent a more or less official report of the voyage, based on Bigges's account, but padded here and there, partly for political, anti-Spanish purposes, and partly to educate the English public as to the nature of the regions that lay beyond the seas.

APPENDIX IV

NOTE ON MAPS

The maps relating to the 1585–86 voyage are of special value, not only as evidence about events, but as examples of the cartographer's art. The importance of having artists on expeditions of the period was recognized, and Richard Hakluyt the elder in 1585 urged that a skilful artist be taken on all voyages of exploration to North America to describe beasts, fish, etc., as well as towns.[1] John White, who had accompanied Frobisher in 1577–78, went out with Grenville to Roanoke in 1585,[2] and the Drake expedition of that year included at least one artist among its personnel.[3] For a venture that was strongly political in nature, drawings of harbours and fortifications at places owned by Spain would be expected.

A rough drawing, evidence of the latter purpose, is the sketch made during the stay at Bayona and Vigo, probably the one sent back by Carleill with his despatch to Walsingham in October 1585. This is the P.R.O. map (MPF 13), approximately $12\frac{1}{4} \times 16\frac{1}{2}$ inches, which has been reproduced as Plate II.[4] The drawing, which clearly shows the signs of having been folded as if in a letter and is crudely done, shows only the outlines of the Bayona islands and harbour, and the river banks inland to a point slightly beyond Vigo. Indicated by a brief key are the place of the first anchorage, of the second, more protected, anchorage near Vigo where the fleet watered, and also the location within Bayona harbour where men were landed briefly. Whether it was drawn by the artist who prepared the finer

---

[1] Paul Hulton and D. B. Quinn, *The American Drawings of John White* (2 vols., London, 1964), I, 34.

[2] Morison, *European Disc. Amer.*, pp. 517, 528–30, 633–6, 641–2.

[3] Drake himself was interested in drawing (Hulton and Quinn, op. cit., I, 34), and others in the expedition, besides the 'official' artist, may have had some skill.

[4] In his despatch Carleill wrote of going in with small boats 'to take the best viewe I might of the place, which I sende herewith described aswell as maybe permitted for the present'. Whether it was a map or a verbal description is not indicated. A note in pencil on the margin of the despatch at the P.R.O. (S.P. 12/183: 10, f. 23) indicates that the enclosure is 'wanting'. Mr P. A. Penfold of the Search Department at the P.R.O. agrees with me that the Bayona–Vigo map (MPF 13) may well be the one to which Carleill referred. Neither the drawing nor the lettering provides a clue for identifying its maker. My original reference to the map was supplied by D. B. Quinn.

maps of places visited later, or by another hand, is impossible to say. It may have been done at Carleill's direction by Boazio, who appears to have been in his company (see below), but no effort seems to have been made afterwards to complete it in a form for publication.

Another manuscript map is a drawing of the Santiago attack that is in the British Library (B.M. Drawing No. 103 C, from the Department of Manuscripts, Egerton MS 2579), reproduced in the present volume as Plate III(A).[1] It resembles the engraved maps of the Santiago action, although it differs in several details and does not agree completely with the account of the action provided in the narratives.[2] If it was by the artist who made the other Santiago maps, then one may surmise that corrections and refinements were made later, in order that the map might more accurately illustrate the *Summarie's* narrative.[3] If this was the case, the Egerton MS map appears to be the first in a series of three representations of the same action (see Plates III(B), (C)).

Most well known are the engraved town plans prepared for the various editions of the *Summarie*, and the general map of the voyage, which may have been planned as a supplement or as a separate item.[4] The latter map bears the name of the artist, Baptista B[oazio], and

[1] This map, with an enlargement of one part, was reproduced in Hulton and Quinn, *The American Drawings of John White*, Plates 155 a and b.

[2] As compared with the engraved maps (see Plates III(B), (C)), this one lacks a key, gives a more crude representation of the ships, representing possibly two different places of anchorage, and provides simpler details on the night march and the formation of the troops for the attack. It locates the little chapel (*BB-25* on the engraved maps) nearer the town, but it also shows more of the interior of the island, including a town, probably the village of Santo Domingo (see p. 231). The figure of the turtle on this drawing shows some resemblance to the turtle of Boazio's Saint Domingo and Saint Augustine maps. It was replaced in the engravings of Santiago by a fish. The imaginary sea creature resembles that on the Saint Domingo and Cartagena Maps.

[3] It is suggested in Hulton and Quinn, *The American Drawings of John White* (p. 132), that this drawing was probably done by the artist of the engraved maps. The more detailed representation of the attacking forces, corresponding well with the *Summarie's* text, would be an example of this sort of change when the engraving was to be done.

[4] The engraved maps are described briefly in George Watson Cole, *Catalogue of Books . . . Library of G. D. Church* (5 vols., N.Y., 1907), Nos. 134A–8 (hereafter, *Church*); in the Wheat-Adams Trial Bibliography (see above, p. 301); in Hans P. Kraus, *Sir Francis Drake* (Amsterdam, 1970), pp. 121–7, 198–9, 214; in Quinn, *Roanoke Voyages*, pp. 34 and 311, n.; and also by D. W. Waters in his introduction to Greepe, *The True and Perfect Newes*, pp. 53–7. Some extant copies of the maps, and also of the broadside letter-press have not been folded. In my study of these maps I am especially indebted to Jeannette D. Black, Curator of Maps, the John Carter Brown Library. The plates for the engraved maps used in this volume are all from copies owned by that library.

the four city maps also are by him, although not until the English edition by Ward did his name appear on the title page of the volume. The town plans present visually not only the military action but many geographical details regarding Santiago in the Cape Verdes, Saint Domingo,¹ Cartagena, and Saint Augustine. Two sets of the four town maps were printed, one being larger than the other (see below), and a key, using numbers or letters for the identifications, was prepared for each. For the larger engravings, the key text was printed in broadside letter-press (either Latin, French, or English) which could be cut and pasted at the bottom of the engraved sheet; but in some instances maps were distributed without that accompanying key. The maps of the smaller size appeared without such a pasted-on key, but had engraved beneath the chart a simple legend – a single or double line in Latin in one state; in a second, with a French translation of the Latin added.² Some of the separate maps, town plans as well as general maps, were coloured by hand.

In the earliest editions the maps were not bound in with the text of the volume, but may have been supplied in a separate pocket or portfolio and afterwards tipped in. The common watermark indicates that at least all of the large town maps were printed at the same time and place. Although the two Leyden editions (1588) had the maps, reference to the mapmaker on the title page did not occur until the English edition of Ward.³ References to the maps in the text were inserted also in the Ward edition;⁴ and in the German edition of the same year the descriptive keys themselves, translated into German with some abbreviation, were printed on pages of the text adjacent to the places at which the small maps were to be inserted.⁵ The preparation of the key in different languages suggests

¹ The town's name is so spelled in the English keys. The Spanish spelling has generally been used elsewhere in the present volume.
² An example of the second state is in an English (Field) edition, No. 136 in *Church*, now owned by the Huntington Library. Examples of the state with the Latin caption only, and used for plates in this volume, are from the German edition at the John Carter Brown Library. That edition inserted a key for the maps in the pages of the narrative text.
³ See p. 210, n. 7, and Appendix III. In Ward's edition instructions for placing the maps were printed below the note about the publishing delay.
⁴ In that edition (pp. 9 and 31), in the descriptions of Santiago and St Augustine, words referring to the specific map are inserted; e.g. (pp. 9-10), 'as in this Plot is plainly shewed.'
⁵ This is true of the volumes of the *Relation oder Beschreibung* . . . (1589) at the B.L.,

that each of the early editions was to be supplied with a key corresponding with the language of its text, but such differentiation was not followed. Among known copies of the Latin edition, one has the letter-press in Latin and another in English, and some have no printed key; few surviving French editions contain maps, but one (at the Huntington Library) has English letter-press. Of the letter-press printed in French, indeed, only one surviving copy is known, and that is in the form of an undivided broadside which never seems to have been attached to a book.¹ Some variations in the texts of the letter-press occur, even among those in English, but, except for the item *II* on the Saint Domingo map,² they are not significant.

As to the town plans, drawn and engraved in two different sizes, there are important differences in detail between the two sets.³ Not only do the smaller ones have simple captions engraved at the bottom instead of letter-press keys,⁴ but they lack an ornate border, have no cartouches, and have fewer embellishments in the way of animals and fish. Since maps of both sizes occur, though not bound in, with the Latin edition of 1588,⁵ and with the London editions of 1589,⁶ no priority regarding date of publication can be established.

---

the John Carter Brown Library, and the New York Public Library. See also *Church*, No. 138. T. De Bry, who used a simplified version of the maps of this edition for his *Grands Voyages*, 'Americana', VIII (1599), omitted some numbers and also reduced the number of items in the descriptive key. Cf. Kraus, *Sir Francis Drake*, pp. 28, 126–7, 198. For this comparison I used the German edition of De Bry (Frankfort, 1599–1623), Part VIII, pp. 20–45, in the Kraus collection.

¹ See below, p. 317, n. 2.

² See below, p. 318.

³ Of the larger size, approx. 39.5 × 53.3 cm. (described in the Trial Bibliography as variant *A*, and 16″ × 21″), some nine full sets are known to be extant. Of the smaller ones, approx. 18.8 × 27.0 cm. (described in the Trial Bibliography as variants *B*, *C*, and *D*, about 7″ × 10″), eight full sets are known, and some incomplete sets. Kraus (*Sir Francis Drake*, p. 198) mentions seven full sets; another set is in a copy of the German *Relation oder Beschreibung* which was advertised in Catalogue 15 (1973) of Nico Israel, Amsterdam. The measurements above were supplied by Jeannette Black. Kraus provides illustrations of both sets and of those in De Bry. See also the dual sets of plates in the present volume.

⁴ See above. The Trial Bibliography variant *D* lacks even a caption.

⁵ Copies at the British Library, the Huntington Library, and the John Carter Brown Library; cf. *Church*, No. 134A. In the Kraus Collection, the Latin *Expeditio* contains three maps of the smaller size. Kraus, *Sir Francis Drake*, p. 198.

⁶ A copy of the earliest Field edition, having four smaller city maps of variant *C*,

A close comparison of details, however, suggests that the smaller engravings come from an earlier set of drawings and that the larger maps represent revisions as well as embellishments, probably done by the same artist. Since no close examination of details seems to have been done previously, the evidence pointing to this view is presented here.

It should be noted first that on the smaller maps numbers rather than letters are used to designate points to be identified, although no printed keys appear with them before the German edition,[1] and that the numbers correspond with the sequence of the letters used on the larger maps, although occasional numbers are missing on the maps themselves. It is significant also that the wording in the cartouche at the left side of each large town plan, in Latin, is almost exactly that of the Latin caption provided for the corresponding smaller map.[2]

If these were the only differences, it might reasonably be concluded that the smaller maps were derived from the larger ones, being simpler in form and with their legends taken from the cartouches. There are, however, some more significant differences. These show most clearly in the maps for Saint Domingo, Cartagena, and Saint Augustine,[3] with the large map in each case showing a significant addition or a correction. The most striking example is that for Saint Domingo. In addition to the generally more ornate appearance of the large map, important changes must be noted for

---

with captions in both Latin and French, is at the Huntington Library. I have used photocopies of these maps for this investigation.

[1] See p. 312 above. The numbers listed in each 'Description' that is inserted in the text of this edition agree exactly with the numbering on the small maps of Santiago and Saint Domingo; they follow the appropriate pattern for Cartagena, even though a few numbers were missed on the map (by the engraver?) and this is true also for Saint Augustine.

[2] There are some differences in abbreviations. Also, for Santiago, whereas the Latin caption of the smaller map refers to *Civitas S. Jacobi*, the cartouche on the larger map begins: *Hoc opidum divi Jacobi*. A similar change shows on the Saint Augustine map, where there are also some slight differences in spelling. See Plates III, VII. In the French caption on the Santiago map (Huntington Library), *Lusitania* (Latin) is erroneously translated as *lombardie*.

[3] The differences in the case of Santiago, while minor, suggest that the smaller one is earlier: (a) the failure of the engraver (or artist?) to show on the larger map the letter *V* for the church although the number *20* is plainly shown on the smaller map; (b) the royal emblem (customarily placed in each drawing on one of the larger ships to represent the flagship) shows clearly on the smaller map but is not reproduced on the larger one.

items *HH, KK* and *MM*, corresponding to numbers *31, 33,* and *35* on the smaller map. The last one *(35)* can probably be explained as a correction, with the figure of the tortoise, omitted from the first set, now being inserted.[1] As to the others, it would appear that space on the right side was needed for the elaborate heraldic design, which follows in close detail the description of the royal escutcheon which Drake seized at Santo Domingo and to which, according to the printed *Summarie,* particular attention is called as an example of King Philip's arrogance.[2] One of the figures replaced by the emblem, *33,* was dropped completely, although *KK* was printed in the letter-press key. The other *(31* or *HH)* was transferred to a different location. The latter change may represent an effort to correct an error,[3] but quite probably it resulted from the desire to make space for an impressive bit of anti-Spanish propaganda.[4]

In the Cartagena maps the larger one shows the insertion of several key letters at places where numbers were missing or incorrectly placed on the smaller one (e.g., *M* for a site not designated by a number; *P* and *Q,* which were shown only as *15; T* for a

[1] It was possibly transferred from the Saint Augustine map (though in reversed position and more carefully drawn), where the number duplicating that of the dolphin indicates a mistake (see Plate VII(A)). On the tortoise see notes on pp. 311, 319.

[2] See above, p. 245. The upper part of the escutcheon follows carefully the heraldry of the Spanish crown.

[3] It is possible that the numbers *31* and *33* were wrongly placed on the small map, and that *33* should have been the 'White Tower', since a building which could be so described shows, without identification, on the large map. (Such a building shows at this place on a map by Johannes Vingboons, *c.* 1665 (Plate 15 in *Monumenta Cartographica,* ed. by F. C. Wieder, the Hague, 1925), although Vingboons, like later artists, may have been following the Boazio drawing.)

As to *HH,* in the large map it identifies a building which was unmarked in the smaller one and is now considerably more impressive. It may have been the chapel referred to in the *Leicester* journal (p. 154), about a mile north of the town, which was used by the Spaniards as a watch tower. Whether it was called Santa Barbara or not I have been unable to discover. That name was most often associated with the large parish church that faced the market place *(AA-24),* and was at such an elevated position that a later official suggested it as a good site for placing guns to defend the harbour (Wright, *Further Eng. Voyages,* p. 222). The English flew a flag from this church soon after they took the city (Castellanos, *Discurso,* p. 294), and it might well have been the artist's intention to identify it on the map. The parish church of Santa Barbara and a corresponding bastion on the city walls that were built later are shown both on the Vingboons drawing and on a late eighteenth-century one which is at the Bibliothèque Nationale, Ge D 8087 (photographs in the Library of Congress Department of Maps and Geography and at the New York Public Library (Manuscript Maps Prior to 1800, French Series, Plate 48)).

[4] See Plates V(A), (B).

missing *18*), and the inclusion of various animals in the countryside, one being a small and rather crudely drawn iguana.[1] More striking is the provision of scenic background for John White's iguana in the inset.[2] A possible correction is the change from a well-defined stretch of wall along the seashore on the Caleta approach to the city to a less formal road.[3]

The Saint Augustine maps reveal still other kinds of change. Some missing key points are clarified (e.g. *I* and *O* are inserted for the missing *9* and *14*); a missing boate is inserted at point *H – 8*; the sign of the compass which, in the small maps had the directions reversed from north to south, is placed in correct position; and the extra creature, two having been given the same number, *15*, is eliminated.[4] In two other respects, however, the larger map does not represent improvement. For the rather realistic dolphin of the smaller map, for which the description under *P* (or *15*) was written, there is the substitution of quite a different creature which has been identified as John White's Dorado fish.[5] Also the flagship, for which the quartered arms of the royal banner show clearly on the smaller map, is less vividly pictured on the larger one.

Although some of the differences noted above may be accounted for by slips that may be expected when copies or new plates are made, the nature of the changes, particularly in the cases of Saint Domingo and Saint Augustine, strongly suggests that the smaller maps pre-date the larger ones, even though both sets appear to have been printed at the same time.[6] Perhaps the smaller ones were considered suitable for fitting into a volume, as in the case of the tipped-in maps of the German edition, whereas the larger ones, with pasted-on letter-press, would require folding and some possible separate packaging.

The relationship of the so-called general map to the others has not been resolved by scholars. It was separately printed under the title,

[1] Near the left-hand border, Plate VI(B).

[2] See p. 319, n. 4 below.

[3] The defences at Cartagena included no such wall.

[4] The figure of the turtle or tortoise was moved to the Saint Domingo map (see above). There is some resemblance to the turtle drawn on the early Santiago map, although the positions are different (see above, p. 311, n. 2). See also p. 319, n. 4 below.

[5] See Kraus, *Sir Francis Drake*, p. 122; and p. 319, n. 4 below.

[6] D. W. Waters commented that the city plans of the smaller maps of the German edition were 'more finely executed' than the others (intro. to Greepe, *The True and Perfect Newes*, p. 54). For some of the military formations they are clearer.

The Famous West Indian Voyadge . . . , and identified as the work of
Baptista B[oazio], and the place names on the map and the text that
is printed in broadside form are in English.[1] Since Boazio was
associated with all five maps, there may have been an expectation
that all might at some time be published together, but most of the
extant copies indicate that this did not occur. The map with its text,
in which the reference for 9 February refers to 'the book or
discourse' of the voyage, could stand alone as evidence of a successful
venture, and its text provides an authentic chronological account of
the major events of the expedition. It may have been published,
perhaps for its propaganda value, during the delay in preparing the
English editions of the *Summarie*.[2]

About Baptista Boazio, the artist whose name is associated with
these five maps, there also has been much conjecture. His name
appeared in full on the title page of the Ward edition of 1589 in
relation to the town plans, and as 'Baptista B' on the general map,
but it has usually been considered that he worked in London from
drawings supplied by some one who had been on the voyage.[3] The
use of the first person 'we' at various points in the general map text
is inconclusive, since there are obvious connections between that
text and the narrative of the *Summarie*.[4] There is, however, another
piece of evidence which has missed the attention of earlier scholars,
and which seems to establish that Boazio was himself a member of
the expedition, travelling in the entourage of the lieutenant general,
Christopher Carleill.

Slight variations occur among the different letter-press keys to

[1] See Plate I, and Document 5, p. 63, n. 1.

[2] Quinn suggested that the general map might have been withheld from the Leyden
publishers for strategic reasons. It has been found, with the text attached, in only one
copy of the *Summarie* (B.L., G. 6509). For further discussion see *Church*, No. 136; the
Wheat-Adams Trial Bibliography; Quinn, *Roanoke Voyages*, pp. 34 and n., 311, n.;
D. W. Waters, intro. to Greepe, *The True and Perfect Newes*, pp. 55–6; notes by
L. C. Wroth in the John Carter Brown Library *Annual Report*, 1939–40, pp. 58–60,
and 1947–48, pp. 17–20; Wright, *Further Eng. Voyages*, p. xiii; and note by S[kelton] in
E. Lynam, *The Mapmaker's Art* (1953), p. 75 n. The German edition (1589), which
includes the smaller town maps, has also a folded engraved map by Hogenberg,
'Americae et proximarum regionus . . . ', which does not show the 1585 voyage.
Cf. *Church*, No. 138, and the Trial Bibliography.

[3] For voyage maps of the period it was customary for the final work before
engraving to be entrusted to a professional cartographer, working from material
brought back by a less skilled artist. Hulton and Quinn, *The American Drawings of
John White*, I, 31.

[4] See above, p. 63, n. 1.

the town maps, most of them of no significance, often simply matters of spelling. For the Saint Domingo map, however, the text has three variants for the item *II*, two of them in English texts and one in French. These relate to a messenger whom Drake sent inland to confer with the city's officials. One English version reads: 'The way which a messenger went from the Generall vp into the countrie to the Lord President of Saint Domingo, being some 12. miles distant from the citie.'[1] Another English text reads: 'The way which *Baptist* the Lieutenant Generals Page went as Messenger from the Generall vp into the countrey to the Lord President. . . .'[2] More explicit is the French text: 'Le chemin par lequel *Baptista Boazio* page de l'lieutenat general fut messagier, envoyé par le general au gouerneur de S. Domingo.'[3]

Nothing is known of Boazio before the appearance of his name in connection with the 1585–86 maps.[4] Since the elder Hakluyt had been urging that a skilful artist be taken on any voyage of exploration to North America, Walsingham, working with Drake and Carleill on the plans for this voyage, had probably decided that one should go. It may be conjectured that Boazio was a young man whose talents had come to the attention of these men – possibly Carleill had met him previously in London or on the continent, or perhaps he was known even by John White, who went that year with Grenville – and that he was assigned a place among Carleill's attendants in order that his skills might be utilized.[5] An Italian, he

---

[1] See Plate opp. p. 28 in the facsimile edition of the *Summarie* (from the map of the B.L., G. 6509), published by Theatrum Orbis Terrarum, Ltd., Amsterdam, 1969.

[2] See Plate V(B) from the John Carter Brown Library copy. This is the form also in an undivided broadside English text owned by the Free Library of Philadelphia (see Plate VIII(A)).

[3] See Plate VIII(B). This is from the rare undivided broadside formerly owned by W. Elkins, and now in the Free Library of Philadelphia. Although several parts of the key were abbreviated for the French translation (e.g. the descriptions for the animals *LL* and *MM*), for some reason the full name of Boazio is given. Possibly he had some reputation on the continent.

[4] See Edward Lynam, *British Museum Quarterly*, XI (1937), 92–5; Leo Bagrow, *History of Cartography*, rev. and enl. by R. A. Skelton (London, 1964), p. 232; and Appendix II, Personnel.

[5] He may indeed have sought the place, since the venture had attracted wide interest (see above, p. 13). Boazio seems to have cultivated connections with various court personages. He was later associated with Essex, as his maps for Cadiz, the Azores, and Ireland indicate (E. Lynam, *British Museum Quarterly*, XI (1937), 93); and he sent at least one map to Robert Cecil about 1601 or 1602 (H.M.C., *Salisbury MSS*, XIV, 195). See also E. Lynam, *British Maps and Map-Makers* (London, 1947), pp. 16, 25; E. Lynam,

may have had some knowledge of Spanish as well, as his employment at Santo Domingo suggests.[1] His artistic skills may have been used as early as the stop at Bayona, although no finished map comparable to the later ones resulted (see above). His Cartagena map was probably the one that was referred to by the writer of the newsletter,[2] and was possibly the one referred to in Alonso Bravo's deposition, although that may have been one which Drake used in planning the attack, or on which Drake himself had worked.[3]

It has been established that various drawings of fish and animals on the large maps were borrowed from John White, the artist of the first Roanoke colony who returned with Drake's fleet to England. The supposition is that the two artists may have compared their materials during the homeward voyage, with the result that White's finer work on animals replaced in several instances the somewhat cruder efforts of the other.[4]

On the identity of the engraver of the maps I have made no special study. It has been suggested that Jodocus Hondius, the Amsterdam engraver who was at this time in London, may have done the work.[5]

The Mapmaker's Art (London, 1953), pp. 75–8; *Maps and Plans in the Public Record Office*, I (1967), Nos. 1943, 3725; E. G. R. Taylor, *Late Tudor and Early Stuart Geography* (London, 1934), pp. 197, 199, 208, 210, 218; and R. V. Tooley, *Map Collectors' Circle*, II (1965), pt 16, p. 41.

[1] A Spanish official stated that Latin, French, and Italian were used in negotiations with Drake there. Cf. p. 31, n. 1.

[2] Its writer, who seems also to have been an associate of Carleill's, mentions a model or plan of the Cartagena attack (see p. 112 above). If the newsletter was planned for Walsingham (see p. 106, n. 5). the drawing might well have been by Boazio, also in Carleill's employ.

[3] Alonso Bravo deposed that he planned to send to the King of Spain a map showing how the city's defences could have been prepared. He added, 'It is exactly like the one the English captain carries.' Wright, *Further Eng. Voyages*, p. 116. Drake's own interest in drawing is pointed out in Hulton and Quinn, *The American Drawings of John White*, I, 34.

[4] See Quinn, *Roanoke Voyages*, pp. 34–5; Hulton and Quinn, *The American Drawings of John White*, I, 7, 15–16, 31, 34; II, Plate 158. Identified as White's drawings on the 1585–86 maps are (a) the trigger fish or sea coney of the general map; (b) the flying fish (GG) of the Santiago map; (c) the alligator of the Saint Domingo map; (d) the iguana of the Cartagena map; and (e) the 'dolphin' of the Saint Augustine map. Each of the references is to the larger version of the Boazio maps. Not considered to be White's is the turtle of Saint Domingo, the one which may have been shown by error on the smaller map for Saint Augustine (see above); the dolphin of that smaller map was not reproduced in any larger one.

[5] Lynam, *British Maps and Map-Makers*, p. 26; Trial Bibliography; Wright, *Further Eng. Voyages*, p. xiii.

Possibly Thomas Cockson, who engraved Boazio's Cadiz map of 1596, might also be considered,[1] although Cockson usually identified his work with his own initials.[2]

[1] In Arthur M. Hind, *Engraving in England* (3 vols., London, 1952–64), I, Plate 133, is a detail from the Cadiz map which is signed by Cockson and which bears the note: 'Baptista Boazio made this description 1596.' The full map, with a pasted-on key at the bottom, is reproduced in the Navy Records Society Naval Miscellany I (1902), J. S. Corbett, ed., *The Voyage to Calis . . . by Sir W. Slyngisbie*, pp. 23–92. The style of the map and the arrangements of the key strongly resemble those of the maps of 1585–86. I am indebted to Jeannette Black for this suggestion.

[2] This comment on Cockson's initials is from P. H. Hulton.

BIBLIOGRAPHY

(Unless stated otherwise, London is the place of publication of printed works.)

A. *Manuscripts*

Public Record Office, London
 Exchequer records (1584–87)
  Declared accounts from the Pipe Office: E 351/2222, 2223, 2224
  Declared accounts from the Audit Office: A.O. 1/1685/20, 20A, 21
  Maps: M P F 13
  Privy Council Register: P.C. 2/14
  State Papers, Domestic: SP 12/180, 183, 185, 186, 187, 188, 189, 191, 195, 202
  State Papers, Ireland: SP 63/112
British Library (formerly British Museum), Department of Manuscripts
 Cotton MSS Otho E. VIII; Titus B. VIII
 Egerton MS 2579
 Harley MSS 167, 364, 2202, 6221
 Lansdowne MSS 51, 52, 100
 Royal MSS 7.C.xvi; 18A.lxvi
Folger Shakespeare Library
 Folger MS L.b.344

B. *Printed Sources*

Acts of the Privy Council of England [1542–1604]. 32 vols. 1890–1907.
ANDREWS, KENNETH RAYMOND, ed. *Elizabethan Privateering Voyages, 1588–1595.* Hakluyt Society. 1959.
——, *The Last Voyage of Drake & Hawkins.* Hakluyt Society. 1972.
ARBER, EDWARD, ed. *A Transcript of the Registers of the Company of Stationers of London, 1554–1640.* 5 vols. P.P. 1875–94.
BIGGES, WALTER [et al.]. *Expeditio Francisci Draki Equitis Angli in*

321

Indias Occidentales A. M. D. LXXXV . . . Additis passim regionum locorumque omnium tabulis Geographicis quam accuratissimis. Leydae, apud Fr. Raphelengium, 1588. Another edition in *Narrationes Duae Admodum Memorabiles.* Noribergae, 1590.

BIGGES, WALTER [*et al.*]. *Le Voyage de Messire François Drake Chevalier, aux Indes Occidentales L'An M.D. LXXXV . . . Avecq Cartes Geographiques de Tout.* Leyden, Fr. de Raphelengien, 1588.

——, *Relation oder Beschreibung der Rheiss und Schiffahrt auss Engellandt in die . . . Indien gethan, durch Einen Englischen Ritter Franciscum Drack genant . . .* [with maps]. [Cologne], 1589.

——, *A Summarie and True Discourse of Sir Frances Drakes West Indian Voyage.* Richard Field, 1589.

——, *A Summarie and True Discourse of Sir Frances Drakes West Indian Voyage . . . With Geographical Mappes.* R. Field, 1589.

——, *A Summarie and True Discourse of Sir Frances Drakes West Indian Voyage . . . With Geographicall Mappes . . . diligently made by Baptista Boazio.* Roger Ward, 1589.

——, *A Summarie and True Discourse of Sir Frances Drakes West Indian Voyage . . . With Geographicall Mappes.* William Ponsonby, 1596.

B[ROWNE] I[OHN], MARCHANT. *The Marchants Avizo.* [1589]. Ed. by Patrick MacGrath. Boston, Mass., [1957].

BLAEU, WILLIAM JANSZOON. *The Light of Navigation.* Amsterdam, 1912. Ed. by R. A. Skelton. [Amsterdam, 1964].

BOURNE, WILLIAM. *A Regiment for the Sea.* Ed. by E. G. R. Taylor. Hakluyt Society. 1963.

BRY, THEODORE DE. *America*, Part VIII. 'Beschreibung der andern Reyss und Kriegssrustung oder Shiffahrt dess Francisci Draken . . . [1585-1586].' Frankfort, 1599. Also an edition in Latin, [Frankfort], 1599.

Calendar of State Papers, Domestic, 1581-1590. 1865. *Addenda, 1580-1625.* 1872.

Calendar of State Papers, Foreign, 1584-1585. 1916. *1585-1586.* 1921. *1586-1588.* Part 1. 1927. Part 2 [*1586-1587*]. 1927.

Calendar of State Papers, Ireland, 1574-1585. 1867.

Calendar of State Papers, Spanish, 1580-1586. 1896.

Calendar of State Papers, Venetian, 1581-1591. 1894.

CARLEILL, CHRISTOPHER. 'A Briefe and Summary Discourse upon the Intended Voyage to the Hithermost Parts of America', printed in Hakluyt, *Principal Navigations* (1903–1905), VIII, 134–47.

CASTELLANOS, JUAN DE. *Discurso de el Captitán Francisco Draque . . . 1586–1587.* [Extracted from Part 3 of his *Elegias.* Ed. with historical intro. by Angel Gonzalez Palencia.] Madrid, 1921.

CORBETT, JULIAN S., ed. *Papers Relating to the Navy during the Spanish War 1585–1587.* Navy Records Society XI. 1898.

——, ed., *The Voyage to Calis . . . by Sir W. Slyngsbie.* Navy Records Society Miscellany I. 1902.

D'EWES, SIMONDS, ed. *The Journals of All the Parliaments during the Reign of Queen Elizabeth. . . .* 1682.

Fugger News-Letters, The. Ed. by Victor von Klarwill. First Ser., trans. [1924], Second Ser., trans. [1926].

GREEPE, THOMAS. *The True and Perfecte Newes of the Worthy and Valiant Exploytes Performed and Donne by . . . Syr Frauncis Drake: Not Onely at Santo Domingo and Carthagena, But Also Now at Cales . . . , 1587.* [1587]. Facsimile edition, with intro. by D. W. Waters. Hartford, 1955.

GREVILLE, FULKE. *The Life of the Renowned Sir Philip Sidney. . . .* 1652. Ed. by Nowell Smith. Oxford, 1907.

HAKLUYT, RICHARD. 'Discourse of Western Planting', in *Original Writings . . . of the Two Richard Hakluyts.* Hakluyt Society. 1935.

——, *Principal Navigations, Voiages, Traffiques, and Discoveries,* 3 vols. 1598–1600. 12 vols. Glasgow, 1903–5.

HAWKINS, RICHARD. *The Observations of Sir Richard Hawkins.* Ed. by J. A. Williamson. 1933.

HISTORICAL MANUSCRIPTS COMMISSION: *Calendar of the Manuscripts of Lord De L'Isle and Dudley.* II. 1934.

——, *Calendar of the Manuscripts of . . . the Marquess of Salisbury . . . Hatfield House.* Part III. 1889. Part XIV. 1923.

——, *Calendar of the Manuscripts of the Duke of Rutland.* Twelfth Report, App. IV–V. 1888, 1891.

HULTON, PAUL and QUINN, DAVID B. *The American Drawings of John White,* 2 vols. 1964.

LACOUR, LOUIS, ed. *Mémoire du Voiage en Russie Fait en 1586 par Jehan Sauvage Suivi de L'Expedition de Fr. Drake en Amérique a la Même Epoque.* Paris, 1855.

LANE, RALPH. 'An Account of the Particularities of the Imploy-

ments of the English men Left in Virginia . . . [1585–1586]',
in Hakluyt, *Principal Navigations* (1903–5), Vol. VIII.

LAUGHTON, JOHN KNOX, ed. *State Papers Relating to the Defeat of
the Spanish Armada Anno 1588*. Navy Records Society I–II. 1894.

LENG, ROBERT. 'Sir Francis Drake's memorable service . . . in
1587.' Ed. by Clarence Hopper. *Camden Miscellany* v (O.S.
LXXXVII), 1864.

Map Texts: Map Text in English, accompanying *The Famous West
Indian Voyadge* . . . by Baptista B[oazio]. [1589]. One copy in
the British Library Field ed. of *A Summarie and True Discourse*.

——: Undivided broadside of the English text for the four town
plans [1588?], owned by The Free Library of Philadelphia.

——: Undivided broadside of the French text for the four town
plans [1588?], owned by The Free Library of Philadelphia.

MURDIN, WILLIAM, ed. *Collection of State Papers . . . Lord Burghley*.
2 vols. 1740–59.

OPPENHEIM, MICHAEL, ed. *The Naval Tracts of Sir William Monson*.
5 vols. Navy Records Society. Vol. 1, 1902.

ORTELIUS, ABRAHAM. *Epistulae*. Ed. by J. H. Hessels. Cambridge,
1887.

QUINN, DAVID B., ed. *The Roanoke Voyages*. 2 vols. Hakluyt
Society. 1955.

——, ed. *The Voyages and Colonising Enterprises of Sir Humphrey
Gilbert*. 2 vols. Hakluyt Society. 1940.

SIMÓN, FRAY PEDRO. *Noticias Historiales de las Conquistas de Tierra
Firme*. [1623]. Excerpts ed. by G. Jenner, *English Historical
Review*, XVI (1901), 46–66.

TAYLOR, E. G. R., ed. *The Original Writings and Correspondence of
the Two Richard Hakluyts*, 2 vols. Hakluyt Society. 1935.

——, ed. *The Troublesome Voyage of Captain Edward Fenton*. Hakluyt
Society. 1959.

WIEDER, F. C., ed. *Monumenta Cartographica: Reproductions of
Unique and Rare Maps. . . .* The Hague, 1925—. Includes Santo
Domingo map by Johannes Vingboons, *c. 1665*.

WRIGHT, IRENE A., ed. *Further English Voyages to Spanish America*.
Hakluyt Society. 1951.

C. Secondary Works

ANDREWS, KENNETH RAYMOND. 'Appraisements of Elizabethan Privateers-men.' *Mariner's Mirror*, XXXVII (1951), 76–9.

ANDREWS, KENNETH RAYMOND. *Drake's Voyages: A Reassessment of Their Place in Elizabethan Maritime Expansion*. 1967.

——, *Elizabethan Privateering* . . . [1585–1603]. Cambridge, 1964.

BAGROW, LEO. *History of Cartography*, rev. and enl. by R. A. Skelton. 1964.

BOULIND, RICHARD. 'Shipwreck and Mutiny in Spain's Galleys on the Santo Domingo Station, 1583.' *Mariner's Mirror*, LVIII (1972), 297–330.

BRADFORD, ERNLE. *Drake*. 1965.

CALLENDAR, GEOFFREY. 'Fresh Light on Drake.' *Mariner's Mirror*, IX (1923), 16–28.

——, 'Drake and His Detractors.' *Mariner's Mirror*, VII (1921), 66–74, 98–105, 142–52.

CAMDEN, WILLIAM. *The History of the Most Renowned and Victorious Princess Elizabeth* . . . , 1688. (Fourth edition of his *Annales*, 1615.)

CHENEY, C. R., ed. *Handbook of Dates for Students of English History*. 1945. 1955.

COLE, GEORGE WATSON. *A Catalogue of Books Relating to the Discovery and Early History of North and South America* . . . [in] *the Library of E. D. Church*. 5 vols. New York, 1907.

CORBETT, JULIAN S. *Drake and the Tudor Navy*. 2 vols. 1898. 1899.

——, *Sir Francis Drake*. 1890.

Dictionary of National Biography.

DUNCAN, T. BENTLEY. *Atlantic Islands: Madeira, the Azores, and the Cape Verdes in Seventeenth Century Commerce and Navigation*. Chicago, 1972.

GLASGOW, THOMAS, JNR. 'List of Ships . . . 1539–1588.' *Mariner's Mirror*, LVI (1970), 299–307.

HIND, ARTHUR M. *Engraving in England*. 3 vols. 1952–1964.

HOWELL, ROGER. *Sir Philip Sidney*. 1968.

HUTH, HENRY. *Catalogue of the Famous Library of* . . . *Henry Huth*. 9 vols. [1911–20].

JAMESON, A. K. 'Some New Spanish Documents.' *English Historical Review*, XLIX (1934), 14–31.

JENNER, G. 'A Spanish Account of Drake's Voyages.' *English Historical Review*, XVI (1901), 146–66.

JONES, ELDRED D. *The Elizabethan Image of Africa*. Folger Shakespeare Library. 1971.

KEELER, MARY FREAR. *The Long Parliament, 1640–1641*. Philadelphia, 1954.

KRAUS, HANS P. *Sir Francis Drake, a Pictorial Biography*. With a historical intro. by D. W. Waters and Richard Boulind. N. Israel, Amsterdam, 1970.

LYNAM, EDWARD. 'Boazio's Map of Ireland, *circa* 1600.' *British Museum Quarterly*, XI (1937), 92–5.

——, *British Maps and Map-Makers*. 1947.

——, *The Mapmaker's Art*. 1953.

MALTBY, WILLIAM S. *The Black Legend in England: The Development of Anti-Spanish Sentiment, 1558–1660*. Duke University Press, 1971.

MARIÉJOL, JEAN HIPPOLYTE. *The Spain of Ferdinand and Isabella*. Trans. and ed. by Benjamin Keen. New Brunswick, N.J., 1961.

MARSDEN, R. G. 'The Vice Admirals of the Coast.' *English Historical Review*, XXII (1907), 468–77; XXIII (1908), 736–57.

MATTINGLY, GARRETT. The *Armada*. Boston, 1959.

MERRIAM, ROGER BIGELOW. *The Rise of the Spanish Empire*. 4 vols. 1918–34. 1962.

METEREN, EMANUEL VAN. *Historia Belgica*. [Antwerp, 1598, 1600?]. Included in *Historie der Nederlandscher*. Delft, 1599, 1609, 1611.

MORISON, SAMUEL ELIOT. *The European Discovery of America: The Northern Voyages*. New York, 1971.

NEALE, JOHN E. *Queen Elizabeth*. 1934.

NEWTON, ARTHUR PERCIVAL. *The European Nations in the West Indies 1493–1688*. 1933.

PARKS, G. B. 'Frobisher's Third Voyage, 1578.' *Huntington Library Bulletin*, VII (1935), 181–90.

PARRY, J. H. *The Spanish Seaborne Empire*. 1966.

POLLARD, G. W. and REDGRAVE, G. R. *A Short-Title Catalogue of Books Printed in England, Scotland, and Ireland . . . 1475–1640*. 1926.

POLLITT, RONALD, 'John Hawkins's Troublesome Voyages.' *Journal of British Studies*, XII (1973), 26–40.

QUINN, DAVID B. 'Some Spanish Reactions to Elizabethan Colonial Enterprises.' *Royal Historical Society Transactions*, 5th Ser., I (1951), 1–23.

READ, CONYERS. *Mr. Secretary Walsingham and the Policy of Queen Elizabeth.* 3 vols. Oxford, 1925.

REBHOLZ, RONALD A. *The Life of Fulke Greville First Lord Brooke.* Oxford, 1971.

ROWSE, A. L. *The Elizabethans and America.* New York, 1959.

SCAMMEL, G. V. 'Shipowning in the Economy and Politics of Early Modern England.' *Historical Journal*, XV (1972), 385–407.

STONE, LAWRENCE. *The Crisis of the Aristocracy, 1558–1640.* Oxford. 1965.

TAYLOR, E. G. R. *Late Tudor and Early Stuart Geography.* 1934.

TOOLEY, R. V. *Maps and Map-Makers.* 1949. 1952.

——, ed. *Map Collectors' Circle.* 1963–

WATERS, D. W. 'The Art of Navigation.' Appendix in K. R. Andrews, *The Last Voyage of Drake & Hawkins.* Hakluyt Society. 1972.

——, 'The Elizabethan Navy and the Armada Campaign.' *Mariner's Mirror*, XXXV (1949), 90–138.

WERNHAM, R. B. 'Elizabethan War Aims and Strategy,' Ch. XII in *Elizabethan Government and Society*, ed. by S. T. Bindoff et. al. 1961.

WHEAT, J. C. and ADAMS, RANDOLPH G. 'Trial Bibliography of Walter Bigges' Narrative of Sir Francis Drake's West Indian Voyage of 1585–1586, and Boazio's Maps Related Thereto.' Unpublished. [Ann Arbor, 1935]. Presently at the John Carter Brown Library, Providence, R. I.

WILLIAMSON, JAMES A. 'Books on Drake.' *History*, XII (1928), 310–21.

——, *Hawkins of Plymouth.* 1949.

——, *Sir John Hawkins. The Time and the Man.* Oxford, 1927.

WOODWARD, JOHN. *A Treatise on Heraldy, British and Foreign.* 2 vols. 1896.

WROTH, LAWRENCE C. Notes on the editions of the Walter Bigges narrative and the Boazio maps in *The John Carter Brown Library Annual Report*, 1939–40, 1942–43, 1947–48, 1948–49.

INDEX

INDEX

340

INDEX

Harte, John, alderman of London, 13*n5*, 56, 60*n1*

Hatteras, 285

Hatton, Sir Christopher, vice chamberlain 12, 16, 49, 49*n8*, 52*n3*, 292

Havana, 6, 27, 33, 38, 68, 113*n6*, 204*n4*, 205, 263*n1*

Hawkins, [Sir] John, treasurer of the navy, advocate of colonial ventures and voyages, 9*n3*, 12, 52*n3*; assists with 1585 preparations, 54, 56; assists with appraisals and audits, 56, 60*n1*; naval accounts of, 283, 286; ships owned by, 14, 15, 283, 286, 287, 288, 294; son Richard, 16; also, 269, 269*n10*, 295

Hawkins, Richard, captain of the *Duck*, 217, 281, 288, 295; his return to England, 40, 40*n4*, 62*n4*, 273*n1*, 295; son of John, 16

Hawkins, William, senior, captain designate of the *Sea Dragon*, his 1582 voyage, 190*n4* (*see also* Voyages; promoter and adventurer in voyage plans, 12, 52*n3*; assists with preparations, 54; his removal from a captaincy, 48; also, 234, 284, 295, 299

Hawkins, William, junior, captain of the *Hawkins*, 16, 50, 83, 216, 281, 287, 295

Hayna River (Hispaniola), 66*n6*, 101*nn 1 and 4*, 238*n4*

Health, Drake's concern about, 99; *see also* Sickness

Heathen practices, 141

Hedgehog, 176*n2*

Henley (Henly), possible author of the *Primrose* journal, 5, 179*n3*, 210, 295

Heneage, Thomas, of London, 13*n5*

Henry III, King of France, 25*n4*, 77*n3*

Hens, 194, 237*n2*

Heraldic design, 315, 316

Herbert, Henry, second earl of Pembroke 12*n6*

Herbs, 229

Heriza, Captain, *see* Erisey, James

Herne, Griffith, shipmaster, 272*n3*, 295

Herring, 133

Hicacos Point (Cartagena), 33*n5*, 161*nn*

Hidalgo Montemayor, Don Diego, Spanish governor of Santa Maria

and investigating judge at Cartagena, 6, 34*n1*, 163*nn*, 176*n1*, 203*n2*, 258*n1*, 295

Hides, 59, 112, 155, 155*n2*, 193, 197, 246, 247, 262

Hierro, *see* Ferro

Hispaniola, 29, 111, 157*n6*, 237, 246, 255*n4*; arrival at, 66, 100*n6*, 111; defences of, 195*n2*; economy of, 246; importance of, 198; natives of, 101*n3*; warnings from, 105*n1*; *see also* Santo Domingo

Hogs, 181

Hogsheads, 46, 47

Holy Gospel, 140, 141

Hondius, Jocodus, engraver, 319

Honey, 47, 221*n2*

Hoops, wooden, 84, 84*n4*

Horsemen, 101, 112, 126, 148, 154, 156, 162, 164, 181, 189, 199, 231, 239, 248, 250

Horses, 115, 148, 154, 188, 269

Hospital, 136, 187, 235

Hostages, at Cartagena, 37, 37*n3*, 175, 176-7; at Vigo, 26, 87, 89, 109, 183, 292

Household goods, 182, 221, 255*n4*

House of Commons, *see* Parliament

Houses, 130, 167, 197

Howard, Charles, second Lord Howard of Effingham, lord high admiral, 45*n1*, 51; adventurer in the voyage and ship owner, 11, 12, 15, 16, 49, 286

Hunsdon, Henry Carey, Lord, *see* Carey, Henry

Hurstpierpoint (Sussex), 294

Hussey, I., on auditing commission, 13*n5*, 60*n1*

Iguanas, 204, 316

Illness in English fleet, *see* Fever, Sickness; in Spanish relief fleet, 37*n2*

Images, religious, 181, 187, 194, 197, 209

Impressment, 255*n4*

Indians, at Cartagena, 33, 162*n1*, 163*n2*, 164, 164*nn*, 250*n6*, 252; in Hispaniola 198, 198*n1*, 246, 246*n5*; in Florida, 38, 115*n4*, 206, 206*n4*, 207, 208, 209; also, 236*n5*, 254

Indian slave from Cuba, 32*n6*

341

Ogle, Thomas, steward of the *Talbot* (or *Aid*,) 111, 148, 148*n1*, 189, 243, 243*n2*, 300

Oil, 28, 47, 110, 112, 139, 149, 155, 185, 187, 190, 194, 200, 221, 228, 247

Olennoise (*Ollenoise*) ships, *see* Sables d'Olonne

Olives (Oliffes), 187, 201, 228, 247

Onions, 84, 138, 229

Opinions regarding the voyage, 42

Oranges, 138, 181, 187, 193, 198, 201, 229

Orange trees, 262

Orchards, 262

Orders, for the fleet, 19, 71, 71*n1*, 82, 82*n2*, 264 (*see also* Articles for the fleet); concerning obedience, 21, 110 (*see also* Oaths); concerning pillage, 130-1, 138, 138*n6*; royal, 51-3

Ordnance, brass and iron, 55, 56, 57, 62, 110, 113, 115, 136-7, 190, 197, 201, 208, 232, 268*n3*, 276-7; English use of, 83, 113, 194, 206, 227, 242, 265; naval, 53, 57, 57*n1*; Spaniards' use of, 102, 102*n2*, 104, 105, 105*n6*, 112, 128, 134, 160*n3*, 162, 162*n5*, 165*n6*, 198, 199, 201, 240, 247, 248, 250*n3*, 267; taken by the English, 28, 39, 50*n5*, 31, 111, 149, 156*n5*, 167, 186, 188, 227, 227*n1*, 244*nn*, 275*n1*, 276-7; transport of, 38, 106, 137, 170, 202, 262; valuation of, 57, 58, 62, 186

Oristan, 208*n8*

Orive (Oribe) Salazar, Tristan de, merchant at Cartagena, 36*n3*, 166, 166*nn*, 176, 177

Ortelius, Abrahamus, 40*n5*

Osorio, Don Diego, captain of the royal galley at Santo Domingo, 101*n2*, 156*n1*, 195*n2*, 243, 243*n1*

Our Lady of the Borge, 81*n3*, 181*n4*

Ovalle, Licentiate Cristóbal de, president of the *Audiencia* at Santo Domingo, 30, 30*n3*, 101*n3*, 154*n5*, 156*n5*, 241*n5*

Overcrowding of ships, 99*n3*

Oxen, 197, 246

Oxford, the earl of, *see* Vere, Edward de, seventeenth earl of Oxford

Oxford, the university of, 296

Oxfordshire, 50

Oynions, *see* Onions

Oysters, 202, 207

Ozama River (Santo Domingo), 29, 194, 241, 241*n5*

Pacific Ocean, 37*n4*

Palace, the royal, at Santo Domingo, 241*n2*

Palavicino, Horatio, English agent in Germany, 44

Palma, island of, arrival and action at, 27, 64, 110, 126-7, 128-9, 184; description of, 129; Drake's intentions regarding, 94, 126, 185, 185*n5*, 223; fleet fired upon, 94, 94*n2*, 110, 128-9, 223; fortifications at, 129, 184, 223; also, 93, 106*n5*, 109*n7*, 125*n6*, 128, 131

Panama, Isthmus of, 11*n7*, 37, 174*n1*, 255

Papal "bulls", 76, 76*n2* for

Paper, 169

Papists, 11*n8*, 77

Paragoses, *see* Porgy

Parleys, at Bayona, 26, 108, 181, 219; at Cartagena, 166; at Dominica, 191-2; at Ferro, 185; at Santiago, 98, 230; at Vigo, 26, 86*n3*, 109, 182, 222, 222*n5*, 223*n1*; *see also* Ransoms, negotiations for

Parliament, English, 10, 52*n2*, 296

Parliament of the Indies, 198

Parrots, 237*n2*

Partisan (a weapon), 155

Pasaje (Passadge), town of, 75, 76, 218

Passadge, *see* Pasaje

Pearls, 56, 159, 197; in ransoms, 156, 167; valuation of, 57-8, 58*n2*, 178

Pease, 47

Pecos (peces), *see* pesos

Pelicans, 193

Pell mell, 241, 251, 251*n8*

Pembroke, earl of, *see* Herbert, Henry, earl of Pembroke

Penalities for violating rules, 96, 130, 169-70

Pepper, 197, 201

Perriers (ordnance), 102*n5*

Perrot, Sir John, lord deputy in Ireland, 291

Personnel, 12, 15-18, 290-300

Pertius Breton, 77*n3*

Peru, 11*n4*, 127*n2*, 184, 263*n1*

Peso de oro, 259*n2*

INDEX

Seamen, 139*n*7, 173, 250*n*5, 257; *see also* Mariners
Seashore, 251, 251*n*1
Secretary, Drake's *see* Cottell
Secretary, Mr., 106*n*5, 108, 111; *see also* Walsingham, Sir Francis
Sedition, 143; *see also* Mutiny
Seelie(y), Captain, *see* Cely, Thomas
Sentinel, 257
Sergeant major, the 47*n*4, 139, 174, 177, 214; *see* Powell, Anthony
Sermon, 142
Serpents, 204
Seville, 157*n*4, 289
Sharpe, —, a merchant, *see* Short
Sheep, 185, 197
Sheriff (high), of Santo Domingo, 153*n*1
Shillings, 259*n*2
Ships, airing of, 29; captains, 48–50 (*also* Captains—sea); logs and journals, 4–6, 23, 73*n*5, 116*n*1; masters (*see* Masters); owners of, 13–14, 283–9; steward of, 148, 189; watches on, 119, 120–5; *see also* Fleet; and Men, complement per ship
Ships, named:
Aid (royal ship), 14, 16, 45, 48, 53, 54, 54*n*3, 128, 144, 147, 148*n*1, 216, 280, 283, 284, 291
Benjamin, 15*n*4, 46, 90*n*3, 157, 216, 281, 287, 296, 297
Bonaventure, see *Elizabeth Bonaventure*
Bond, a bark, 46, 49, 145, 145*n*2, 216, 280, 286, 292
Bonner, a bark, 46, 49, 145, 145*n*2, 174, 216, 274*n*1, 281, 286, 293
"Burton bark", *see* Drake
Capitana (Sp. galley), 104*n*1
Drake (French "Burton" prize, *La Magdelaine*), 15, 16, 25, 77*n*3, 91*n*2, 120*n*5, 180*n*6, 184*n*1, 216, 216*n*5, 218, 281, 282, 289
Drake of London, 289
Duck, the galley, 15, 16, 46, 83, 84, 217, 219*n*3, 273*n*1, 281, 288, 295
Dudley (in Armada), 293
Elizabeth, or *Elizabeth Drake*, 15, 89, 216*n*6, 282, 288, 289, 299
Elizabeth Bonaventure, royal ship, "admiral" of the fleet, 14, 16, 45, 48, 53, 54, 122*n*1, 128–9, 133, 133*n*2, 215*n*2, 216, 280, 284, 289, 293

Elizabeth Fownes (1588), 289
Elizabeth Jonas (1588), 284
Francis, 14, 15, 15*n*6, 40*n*2, 46, 50, 62*n*4, 84, 92, 92*n*1, 93, 94, 95, 120*n*3, 122, 144, 145, 145*n*2, 149*n*4, 150*n*5, 185*n*4, 216, 238, 257*n*3, 272, 272*nn*, 273, 281, 287
George, 46, 91, 122, 183, 216, 216*n*6, 257*n*3, 281, 288, 299
George Bonaventure, London merchantman, 77*n*1, 86, 89, 180*n*7
Golden Hind (1577), 49*n*8
Hastings, a bark, *see Thomas*, alias *Hastings*
Hawkins, a bark, 46, 50, 81, 81*n*6, 83, 94, 95, 108*n*9, 150, 150*n*5, 156, 185*n*4, 216, 221, 281, 282, 286, 295, 305
Hope, 15*n*4, 16, 46, 50, 93, 94, 95, 127*n*4, 128, 157, 185*n*4, 216, 281, 286, 290
Hope, the new, 112, 157, 158
Hope, royal ship, 286
Hope Hawkins (1588), 286, 298
Jonas, a London ship, 90*n*4
La Magdelaine, French prize, *see* Drake
Leicester (*Lettice Leicester*), the galleon, "rear admiral" of the fleet, 4, 14, 15, 16, 22, 45, 47*n*4, 48, 91, 94, 110, 116*n*1, 119, 128, 134*n*7, 137, 144*n*4, 149, 165*n*4, 215*n*2, 216, 253*n*6, 280, 283, 296, 298, 299
Marigold (*Mary Goolld*), of Hampton, 77*n*1
Mathew, 15, 46, 281, 288
Minion of London, (1588) 285
Minion of Plymouth, 14, 16, 45, 49, 71, 216, 280, 285, 291, 300
Napolitana, Spanish frigate, 104*n*1, 201*n*5
New Year's Gift, ship taken at Santo Domingo, 15, 31, 36, 105, 106, 112, 113, 157, 170, 202, 202*n*6, 262, 281, 282, 289
Ocasion, Spanish galley, 104*n*1
Primrose, "vice admiral" of the fleet, 4, 5, 10*n*4, 14, 15, 25, 45, 48, 48*n*3, 90, 91, 120*n*3, 150, 184, 209, 216, 280, 283, 293, 294, 295
Primrose of London, 11, 283
Rainbow, royal ship (1587), 294
Ramaldes, a London bark, 81*n*6
Revenge, royal ship (1588), 284, 293